Canadian Literature

Two Centuries in Prose

Canadian Literature

Two Centuries in Prose

edited by Brita Mickleburgh

with a foreword by Malcolm Ross

McClelland and Stewart Limited

McClelland and Stewart Limited
The Canadian Publishers
25 Hollinger Road, Toronto 374

PRINTED AND BOUND IN CANADA

0-7710-5823-3

Contents

Preface

This book is a response to the many inquiries I have had regarding the teaching of Canadian literature. It may also, however, be of interest to those readers wishing to extend their present knowledge of this country's literary heritage.

From a cultural point of view, Canada is fortunate in having two distinct literatures, one in English and one in French. I have attempted to deal with the former only, although I have included two selections from a growing body of writing available to English-speaking Canadians, namely, the literature of French Canada in English translation.

The general aim of the selections included in this book is that of representing our major writers in English. The criteria used in assessing "major" writers is based on qualitative as well as more popular considerations, and in some cases both. Where, then, are writers like Pierre Berton, Northrop Frye, Ernest Buckler, and Eric Nicol? Space restriction accounts for their omission, and for the omission of other prominent Canadian writers.

Intended as an introduction to Canadian literature, the structural pattern of the book is historical, showing the origins and subsequent development of Canadian writing. I have purposely chosen selections with themes emphasizing the relationship between man and his social environment, as I feel that the "bush" has been rather over-explored in many anthologies. For example, Hugh Garner's short story, *E Equals MC Squared*, reflects an important aspect of urban life. At the same time, we are reminded by Grant Huffman that, "If you grant that the realistic animal story is a legitimate literary genre, then it is the one original contribution that Canada has made to world literature. It was originated by Ernest Thompson Seton and Charles G. D. Roberts."

Decisive criteria in selection choice have been student interest and opportunity for student scholarship. At this time, when literature as a study is undergoing so much evaluation, it is my personal view that the mastery of critical method remains a fundamental aim in the teaching of literature. A number of approaches to the selections may be found in the critiques which accompany some of them. Since many writers, particularly those writing today or in the recent past, have had a great deal of critical material devoted to them, I did not consider it essential, or indeed particularly desirable, to provide critiques in every case.

The list of study resources following each selection does not reflect the total output of the author, or the totality of criticism about him and his work, but only what is available for purchase. One purpose of these bibliographies is that they serve as a guide for librarians, as well as for teachers of Canadian literature. Because cost is so often a decisive factor in the building of a library of Canadian literature, I have listed paperbacks in preference to more expensive editions. Students may find the outlines useful in suggesting areas for individual research; teachers, on the other hand, may take one or more of the study programs and use them as units in a course of Canadian literature. The content and organization of the book are meant to facilitate adaptation and flexibility. Not mentioned in any of the lists, but indispensable as a work of reference, is *Literary History of Canada*, edited by Carl F. Klinck and published by the University of Toronto Press.

The selections are arranged chronologically; in most instances I have considered the date of writing, rather than the date of publication. For example, Malcolm Lowry's collection of short stories, *Hear Us O Lord from Heaven Thy Dwelling Place*, was published in 1961, but the stories were written at least seven years earlier. Again, it was not until 1971 that Desmond Pacey gathered twenty-five of Frederick Philip Grove's short stories into a posthumous collection. Of these stories from *Tales from the Margin*, thirteen were appearing in print for the first time. I have used selections from these two anthologies to conclude Part One, which takes the reader from early Canadian writing to modern fiction. Part Two wholly concerns contemporary writers, almost all of whom are still writing.

In conclusion, I give grateful thanks to the following: S. L. G. Chapman, J. R. Frizzell, Larry Bone, and Jennifer Ireland for making my leave of absence possible; Irene Howard who did biography research; Kay Dorken and Pauline Mickleburgh who typed the manuscript; and, finally, the students, colleagues, friends, and family who sustained me with their interest and encouragement.

Brita Mickleburgh

Foreword

Ten years ago no one would have dared to predict the "boom" in Canadian literary studies which we are now experiencing not only in our universities but also in our community colleges and our high schools. Twenty years ago only two or three universities offered full courses in Canadian literature. The usual pattern in those days was an American literature course with the last two weeks given over to Canadian writing. Not infrequently these last two weeks were ushered in with uneasy apology. It was explained that we were, after all, a "new country," that we had been so engrossed as a people with pushing back the wilderness and building the CPR that there was no energy left for writing "The Great Canadian Novel" – or even a couple of readable sonnets.

Then, of course, we suffered from the blight of "colonialism" and, what was worse, "puritanism." As a "transplanted culture" we sought, it was said, to perpetuate on alien soil the literary traditions of Britain. Thus it was that we reared a brood of mute, inglorious Tennysons. Our very images and symbols had been prefabricated for us abroad. Our robins, under the feather, were nightingales or larks, and even the maple tree, under the bark, had the look of the laburnum.

From colony to nation – and back again, as New York (and Hollywood) at last drove London out of mind, and film and television killed the book, as it were, in the eye. Culturally, it was contended, we became (and we are) a colony of the United States, putting off our British apron strings only to put on our brand new American diapers.

And until only yesterday we were, they told us, frozen to the bone by our cold northern Puritan morality. It was not just that Canadians did not dare write about "the facts of life." We were led to believe that to write at all, except for the advertising pages or in the office ledger, was to engage in a profitless and therefore immoral exercise in frivolity.

No wonder, then, that students of twenty years ago expected very little of a native literature. No wonder that they pushed aside the little scraps of Roberts, Carman, and Callaghan flung to them after the great American feast of Whitman, Melville, and Hemingway.

I suppose we were taught to be ashamed of ourselves. And perhaps this is why we tried so desperately to be superior to ourselves and to look down our noses at the dollar-chasing lumberjack culture of our kith and kin.

But that was twenty years ago. We are at last beginning to grow into our own size. We are not disposed nowadays to look down our noses at writers like Margaret Laurence, Mordecai Richler, Robertson Davies, Thomas Raddall – or at Roberts, Carman, and Callaghan.

True, eminent critics in our midst still write laments for a dying nation, a nation dying before it could be born. One very eminent critic has recently informed us that Canada is now the only truly colonial country left in the modern world, and that Canadians fear annexation to the United States only because, once inside the Union, it would be discovered that we had brought with us nothing of our own except natural resources – oil, water, minerals, but nothing for the mind.

I suppose the phrase that best sums up what are said to be our besetting sins ("colonialism" and "puritanism") is "the garrison mentality." The phrase is Northrop Frye's and he used it, first of all, to describe the state of mind our early pioneers huddling together in lonely settlements along the lakes or behind the wooden palisades of forts from Halifax and Chignecto to the reaches of the Red River. The "garrison mentality" was the defensive mentality of men threatened by Indians, by wolves, by the vast snows, by the meaningless blankness of unpeopled space.

Since Frye, other critics have seen this defensiveness as the dominant mark of the Canadian culture. In this view, we are, as a people, ruled by fear, fear not just of the wilderness without, but fear, too, of the wilderness within us. We fear now not the red Indian but our own red blood. We fear our impulses, our desires, our very flesh. An interesting new book, *Butterfly on Rock* by D. G. Jones, is a study of Canadian writing as a war, long-drawn-out, between the "garrison mentality" and a militant spirit, now growing in force, which says "Yes" not only to the wilderness "out there" but to all the passions and pulses and itches that lurk within us. And as we say "Yes," words like "colonial" and "puritan" fall from us like dead fleas and we are able to stand forward in our own true flesh.

Perhaps.

It may have occurred to you that the most terrifying example of the "garrison mentality" in the world today is that of the New York apartment dweller who depends on closed circuit television in his elevator to reveal to his "keeper" the presence of mugger and marauder. One wonders if there is, or ever was, anything peculiarly Canadian about fear or defensiveness. And man's war with the wilderness of his own desires did not, one suspects, begin in the world at the time of Jacques Cartier, nor is it a war that is only waged north of the 49th parallel.

Nevertheless, the critical attitudes which I have attempted to summarize present useful approaches to the material collected in this book. For here you have representative Canadian prose writing from the earliest colonial days to the present. Note in Frances Brooke, for instance, an actual garrison town. But do not be surprised when the pent-up denizens of this garrison break out in their sleighs, soon exulting in the flashing white beauty of the winter world beyond the palisades. And in Mrs. Moodie, and much later in Ralph Connor you may be able to observe how the man of the bush comes to terms with nature and begins to come to terms with himself. I am sure you will find evidence of a "colonial" mentality in the passages taken from L. M. Montgomery and Mazo de la Roche. But any hint of a "puritan" reticence that you may be able to detect in some of the earlier work is surely quite absent in the passages from Mordecai Richler and Leonard Cohen.

The book, historical in pattern, is not designed as a set of neatly illustrated Canadian themes. But you will find the kinds of theme and issue that I have talked about at almost every turn of the page. And you will find an exciting variety of tone, texture, and intention. Violence, laughter, social awareness, compassion – and no little sophistication. Above all, I think you will find the sense of place. Not the great, wide, abstract political place – "from sea to sea." Rather Quebec under snow, the log-plunging river of Ontario, a harsh winter-set in Nova Scotia made warm by human flesh.

Now it may be that it was the first task of our writers to make human the land. Not all of it at once. First this river, then that hill and wood and town. Perhaps, before anything else was possible to the Canadian imagination, place had to be peopled. Perhaps it is by this very peopling of the mind that we become at last "a people."

Malcolm Ross
Professor of English
Dalhousie University
and Editor of the
New Canadian Library

Part One

Frances Brooke

Frances Brooke (1724-89), née Moore, was an Englishwoman who lived in Canada for five years, having come in 1763 to join her husband, chaplain to the Quebec garrison. They returned in 1768. In England she had already written The History of Lady Julia Mandeville, *an epistolary novel with Canadian scenes. While in Canada she wrote* The History of Emily Montague, *a novel consisting of 228 letters revolving about a pleasant love story, and providing at the same time a social history of Quebec City in the years following the British capture and occupation of New France. She is also the author of a two-act comic opera and the translator of a French romance.*

Because *The History of Emily Montague* touches the literatures of Canada, the United States, and England, it is of particular interest to anyone concerned with literary history. Published in 1769 in England, it is considered the first Canadian novel; the absence of a Canadian imprint indicates only the absence at the time of Canadian publishers of fiction. Novels read in British North America were imported from London.

In his introduction to the New Canadian Library edition of *Emily Montague*, Carl Klinck writes, "By ignoring Mrs. Brooke, Canadians could lose the principal artistic attempt to recreate life in the early northern colonies. Commonwealth literature could lose its first novel."

Lionel Stevenson, in *The English Novel*, accords *Emily Montague* a second distinction, one related to the history of English literature:

> A touch of novelty appeared in Frances Brooke's second novel, *The History of Emily Montague* (1769), because of its unusual setting. Shortly after her *Lady Julia Mandeville* came out, her husband was appointed chaplain of the forces in Quebec, and she spent several years with him in Canada. She therefore provided *Emily Montague* with a regional background, including

both the picturesque Canadian scenery and the unconventional habits of the people. Most other novelists of the time felt no need for much description of setting, since their books were laid either in the contemporary England that the readers knew familiarly or else in remote oriental lands that the authors knew not at all. *Emily Montague* can be termed the first novel of local colour.

Appearing, as it does, during the brief existence of British North America between 1760 and 1776, *Emily Montague* is not only the first Canadian novel but the first American novel as well. The earliest date in a standard book list of American fiction is 1774.

To identify the novel historically, were one ignorant of its author and period, would present little difficulty. Samuel Richardson had introduced the epistolary novel into England when he wrote *Pamela* in 1741, and *Clarissa* in 1748. Later, Fanny Burney, with many others, used the form when she wrote *Evelina*. Frances Brooke knew both these writers personally; in the London of the mid-eighteenth century she was very much in the centre of the literary scene. It was no accident, then, that she chose to develop the plot in *Emily Montague* through letters exchanged between characters.

The tone of the novel also reflects the taste for sentimental fiction current in the eighteenth century. The popularity of French novels with their emphasis on *sensibilité*, had been influential in the development of the English novel of sentiment. When Arabella writes, "I sent a thousand sighs and a thousand tender wishes to dear England", her words seem to us affected, and even silly, because we have grown up accustomed to different conventions in literature.

Polished, graceful, and witty, the prose in *Emily Montague* is marked by the elegance in style demanded by eighteenth century upper class standards:

We had a million of beaux here yesterday, notwithstanding the severe cold; 'tis the Canadian custom, calculated I suppose for the climate, to visit all the ladies on New-Year's-day, who sit dressed in form to be kissed: I assure you, however, our kisses could not warm them; but we were obliged, to our eternal disgrace, to call in rasberry brandy as an auxiliary.

The eighteenth century fondness for the maxim is also evident: "Two moderate letters are vastly better than one long one."

In describing Montmorency Falls, however, Arabella Fermor strays from then acceptable ideas of beauty. These ideas were based on principles of control, formality, regularity, balance, dignity and elegance—all characteristics of the Age of Reason. Arabella's idea of beauty is much more in line with romanticism which was to dominate the following century. An appreciation of irregularity in line and form, asymmetry, variety, surprise, and contrast in nature became part of the romanticist creed. Contrast and variety were basic to the concept of the picturesque:

> While the outstanding qualities of the sublime were vastness and obscurity; and those of the beautiful, smoothness and gentleness; the characteristics of the picturesque were roughness and sudden variation joined to irregularity of form, colour, lighting, and even sound.
>
> (from A. O. Lovejoy, *Essays in the History of Ideas*)

The new liking for wildness, broken contours and unlimited views in natural landscape was, actually, an early sign of the Gothic revival in England. It is evident in Arabella's picture of the falls which concludes, "I have not told you half the grandeur, half the beauty, half the lovely wildness of this scene . . ."

What Frances Brooke painted in words, Cornelius Krieghoff in 1853 painted in oil: *The Montmorency Falls in Winter.* Two other Krieghoff paintings with subjects related to *The History of Emily Montague* are, *Royal Mail Crossing the Ice at Quebec* (1858), and *Sillery Cove, Quebec* (1859).

Everything said so far points to English characteristics in *Emily Montague.* Is the "made-in-Canada" label on the novel based on geography alone? Hardly.

When Arabella writes about the coming of winter, she does not restrict herself to matters of climate. Instead, she describes the effect that winter has on the human spirit: "I have been seeing the last ship go out of the port, Lucy; you have no notion what a melancholy sight it is: we are now left to ourselves, and shut up from all the world for the winter; somehow we seem so forsaken, so cut off from the rest of human kind."

Here is a first expression in Canadian literature of what Northrop Frye calls the "garrison mentality." This is a frame of mind which develops in "small and isolated communities surrounded with a physical or psychological 'frontier,' separated from one another and from their American and British cultural sources." (From *Literary History of Canada*)

From its very beginning we recognize in this literature the theme of the hostile landscape, a landscape which both beckons and threatens. Its ambivalence we see in Arabella's words, "we passed the ice from thence to Orleans, and dined out of doors on six feet of snow, in the charming enlivening warmth of the sun."

Already there is evident foreshadowing of Hugh MacLennan's

Two Solitudes: "They are squabbling at Quebec, I hear, about I cannot tell what, therefore shall not attempt to explain: some dregs of old disputes, it seems which have had not time to settle."

WINTER IN QUEBEC

TO MISS RIVERS, CLARGES STREET

LETTER 45 SILLERI, NOV. 23: I have been seeing the last ship go out of the port, Lucy; you have no notion what a melancholy sight it is: we are now left to ourselves, and shut up from all the world for the winter: somehow we seem so forsaken, so cut off from the rest of human kind, I cannot bear the idea: I sent a thousand sighs and a thousand tender wishes to dear England, which I never loved so much as at this moment.

Do you know, my dear, I could cry if I was not ashamed? I shall not absolutely be in spirits again this week.

'Tis the first time I have felt any thing like bad spirits in Canada: I followed the ship with my eyes till it turned Point Levi, and, when I lost sight of it, felt as if I had lost every thing dear to me on earth. I am not particular: I see a gloom on every countenance; I have been at church, and think I never saw so many dejected faces in my life.

Adieu! for the present: it will be a fortnight before I can send this letter; another agreeable circumstance that: would to Heaven I were in England, though I changed the bright sun of Canada for a fog!

Dec. 1

We have had a week's snow without intermission: happily for us, your brother and the Fitz have been weatherbound all the time at Silleri, and cannot possibly get away.

We have amused ourselves within doors, for there is no stirring abroad, with playing cards, playing at shuttlecock, playing the fool, making love, and making moral reflections: upon the whole, the week has not been very disagreeable.

The snow is when we wake constantly up to our chamber windows; we are literally dug out of it every morning.

From: Frances Brooke, *The History of Emily Montague* (Toronto: McClelland and Stewart, New Canadian Library Series, 1961). Reprinted by permission of McClelland and Stewart Limited, The Canadian Publishers.

As to Quebec, I give up all hopes of ever seeing it again: but my comfort is, that the people there cannot possibly get to their neighbours; and I flatter myself very few of them have been half so well entertained at home.

We shall be abused, I know, for (what is really the fault of the weather) keeping these two creatures here this week; the ladies hate us for engrossing two such fine fellows as your brother and Fitzgerald, as well as for having vastly more than our share of all the men: we generally go out attended by at least a dozen, without any other woman but a lively old French lady, who is a flirt of my father's, and will certainly be my mamma.

We sweep into the general's assembly on Thursdays with such a train of beaux as draws every eye upon us; the rest of the fellows crowd round us; the misses draw up, blush, and flutter their fans; and your little Bell sits down with such a fancy impertinent consciousness in her countenance as is really provoking: Emily on the contrary looks mild and humble, and seems by her civil decent air to apologize to them for being so much more agreeable than themselves, which is a fault I for my part am not in the least inclined to be ashamed of.

Your idea of Quebec, my dear, is perfectly just; it is like a third or fourth rate country town in England; much hospitality, little society; cards, scandal, dancing, and good chear; all excellent things to pass away a winter evening, and peculiarly adapted to what I am told, and what I begin to feel, of the severity of the climate.

I am told they abuse me, which I can easily believe, because my impertinence to them deserves it: but what care I, you know, Lucy, so long as I please myself, and am at Silleri out of the sound?

They are squabbling at Quebec, I hear, about I cannot tell what, therefore shall not attempt to explain: some dregs of old disputes, it seems, which have had not time to settle: however, we new comers have certainly nothing to do with these matters: you can't think how comfortable we feel at Silleri, out of the way.

My father says, the politics of Canada are as complex and as difficult to be understood as those of the Germanic system.

For my part, I think no politics worth attending to but those of the little commonwealth of woman: if I can maintain my empire over hearts, I leave the men to quarrel for every thing else.

I observe a strict neutrality, that I may have a chance for admirers amongst both parties. Adieu! the post is just going out.

Your faithful

A. Fermor

LETTER 49 SILLERI, JAN. 1: It is with difficulty I breathe, my dear; the cold is so amazingly intense as almost totally to stop respiration. I have business, the business of pleasure, at Quebec; but have not courage to stir from the stove.

We have had five days, the severity of which none of the natives remember to have ever seen equalled: 'tis said, the cold is beyond all the thermometers here, tho' intended for the climate.

The strongest wine freezes in a room which has a stove in it; even brandy is thickened to the consistence of oil: the largest wood fire, in a wide chimney, does not throw out its heat a quarter of a yard.

I must venture to Quebec to-morrow, or have company at home: amusements are here necessary to life; we must be jovial, or the blood will freeze in our veins.

I no longer wonder the elegant arts are unknown here; the rigour of the climate suspends the very powers of the understanding: what then must become of those of the imagination? Those who expect to see

"A new Athens rising near the pole,"

will find themselves extremely disappointed. Genius will never mount high, where the faculties of the mind are benumbed half the year.

'Tis sufficient employment for the most lively spirit here to contrive how to preserve an existence, of which there are moments that one is hardly conscious: the cold really sometimes brings on a sort of stupefaction.

We had a million of beaux here yesterday, notwithstanding the severe cold: 'tis the Canadian custom, calculated I suppose for the climate, to visit all the ladies on New-year's-day, who sit dressed in form to be kissed: I assure you, however, our kisses could not warm them; but we were obliged, to our eternal disgrace, to call in rasberry brandy as an auxiliary.

You would have died to see the men; they look just like so many bears in their open carrioles, all wrapped in furs from head to foot; you see nothing of the human form appear, but the tip of a nose.

They have intire coats of beaver skin exactly like Friday's in Robinson Crusoe, and casques on their heads like the old knights errant in romance; you never saw such tremendous figures; but without this kind of clothing it would be impossible to stir out at present.

The ladies are equally covered up, tho' in a less unbecoming style; they have long cloth cloaks with loose hoods, like those worn by the market-women in the north of England. I have one in scarlet, the hood lined with sable, the prettiest ever seen here, in which I assure you I look amazingly handsome; the men think so, and call me the *Little red riding-hood*; a name which becomes me as well as the hood.

The Canadian ladies wear these cloaks in India silk in summer, which, fluttering in the wind, look really graceful on a fine woman.

Besides our riding-hoods, when we go out, we have a large buffaloe's skin under our feet, which turns up, and wraps round us almost to our shoulders; so that, upon the whole, we are pretty well guarded from the weather as well as the men.

Our covered carrioles too have not only canvas windows (we dare not have glass, because we often overturn), but cloth curtains to draw all round us; the extreme swiftness of these carriages also, which dart along like lightening, helps to keep one warm, by promoting the circulation of the blood.

I pity the Fitz; no tiger was ever so hard-hearted as I am this weather: the little god has taken his flight, like the swallows. I say nothing, but cruelty is no virtue in Canada; at least at this season.

I suppose Pygmalion's statue was some frozen Canadian gentlewoman, and a sudden warm day thawed her. I love to expound ancient fables, and I think no exposition can be more natural than this.

Would you know what makes me chatter so this morning? Papa has made me take some excellent *liqueur*; 'tis the mode here; all the Canadian ladies take a little, which makes them so coquet and agreeable. Certainly brandy makes a woman talk like an angel. Adieu!

Yours,

A. Fermor

TO MISS RIVERS, CLARGES STREET

LETTER 80 SILLERI, FEB. 25: Those who have heard no more of a Canadian winter than what regards the intenseness of its cold, must suppose it a very joyless season: 'tis, I assure you, quite otherwise; there are indeed some days here of the severity of which those who were never out of England can form no conception; but those days seldom exceed a dozen in a whole winter; nor do they come in succession, but at intermediate periods, as the winds set in from the North-West; which, coming some hundred leagues, from frozen lakes and rivers, over woods and mountains covered with snow, would be insupportable, were it not for the furs with which the country abounds, in such variety and plenty as to be within the reach of all its inhabitants.

Thus defended, the British belles set the winter of Canada at defiance; and the season of which you seem to entertain such terrible ideas, is that of the utmost chearfulness and festivity.

But what particularly pleases me is, there is no place where women are of such importance: not one of the sex, who has the least share of attractions, is without a levee of beaux interceding for the honour of attending her on some party, of which every day produces three or four.

I am just returned from one of the most agreeable jaunts imagination can paint, to the island of Orleans, by the falls of Montmorenci; the latter is almost nine miles distant, across the great bason of Quebec; but as we are obliged to reach it in winter by the waving line, our direct road being intercepted by the inequalities of the ice, it is now perhaps a third more. You will possibly suppose a ride of this kind must want one of the greatest essentials to entertainment, that of variety, and imagine it only one dull whirl over an unvaried plain of snow: on the contrary, my dear, we pass hills and mountains of ice in the trifling space of these few miles. The bason of Quebec is formed by the conflux of the rivers of St. Charles and Montmorenci with the great river St. Lawrence, the rapidity of whose flood-tide, as these rivers are gradually seized by the frost, breaks up the ice, and drives it back in heaps, till it forms ridges of transparent rock to an height that is astonishing, and of a strength which bids defiance to the utmost rage of the most furiously rushing tide.

This circumstance makes this little journey more pleasing than you can possibly conceive: the serene blue sky above, the dazzling brightness of the sun, and the colours from the refraction of its rays on the transparent part of these ridges of ice, the winding course these oblige you to make, the sudden disappearing of a train of fifteen or twenty carrioles, as these ridges intervene, which again discover themselves on your rising to the top of the frozen mount, the tremendous appearance both of the ascent and descent, which however are not attended with the least danger; all together give a grandeur and variety to the scene, which almost rise to enchantment.

Your dull foggy climate affords nothing that can give you the least idea of our frost-pieces in Canada; nor can you form any notion of our amusements, of the agreeableness of a covered carriole, with a sprightly fellow, rendered more sprightly by the keen air and romantic scene about him; to say nothing of the fair lady at his side.

Even an overturning has nothing alarming in it; you are laid gently down on a soft bed of snow, without the least danger of any kind; and an accident of this sort only gives a pretty fellow occasion to vary the style of his civilities, and shew a greater degree of attention.

But it is almost time to come to Montmorenci; to avoid, however, fatiguing you or myself. I shall refer the rest of our tour to another letter, which will probably accompany this: my meaning is, that two moderate letters are vastly better than one long one; in which sentiment I know you agree with.

Yours,

A. Fermor

TO MISS RIVERS, CLARGES STREET

LETTER 81 SILLERI, FEB. 25, AFTERNOON: So, my dear, as I was saying, this same ride to Montmorenci–where was I, Lucy? I forget–O, I believe pretty near the mouth of the bay, embosomed in which lies the lovely cascade of which I am to give you a winter description, and which I only slightly mentioned when I gave you an account of the rivers by which it is supplied.

The road, about a mile before you reach this bay, is a regular glassy level, without any of those intervening hills of ice which I have mentioned, hills, which with the ideas, though false ones, of danger and dificulty, give those of beauty and magnificence too.

As you gradually approach the bay, you are struck with an awe, which increases every moment, as you come nearer, from the grandeur of a scene, which is one of the noblest works of nature: the beauty, the proportion, the solemnity, the wild magnificence of which, surpassing every possible effect of art, impress one strongly with the idea of its Divine Almighty Architect.

The rock on the east side, which is first in view as you approach, is a smooth and almost perpendicular precipice, of the same height as the fall; the top, which a little over-hangs, is beautifully covered with pines, firs, and ever-greens of various kinds, whose verdant lustre is rendered at this season more shining and lovely by the surrounding snow, as well as by that which is sprinkled irregularly on their branches, and glitters half melted in the sun-beams: a thousand smaller shrubs are scattered on the side of the ascent, and, having their roots in almost imperceptible clefts of the rock, seem to those below to grow in air.

The west side is equally lofty, but more sloping, which from that circumstance, affords soil all the way, upon shelving inequalities of the rock, at little distances, for the growth of trees and shrubs, by which it is almost entirely hid.

The most pleasing view of this miracle of nature is certainly in summer, and in the early part of it, when every tree is in foliage and full verdure, every shrub in flower; and when the river, swelled with a waste of waters from the mountains from which it derives its source, pours down in a tumultuous torrent, that equally charms and astonishes the beholder.

The winter scene has, notwithstanding, its beauties, though of a different kind, more resembling the stillness and inactivity of the season.

The river being on its sides bound up in frost, and its channel rendered narrower than in the summer, affords a less body of water to supply the cascade; and the fall, though very steep, yet not being exactly perpendicular, masses of ice are formed, on different shelving projections of the rock, in a great variety of forms and proportions.

The torrent, which before rushed with such impetuosity down the deep descent in one vast sheet of water, now descends in some parts with a slow and majestic pace; in others seems almost suspended in mid air; and in others, bursting through the obstacles which interrupt its course, pours down with redoubled fury into the foaming bason below, from whence a spray arises, which, freezing in its ascent, becomes on each side a wide and irregular frozen breast-work; and in front, the spray being there much greater, a lofty and magnificent pyramid of solid ice.

I have not told you half the grandeur, half the beauty, half the lovely wildness of this scene: if you would know what it is, you must take no information but that of your own eyes, which I pronounce strangers to the loveliest work of creation till they have seen the river and fall of Montmorenci.

In short, my dear, I am Montmorenci-mad.

I can hardly descend to tell you, we passed the ice from thence to Orleans, and dined out of doors on six feet of snow, in the charming enlivening warmth of the sun, though in the month of February, at a time when you in England scarce feel his beams.

Fitzgerald made violent love to me all the way, and I never felt myself listen with such complacency.

Adieu!

Adieu! I have wrote two immense letters. Write oftener; you are lazy, yet expect me to be an absolute slave in the scribbling way.

Your faithful

A. Fermor

Do you know your brother has admirable ideas? He contrived to lose his way on our return, and kept Emily ten minutes behind the rest of the company. I am apt to fancy there was something like a declaration, for she blushed.

"Celestial rosy red,"

when he led her into the dining-room at Silleri.

Once more, Adieu!

FURTHER READING

THE EPISTOLARY NOVEL IN THE EIGHTEENTH CENTURY
Samuel Richardson, *Pamela*, 1740 (New York: W. W. Norton Co. Ltd., The Norton Library, 1958).
Frances Brooke, *The History of Emily Montague*, 1769 (Toronto: McClelland and Stewart, New Canadian Library, 1969).
Fanny Burney, *Evelina*, 1778 (New York: W. W. Norton Co. Ltd., The Norton Library).
(For reference) Lionel Stevenson, *The English Novel* (Boston: Houghton Mifflin Company; Cambridge: The Riverside Press, 1960).
LETTERS FROM CANADA
Frances Brooke, *The History of Emily Montague* (publisher's details above).
Marchioness of Dufferin and Ava, *My Canadian Journal* (Toronto: Coles Publishing Company). Extracts from *My Letters Home*, written while Lord Dufferin was Governor General, 1872-8.
NOVELS OF FRANCES BROOKE
Lady Julia Mandeville, 1763. Out of print, available in university libraries only.
The History of Emily Montague (publisher's details above).

Thomas C. Haliburton

Thomas Chandler Haliburton (1796-1865) was the Nova Scotia-born lawyer, politician, judge and humourist who created the character of Sam Slick, the Yankee clock peddler. He began writing humour when he met with Joseph Howe and others as "The Club" to supply sketches in Scottish dialect for Howe's Nova Scotian, *and contributed his first Sam Slick pieces to the same newspaper. These were published by Howe as* The Clockmaker *in 1836. Haliburton subsequently wrote several more Sam Slick books, but none so popular as the first, which has gone through more than seventy printings. His political commentary includes* A Reply to the Report of the Earl of Durham *(1839), in which he opposes responsible government for Canada. He was appointed to the Supreme Court in 1841 and on his retirement went to live in England.*

The idea of tying together a collection of stories into a framework is well-known in literature. One of the most famous of such framed tales are the *Canterbury Tales*, exchanged by pilgrims on their way to Canterbury.

Thomas Chandler Haliburton tells his stories through the medium of two characters travelling about Nova Scotia in the thirties of the last century: a Yankee clock peddler, Sam Slick; and his travelling companion, the Squire. Squire is the narrator, but he tells us Sam Slick's yarns. The anecdotes and social comment appear to be quoted word for word as they roll off Sam's tongue in his rich vernacular; one can almost imagine that they have been put on tape. In some ways the stories resemble a type of early travelling salesman folk lore.

Haliburton's sketches appeared originally in Joseph Howe's newspaper, the *Nova Scotian*, but because of their popularity the editor decided to publish them in book form: first, in a series in 1836, later in two additional series in 1838 and 1840. The title was, *The Clockmaker or The Sayings and Doings of Samuel Slick of Slickville*. Since that first edition, the book has gone through at least seventy editions.

The title of one of the sketches sounds strangely modern: *The White Nigger*. "Bluenose approbates no distinction in colours, and when reduced to poverty, is reduced to slavery, and is sold–*a white nigger*." According to the author, this meaning lies at the heart of Pierre Vallières' book, *White Niggers of America*.

The pamphlet, given out at the Haliburton Memorial Museum in Windsor, Nova Scotia, reminds us how contemporary *Sam Slick* can be:

> Many of Sam Slick's sayings are still in common use today, such as "An ounce of prevention is worth a pound of cure"; "Facts are stranger than fiction"; "Circumstances alter cases", to mention a few. Haliburton's statement, "May our government never degenerate into a mob, nor our mobs grow strong enough to become our government," is often quoted, and many of the expressions he used have a familiar ring even with the passing of more than a century: "raining cats and dogs"; "jack of all trades and master of none"; "quick as a wink"; and "barking up the wrong tree".

Haliburton is a skilled practitioner in the art of humour. Usually he begins with a comic situation which he then develops. Often, his choice is not original; for example, the comedy associated with a person's getting into a wrong room is as old as the "pie-in-the-face" routine. But Haliburton manages to extract maximum amusement out of what begins as a stock situation.

First of all, his use of imagery is pungent: the wife's hair is "all stuck chock full of paper and pins, like porcupine quills"; Mrs. Sproul carries on "like a ravin' distracted bedbug"; "seezin' her dressin' gownd, instead of his trousers," Mr. Zwicker puts "his legs into the arms of it," and is seen "arunnin' out of the room aholdin' up of the skirts with his hands."

Haliburton is also a master at using a disruption as a source of humour, because it allows him to bring into a central vortex a multiplicity of characters and events. Note how the key incident in *The Wrong Room* is exploited in this way. Another of his techniques is the use of a gimmick to induce laughter–the gimlet, for instance. The whole comic disaster is precipitated by Mister Zwicker's neglect to take a gimlet with him on his journey. The unexpected twist at the end of a story is a device which Mark Twain recognized as a characteristic of the oral anecdote. Anti-climax, too, is used with telling effect, "He's asleep, now, says she; I hope he won't disturb me ag'in. No, I ain't asleep, mynheer stranger, says old Zwicker, a Dutch merchant from Albany . . ."

By itself, each peculiarity of language would contribute to the sense of the comic which dominates *The Wrong Room*; together, Sam's New England dialect and Mr. Zwicker's Dutch accent turn the story into a Haliburton bedroom farce.

But Haliburton was also well aware that, "Laughing is a very serious thing and ought to be tempered with a great deal of gravity," a thought given expression by Mephibosheth Stepsure. Who can mistake the irony in Sam's description of the Fourth of July:

> A great day that, squire; a great national festival; a splendid spectacle; fifteen millions of free men and three millions of slaves acelebratin' the birthday of liberty; rejoicin' in their strength, their freedom and enlightenment?

As a satirist, Haliburton does not choose to be subtle:

> It's a bright page of history that. It exasperates the young–it makes their blood boil at the wrongs of their forefathers; it makes them clean their rifles, and run their bullets. It prepares them for that great day, that comin' day, that no distant day neither, that must come and will come, and can't help a comin', when Britain will be a colony to our great nation, and when her colonies will be states in our Union.

As a political prophet, Haliburton was remarkably acute. Thirty years before the outbreak of the Civil War in the United States, Sam Slick tells Squire:

> You have heerd tell of cotton rags dipped in turpentine, haven't you, how they produce combustion? Well, I guess we have the elements of spontaneous combustion among us in abundance; when it does break out, if you don't see an eruption of human gore worse than Etna lava, then I'm mistaken. There'll be the very devil to pay, that's a fact. I expect the blacks will butcher Southern Whites, and the Northerners will have to turn out and butcher them again; and all this shoot, hang, cut, stab, and burn business will sweeten our folks' temper, as raw meat does that of a dog; it fairly makes me sick to think on it.

There may be, however, subtle ambiguity in the story of *The Wrong Room*: "I takes my leetle gimblet out and bores wid it over de latch of de toor, and dat fastens it, and keeps out de tief and de villain and de womans." Good advice to travellers–and Canadians?

THE WRONG ROOM

You may talk about the domestic hearth, and the pleasures of home, and the family circle, and all that sort o' thin', squire: it sounds very clever, and reads dreadful pretty; but what does it eend in at last? why, a scoldin' wife with her shoes down to heel, a-see-sawin' in a rocking chair; her hair either not done up at all, or all stuck chock full of paper and pins, like porcupine quills; a smoky chimbly aputtin' of your eyes out; cryin' children ascreamin' of your ears out; extravagant, wasteful helps, a-emptying of your pockets out, and the whole thing awearin' of your patience out. No, there's nothing' like a great boardin' house, for married folks; it don't cost nothin' like keepin' house, and there's plenty o' company all the time, and the women folks never feel lonely like, when their husbands are not at home. The only thing is to larn the geography of the house well, and know their own number. If they don't do that, they may get into a most adeuce of a scrape, that it ain't so easy to back out of. I recollect a most curious accident that happened that way once, agettin' into the wrong room.

I had gone down to Boston to keep 4th of July, our great Annivarsary-day. A great day that, squire; a great national festival; a splendid spectacle; fifteen millions of free men and three millions of slaves acelebratin' the birth-day of liberty; rejoicin' in their strength, their freedom and enlightenment. Perhaps the sun never shone on such a sight before, nor the moon, nor the stars, for their planetary system ain't more perfect than our political system. The sun typifies our splendour; the moon in its changes figures our rotation of office, and eclipses of Presidents,–and the stars are emblems of our states, as painted on our flags. If the British don't catch it that day, it's a pity. All over our Union, in every town and village, there are orations made, jist about as beautiful pieces of workmanship, and as nicely dove-tailed and mortised, and as prettily put together as well can be, and the English catch it everywhere. All our battles are fought over ag'in, and you can e'en a'most see the British aflyin' afore them like the wind, full split, or layin' down their arms as humble as you please, or marchin' off as prisoners tied two and two, like runaway niggers, as plain as if you was in the engagements, and Washington on his great big war-horse aridin' over them, and our free and enlightened citizens askiverin' of them; or the proud impudent officers akneelin' down to him, givin' up their swords, and abeggin' for dear life for quarter. Then you think you can e'en a'most see that infernal spy André nabbed and sarched, and the scorn that sot on the brows of our heroes as they threw into the dirt the money he offered to be released, and heerd him beg like an Indgian to be shot like a gentleman, and not hanged like a thief, and Washington's noble and magnanimous answer,–"I guess they'll think we are afeerd if we don't,"–so simple, so sublime. The hammerin' of the carpenters seems to strike your ears as they erect the gallus; and then his struggles, like a dog tucked up for sheep-stealin', are as nateral as life. I must say I do like to hear them orations,–to hear of the deeds of our heroes by land and by sea. It's a bright page of history that. It exasperates the young–it makes their blood boil at the wrongs of their forefathers; it makes them clean their rifles, and run their bullets. It prepares them for that great day, that comin' day, that no distant day neither, that must come and will come, and can't help a comin', when Britain will be a colony to our great nation, and when her colonies will be states in our Union.

Many's the disputes, and pretty hot disputes too, I've had with minister about these orations. He never would go near one on 'em; he said they were in bad taste–(a great phrase of his'n that, poor dear good old man; I believe his heart yarns arter old times, and I must think sometimes he ought to have joined the refugees,)–bad taste, Sam. It smells o' braggin', it's ongentlemanly; and what's worse –it's onchristian.

But ministers don't know much of this world;–they may know the road to the next; but they don't know the crossroads and by-paths of this one–that's a fact. But I was agoin' to tell you what happened that day–I was stayin' to General Peep's boardin' house to Boston, to enjoy, as I was asayin', the anniversary. There was an amazin' crowd of folks there; the house was chock full of strangers. Well, there was a gentleman and a lady, one Major Ebenezer Sproul and his wife, aboardin' there, that had one child, the most cryenest critter I ever seed; it boohood all night a'most, and the boarders said it must be sent up to the garret to the helps, for no soul could sleep a'most for it. Well, most every night Mrs. Sproul had to go up there to quiet the little varmint,–for it wouldn't give over yellin' for no one but her. That night, in partikelar, the critter screeched and screamed like Old Scratch; and at last Mrs. Sproul slipped on her dressin' gownd, and went up stairs to it,–and left her door ajar, so as not to disturb her husband acomin' back; and when she returned, she pushed the door open softly, and shot it to, and got into bed. He's asleep, now, says she; I hope he won't disturb me ag'in. No, I ain't asleep, mynheer stranger, says old Zwicker, a Dutch merchant from Albany, (for she had got into the wrong room, and got in his bed by mistake,) nor I don't dank you, nor Gineral Beep needer, for puddin' you into my bed mid me, widout my leave nor lichense, nor abbrobation, needer. I liksh your place more better as your company! Oh, I got no gimblet! Het is jammer, it is a pity! Oh dear! if she didn't let go, it's a pity; she kicked and screamed, and carried on like a ravin' distracted bedbug. Tousand teyvils, said he, what ails te man? I pelieve he is pewitched. Murder! murder! said she, and she cried out at the very tip eend of her voice, murder! murder! Well,

Zwicker, he jumped out o' bed in an all-fired hurry, most properly frightened, you may depend; and seezin' her dressin'gownd, instead of his trousers, he put his legs into the arms of it, and was arunnin' out of the room aholdin' up of the skirts with his hands, as I came in with the candle. De ferry teyvil hisself is in te man, and in de trousher too, said he; for I pelieve te coat has grow'd to it in te night, it is so tam long. Oh, tear! what a pity! Stop, says I, Mister Zwicker, and I pulled him back by the gownd (I thought I should adied larfin' to see him in his red night-cap, his eyes startin' out o' his head, and those short-legged trousers on, for the sleeves of the dressin' gownd didn't come further than his knees, with a great long tail to 'em.) Stop, says I, and tell us what all this everlastin' hubbub is about: who's dead and what's to pay now?

All this time Mrs. Sproul lay curled up like a cat, covered all over in the bed clothes, ayellin' and ascreamin' like mad; 'most all the house was gathered there, some ondressed, and some half-dressed– some had sticks and pokers, and some had swords. Hullo! says I, who on airth is makin' all this touss? Goten Hymel, said he, old Saydon himself, I do pelieve; he came tru de door and jumped right into ped, and yelled so loud in mine ear as to deefen my head a'most: pull him out by de cloven foot, and kill him, tam him! I had no gimblet no more, and he know'd it, and dat is te cause, and nothin' else. Well, the folks got hold of the clothes, and pulled and hauled away till her head showed above the sheet. Dear, dear, said Major Ebenezer Sproul;–If it ain't Mrs. Sproul, my wife, as I am alive! Why, Mary dear, what brought you here?–what on airth are you adoin' of in Mr. Zwicker's room here? I take my oat', she prought herself here, said Zwicker, and peg she take herself away ag'in so fast as she came, and more faster too. What will Vrou Zwicker say to this woman's tale?–was te likeesh ever heerd afore? Tear, tear, but 'tis too pad! Well, well, says the folks, who'd athought it?–such a steady old gentleman as Mr. Zwicker,–and young Marm Sproul, says they,–only think of her!–ain't it horrid? The hussy! says the women house-helps: she's nicely caught, ain't she? She's no great things any how to take up with that nasty smoky old Dutchman: it sarves her right,–it does, the good-for-nothin' jade! I wouldn't ahad it happen, says the major, for fifty dollars, I vow; and he walked up and down, and wrung his hands, and looked streaked enough, you may depend:–no, nor I don't know, said he, as I would for a hundred dollars a'most. Have what happened, says Zwicker; upon my vort and honour and sole, nothin' happened, only I had no gimblet. Het is jammer; it is a pity. I went to see the baby, said Mrs. Sproul, –asobbin' ready to kill herself, poor thing!–and–Well, I don't want, nor have occasion, nor require a nurse, said Zwicker.–And I mistook the room, said she, and come here athinkin' it was ourn. Couldn't pe possible, said he, to take me for te papy, dat has papys hisself,– but it was to ruin my character, and name, and reputation. Oh, Goten Hymel! what will Vrou Zwicker say to dis wooman's tale? but then she knowd I had no gimblet, she did. Folks snickered and larfed a good deal, I tell you; but they soon cleared out and went to bed ag'in. The story ran all over Boston like wild fire; nothin' else a'most was talked of; and like most stories, it grew worse and worse every day. Zwicker returned next mornin' to Albany, and has never been to Boston since; and the Sprouls kept close for some time, and then moved away to the western territory. I actilly believe they changed their name, for I never heerd tell of any one that ever seed them since.

Mr. Slick, says Zwicker, the mornin' he started, I have one leetle gimblet; I always travel with my leetle gimblet; take it mid me wherever I go; and when I goes to ped, I takes my leetle gimblet out and bores wid it over de latch of de toor, and dat fastens it, and keeps out de tief and de villain and de womans. I left it to home dat time mid the old vrou, and it was all because I had no gimblet, de row and te noise and te rumpush wash made. Tam it! said he, Mr. Slick, 'tis no use talkin', but tere is always de teyvil to pay when there is a woman and no gimblet.

Yes, said the Clockmaker, if they don't mind the number of the room, they'd better stay away,–but a little attention that way cures all. We are all in a hurry in the States; we eat in a hurry, drink in a hurry, and sleep in a hurry. We all go ahead so fast it keeps one full spring to keep up with others, and one must go it hot foot, if he wants to pass his neighbours. Now, it is a great comfort to have your dinner to the minute, as you do at a boardin'-house, when you are in a hurry—only you must look out sharp arter the dishes, or you won't get nothin'. Things vanish like a wink. I recollect once when quails first came in that season; there was an old chap at Peep's boardin'-house, that used to take the whole dish of 'em, empty it on his plate, and gobble 'em up like a turkeycock,–no one else ever got none. We were all a good deal ryled at it, seein' that he didn't pay no more for his dinner than us, so I nicknamed him "Old Quail," and it cured him; he always left half arter that, for a scramb. No systim is quite perfect, squire; accidents will happen in the best regulated places, like that of Marm Sproul's and Old Quail's; but still there is nothin' arter all like a boardin'-house,–the only thing is, keep out of the *wrong room*.

FURTHER READING

WORKS BY THOMAS HALIBURTON

The Clockmaker or *The Sayings and Doings of Samuel Slick of Slickville* (Toronto: McClelland and Stewart, New Canadian Library, 1958).

Sam Slick in Pictures: The Best of the Humour of Thomas Chandler Haliburton, edited, with an introduction by, Lorne Pierce, illustrated by C. W. Jefferys (Toronto: Ryerson Press, 1956).

The Sam Slick Anthology, selected and introduced by R. E. Watters (Toronto: Clarke Irwin, 1969).

The Old Judge or *Life in a Colony*, edited by R. E. Watters (Toronto: Clarke Irwin, 1968).

CRITICISM

Haliburton's work is discussed in *Masks of Fiction*, edited by A. J. M. Smith (Toronto: McClelland and Stewart, New Canadian Library, 1961).

RELATED STUDY

Herman Melville, *The Confidence Man*, 1857 (Toronto: Ryerson Press, Airmont Classics).

LITERARY SITE

Haliburton Memorial Museum, Windsor, Nova Scotia, which used to be Haliburton's home, *Clifton*.

Susanna Moodie

Susanna Moodie (1803-85), née Strickland, was an English-woman who married a half-pay officer and in 1832 emigrated with him to Upper Canada where they lived for two years on a farm near Cobourg. They then took up wild land in Douro township, and she tells the story of their struggles to establish a farm in the backwoods in her first Canadian book, Roughing It in the Bush *(1852). They moved to Belleville in 1840; and* Life in the Clearings *(1853) is an account of her experiences there. Mrs. Moodie also pioneered in Canadian literary journalism. She was a leading contributor to the Montreal* Literary Garland *from 1839 until its demise in 1851 because of American competition. She and her husband also contributed to and edited the* Victoria Magazine: a Cheap Periodical for the Canadian People.

So much has been written in the twentieth century about the alienated individual in society, that the modern reader is surprised to meet a nineteenth century character cast in the role of outsider.

Susanna Moodie's portrayal of Brian B— stands in sharp contrast to the backwoodsman cliché. Brian is much more Byronic hero than he is *coureur de bois.* In appearance he fits the romantic image: black curling hair, high features, brightly dark complexion, hawk-like eyes, face sorrowful and taciturn. His despondency and melancholy come from self-accusation, a sense of personal guilt, and remorse: "I felt deeply my degradation–felt that I had become the slave to low vice . . . How sad and gloomy I felt! I thought that there was no creature in the world so miserable as myself."

In Brian's occupation he is marked for aloneness; the still-hunter tracks down and creeps up on his quarry through deep soft snow. Brian's loneliness sharpens the impression we have of Mrs. Moodie's own sense of isolation. She admits herself: "My recollections of Brian seem more particularly to concentrate in the adventures of one night, when I happened to be left alone." They both undergo an intense emotional experience involving a pack of wolves. So closely related in event, situation, and feeling are the phrases and images they use that these could be interchanged in their separate accounts. The cynic might comment that this is not surprising, since Mrs. Moodie is, after all, the primary narrator in both instances. However, that is the point exactly: Brian is, in effect, Mrs. Moodie's emotional counterpart. Even at the end of the story, the two characters are bound together by the dismal prospect the future holds for them. The Moodies embark upon the "ruinous scheme" of selling their farm and taking up a grant of land in the backwoods where new "trials and sorrows" await them. Brian's life ends in self-destruction.

Throughout the narrative we are made aware of the author's conscious efforts to create and sustain an atmosphere of melancholy. Sometimes this melancholy is further darkened by violence; other times it is lessened by instances of human warmth. In Mrs. Moodie's other narratives as well, the treatment of her material is much more fictional than documentary. George Woodcock comments in *Canada and The Canadians*:

> Pioneers are people whose creativity goes into the reshaping of the land. They have neither the time nor the energy to turn their minds to original thought or artistic creation, and they are usually so engrossed in the idea of reproducing in a strange land the world from which they came that the thought of giving a novel expression to what they see is remote from their minds . . . There are a few exceptions, created by peculiar circumstances, among them the indefatigable Strickland sisters, Susanna Moodie and Catherine Parr Traill, who wrote out of a bitter experience of trying to combine gentility with pioneering and, later, of attempting to establish literary journalism in early Upper Canada. Susanna's *Roughing it in the Bush* and *Life in the Clearings*, and Catherine's *The Backwoods of Canada*, are memoirs which together provide an excellent if idiosyncratic picture of life during the 1830's in the rural areas and small towns of Upper Canada, a picture far more convincing than one will get from any Canadian novel before the end of the century.

Carl Klinck, in his introduction to the New Canadian Library edition of *Roughing It*, states categorically, "The sketches in *Roughing it in the Bush* were written by a novelist."

But Mrs. Moodie was not only a kind of early Canadian novelist, she was also an early social critic who spoke out strongly about conditions that were to her, unjust. Here is what she had to say to land speculators in her introduction to the first edition of *Roughing it in the Bush*:

You had your acres to sell, and what to you were the worn-down frames and broken hearts of the infatuated purchasers? The public believed the plausible statements you made with such earnestness, and men of all grades rushed to hear your hired orators declaim upon the blessings to be obtained by the clearers of the wilderness . . . Too many of these brave and honourable men were easy dupes to the designing land-speculators. Not having counted the cost, but only looked upon the bright side of the picture held up to their admiring gaze, they fell easily into the snares of their artful seducers.

She had concern too for the natives of Canada:

An Indian is Nature's gentleman—never familiar, coarse, or vulgar . . . Often have I grieved that people with such generous impulses should be degraded and corrupted by civilized men; that a mysterious destiny involves and hangs over them, pressing them back into the wilderness, and slowly and surely sweeping them from the earth.

BRIAN, THE STILL-HUNTER

It was early day. I was alone in the old shanty, preparing breakfast, and now and then stirring the cradle with my foot, when a tall, thin, middle-aged man walked into the house, followed by two large, strong dogs.

Placing the rifle he had carried on his shoulder in a corner of the room, he advanced to the hearth, and, without speaking, or seemingly looking at me, lighted his pipe and commenced smoking. The dogs, after growling and snapping at the cat, who had not given the strangers a very courteous reception, sat down on the hearth-stone on either side of their taciturn master, eyeing him from time to time, as if long habit had made them understand all his motions. There was a great contrast between the dogs. The one was a brindled bull-dog of the largest size, a most formidable and powerful brute; the other a staghound, tawny, deep-chested, and strong-limbed. I regarded the man and his hairy companions with silent curiosity.

He was between forty and fifty years of age; his head, nearly bald, was studded at the sides with strong, coarse, black curling hair. His features were high, his complexion brightly dark, and his eyes in size,

From: Susanna Moodie, *Roughing it in the Bush* (Toronto: McClelland and Stewart, New Canadian Library, 1962). Reprinted by permission of McClelland and Stewart Limited, the Canadian Publishers.

shape, and colour greatly resembling the eyes of a hawk. The face itself was sorrowful and taciturn; and his thin, compressed lips looked as if they were not much accustomed to smile, or often to unclose to hold social communion with anyone. He stood at the side of the huge hearth, silently smoking, his eyes bent on the fire, and now and then he patted the heads of his dogs, reproving their exuberant expressions of attachment with, "Down, Music; down, Chance!"

"A cold, clear morning," said I, in order to attract his attention and draw him into conversation.

A nod, without raising his head, or withdrawing his eyes from the fire, was his only answer; and, turning from my unsociable guest, I took up the baby, who just then awoke, sat down on a low stool by the table, and began feeding her. During this operation, I once or twice caught the stranger's hawk-eye fixed upon me and the child, but word spoke he none; and presently, after whistling to his dogs, he resumed his gun, and strode out.

When Moodie and Monaghan came in to breakfast, I told them what a strange visitor I had had; and Moodie laughed at my vain attempt to induce him to talk.

"He is a strange being," I said; "I must find out who and what he is."

In the afternoon an old soldier, called Layton, who had served during the American war, and got a grant of land about a mile in the rear of our location, came in to trade for a cow. Now, this Layton was a perfect ruffian, a man whom no one liked, and whom all feared. He was a deep drinker, a great swearer, in short, a perfect reprobate, who never cultivated his land, but went jobbing about from farm to farm, trading horses and cattle, and cheating in a pettifogging way. Uncle Joe had employed him to sell Moodie a young heifer, and he had brought her over for him to look at. When he came in to be paid, I described the stranger of the morning; and as I knew that he was familiar with everyone in the neighbourhood, I asked if he knew him.

"No one should know him better than myself," he said; "'tis old Brian B——, the still-hunter, and a near neighbour of your'n. A sour, morose, queer chap he is, and as mad as a March hare! He's from Lancashire, in England, and came to this country some twenty years ago, with his wife, who was a pretty young lass in those days, and slim enough then, though she's so awfully fleshy now. He had lots of money, too, and he bought four hundred acres of land, just at the corner of the concession line, where it meets the main road. And excellent land it is; and a better farmer, while he stuck to his business, never went into the bush, for it was all bush here then. He was a dashing, handsome fellow, too, and did not hoard the money either;

he loved his pipe and his pot too well; and at last he left off farming, and gave himself to them altogether. Many a jolly booze he and I have had, I can tell you. Brian was an awful passionate man, and, when the liquor was in, and the wit was out, as savage and as quarrelsome as a bear. At such times there was no one but Ned Layton dared go near him. We once had a pitched battle, in which I was conqueror, and ever arter he yielded a sort of sulky obedience to all I said to him. Arter being on the spree for a week or two, he would take fits of remorse, and return home to his wife; would fall down at her knees, and ask her forgiveness, and cry like a child. At other times he would hide himself up in the woods, and steal home at night, and get what he wanted out of the pantry, without speaking a word to any one. He went on with these pranks for some years, till he took a fit of the blue devils.

" 'Come away, Ned, to the — lake, with me,' said he; 'I am weary of my life, and I want a change.'

" 'Shall we take the fishing-tackle?' says I. 'The black bass are in prime season, and F— will lend us the old canoe. He's got some capital rum up from Kingston. We'll fish all day, and have a spree at night.'

" 'It's not to fish I'm going,' says he.

" 'To shoot, then? I've bought Rockwood's new rifle.'

" 'It's neither to fish nor to shoot, Ned; it's a new game I'm going to try; so come along.'

"Well, to the — lake we went. The day was very hot, and our path lay through the woods, and over those scorching plains, for eight long miles. I thought I should have dropped by the way; but during our long walk my companion never opened his lips. He strode on before me, at a half-run, never once turning his head.

" 'The man must be a devil!' says I, 'and accustomed to a warmer place, or he must feel this. Hollo, Brian! Stop there! Do you mean to kill me?'

" 'Take it easy,' says he; 'you'll see another day arter this–I've business on hand and cannot wait.'

"Well, on we went, at the same awful rate, and it was midday when we got to the little tavern on the lake shore, kept by one F—, who had a boat for the convenience of strangers who came to visit the place. Here we got our dinner, and a glass of rum to wash it down. But Brian was moody, and to all my jokes he only returned a sort of grunt; and while I was talking with F—, he steps out and a few minutes arter we saw him crossing the lake in the old canoe.

" 'What's the matter with Brian?' says F—; 'all does not seem right with him, Ned. You had better take the boat and look arter him.'

" 'Pooh!' says I; 'he's often so, and grows so glum nowadays that I will cut his acquaintance altogether if he does not improve.'

" 'He drinks awful hard,' says F—; 'may be he's got a fit of the delirium-tremulous. There is no telling what he may be up to at this minute.'

"My mind misgave me too, so I e'en takes the oars, and pushes out, right upon Brian's track; and by the Lord Harry! if I did not find him, upon my landing on the opposite shore, lying wallowing in his blood, with his throat cut. 'Is that you, Brian?' says I, giving him a kick with my foot, to see if he was alive or dead. 'What upon earth tempted you to play me and F— such a dirty, mean trick, as to go and stick yourself like a pig, bringing such a discredit upon the house?–and you so far from home and those who should nurse you.'

"I was so mad with him, that (saving your presence, ma'am) I swore awfully, and called him names that would be ondacent to repeat here; but he only answered with groans and a horrid gurgling in his throat. 'It's a-choking you are,' said I; 'but you shan't have your own way and die so easily either, if I can punish you by keeping you alive.' So I just turned him upon his stomach, with his head down the steep bank; but he still kept choking and growing black in the face."

Layton then detailed some particulars of his surgical practice which it is not necessary to repeat. He continued:

"I bound up his throat with my handkerchief, and took him neck and heels, and threw him into the bottom of the boat. Presently he came to himself a little, and sat up in the boat; and–would you believe it?–made several attempts to throw himself into the water. 'This will not do,' says I; 'you've done mischief enough already by cutting your weasand! If you dare to try that again, I will kill you with the oar.' I held it up to threaten him; he was scared, and lay down quiet as a lamb. I put my foot upon his breast, 'Lie still, now! or you'll catch it!' He looked piteously at me; he could not speak, but his eyes seemed to say, 'Have pity upon me, Ned; don't kill me.'

"Yes, ma'am, this man, who had just cut his throat, and twice arter that had tried to drown himself, was afraid that I should knock him on the head and kill him. Ha! ha! I never shall forget the work that F— and I had with him arter I got him up to the house.

"The doctor came and sewed up his throat; and his wife–poor crittur!–came to nurse him. Bad as he was, she was mortal fond of him. He lay there, sick and unable to leave his bed, for three months, and did nothing but pray to God to forgive him, for he thought the devil would surely have him for cutting his own throat; and when he got about again, which is now twelve years ago, he left off drinking entirely, and wanders about the woods with his dogs, hunting. He seldom speaks to any one, and his wife's brother carries on the farm for the family. He is so shy of strangers that 'tis a wonder he came in here. The old wives are afraid of him; but you need not heed him –his troubles are to himself, he harms no one."

Layton departed, and left me brooding over the sad tale which he had told in such an absurd and jesting manner. It was evident from the account he had given of Brian's attempt at suicide, that the hapless hunter was not wholly answerable for his conduct–that he was a harmless maniac.

The next morning, at the very same hour, Brian again made his appearance; but instead of the rifle across his shoulder, a large stone jar occupied the place, suspended by a stout leather thong. Without saying a word, but with a truly benevolent smile that flitted slowly over his stern features, and lighted them up like a sunbeam breaking from beneath a stormy cloud, he advanced to the table, and unslinging the jar, set it down before me, and in a low and gruff, but by no means an unfriendly, voice, said, "Milk, for the child," and vanished.

"How good it was of him! How kind!" I exclaimed, as I poured the precious gift of four quarts of pure new milk out into a deep pan. I had not asked him–had never said that the poor weanling wanted milk. It was the courtesy of a gentleman–of a man of benevolence and refinement.

For weeks did my strange, silent friend steal in, take up the empty jar, and supply its place with another replenished with milk. The baby knew his step, and would hold out her hands to him and cry, "Milk!" and Brian would stoop down and kiss her, and his two great dogs lick her face.

"Have you any children, Mr. B—?"

"Yes, five; but none like this."

"My little girl is greatly indebted to you for your kindness."

"She's welcome, or she would not get it. You are strangers; but I like you all. You look kind, and I would like to know more about you."

Moodie shook hands with the old hunter, and assured him that we should always be glad to see him. After this invitation, Brian became a frequent guest. He would sit and listen with delight to Moodie while he described to him elephant-hunting at the Cape, grasping his rifle in a determined manner, and whistling an encouraging air to his dogs. I asked him one evening what made him so fond of hunting.

"'Tis the excitement," he said; "it drowns thought, and I love to be alone. I am sorry for the creatures, too, for they are free and happy; yet I am led by an instinct I cannot restrain to kill them.

Sometimes the sight of their dying agonies recalls painful feelings, and then I lay aside the gun, and do not hunt for days. But 'tis fine to be alone with God in the great woods–to watch the sunbeams stealing through the thick branches, the blue sky breaking in upon you in patches, and to know that all is bright and shiny above you, in spite of the gloom that surrounds you."

After a long pause, he continued, with much solemn feeling in his look and tone:

"I lived a life of folly for years, for I was respectably born and educated, and had seen something of the world, perhaps more than was good, before I left home for the woods; and from the teaching I had received from kind relatives and parents I should have known how to have conducted myself better. But, madam, if we associate long with the depraved and ignorant, we learn to become even worse than they. I felt deeply my degradation–felt that I had become the slave to low vice, and, in order to emancipate myself from the hateful tyranny of evil passions, I did a very rash and foolish thing. I need not mention the manner in which I transgressed God's holy laws; all the neighbours know it, and must have told you long ago. I could have borne reproof, but they turned my sorrow into indecent jests, and, unable to bear their coarse ridicule, I made companions of my dogs and gun, and went forth into the wilderness. Hunting became a habit. I could no longer live without it, and it supplies the stimulant which I lost when I renounced the cursed whiskey-bottle.

"I remember the first hunting excursion I took alone in the forest. How sad and gloomy I felt! I thought that there was no creature in the world so miserable as myself. I was tired and hungry, and I sat down upon a fallen tree to rest. All was still as death around me, and I was sinking to sleep, when my attention was aroused by a long, wild cry. My dog, for I had not Chance then, and he's no hunter, pricked up his ears, but instead of answering with a bark of defiance, he crouched down, trembling, at my feet. 'What does this mean?' I cried, and I cocked my rifle and sprang upon the log. The sound came nearer upon the wind. It was like the deep baying of a pack of hounds in full cry. Presently a noble deer rushed past me, and fast upon his trail–I see them now, like so many black devils– swept by a pack of ten or fifteen large, fierce wolves, with fiery eyes and bristling hair, and paws that seemed hardly to touch the ground in their eager haste. I thought not of danger, for, with their prey in view, I was safe; but I felt every nerve within me tremble for the fate of the poor deer. The wolves gained upon him at every bound. A close thicket intercepted his path, and, rendered desperate, he turned at bay. His nostrils were dilated, and his eyes seemed to send forth long streams of light. It was wonderful to witness the courage of the beast. How bravely he repelled the attacks of his deadly enemies, how gallantly he tossed them to the right and left, and spurned them from beneath his hoofs; yet all his struggles were useless, and he was quickly overcome and torn to pieces by his ravenous foes. At that moment he seemed more unfortunate even than myself, for I could not see in what manner he had deserved his fate. All his speed and energy, his courage and fortitude, had been exerted in vain. I had tried to destroy myself; but he, with every effort vigorously made for self-preservation, was doomed to meet the fate he dreaded! Is God just to his creatures?"

With this sentence on his lips, he started abruptly from his seat and left the house . . .

My recollections of Brian seem more particularly to concentrate in the adventures of one night, when I happened to be left alone, for the first time since my arrival in Canada. I cannot now imagine how I could have been such a fool as to give way for four-and-twenty hours to such childish fears; but so it was, and I will not disguise my weakness from my indulgent reader.

Moodie had bought a very fine cow of a black man, named Mollineux, for which he was to give twenty-seven dollars. The man lived twelve miles back in the woods, and one fine frosty spring day– (don't smile at the term frosty, thus connected with the genial season of the year; the term is perfectly correct when applied to the Canadian spring, which, until the middle of May, is the most dismal season in the year)–he and John Monaghan took a rope and the dog, and sallied forth to fetch the cow home. Moodie said that they should be back by six o'clock in the evening, and charged me to have something cooked for supper when they returned, as he doubted not their long walk in the sharp air would give them a good appetite. This was during the time that I was without a servant, and living in old Mrs. —'s shanty.

The day was so bright and clear, and Katie was so full of frolic and play, rolling upon the floor, or toddling from chair to chair, that the day passed on without my feeling remarkably lonely. At length the evening drew nigh, and I began to expect my husband's return, and to think of the supper that I was to prepare for his reception. The red heifer that we had bought of Layton, came lowing to the door to be milked, but I did not know how to milk in those days, and, besides this, I was terribly afraid of cattle. Yet, as I knew that milk would be required for the tea, I ran across the meadow to Mrs. Joe, and begged that one of her girls would be so kind as to milk for me. My request was greeted with a rude burst of laughter from the whole set.

"If you can't milk," said Mrs. Joe, "It's high time you should learn. My girls are above being helps."

"I would not ask you but as a great favour; I am afraid of cows."

"*Afraid of cows*! Lord bless the woman! A farmer's wife and afraid of cows!"

Here followed another laugh at my expense; and, indignant at the refusal of my first and last request, when they had all borrowed so much from me, I shut the inhospitable door, and returned home.

After many ineffectual attempts, I succeeded at last, and bore my half-pail of milk in triumph to the house. Yes! I felt prouder of that milk than many an author of the best thing he ever wrote, whether in verse or prose; and it was doubly sweet when I considered that I had procured it without being under any obligation to my ill-natured neighbours. I had learned a useful lesson of independence, to which in after years I had often again to refer. I fed little Katie and put her to bed, made the hot cakes for tea, boiled the potatoes, and laid the ham, cut in nice slices, in the pan, ready to cook the moment I saw the men enter the meadow, and arranged the little room with scrupulous care and neatness. A glorious fire was blazing on the hearth, and everything was ready for their supper, and I began to look out anxiously for their arrival.

The night had closed in cold and foggy, and I could no longer distinguish any object at more than a few yards from the door. Bringing in as much wood as I thought would last me for several hours, I closed the door; and for the first time in my life I found myself at night in a house entirely alone. Then I began to ask myself a thousand torturing questions as to the reason of their unusual absence. Had they lost their way in the woods? Could they have fallen in with wolves (one of my early bugbears)? Could any fatal accident have befallen them? I started up, opened the door, held my breath, and listened. The little brook lifted up its voice in loud, hoarse wailing, or mocked, in its babbling to the stones, the sound of human voices. As it became later, my fears increased in proportion. I grew too superstitious and nervous to keep the door open. I not only closed it, but dragged a heavy box in front, for bolt there was none. Several ill-looking men had, during the day, asked their way to Toronto. I felt alarmed lest such rude wayfarers should come tonight and demand a lodging, and find me alone and unprotected. Once I thought of running across to Mrs. Joe and asking her to let one of the girls stay with me until Moodie returned; but the way in which I had been repulsed in the evening prevented me from making a second appeal to their charity.

Hour after hour wore away, and the crowing of the cocks proclaimed midnight, and yet they came not. I had burnt out all my wood, and I dared not open the door to fetch in more. The candle was expiring in the socket, and I had not courage to go up into the loft and procure another before it went finally out. Cold, heart-weary, and faint, I sat and cried. Every now and then the furious barking of the dogs at the neighbouring farms, and the loud cackling of the geese upon our own, made me hope that they were coming; and then I listened till the beating of my own heart excluded all other sounds. Oh, that unwearied brook! how it sobbed and moaned like a fretful child;–what unreal terrors and fanciful illusions my too active mind conjured up, whilst listening to its mysterious tones!

Just as the moon rose, the howling of a pack of wolves, from the great swamp in our rear, filled the whole air. Their yells were answered by the barking of all the dogs in the vicinity, and the geese, unwilling to be behind-hand in the general confusion, set up the most discordant screams. I had often heard, and even been amused, during the winter, particularly on thaw nights, with hearing the howls of these formidable wild beasts, but I had never before heard them alone, and when one dear to me was abroad amid their haunts. They were directly in the track that Moodie and Monaghan must have taken; and I now had no doubt that they had been attacked and killed on their return through the woods with the cow, and I wept and sobbed until the cold grey dawn peered in upon me through the small dim window. I have passed many a long cheerless night, when my dear husband was away from me during the rebellion, and I was left in my forest home with five little children, and only an old Irishwoman to draw and cut wood for my fire and attend to the wants of the family, but that was the saddest and longest night I ever remember.

Just as the day broke my friends the wolves set up a parting benediction, so loud and wild, and near to the house, that I was afraid lest they should break through the frail window, or come down the low, wide chimney, and rob me of my child. But their detestable howls died away in the distance, and the bright sun rose up and dispersed the wild horrors of the night, and I looked once more timidly around me. The sight of the table spread, and the uneaten supper, renewed my grief, for I could not divest myself of the idea that Moodie was dead. I opened the door, and stepped forth into the pure air of the early day. A solemn and beautiful repose still hung like a veil over the face of Nature. The mists of night still rested upon the majestic woods, and not a sound but the flowing of the waters went up in the vast stillness. The earth had not yet raised her matin hymn to the throne of the Creator. Sad at heart, and weary and worn in spirit, I went down to the spring and washed my face and head, and drank a deep draught of its icy waters. On returning to the house, I met, near the door, old Brian the hunter, with a large fox dangling across his shoulder, and the dogs following at his heels.

"Why! Mrs. Moodie, what is the matter? You are early abroad this morning, and look dreadful ill. Is anything wrong at home? Is the baby or your husband sick?"

"Oh!" I cried, bursting into tears, "I fear he is killed by the wolves."

The man stared at me, as if he doubted the evidence of his senses, and well he might; but this one idea had taken such strong possession of my mind that I could admit no other. I then told him, as well as I could find words, the cause of my alarm, to which he listened very kindly and patiently.

"Set your heart at rest; your husband is safe. It is a long journey on foot to Mollineux, to one unacquainted with a blazed path in a bush road. They have stayed all night at the black man's shanty, and you will see them back at noon."

I shook my head, and continued to weep.

"Well, now, in order to satisfy you, I will saddle my mare and ride over to the nigger's, and bring you word as fast as I can."

I thanked him sincerely for his kindness, and returned, in somewhat better spirits, to the house. At ten o'clock my good messenger returned with the glad tidings that all was well.

The day before, when half the journey had been accomplished, John Monaghan let go the rope by which he led the cow, and she had broken away through the woods and returned to her old master; and when they again reached his place, night had set in, and they were obliged to wait until the return of day. Moodie laughed heartily at all my fears; but indeed I found them no joke . . .

When our resolution was formed to sell our farm, and take up our grant of land in the backwoods, no one was so earnest in trying to persuade us to give up this ruinous scheme as our friend Brian B—, who became quite eloquent in his description of the trials and sorrows that awaited us. During the last week of our stay in the township of H—, he visited us every evening, and never bade us good-night without a tear moistening his cheek. We parted with the hunter as with an old friend; and we never met again. His fate was a sad one. After we left that part of the country, he fell into a moping melancholy, which ended in self-destruction. But a kinder or warmer-hearted man, while he enjoyed the light of reason, has seldom crossed our path.

FURTHER READING

WORKS BY SUSANNA MOODIE

Roughing it in the Bush (Toronto: McClelland and Stewart, New Canadian Library, 1962).
Life in the Clearings (Toronto: The Macmillan Company of Canada, 1959).

RELATED WORKS—FROM THE PAST

Mary Quayle Innis, ed., *Mrs. Simcoe's Diary* (Toronto: The Macmillan Company of Canada, 1965).
H. H. Langton, ed., *A Gentlewoman in Upper Canada: The Journals of Anne Langton* (Toronto: Clarke Irwin).
W. Dunlop, *Tiger Dunlop's Upper Canada* (Toronto: McClelland and Stewart, New Canadian Library, 1967).
Catherine Parr Traill, *The Backwoods of Canada* (Toronto: McClelland and Stewart, New Canadian Library, 1966). Catherine Parr Traill was a sister of Susanna Moodie.
Catherine Parr Traill, *A Canadian Settler's Guide* (Toronto: McClelland and Stewart, New Canadian Library, 1969).
Anna B. Jameson, *Winter Studies and Summer Rambles in Canada* (Toronto: McClelland and Stewart, New Canadian Library, 1965).

RELATED WORKS—MODERN

Robertson Davies, *At my Heart's Core*, an historical play (Toronto: Clarke Irwin, 1950).
Margaret Atwood, *The Journals of Susanna Moodie* (Toronto: Oxford University Press). "A cycle of poems invoking the life and thoughts of an immigrant to Canada from England in the 1800's . . . The poems were inspired by two books about early Canada written by Susanna Moodie."

CRITICISM

A. J. M. Smith, ed., *Masks of Fiction* (Toronto: McClelland and Stewart, New Canadian Library, 1961). Susanna Moodie's work is discussed.

BIOGRAPHY

Audrey Y. Morris, *Gentle Pioneers* (Toronto: Musson Book Company, 1967). The story of the Moodie, Traill, and Strickland families in Upper Canada.

ILLUSTRATIONS

Edwin C. Guillet, *The Valley of the Trent* (Toronto: Ontario Government Series of the Champlain Society; and University of Toronto Press). May be ordered through the University of Toronto Press.

RECORDINGS

The Journals of Susanna Moodie, poems by Margaret Atwood, read by Mia Anderson. May be obtained from CBC Publications, Box 500, Terminal "A", Toronto 116, Ontario.

LITERARY SITE

Catherine Parr Traill's home, *Westove,* is now the home of a Peterborough lawyer, Mr. W. C. Grant.

James De Mille

Scholar and professor, James De Mille (1836-80) was born in St. John, New Brunswick, and educated at Acadia College and Brown University. After an unsuccessful attempt at bookselling he spent four years teaching classics at Acadia before going to a permanent position teaching English at Dalhousie. To supplement his income he wrote popular novels, historical romances and adventure stories for boys for the American market–thirty volumes in all in less than twenty years. Among these are The Dodge Club; or Italy in MDCCCLVIII *(1869) in the "innocents abroad" manner, and* The Lady of the Ice *(1870), set in Quebec. The sombrely satirical mock-utopia,* A Strange Manuscript Found in a Copper Cylinder *(1888), though not characteristic of his writing, is his best book.*

This excerpt is taken from a novel which should excite followers of Edgar Allan Poe, Jules Verne, Aldous Huxley and George Orwell–indeed, it should excite anyone whose bent is fantasy. The plot of *A Strange Manuscript Found in a Copper Cylinder* strongly brings to mind Jules Verne techniques. Although the book is almost one hundred years old, its author examines basically the same question which concerns Huxley and Orwell in *Brave New World* and *Nineteen Eighty-Four*: the nature of man's relationship to society and its values.

The mood and setting of *A Strange Manuscript* is reminiscent of Edgar Allan Poe–there is the same consistent emphasis on darkness, often extended into horror, and lightened only in preparation for further shock. As a matter of fact, Edgar Allan Poe's first short story, published in 1833, was named, *A Manuscript Found in a Bottle*. There are striking similarities in the two works. Both stories involve two characters, later reduced to one, cast adrift in south polar regions where they experience every degree of suffering in a nightmare of rock, darkness, whirlpool, terror, and corpse-like human beings.

De Mille's description and analysis of life among the Kosekin place *Strange Manuscript* in the negative or anti-utopia genre. Utopian literature traces the structure of society in an imaginary state where perfection in human living conditions has been achieved. Plato's *Republic*, Thomas More's *Utopia* (1516) and Samuel Butler's *Erewhon* (1872) are examples. Writers of the twentieth century have preferred the mock-utopia, a satirical form which ridicules modern man's attempt to engineer a model society based on advanced technology.

Good fantasy develops out of recognizable situations from which events appear to flow in a logical sequence. The science fiction writer, for example, who drops his reader without preparation into the unknown makes too heavy a demand on that reader's credulity. Jules Verne, Edgar Allan Poe, Jonathan Swift, all begin our journey into the fantastic from familiar territory. For example, the opening scene, in both *Brave New World* and *Nineteen Eighty-Four* is set in a London building.

This selection, "The Sight of Human Beings," from *A Strange Manuscript Found in a Copper Cylinder* is part of the briefing De Mille provides for the fantastic journey ahead.

THE SIGHT OF HUMAN BEINGS

The channel had now lessened to a width of not more than two miles; the shores on either side were precipitous cliffs, broken by occasional declivities, but all of solid rock, so dark as to be almost black, and evidently of volcanic origin. At times there arose rugged eminences, scarred and riven, indescribably dismal and appalling. There was not only an utter absence of life here in these abhorrent regions, but an actual impossibility of life which was enough to make the stoutest heart quail. The rocks looked like iron. It seemed a land of iron penetrated by this ocean stream which had made for itself a channel, and now bore us onward to a destination which was beyond all conjecture.

Through such scenes we drifted all that day. Night came, and in the skies overhead there arose a brilliant display of the aurora australis, while towards the north the volcanic fires glowed with intense lustre. That night we slept. On awakening we noticed a change in the scene. The shores, though still black and forbidding,

From: James De Mille, *A Strange Manuscript found in a Copper Cylinder* (Toronto: McClelland and Stewart, New Canadian Library, 1969). Reprinted by permission of McClelland and Stewart Limited, the Canadian Publishers.

were no longer precipitous, but sloped down gradually to the water; the climate was sensibly milder, and far away before us there arose a line of giant mountains, whose summits were covered with ice and snow that gleamed white and purple in the rays of the sun.

Suddenly Agnew gave a cry, and pointed to the opposite shore.

"Look!" he cried—"do you see? They are men!"

I looked, and there I saw plainly some moving figures that were, beyond a doubt, human beings.

The sight of human beings, thus unexpectedly found, filled us with strange feelings—feelings which I cannot explain. The country was still iron-bound and dark and forbidding, and the stream ran on in a strong current, deep, black as ink, and resistless as fate; the sky behind was lighted up by the volcanic glare which still shone from afar; and in front the view was bounded by the icy heights of a mountain chain. Here was, indeed, a strange country for a human habitation; and strange, indeed, were the human beings whom we saw.

"Shall we land?" said Agnew.

"Oh, no," said I. "Don't be hasty. The elements are sometimes kinder than men, and I feel safer here, even in this river of death, than ashore with such creatures as those."

Agnew made no reply. We watched the figures on the shore. We saw them coming down, staring and gesticulating. We drew on nearer to them till we were able to see them better. A nearer view did not improve them. They were human beings, certainly, but of such an appalling aspect that they could only be likened to animated mummies. They were small, thin, shrivelled, black, with long spears, and wore about the waist short skirts that seemed to be made of the skin of some sea-fowl.

We could not imagine how these creatures lived, or where. There were no signs of vegetation of any kind—not a tree or a shrub. There were no animals; but there were great flocks of birds, some of which seemed different from anything that we had ever seen before. The long spears which the natives carried might possibly be used for catching these, or for fishing purposes. This thought made them seem less formidable, since they would thus be instruments of food rather than weapons of war. Meanwhile we drifted on as before, and the natives watched us, running along the shore abreast of us, so as to keep up with the boat. There seemed over a hundred of them. We could see no signs of any habitations—no huts, however humble; but we concluded that their abodes were farther inland. As for the natives themselves, the longer we looked at them the more abhorrent they grew. Even the wretched aborigines of Van Dieman's Land, who have been classed lowest in the scale of humanity, were pleasing and congenial when compared with these, and the land looked worse than Tierra del Fuego. It looked like a land of iron, and its inhabitants like fiends.

Agnew again proposed to land, but I refused.

"No," I said; "I'd rather starve for a week, and live on hope. Let us drift on. If we go on we may have hope if we choose, but if we land here we shall lose even that. Can we hope for anything from such things as these? Even if they prove friendly, can we live among them? To stay here is worse than death; our only hope is to go on."

Agnew made no reply, and we drifted on for two hours, still followed by the natives. They made no hostile demonstrations. They merely watched us, apparently from motives of curiosity. All this time we were drawing steadily nearer to the line of lofty mountains, which with their icy crests rose before us like an inaccessible and impassable barrier, apparently closing up all farther progress; nor was there any indication of any pass or any opening, however narrow, through which the great stream might run. Nothing was there but one unbroken wall of iron cliffs and icy summits. At last we saw that the sloping shores grew steeper, until, about a mile or two before us, they changed to towering cliffs that rose up on each side for about a thousand feet above the water; here the stream ran, and became lost to view as completely as though swallowed up by the earth.

"We can go no farther," said Agnew. "See–this stream seems to make a plunge there into the mountains. There must be some deep canyon there with cataracts. To go on is certain death. We must stop here, if only to deliberate. Say, shall we risk it among these natives? After all, there is not, perhaps, any danger among them. They are little creatures and seem harmless. They are certainly not very good-looking; but then, you know, appearances often deceive, and the devil's not so black as he's painted. What do you say?"

"I suppose we can do nothing else," said I.

In fact, I could see that we had reached a crisis in our fate. To go on seemed certain death. To stop was our only alternative; and as we were armed we should not be altogether at the mercy of these creatures. Having made this decision we acted upon it at once, for in such a current there was no time for delay; and so, seizing the oars, we soon brought the boat ashore.

As we approached, the crowd of natives stood awaiting us, and looked more repulsive than ever. We could see the emaciation of their bony frames; their toes and fingers were like birds' claws; their eyes were small and dull and weak, and sunken in cavernous hollows, from which they looked at us like corpses—a horrible sight. They stood quietly, however, and without any hostile demonstration, holding their spears carelessly resting upon the ground.

"I don't like the looks of them," said I. "I think I had better fire a gun."

"Why?" cried Agnew. "For Heaven's sake, man, don't hurt any of them!"

"Oh, no," said I; "I only mean to inspire a little wholesome respect."

Saying this I fired in the air. The report rang out with long echoes, and as the smoke swept away it showed us all the natives on the ground. They had seated themselves with their hands crossed on their laps, and there they sat looking at us as before, but with no manifestation of fear or even surprise. I had expected to see them run, but there was nothing of the kind. This puzzled us. Still, there was no time now for any further hesitation. The current was sweeping us towards the chasm between the cliffs, and we had to land without delay. This we did, and as I had another barrel still loaded and a pistol, I felt that with these arms and those of Agnew we should be able to defend ourselves. It was in this state of mind that we landed, and secured the boat by means of the grappling-iron.

The natives now all crowded around us, making many strange gestures, which we did not understand. Some of them bowed low, others prostrated themselves; on the whole these seemed like marks of respect, and it occurred to me that they regarded us as superior beings of some sort. It was evident that there was nothing like hostility in their minds. At the same time, the closer survey which I now made of them filled me with renewed horror; their meagre frames, small, watery, lack-lustre eyes, hollow, cavernous sockets, sunken cheeks, protruding teeth, claw-like fingers, and withered skins, all made them look more than ever like animated mummies, and I shrank from them involuntarily, as one shrinks from contact with a corpse.

Agnew, however, was very different, and it was evident that he felt no repugnance whatever. He bowed and smiled at them, and shook hands with half a dozen of them in succession. The hand-shaking was a new thing to them, but they accepted it in a proper spirit, and renewed their bows and prostrations. After this they all offered us their lances. This certainly seemed like an act of peace and good-will. I shook my head and declined to touch them; but Agnew accepted one of them, and offered his rifle in return. The one to whom he offered it refused to take it. He seemed immensely gratified because Agnew had taken his lance, and the others seemed disappointed at his refusal to take theirs. But I felt my heart quake as I saw him offer his rifle, and still more when he offered it to one or two others, and only regained my composure as I perceived that his offer was refused by all.

They now made motions to us to follow, and we all set forth together.

"My dear More," said Agnew, cheerily, "they're not a bad lot. They mean well. They can't help their looks. You're too suspicious and reserved. Let's make friends with them, and get them to help us. Do as I do."

I tried to, but found it impossible, for my repugnance was immovable. It was like the horror which one feels towards rats, cockroaches, earwigs, or serpents. It was something that defied reason. These creatures seemed like human vermin.

We marched inland for about half a mile, crossed a ridge, and came to a valley, or rather a kind of hollow, at the other side of which we found a cave with a smouldering fire in front. The fire was made of coal, which must exist here somewhere. It was highly bituminous, and burned with a great blaze.

The day was now drawing to a close; far away I could see the lurid glow of the volcanoes, which grew brighter as the day declined: above, the skies twinkled with innumerable stars, and the air was filled with the moan of rushing waters.

We entered the cave. As we did so the natives heaped coal upon the fire, and the flames arose, lighting up the interior. We found here a number of women and children, who looked at us without either fear or curiosity. The children looked like little dwarfs; the women were hags, hideous beyond description. One old woman in particular, who seemed to be in authority, was actually terrible in her awful and repulsive ugliness. A nightmare dream never furnished forth a more frightful object. This nightmare hag prostrated herself before each of us with such an air of self-immolation that she looked as though she wished us to kill her at once. The rough cave, the red light of the fire, all made the scene more awful; and a wild thought came to me that we had actually reached, while yet living, the infernal world, and that this was the abode of devils. Yet their actions, it must be confessed, were far from devilish. Every one seemed eager to serve us. Some spread out couches formed of the skins of birds for us to sit on; others attended to the fire; others offered us gifts of large and beautiful feathers, together with numerous trinkets of rare and curious workmanship. This kind attention on their part was a great puzzle to me, and I could not help suspecting that beneath all this there must be some sinister design. Resolving to be prepared for the worst, I quietly reloaded the empty barrel of my rifle and watched with the utmost vigilance. As for Agnew, he took it all in the most unsuspicious manner. He made signs to them, shook hands with them, accepted their gifts, and even tried to do the agreeable to the formidable hags and the child-fiends around him. He soon attracted the chief attention, and while all looked admiringly upon him, I was left to languish in comparative neglect.

At length a savory odor came through the cave, and a repast was spread before us. It consisted of some large fowl that looked like a goose, but was twice as large as the largest turkey that I had ever seen. The taste was like that of a wild-goose, but rather fishy. Still to us it seemed delicious, for our prolonged diet of raw seal had made us ready to welcome any other food whatever; and this fowl, whatever it was, would not have been unwelcome to any hungry man. It was evident that these people lived on the flesh of birds of various sorts. All around us we saw the skins of birds dried with the feathers on, and used for clothing, for mats, and for ornaments.

The repast being finished, we both felt greatly strengthened and refreshed. Agnew continued to cultivate his new acquaintances, and seeing me holding back, he said,

"More, old fellow, these good people give me to understand that there is another place better than this, and want me to go with them. Will you go?"

At this a great fear seized me.

"Don't go!" I cried–"don't go! We are close by the boat here, and if anything happens we can easily get to it."

Agnew laughed in my face.

"Why, you don't mean to tell me," said he, "that you are still suspicious, and after that dinner? Why, man, if they wanted to harm us, would they feast us in this style? Nonsense, man! Drop your suspicions and come along."

I shook my head obstinately.

"Well," said he, "if I thought there was anything in your suspicions I would stay by you; but I'm confident they mean nothing but kindness, so I'm going off to see the place."

"You'll be back again?" said I.

"Oh, yes," said he, "of course I'll come back, and sleep here."

With these words he left, and nearly all the people accompanied him. I was left behind with the women and children and about a dozen men. These men busied themselves with some work over bird-skins; the women were occupied with some other work over feathers. No one took any notice of me. There did not seem to be any restraint upon me, nor was I watched in any way. Once the nightmare hag came and offered me a small roasted fowl, about the size of a woodcock. I declined it, but at the same time this delicate attention certainly surprised me.

I was now beginning to struggle with some success against my feelings of abhorrence, when suddenly I caught sight of something which chased away every other thought, and made my blood turn cold in my veins. It was something outside. At the mouth of the cave–by the fire which was still blazing bright, and lighting up the scene–I saw four men who had just come to the cave: they were carrying something which I at first supposed to be a sick or wounded companion. On reaching the fire they put it down, and I saw, with a thrill of dismay, that their burden was neither sick nor wounded, but dead, for the corpse lay rigid as they had placed it. Then I saw the nightmare hag approach it with a knife. An awful thought came to me–the crowning horror! The thought soon proved to be but too well founded. The nightmare hag began to cut, and in an instant had detached the arm of the corpse, which she thrust among the coals in the very place where lately she had cooked the fowl. Then she went back for more.

For a moment my brain reeled, and I gasped for breath. Then I rose and staggered out, I know not how. No one tried to stop me, nor did any one follow me; and, for my part, I was ready to blow out the brains of the first who dared to approach me. In this way I reached the open air, and passed by the hag and the four men as they were busy at their awful work. But at this point I was observed and followed. A number of men and women came after me, jabbering their uncouth language and gesticulating. I warned them off, angrily. They persisted, and though none of them were armed, yet I saw that they were unwilling to have me leave the cave, and I supposed that they would try to prevent me by force.

The absence of Agnew made my position a difficult one. Had it not been for this I would have burst through them and fled to the boat; but as long as he was away I felt bound to wait; and though I longed to fly, I could not for his sake. The boat seemed to be a haven of rest. I longed to be in her once more, and drift away, even if it should be to my death. Nature was here less terrible than man; and it seemed better to drown in the waters, to perish amid rocks and whirlpools, than to linger here amid such horrors as these. These people were not like human beings. The vilest and lowest savages that I had ever seen were not so odious as these. A herd of monkeys would be far more congenial, a flock of wolves less abhorrent. They had the caricature of the human form; they were the lowest of humanity; their speech was a mockery of language; their faces devilish, their kindness a cunning pretence; and most hideous of all was the nightmare hag that prepared the cannibal repast.

I could not begin hostilities, for I had to wait for Agnew; so I stood and looked, and then walked away for a little distance. They followed me closely, with eager words and gesticulations, though as yet no one touched me or threatened me. Their tone seemed rather

one of persuasion. After a few paces I stood still, with all of them
around me. The horrible repast showed plainly all that was in store
for us. They received us kindly and fed us well only to devote us
to the most abhorrent of deaths. Agnew, in his mad confidence, was
only insuring his own doom. He was putting himself completely in
the power of devils, who were incapable of pity and strangers to
humanity. To make friends with such fiends was impossible, and I
felt sure that our only plan was to rule by terror–to seize, to slay,
to conquer. But still I had to wait for him, and did not dare to resort
to violence while he was absent; so I waited, while the savages
gathered round me, contenting themselves with guarding me, and
neither touching me nor threatening me. And all this time the hag
went on, intent on her preparation of the horrible repast.

While standing there looking, listening, waiting for Agnew, I noticed many things. Far away the volcanoes blazed, and the northern
sky was red with a lurid light. There, too, higher up, the moon was
shining overhead, the sky was gleaming with stars; and all over the
heavens there shone the lustre of the aurora australis, brighter than
any I had ever seen–surpassing the moon and illuminating all. It
lighted up the haggard faces of the devils around me, and it again
seemed to me as though I had died and gone to the land of woe–an
iron land, a land of despair, with lurid fires all aglow and faces of
fear.

Suddenly, there burst upon my ears the report of a gun, which
sounded like a thunder-peal, and echoed in long reverberations. At
once I understood it. My fears had proved true. These savages had
enticed Agnew away to destroy him. In an instant I burst through
the crowd around me, and ran wildly in the direction of that sound,
calling his name, as I ran, at the top of my voice.

I heard a loud cry; then another report. I hurried on, shouting
his name in a kind of frenzy. The strange courage of these savages
had already impressed me deeply. They did not fear our guns. They
were all attacking him, and he was alone, fighting for his life.

Then there was another report; it was his pistol. I still ran on, and
still shouted to him.

At last I received an answer. He had perhaps heard me, and was
answering, or, at any rate, he was warning me.

"More," he cried, "fly, fly, fly to the boat! Save yourself!"

"Where are you?" I cried, as I still rushed on.

"Fly, More, fly! Save yourself! You can't save me. I'm lost. Fly
for your life!"

Judging from his cries, he did not seem far away. I hurried on.
I could see nothing of him. All the time the savages followed me.
None were armed; but it seemed to me that they were preparing to
fling themselves upon me and overpower me with their numbers.

They would capture me alive, I thought, bind me, and carry me back, reserving me for a future time!

I turned and waved them back. They took no notice of my gesture. Then I ran on once more. They followed. They could not run so fast as I did, and so I gained on them rapidly, still shouting to Agnew. But there was no response. I ran backward and forward, crossing and recrossing, doubling and turning, pursued all the time by the savages. At last, in rage and despair, I fired upon them, and one of them fell. But, to my dismay, the others did not seem to care one whit; they did not stop for one moment, but pursued as before.

My situation was now plain in all its truth. They had enticed Agnew away; they had attacked him. He had fought, and had been overpowered. He had tried to give me warning. His last words had been for me to fly–to fly: yes, for he well knew that it was better far for me to go to death through the raging torrent than to meet the fate which had fallen upon himself. For him there was now no more hope. That he was lost was plain. If he were still alive he would call to me; but his voice had been silenced for some time. All was over, and that noble heart that had withstood so bravely and cheerily the rigors of the storm, and the horrors of our desperate voyage, had been stilled in death by the vilest of miscreants.

I paused for a moment. Even though Agnew was dead, I could not bear to leave him, but felt as though I ought to share his fate. The savages came nearer. At their approach I hesitated no longer. That fate was too terrible: I must fly.

But before I fled I turned in fury to wreak vengeance upon them for their crimes. Full of rage and despair, I discharged my remaining rifle-barrel into the midst of the crowd. Then I fled towards the boat. On the way I had a frightful thought that she might have been sent adrift; but, on approaching the place, I found her there just as I had left her. The savages, with their usual fearlessness, still pursued. For a moment I stood on the shore, with the grapple in my hand and the boat close by, and as they came near I discharged my pistol into the midst of them. Then I sprang into the boat; the swift current bore me away, and in a few minutes the crowd of pursuing demons disappeared from view.

FURTHER READING

MOCK-UTOPIAS
Jonathan Swift, *Gulliver's Travels*, Section III (Harmondsworth: Penguin Books).
James De Mille, *A Strange Manuscript found in a Copper Cylinder* (Toronto: McClelland and Stewart, New Canadian Library, 1969).

Aldous Huxley, *Brave New World* (Harmondsworth: Penguin Books).
George Orwell, *Nineteen Eighty-Four* (Harmondsworth: Penguin Books).

NINETEENTH CENTURY UTOPIAS

Samuel Butler, *Erewhon*, 1872 (Toronto: Ryerson Press, Airmont Classics). Also available in Penguin and Signet paperbacks.
James De Mille, *A Strange Manuscript found in a Copper Cylinder*, written before 1880, published 1888 (publisher's details above).
Edward Bellamy, *Looking Backward*, 1887 (Signet paperback).
William Morris, *News from Nowhere*, 1890 (Toronto: Holt, Rinehart and Winston).

SCIENCE FICTION

Jules Verne, *Journey to the Centre of the Earth* (Toronto: Ryerson Press, Airmont Classics).
James De Mille, *A Strange Manuscript found in a Copper Cylinder* (publisher's details above).

Gilbert Parker

Gilbert Parker (1862-1932) was born in Camden East, Ontario. He was educated in Ontario public schools, attended Ottawa Normal School, and became a teacher. When he had saved enough money he went to Trinity College, University of Toronto, where he was ordained a deacon in the Anglican Church. After serving for a short time in the parish of Trenton, he went to Australia, mainly for health reasons, and became a newspaperman. In 1889 he settled in England where for eighteen years he served as a member of the British House of Commons.

What are some of Gilbert Parker's accomplishments? His first book, *Pierre and His People*, appeared in 1892. This is a collection of short stories about early days in the Canadian North West; the characters are mainly ranchers, cowboys, bushworkers, miners, mounted police, Indians, trappers, and Hudson's Bay men. This work proved so popular that it went through twenty-seven editions in twenty years. It was followed by others; in all, Gilbert Parker wrote some thirty-six works: romances, novels, and short stories, about half of them having their setting in Canada. One of them, *The Lane that Had No Turning*, Parker dedicated to Sir Wilfred Laurier:

> For many years your name has stood for a high and noble compromise between the temperaments and the intellectual and social habits of two races, and I am not singular in thinking that you have done more than most other men to make the English and French of the Dominion understand each other better. To you, sir, I come with this book, which contains the first things I ever wrote out of the life of the province so dear to you, and the last things also that I shall ever write about it. I beg you to receive it as the loving re-creation of one who sympathizes with the people of whom you come, and honours their virtues, and who has no fear for the unity, and no doubt as to the

splendid future, of the nation, whose fibre is got of the two
great civilizing races of Europe.
Dated August 14, 1900.

Gilbert Parker merited the publication by Scribners' in New York
of his collected works in the same series as the collected works of
Dickens, Turgeniev, Kipling, Meredith and Henry James. Between
the years 1912 and 1923, twenty-three volumes of Parker's work
were published.

In 1902 Gilbert Parker was knighted by King Edward VII; in
1915 he was created a baronet. He died in England, but according
to his previously expressed wish, his body was brought to Canada
for burial.

The *Globe and Mail* edition of September 28, 1932, carries a full
account of the funeral service held in the old Parish Church of
St. Thomas in Belleville, Ontario. Sir Gilbert was buried in the
Parker Mausoleum, overlooking the Bay of Quinte.

"Gilbert Parker was first and last a Canadian," said the Right
Reverend John Lyons, Bishop of Ontario, in his funeral oration. He
also quoted a few lines of verse:

Lives of great men all remind us
We can make our lives sublime
And in departing leave behind us
Footprints on the sands of time.

The Prime Minister of Canada, R. B. Bennett, was only one of
the many distinguished pall bearers.

"One of the most touching incidents of the funeral", says the
Globe and Mail story, "was the attendance of the surviving students
of the class which Sir Gilbert taught at Marsh Hill, but a few miles
from this city. There were fifteen of these students."

The account concludes, "He sleeps with his fathers."

Today, with the exception of *The Seats of the Mighty* in the New
Canadian Library, there is not a single book by Sir Gilbert Parker
in print in the United States, in Great Britain—or, in Canada.

THE STONE

The Stone hung on a jutting crag of Purple Hill. On one side of it,
far beneath, lay the village, huddled together as if, through being
close compacted, its handful of humanity should not be a mere dust
in the balance beside Nature's portentousness. Yet if one stood beside

The Stone, and looked down, the flimsy wooden huts looked like a barrier at the end of a great flume. For the hill hollowed and narrowed from The Stone to the village, as if giants had made this concave path by trundling boulders to that point like a funnel where the miners' houses now formed a *cul-de-sac*. On the other side of the crag was a valley also; but it was lonely and untenanted; and at one flank of The Stone were serried legions of trees.

The Stone was a mighty and wonderful thing. Looked at from the village direct, it had nothing but the sky for a background. At times, also, it appeared to rest on nothing; and many declared that they could see clean between it and the oval floor of the crag on which it rested. That was generally in the evening, when the sun was setting behind it. Then the light coiled round its base, between it and its pedestal, thus making it appear to hover above the hill-point, or, planet-like, to be just settling on it. At other times, when the light was perfectly clear and not too strong, and the village side of the crag was brighter than the other, more accurate relations of The Stone to its pedestal could be discovered. Then one would say that it balanced on a tiny base, a toe of granite. But if one looked long, especially in the summer, when the air throbbed, it evidently rocked upon that toe; if steadily, and very long, he grew tremulous, perhaps afraid. Once, a woman who was about to become a mother went mad, because she thought The Stone would hurtle down the hill at her great moment and destroy her and her child. Indians would not live either on the village side of The Stone or in the valley beyond. They had a legend that, some day, one, whom they called The Man Who Sleeps, would rise from his hidden couch in the mountains, and, being angry that any dared to cumber his playground, would hurl The Stone upon them that dwelt at Purple Hill. But white men pay little heed to Indian legends.

At one time or another every person who had come to the village visited The Stone. Colossal as it was, the real base on which its weight rested was actually very small: the view from the village had not been all deceitful. It is possible, indeed, that at one time it had really rocked, and that the rocking had worn for it a shallow cup, or socket, in which it poised. The first man who came to Purple Valley prospecting had often stopped his work and looked at The Stone in a half-fear that it would spring upon him unawares. And yet he had as often laughed at himself for doing so, since, as he said, it must have been there hundreds of thousands of years. Strangers, when they came to the village, went to sleep somewhat timidly the first night of their stay, and not infrequently left their beds to go and look at The Stone, as it hung there ominously in the light of the moon; or listened towards it if it was dark. When the moon rose late, and The Stone chanced to be directly in front of it, a black sphere seemed to be rolling into the light to blot it out.

But none who lived in the village looked upon The Stone in quite the same fashion as did that first man who had come to the valley. He had seen it through three changing seasons, with no human being near him, and only occasionally a shy, wandering elk, or a cloud of wild ducks whirring down the pass, to share his companionship with it. Once he had waked in the early morning, and, possessed of a strange feeling, had gone out to look at The Stone. There, perched upon it, was an eagle; and though he said to himself that an eagle's weight was to The Stone as a feather upon the world, he kept his face turned towards it all day; for all day the eagle stayed. He was a man of great stature and immense strength. The thews of his limbs stood out like soft unbreakable steel. Yet, as if to cast derision on his strength and great proportions, God or Fate turned his bread to ashes, gave failure into his hands where he hugely grasped at fortune, and hung him about with misery. He discovered gold, but others gathered it. It was his daughter that went mad, and gave birth to a dead child in fearsome thought of The Stone. Once, when he had gone over the hills to another mining field, and had been prevented from coming back by unexpected and heavy snows, his wife was taken ill, and died alone of starvation, because none in the village remembered of her and her needs. Again, one wild night, long after, his only son was taken from his bed and lynched for a crime that was none of his, as was discovered by his murderers next day. Then they killed horribly the real criminal, and offered the father such satisfaction as they could. They said that any one of them was ready there to be killed by him; and they threw a weapon at his feet. At this he stood looking upon them for a moment, his great breast heaving, and his eyes glowering; but presently he reached out his arms, and taking two of them by the throat, brought their heads together heavily, breaking their skulls; and, with a cry in his throat like a wounded animal, left them, and entered the village no more. But it became known that he had built a rude hut on Purple Hill, and that he had been seen standing beside The Stone or sitting among the boulders below it, with his face bent upon the village. Those who had come near to him said that he had greatly changed; that his hair and beard had grown long and strong, and, in effect, that he looked like some rugged fragment of an antique world.

The time came when they associated The Man with The Stone: they grew to speak of him simply as The Man. There was something natural and apt in the association. Then they avoided these two singular dwellers on the height. What had happened to The Man when he lived in the village became almost as great a legend as the Indian fable concerning The Stone. In the minds of the people one seemed as old as the other. Women who knew the awful disasters which had befallen The Man brooded at times most timidly, regarding him as they did at first–and even still–The Stone. Women who carried life unborn about with them had a strange dread of both The Stone and The Man. Time passed on, and the feeling grew that The Man's grief must be a terrible thing, since he lived alone with The Stone and God. But this did not prevent the men of the village from digging gold, drinking liquor, and doing many kinds of evil. One day, again, they did an unjust and cruel thing. They took Pierre, the gambler, whom they had at first sought to vanquish at his own art, and, possessed suddenly of the high duty of citizenship, carried him to the edge of a hill and dropped him over, thinking thereby to give him a quick death, while the vultures would provide him a tomb. But Pierre was not killed, though to his grave–unprepared as yet–he would bear an arm which should never be lifted higher than his shoulder. When he waked from the crashing gloom which succeeded the fall, he was in the presence of a being whose appearance was awesome and massive–an out-lawed god: whose hair and beard were white, whose eye was piercing, absorbing, painful, in the long perspective of its woe. This being sat with his great hand clasped to the side of his head. The beginning of his look was the village, and–though the vision seemed infinite–the village was the end of it too. Pierre, looking through the doorway beside which he lay, drew in his breath sharply, for it seemed at first as if The Man was an unnatural fancy, and not a thing. Behind The Man was The Stone, which was not more motionless nor more full of age than this its comrade. Indeed, The Stone seemed more a thing of life as it poised above the hill: The Man was sculptured rock. His white hair was chiselled on his broad brow, his face was a solemn pathos petrified, his lips were curled with an iron contempt, an incalculable anger.

The sun went down, and darkness gathered about The Man. Pierre reached out his hand, and drank the water and ate the coarse bread that had been put near him. He guessed that trees or protruding ledges had broken his fall, and that he had been rescued and brought here. As he lay thinking, The Man entered the doorway, stooping much to do so. With flints he lighted a wick which hung from a wooden bowl of bear's oil; then kneeling, held it above his head, and looked at Pierre. And Pierre, who had never feared anyone, shrank from the look in The Man's eyes. But when the other saw that Pierre was awake, a distant kindness came upon his face, and he nodded gravely; but he did not speak. Presently a great tremor as of pain shook all his limbs, and he set the candle on the ground, and with his stalwart hands arranged afresh the bandages about Pierre's injured arm and leg. Pierre spoke at last.

"You are The Man?" he said.

The other bowed his head.

"You saved me from those devils in the valley?" A look of impregnable hardness came into The Man's face, but he pressed Pierre's hand for answer; and though the pressure was meant to be gentle, Pierre winced painfully. The candle spluttered, and the hut filled with a sickly smoke. The Man brought some bear skins and covered the sufferer, for, the season being autumn, the night was cold. Pierre, who had thus spent his first sane and conscious hour in many days, fell asleep. What time it was when he waked he was not sure, but it was to hear a metallic *click-click* come to him through the clear air of night. It was a pleasant noise as of steel and rock: the work of some lonely stone-cutter of the hills. The sound reached him with strange, increasing distinctness. Was this Titan that had saved him sculpturing some figure from the metal hill? *Click-click!* it vibrated as regularly as the keen pulse of a watch. He lay and wondered for a long time, but fell asleep again; and the steely iteration went on in his dreams.

In the morning The Man came to him, and cared for his hurts, and gave him food; but still would speak no word. He was gone nearly all day in the hills; yet when evening came he sought the place where Pierre had seen him the night before, and the same weird scene was re-enacted. And again in the night the clicking sound went on; and every night it was renewed. Pierre grew stronger, and could, with difficulty, stand upon his feet. One night he crept out, and made his way softly, slowly, towards the sound. He saw The Man kneeling beside The Stone, he saw a hammer rise and fall upon a chisel; and the chisel was at the base of The Stone. The hammer rose and fell with perfect but dreadful precision. Pierre turned and looked towards the village below, whose lights were burning like a bunch of fire-flies in the gloom. Again he looked at The Stone and The Man.

Then the thing came to him sharply. The Man was chiselling away the socket of The Stone, bringing it to that point of balance where the touch of a finger, the wing of a bird, or the whistle of a northwest wind, would send it down upon the offending and unsuspecting village.

The thought held him paralysed. The Man had nursed his revenge long past the thought of its probability by the people beneath. He had at first sat and watched the village, hated, and mused dreadfully upon the thing he had determined to do. Then he had worked a little, afterwards more, and now, lastly, since he had seen what they had done to Pierre, with the hot but firm eagerness of an avenging giant. Pierre had done some sad deeds in his time, and had tasted some sweet revenges, but nothing like to this had ever entered his brain. In that village were men who–as they thought–had cast him to a death fit only for a coward or a cur. Well, here was the most exquisite retaliation. Though his hand should not be in the thing, he could still be the cynical and approving spectator.

But yet: had all those people hovering about those lights below done harm to him? He thought there were a few–and they were women–who would not have followed his tumbril to his death with cries of execration. The rest would have done so,–not because he was a criminal, but because he was a victim, and because human nature as it is thirsts inordinately at times for blood and sacrifice–a living strain of the old barbaric instinct. He remembered that most of these people were concerned in having injured The Man. The few good women there had vile husbands; the few pardonable men had hateful wives: the village of Purple Hill was an ill affair.

He thought: now doubtfully, now savagely, now with irony.

The hammer and steel clicked on.

He looked at the lights of the village again.

Suddenly there came to his mind the words of a great man who sought to save a city manifold centuries ago. He was not sure that he wished to save this village; but there was a grim, almost grotesque, fitness in the thing that he now intended. He spoke out clearly through the night:

" *'Oh, let not the Lord be angry, and I will speak yet but this once: Peradventure ten righteous shall be found there.'* "

The hammer stopped. There was a silence, in which the pines sighed lightly. Then, as if speaking was a labour, The Man replied in a deep, harsh voice:

"I will not spare it for ten's sake."

Again there was a silence, in which Pierre felt his maimed body bend beneath him; but presently the voice said,–"*Now!*"

At this the moon swung from behind a cloud. The Man stood behind The Stone. His arm was raised to it. There was a moment's pause–it seemed like years to Pierre; a wind came softly crying out of the west, the moon hurried into the dark, and then a monster sprang from its pedestal upon Purple Hill, and, with a sound of thunder and an awful speed, raced upon the village below. The boulders of the hillside crumbled after it.

And Pierre saw the lights go out.

The moon shone out again for an instant, and Pierre saw that The Man stood where The Stone had been; but when he reached the place The Man was gone. Forever!

FURTHER READING

WORKS IN PRINT
The Seats of the Mighty (Toronto: McClelland and Stewart, New Canadian Library, 1971).
The following books are available only through:
  Books for Libraries Inc.,
  50 Liberty Avenue,
  Freeport,
  New York 11520, N.Y.

Adventurer of the North
Pierre and his People
Romany of the Snows

Your nearest university may place an order for you. In addition, there are many Gilbert Parker books in public and school libraries, homes, and second-hand book stores.

Ralph Connor

Ralph Connor is the pseudonym of the Presbyterian minister-cum-novelist, Charles William Gordon (1860-1937). Born in Glengarry County, Ontario (then Canada West) and educated at the Universities of Toronto and Edinburgh, he was ordained in 1890 and sent out west, mission headquarters in Banff, to preach in frontier camps and pioneer settlements. In 1894 he became pastor of St. Stephen's parish then near, now within Winnipeg, and kept that parish until his death, leaving it only to serve as a chaplain in the First World War. He was chairman of the Manitoba Council of Industry, organized after the Winnipeg General Strike of 1919, and a leading spokesman in the campaign for the union of the Presbyterian and Methodist Churches. In 1931 he accompanied the representatives of the League of Nations' International Labour Office on a visit to the newly-formed Spanish Republic, and preached the opening sermon for the League's meeting of 1932. His last public statement was a letter criticizing the church for not speaking out against fascism. He wrote more than twenty novels, all embracing and explicitly stating a vigorous Christian morality. Among them are Black Rock *(1898),* The Foreigner *(1909),* To Him that Hath *(1921),* The Arm of Gold *(1932) and the* Glengarry *books.*

James Gray in his book, *Red Lights on the Prairies*, gives us a version of early western community life that is not always found in history books. He describes it in the following words:

> Nothing like the great mass migration into Canada's West during the first decades of the 20th century had ever happened in the world before. Between 1900 and 1915, the combined efforts of government, railways and free-lance land agents lured more than one million immigrants to the three prairie provinces. Their coming ushered in the bawdiest, brawlingest, drunkenest

and backbreakingest era in prairie history. It was also the most puritanical, law-abiding, Sabbatarian and pietistic. It was an era in which the forces of self-righteousness collided head on with the entrenched forces of prostitution. That was a collision which generated uproarious civic turmoil, made and unmade reputations and political careers, disrupted the even tenor of law enforcement, and turned Protestant pulpits into launching pads for morality crusades.

Into one of those pulpits walked the Reverend Charles Gordon –later known by his pen-name, Ralph Connor–in 1894 when he became Pastor of St. Stephen's Church in Winnipeg. In spite of his busy life as a minister, Charles Gordon produced some thirty novels, achieving great fame as an author (sales of his books surpassed the five million mark).

What lay behind Ralph Connor's tremendous success as a writer of fiction, apart from his professional skill with words, was his weaving together of the two strands that Gray describes: sin and salvation. Both are clearly defined in the selection, *The Open River,* although *The Man from Glengarry*, from which it is taken, is set in Ontario, not the prairies.

Remote from the restraints of law and of society, and living in wild surroundings and in hourly touch with danger, small wonder that often the shanty-men were wild and reckless. So that many a poor fellow in a single wild carouse in Quebec, or more frequently in some river town, would fling into the hands of sharks and harlots and tavern-keepers, with whom the bosses were sometimes in league, the earnings of his long winter's work . . .

Standing against that kind of life is the towering figure of Macdonald Bhain whose turning to God has had the effect of imposing on his men the "strictest discipline."

When Connor describes the battle between Macdonald's and Murphy's gangs, the authenticity of his account can be verified by placing it beside an historical description from Richard Dorson's, *Folk Traditions of the Upper Peninsula*. In this work the old-time lumberjack is said to be, "hard-drinking, hard-fighting, hard-working, respectful to women, loyal to his camp, titanic in endurance, hopelessly spendthrift." Cases of eye-gouging and thumb-biting in fights were common, says Dorson, and often the winner would stamp his caulked boots on the face of his prostrate opponent, as indeed Le Noir does to Black Hugh. The opening pages from *The Man from Glengarry* show the community of men Connor tries to recreate for the reader. The tavern fight is only the first of a series of colourful, action-packed incidents.

It is not difficult to recognize in Macdonald Bhain the hero archetype, whose best known antecedent is Hercules. His presence is first announced by the door's crashing in, followed by "a mighty roar." He stands for a moment, "his great head and shoulders towering above the crowd, his tawny hair and beard falling around his face like a great mane, his blue eyes gleaming from under his shaggy eyebrows like livid lightning." He seizes the nearest Frenchman, lifts him high, and hurls him "smashing into the bottles behind the counter." There is more than a hint in Macdonald's character of Paul Bunyan, the prototype of the powerful logger. The heroic proportions of the Glengarry men as shown in this scene may be related to a nostalgia Connor would feel in thinking back to his boyhood in Glengarry County and the men who had made up his father's congregation.

In staging the fight, Connor observes some of the rituals of the bar-room brawl in the western. However, he manages to maintain savagery in the conflict without relying on guns and slaughter. What is distinctive–and perhaps essentially Canadian–is the way the good guys and the bad guys are separated along racial and denominational lines: the Irish "Papishes" and French "Crapeaux" against Scottish Presbyterians. A lot of the colour in the dialogue comes from the intermingling of the three dialects.

Different also from the western convention is the degree of spiritual conflict that Macdonald experiences when confronted by his enemies. The hand of the Lord has been laid upon him and he must not kill Le Noir though the temptation is strong.

Two curses close the scene: Ranald's shrill promise to avenge his father's injuries, and Macdonald Bhain's warning to Murphy to repent or risk "the curse of God."

THE OPEN RIVER

The winter had broken early and the Scotch River was running ice-free and full from bank to bank. There was still snow in the woods, and with good sleighing and open rivers, every day was golden to the lumbermen who had stuff to get down to the big water.

From: Ralph Connor, *The Man from Glengarry* (Toronto: McClelland and Stewart, New Canadian Library, 1960). Reprinted by permission of McClelland and Stewart Limited, the Canadian Publishers.

A day gained now might save weeks at a chute farther down, where the rafts would crowd one another and strive for right of way.

Dan Murphy was mightily pleased with himself and with the bit of the world about him, for there lay his winter's cut of logs in the river below him, snug and secure and held tight by a boom across the mouth, just where it flowed into the Nation. In a few days he would have his crib made and his outfit ready to start for the Ottawa mills. He was sure to be ahead of the big timber rafts that took up so much space, and whose crews with unbearable effrontery considered themselves the aristocrats of the river.

Yes, it was a pleasant and satisfying sight, some three solid miles of logs boomed at the head of the big water. Suddenly Murphy turned his face up the river.

"What's that now, d'ye think, LeNware?" he asked.

LeNoir, or "LeNware," as they all called it in that country, was Dan Murphy's foreman, and as he himself said, "for haxe, for hit (eat), for fight de boss on de reever Hottawa! by Gar!" Louis LeNoir was a French Canadian, handsome, active, hardy, and powerfully built. He had come from the New Brunswick woods some three years ago, and had wrought and fought his way, as he thought, against all rivals to the proud position of "boss on de reever," the top-most pinnacle of a lumberman's ambition. It was something to see LeNoir "run a log" across the river and back; that is, he would balance himself upon a floating log, and by spinning it round, would send it whither he would. At Murphy's question LeNoir stood listening with bent head and open mouth. Down the river came the sound of singing. "Don-no me! Ah oui! be dam! Das Macdonald gang for sure! De men from Glengarrie, les diables! Dey not hout de reever yet." His boss went off into a volley of oaths–

"They'll be wanting the river now, an' they're devils to fight."

"We give em de full belly, heh? Bon!" said LeNoir, throwing back his head. His only unconquered rival on the river was the boss of the Macdonald gang.

Ho ro, mo nighean donn bhoidheach,
Hi-ri, mo nighean donn bhoidheach,
Mo chaileag, laghach, bhoidheach,
    Cha phosainn ach thu.

Down the river came the strong, clear chorus of men's voices, and soon a "pointer" pulled by six stalwart men with a lad in the stern swung round the bend into view. A single voice took up the song–

'S ann tha mo run's na beanntaibh,
Far bheil no ribhinn ghreannar,

Mar ros am fasach shamhraidh
  An gleann fad o shuil.
After the verse the full chorus broke forth again–
Ho ro, mo nighean, etc.

Swiftly the pointer shot down the current, the swaying bodies and swinging oars in perfect rhythm with the song that rose and fell with melancholy but musical cadence. The men on the high bank stood looking down upon the approaching singers. "You know dem fellers?" said LeNoir. Murphy nodded. "Ivery divil iv thim–Big Mack Cameron, Dannie Ross, Finlay Campbell–the redheaded one–the next I don't know, and yes! be dad! there's that blanked Yankee, Yankee Jim, they call him, an' bad luck till him. The divil will have to take the poker till him, for he'll bate him wid his fists, and so he will– and that big black divil is Black Hugh, the brother iv the boss Macdonald. He'll be up in the camp beyant, and a mighty lucky thing for you, LeNoir, he is."

"Bah!" spat LeNoir. "Dat beeg Macdonald I mak heem run like one leetle sheep, one tam at de long Sault, bah! No good!" LeNoir's contempt for Macdonald was genuine and complete. For two years he had tried to meet the boss Macdonald, but his rival had always avoided him.

Meantime, the pointer came swinging along. As it turned the point the boy uttered an exclamation–"Look there!" The song and the rowing stopped abruptly; the big, dark man stood up and gazed down the river, packed from bank to bank with the brown saw-logs; deep curses broke from him. Then he caught sight of the men on the bank. A word of command and the pointer shot into the shore, and the next moment Macdonald Dubh, or Black Hugh, as he was sometimes called, followed by his men, was climbing up the steep bank.

"What the blank, blank, do these logs mean, Murphy?" he demanded, without pause for salutation.

"Tis a foine avenin' Misther Macdonald," said Murphy, blandly offering his hand, "an' Hiven bliss ye."

Macdonald checked himself with an effort and reluctantly shook hands with Murphy and LeNoir, whom he slightly knew. "It is a fery goot evening, indeed," he said, in as quiet a voice as he could command, "but I am inquiring about these logs."

"Shure, an' it is a dhry night, and onpolite to kape yez talking here. Come in wid yez," and much against his will Black Hugh followed Murphy to the tavern, the most pretentious of a group of log buildings–once a lumber camp–which stood back a little distance from the river, and about which Murphy's men, some sixty of them, were now camped.

The tavern was full of Murphy's gang, a motley crew, mostly French Canadians and Irish, just out of the woods and ready for any devilment that promised excitement. Most of them knew by sight, and all by reputation, Macdonald and his gang, for from the farthest reaches of the Ottawa down the St. Lawrence to Quebec the Macdonald gang of Glengarry men was famous. They came, most of them, from that strip of country running back from the St. Lawrence through Glengarry County, known as the Indian Lands—once an Indian reservation. They were sons of the men who had come from the highlands and islands of Scotland in the early years of the last century. Driven from homes in the land of their fathers, they had set themselves with indomitable faith and courage to hew from the solid forest homes for themselves and their children that none might take from them. These pioneers were bound together by ties of blood, but also by bonds stronger than those of blood. Their loneliness, their triumphs, their sorrows, born of their common life-long conflict with the forest and its fierce beasts, knit them in bonds close and enduring. The sons born to them and reared in the heart of the pine forests grew up to witness that heroic struggle with stern nature and to take their part in it. And mighty men they were. Their life bred in them hardiness of frame, alertness of sense, readiness of resource, endurance, superb self-reliance, a courage that grew with peril, and withal a certain wildness which at times deepened into ferocity. By their fathers the forest was dreaded and hated, but the sons, with rifles in hand, trod its pathless stretches without fear, and with their broad-axes they took toll of their ancient foe. For while in spring and summer they farmed their narrow fields, and rescued new lands from the brûlé, in winter they sought the forest, and back on their own farms or in "the shanties" they cut sawlogs, or made square timber, their only source of wealth. The shanty life of the early fifties of the last century was not the luxurious thing of today. It was full of privation, for the men were poorly housed and fed, and of peril, for the making of the timber and the getting it down the smaller rivers to the big water was a work of hardship and danger. Remote from the restraints of law and of society, and living in wild surroundings and in hourly touch with danger, small wonder that often the shanty-men were wild and reckless. So that many a poor fellow in a single wild carouse in Quebec, or more frequently in some river town, would fling into the hands of sharks and harlots and tavern-keepers, with whom the bosses were sometimes in league, the earnings of his long winter's work, and would wake to find himself sick and penniless, far from home and broken in spirit.

Of all the shanty-men of the Ottawa, the men of Glengarry—and of Glengarry men, Macdonald's gang–were easily first, and of the gang, Donald Bhain Macdonald, or Macdonald More, or the Big Macdonald, for he was variously known, was not only the "boss" but best and chief. There was none like him. A giant in size and strength, a prince of broad-axe men, at home in the woods, sure-footed and daring on the water, free with his wages, and always ready to drink with friend or fight with foe, the whole river admired, feared, or hated him, while his own men followed him into the woods, onto a jam, or into a fight with equal joyousness and devotion. Fighting was like wine to him, when the fight was worth-while, and he went into the fights his admirers were always arranging for him with the easiest good humour and with a smile on his face. But Macdonald Bhain's carousing, fighting days came to an abrupt stop about three years before the opening of this tale, for on one of his summer visits to his home, "The word of the Lord in the mouth of his servant Alexander Murray," as he was wont to say, "found him and he was a new man." He went into his new life with the same whole-souled joyousness as had marked the old, and he announced that with the shanty and the river he was "done for ever more." But after the summer's work was done, and the logging over, and when the snap of the first frost nipped the leaves from the trees, Macdonald became restless. He took down his broad-axe and spent hours polishing it and bringing it to an edge, then he put it in its wooden sheath and laid it away. But the fever was upon him, ten thousand voices from the forest were shouting for him. He went away troubled to his minister. In an hour he came back with the old good humour in his face, took down the broad-axe again, and retouched it, lovingly, humming the while the old river song of the Glengarry men–

Ho ro mo nighean, etc.

He was going back to the bush and to the biggest fight of his life. No wonder he was glad. Then his good little wife began to get ready his long, heavy stockings, his thick mits, his homespun smock, and other gear, for she knew well that soon she would be alone for another winter. Before long the word went round that Macdonald Bhain was for the shanties again, and his men came to him for their orders.

But it was not to the old life that Macdonald was going, and he gravely told those that came to him that he would take no man who could not behave himself. "Behaving himself" meant taking no more whiskey than a man could carry, and refusing all invitations to fight unless "necessity was laid upon him." The only man to object was his own brother, Macdonald Dubh, whose temper was swift to blaze, and with whom the blow was quicker than the word. But after the second year of the new order even Black Hugh fell into line. Macdonald soon became famous on the Ottawa. He picked only the best men, he fed them well, paid them the highest wages, and cared for their comfort, but held them in strictest discipline. They would drink but kept sober, they would spend money but knew how much was coming to them. They feared no men even of "twice their own heavy and big," but would never fight except under necessity. Contracts began to come their way. They made money, and what was better, they brought it home. The best men sought to join them, but by rival gangs and by men rejected from their ranks they were hated with deepest hatred. But the men from Glengarry knew no fear and sought no favour. They asked only a good belt of pine and an open river. As a rule they got both and it was peculiarly maddening to Black Hugh to find two or three miles of solid logs between his timber and the open water of the Nation. Black Hugh had a temper fierce and quick, and when in full flame he was a man to avoid, for from neither man nor devil would he turn. The only man who could hold him was his brother Macdonald Bhain, for strong man as he was, Black Hugh knew well that his brother could with a single swift grip bring him to his knees.

It was unfortunate that the command of the party this day should have been Macdonald Dubh's. Unfortunate, too, that it was Dan Murphy and his men that happened to be blocking the river mouth. For the Glengarry men, who handled only square timber, despised the Murphy gang as sawlog-men: "log-rollers" or "mushrats" they called them, and hated them as Irish "Papishes" and French "Crapeaux," while between Dan Murphy and Macdonald Dubh there was an ancient personal grudge, and today Murphy thought he had found his time. There were only six of the enemy, he had ten times the number with him, many of them eager to pay off old scores; and besides there was Louis LeNoir as the "Boss Bully" of the river. The Frenchman was not only a powerful man, active with hands and feet, but he was an adept in all kinds of fighting tricks. Since coming to the Ottawa he had heard of the big Macdonald, and he sought to meet him. But Macdonald avoided him once and again till LeNoir, having never known any one avoiding a fight for any reason other than fear, proclaimed Macdonald a coward, and himself "de boss on de reever." Now there was a chance of meeting his rival and of forcing a fight, for the Glengarry camp could not be far away where the big Macdonald himself would be. So Dan Murphy, backed up with numbers, and the boss bully LeNoir, determined that for these Macdonald men the day of settlement had come. But they were dangerous men, and it would be well to take all precautions, and hence his friendly invitation to the tavern for drinks.

Macdonald Dubh, scorning to show hesitation, though he suspected treachery, strode after Murphy to the tavern door and through the crowd of shanty-men filling the room. They were as ferocious looking a lot of men as could well be got together, even in that country and in those days–shaggy of hair and beard, dressed out in red and blue and green jerseys, with knitted sashes about their waists, and red and blue and green tuques on their heads. Drunken rows were their delight, and fights so fierce that many a man came out battered and bruised to death or to life-long decrepitude. They were sitting on the benches that ran round the room, or lounging against the bar singing, talking, blaspheming. At the sight of Macdonald Dubh and his men there fell a dead silence, and then growls of recognition, but Murphy was not yet ready, and roaring out "Dhr-r-i-n-k-s," he seized a couple of his men leaning against the bar, and hurling them to right and left, cried, "Ma-a-ke room for yer betthers, be the powers! Sthand up, bhoys, and fill yirsilves!"

Black Hugh and his men lined up gravely to the bar and were straightway surrounded by the crowd yelling hideously. But if Murphy and his gang thought to intimidate those grave Highlanders with noise, they were greatly mistaken, for they stood quietly waiting for their glasses to be filled, alert, but with an air of perfect indifference. Some eight or ten glasses were set down and filled when Murphy, snatching a couple of bottles from the shelf behind the bar, handed them out to his men, crying, "Here, ye bluddy thaves, lave the glasses to the gintlemen!"

There was no mistaking the insolence in his tone, and the chorus of derisive yells that answered him showed that his remark had gone to the spot.

Yankee Jim, who had kept close to Black Hugh, saw the veins in his neck beginning to swell, and face to grow dark. He was longing to be at Murphy's throat. "Speak him fair," he said in a low tone, "there's rather a good string of 'em around." Macdonald Dubh glanced about him. His eye fell on his boy, and for the first time his face became anxious. "Ranald," he said angrily, "take yourself out of this. It is no place for you whatever." The boy, a slight lad of seventeen, but tall and well-knit and with his father's fierce, wild, dark face, hesitated.

"Go," said his father, giving him a slight cuff.

"Here, boy!" yelled LeNoir, catching him by the arm and holding the bottle to his mouth, "drink." The boy took a gulp, choked, and spat it out. LeNoir and his men roared. "Dat good whiskey," he cried, still holding the boy. "You not lak dat, hey?"

"No," said the boy, "it is not good at all."

"Try heem some more," said LeNoir, thrusting the bottle at him again.

"I will not," said Ranald, looking at LeNoir straight and fearless.

"Ho-ho! mon brave enfant! But you have not de good mannere. Come, drink!" He caught the boy by the back of the neck, and made as if to pour the whiskey down his throat. Black Hugh, who had been kept back by Yankee Jim all this time, started forward, but before he could take a second step Ranald, squirming round like a cat, had sunk his teeth into LeNoir's wrist. With a cry of rage and pain LeNoir raised the bottle and was bringing it down on Ranald's head, when Black Hugh, with one hand caught the falling blow, and with the other seized Ranald, and crying, "Get out of this!" he flung him towards the door. Then turning to LeNoir he said, with surprising self-control, "It is myself that is sorry that a boy of mine should be guilty of biting like a dog."

"Sa-c-r-ré le chien!" yelled LeNoir, shaking off Macdonald Dubh; "he is one dog, and the son of a dog!" He turned and started for the boy. But Yankee Jim had got Ranald to the door and was whispering to him. "Run!" cried Yankee Jim, pushing him out of the door, and the boy was off like the wind. LeNoir pursued him a short way and returning raging.

Yankee Jim, or Yankee, as he was called for short, came back to Macdonald Dubh's side, and whispering to the other Highlanders, "Keep your backs clear," sat up coolly on the counter. The fight was sure to come and there were seven to one against them in the room. If he could only gain time. Every minute was precious. It would take the boy fifteen minutes to run the two miles to camp. It would be half an hour before the rest of the Glengarry men could arrive, and much fighting may be done in that time. He must avert attention from Macdonald Dubh, who was waiting to cram LeNoir's insult down his throat. Yankee Jim had not only all the cool courage but also the shrewd, calculating spirit of his race. He was ready to fight, and if need be against odds, but he preferred to fight on as even terms as possible.

Soon LeNoir came back, wild with fury, and yelling curses at the top of his voice. He hurled himself into the room, the crowd falling back from him on either hand.

"Hola!" he yelled, "*Sacré bleu!*" He took two quick steps, and springing up into the air he kicked the stovepipe that ran along some seven feet above the floor.

"Purty good kicking," called out Yankee, sliding down from his seat. "Used to kick some myself. Excuse me." He stood for a moment looking up at the stovepipe, then without apparent effort he sprang into the air, shot up his long legs, and knocked the stovepipe with a bang against the ceiling. There was a shout of admiration.

"My damages," he said to Pat Murphy, who stood behind the

counter. "Good thing there ain't no fire. Thought it was higher. Wouldn't care to kick for the drinks, would ye?" he added to LeNoir.

LeNoir was too furious to enter into any contest so peaceful, but as he specially prided himself on his high kick, he paused a moment and was about to agree when Black Hugh broke in, harshly, spoiling all Yankee's plans.

"There is no time for such foolishness," he said, turning to Dan Murphy. "I want to know when we can get our timber out."

"Depinds intoirly on yirsilf," said Murphy.

"When will your logs be out of the way?"

"Indade an' that's a ha-r-r-d one," laughed Murphy.

"And will you tell me what right hev you to close up the river?" Black Hugh's wrath was rising.

"You wud think now it wuz yirsilf that owned the river. An' bedad it's the thought of yir mind, it is. An' it's not the river only, but the whole creation ye an' yir brother thinks is yours." Dan Murphy was close up to Macdonald Dubh by this time. "Yis, blank, blank, yir faces, an' ye'd like to turn better than yirsilves from aff the river, so ye wud, ye black-hearted thaves that ye are."

This, of course, was beyond all endurance. For answer Black Hugh smote him sudden and fierce on the mouth, and Murphy went down.

"Purty one," sang out Yankee cheerily. "Now, boys, back to the wall."

Before Murphy could rise, LeNoir sprang over him and lit upon Macdonald like a cat, but Macdonald shook himself free and sprang back to the Glengarry line at the wall.

"Mac an' Diabhoil," he roared, "Glengarry forever!"

"Glengarry!" yelled the four Highlanders beside him, wild with the delight of battle. It was a plain necessity, and they went into it with free consciences and happy hearts.

"Let me at him," cried Murphy, struggling past LeNoir towards Macdonald.

"Non! He is to me!" yelled LeNoir, dancing in front of Macdonald.

"Here, Murphy," called out Yankee obligingly, "help yourself this way." Murphy dashed at him, but Yankee's long arm shot out to meet him, and Murphy again found the floor.

"Come on, boys," cried Pat Murphy, Dan's brother, and followed by half a dozen others, he flung himself at Yankee and the line of men standing up against the wall. But Yankee's arms flashed out once, twice, thrice, and Pat Murphy fell back over his brother; two others staggered across and checked the oncoming rush, while Dannie Ross and big Mack Cameron had each beaten back their man, and the Glengarry line stood unbroken. Man for man they were far more than a match for their opponents, and standing shoulder to shoulder.

with their backs to the wall, they taunted Murphy and his gang with all the wealth of gibes and oaths at their command.

"Where's the rest of your outfit, Murphy?" drawled Yankee. "Don't seem's if you'd counted right."

"It is a cold day for the parley voos," laughed Big Mack Cameron. "Come up, lads, and take a taste of something hot."

Then the Murphy men, clearing away the fallen, rushed again. They strove to bring the Highlanders to a clinch, but Yankee's voice was high and clear in command.

"Keep the line, boys! Don't let 'em draw you!" And the Glengarry men waited till they could strike, and when they struck men went down and were pulled back by their friends.

"Intil them, bhoys!" yelled Dan Murphy, keeping out of range himself. "Intil the divils!" And again and again his men crowded down upon the line against the wall, but again and again they were beaten down or hurled back bruised and bleeding.

Meantime LeNoir was devoting himself to Black Hugh at one end of the line, dancing in upon him and away again, but without much result. Black Hugh refused to be drawn out, and fought warily on defence, knowing the odds were great and waiting his chance to deliver one good blow, which was all he asked.

The Glengarry men were enjoying themselves hugely, and when not shouting their battle-cry, "Glengarry forever!" or taunting their foes, they were joking each other on the fortunes of war. Big Mack Cameron, who held the centre, drew most of the sallies. He was easy-tempered and good-natured, and took his knocks with the utmost good humour.

"That was a good one, Mack," said Dannie Ross, his special chum, as a sounding whack came in on Big Mack's face. "As true as death I will be telling it to Bella Peter." Bella, the daughter of Peter McGregor, was supposed to be dear to Big Mack's heart.

"What a peety she could not see him the now," said Finlay Campbell. "Man alive, she would say the word queeck!"

"'Tis more than she will do to you whatever, if you cannot keep off that *crapeau* yonder a little better," said Big Mack, reaching for a Frenchman who kept dodging in upon him with annoying persistence. Then Mack began to swear Gaelic oaths.

"'Tain't fair, Mack!" called out Yankee from his end of the line, "bad language in English is bad enough, but in Gaelic it must be uncommon rough." So they gibed each other. But the tactics of the enemy were exceedingly irritating, and were beginning to tell upon the tempers of the Highlanders.

"Come to me ye cowardly little devil," roared Mack to his persisting assailant. "No one will hurt you! Come away, man! A-a-ah-ouch!" His cry of satisfaction at having grabbed his man ended in a howl of pain, for the Frenchman had got Mack's thumb between his teeth, and was chewing it vigorously.

"Ye would, would you, ye dog?" roared Big Mack. He closed his fingers into the Frenchman's gullet, and drew him up to strike, but on every side hands reached for him and stayed his blow. Then he lost himself. With a yell of rage he jammed his man back into the crowd, sinking his fingers deeper and deeper into his enemy's throat till his face grew black and his head fell over on one side. But it was a fatal move for Mack, and overcome by numbers that crowded upon him, he went down fighting wildly and bearing the Frenchman beneath him. The Glengarry line was broken. Black Hugh saw Mack's peril, and knew that it meant destruction to all. With a wilder cry than usual, "Glengarry! Glengarry!" he dashed straight into LeNoir, who gave back swiftly, caught two men who were beating Big Mack's life out, and hurled them aside, and grasping his friend's collar, hauled him to his feet, and threw him back against the wall and into the line again with his grip still upon his Frenchman's throat.

"Let dead men go, Mack," he cried, but even as he spoke LeNoir, seeing his opportunity, sprang at him and with a backward kick caught Macdonald fair in the face and lashed him hard against the wall. It was the terrible French *lash* and was one of LeNoir's special tricks. Black Hugh, stunned and dazed, leaned back against the wall, spreading out his hands weakly before his face. LeNoir, seeing victory within his grasp, rushed in to finish off his special foe. But Yankee Jim, who, while engaged in cheerfully knocking back the two Murphys and others who took their turn at him, had been keeping an eye on the line of battle, saw Macdonald's danger, and knowing that the crisis had come, dashed across the line, crying "Follow me, boys." His long arms swung round his head like the sails of a windmill, and men fell back from him as if they had been made of wood. As LeNoir sprang, Yankee shot fiercely at him, but the Frenchman, too quick for him, ducked and leaped upon Black Hugh, who was still swaying against the wall, bore him down and jumped with his heavy "corked" boots on his breast and face. Again the Glengarry line was broken. At once the crowd surged about the Glengarry men, who now stood back to back, beating off the men leaping at them from every side, as a stag beats off dogs, and still chanting high their dauntless cry, "Glengarry forever," to which Big Mack added at intervals, "To hell with the Papishes!" Yankee, failing to check LeNoir's attack upon Black Hugh, fought off the men crowding upon him, and made his way to the corner where the Frenchman was still engaged in kicking the prostrate Highlander to death.

"Take that, you blamed cuss," he said, catching LeNoir in the jaw and knocking his head with a thud against the wall. Before he could strike again he was thrown against his enemy, who clutched him and held like a vice.

The Glengarry men had fought their fight, and it only remained for their foes to wreak their vengeance upon them and wipe out old scores. One minute more would have done for them, but in that minute the door came crashing in. There was a mighty roar, "Glengarry! Glengarry!" and the great Macdonald himself, with the boy Ranald and some half-dozen of his men behind him, stood among them. On all hands the fight stopped. A moment he stood, his great head and shoulders towering above the crowd, his tawny hair and beard falling around his face like a great mane, his blue eyes gleaming from under his shaggy eyebrows like vivid lightning. A single glance around the room, and again raising his battle-cry, "Glengarry!" he seized the nearest shrinking Frenchman, lifted him high, and hurled him smashing into the bottles behind the counter. His men, following him, bounded like tigers on their prey. A few minutes of fierce, eager fighting, and the Glengarry men were all freed and on their feet, all except Black Hugh, who lay groaning in his corner. "Hold, lads!" Macdonald Bhain cried, in his mighty voice. "Stop, I'm telling you." The fighting ceased.

"Dan Murphy!" he cried, casting his eye round the room, "where are you, ye son of Belial?'

Murphy, crouching at the back of the crowd near the door, sought to escape.

"Ah! there you are!" cried Macdonald, and reaching through the crowd with his great, long arm, he caught Murphy by the hair of the head and dragged him forward.

"R-r-r-a-a-t! R-r-r-a-a-t! R-r-r-a-a-t!" he snarled, shaking him till his teeth rattled. "It is yourself that is the cause of this wickedness. Now, may the Lord have mercy on your soul." With one hand he gripped Murphy by the throat, holding him at arm's length, and raised his huge fist to strike. But before the blow fell he paused.

"No!" he muttered, in a disappointed tone, "it is not good enough. I will not be demeaning myself. Hence, you r-r-a-a-t!" As he spoke he lifted the shaking wretch as if he had been a bundle of clothes, swung him half round and hurled him crashing through the window.

"Is there no goot man here at all who will stand before me?" he raged in a wild, joyous fury. "Will not two of you come forth, then?" No one moved. "Come to me!" he suddenly cried, and snatching two of the enemy, he dashed their heads together, and threw them insensible on the floor.

Then he caught sight of his brother for the first time lying in the corner with Big Mack supporting his head, and LeNoir standing near.

"What is this? What is this?" he cried, striding towards LeNoir. "And is it you that has done this work?" he asked, in a voice of subdued rage.

"Oui!" cried LeNoir, stepping back and putting up his hands, "das me; Louis LeNoir! by Gar!" He struck himself on the breast as he spoke.

"Out of my way!" cried Macdonald, swinging his open hand on the Frenchman's ear. With a swift sweep he brushed LeNoir aside from his place and, ignoring him, stooped over his brother. But LeNoir was no coward, and besides his boasted reputation was at stake. He thought he saw his chance, and rushing at Macdonald as he was bending over his brother, delivered his terrible *lash*. But Macdonald had not lived with and fought with Frenchmen all these years without knowing their tricks and ways. He saw LeNoir's *lash* coming, and quickly turning his head, avoided the blow.

"Ah! would ye? Take that, then, and be quate!" and so saying, he caught LeNoir on the side of the head and sent him to the floor.

"Keep him off a while, Yankee!" said Macdonald, for LeNoir was up again, and coming at him.

Then kneeling beside his brother he wiped the bloody froth that was oozing from his lips, and said in a low, anxious tone:

"Hugh, bhodaich (old man), are ye hurted? Can ye not speak to me, Hugh?"

"Oich-oh," Black Hugh groaned. "It was a necessity–Donald man –and–he took me–unawares–with his–keeck."

"Indeed, and I'll warrant you!" agreed his brother, "but I will be attending to him, never you fear."

Macdonald was about to rise, when his brother caught his arm.

"You will–not be–killing him," he urged, between his painful gasps, "because I will be doing that myself some day, by God's help."

His words and the eager hate in his face seemed to quiet Macdonald.

"Alas! Alas!" he said sadly, "it is not allowed me to smite him as he deserves–'Vengeance is mine saith the Lord,' and I have solemnly promised the minister not to smite for glory or for revenge! Alas! alas!"

Then turning to LeNoir, he said gravely: "It is not given me to punish you for your coward's blow. Go from me!" But LeNoir misjudged him.

"Bah!" he cried contemptuously, "you tink me one baby, you strike me on de head side like one little boy. Bon! Louis LeNware, de bes bully on de Hottawa, he's not 'fraid for hany man, by Gar!" He pranced up and down before Macdonald, working himself into a great rage, as Macdonald grew more and more controlled.

Macdonald turned to his men with a kind of appeal—"I hev given my promise, and Macdonald will not break his word."

"Bah!" cried LeNoir again, mistaking Macdonald's quietness and self-control for fear. "You no good! Your brother is no good! Beeg sheep! Beeg sheep! Bah!"

"God help me," said Macdonald as if to himself. "I am a man of grace! But must this dog go unpunished?"

LeNoir continued striding up and down, now and then springing high in the air and knocking his heels together with blood-curdling yells. He seemed to feel that Macdonald would not fight, and his courage and desire for blood grew accordingly.

"Will you not be quate?" said Macdonald, rising after a few moments from his brother's side, where he had been wiping his lips and giving him water to drink. "You will be better outside."

"Oui! you strike me on the head side. Bon! I strike you de same way! By Gar!" So saying he approached Macdonald lightly, and struck him a slight blow on the cheek.

"Aye," said Macdonald, growing white and rigid, "I struck you twice, LeNoir. Here!" he offered the other side of his face. LeNoir danced up carefully, made a slight pass, and struck the offered cheek.

"Now, that is done, will it please you to do it again?" said Macdonald, with earnest entreaty in his voice. LeNoir must have been mad with his rage and vanity, else he had caught the glitter in the blue eyes looking through the shaggy hair. Again LeNoir approached, this time with greater confidence, and dealt Macdonald a stinging blow on the side of the head.

"Now the Lord be praised," he cried, joy breaking out in his face. "He has delivered my enemy into my hand. For it is the third time he has smitten me, and that is beyond the limit appointed by Himself." With this he advanced upon LeNoir with a glad heart. His conscience was clear at last.

LeNoir stood up against his antagonist. He well knew he was about to make the fight of his life. He had beaten men as big as Macdonald, but he knew that his hope lay in keeping out of the enemy's reach. So he danced around warily. Macdonald followed him slowly. LeNoir opened with a swift and savage reach for Macdonald's neck, but failed to break the guard and danced out again, Macdonald still pressing on him. Again and again LeNoir rushed, but the guard was impregnable, and steadily Macdonald advanced. That steady, relentless advance began to tell on the Frenchman's nerves. The sweat gathered in big drops on his forehead and ran down his face. He prepared for a supreme effort. Swiftly retreating, he lured Macdonald to a more rapid advance, then with a yell he doubled himself into a ball and delivered himself head, hands, and feet into Macdonald's stomach. It is a trick that sometimes avails to break an unsteady guard and to secure a clinch with an unwary opponent. But Macdonald had been waiting for that trick. Stopping short, he leaned over to one side, and stooping slightly, caught LeNoir low and tossed him clear over his head. LeNoir fell with a terrible thud on his back, but was on his feet again like a cat and ready for the ever-advancing Macdonald. But though he had not been struck a single blow he knew that he had met his master. That unbreakable guard, the smiling face with the gleaming, unsmiling eyes, that awful unwavering advance, were too much for him. He was pale, his breath came in quick gasps, and his eyes showed the fear of a hunted beast. He prepared for a final effort. Feigning a greater distress than he felt, he yielded weakly to Macdonald's advance, then suddenly gathering his full strength he sprang into the air and lashed out backward at that hated, smiling face. His boot found its mark, not on Macdonald's face, but fair on his neck. The effect was terrific. Macdonald staggered back two or three paces, but before LeNoir could be at him, he had recovered sufficiently to maintain his guard, and shake off his foe. At the yell that went up from Murphy's men, the big Highlander's face lost its smile and became keen and cruel, his eyes glittered with the flash of steel and he came forward once more with a quick, light tread. His great body seemed to lose both size and weight, so lightly did he step on tiptoe. There was no more pause, but lightly, swiftly, and eagerly he glided upon LeNoir. There was something terrifying in that swift, cat-like movement. In vain the Frenchman backed and dodged and tried to guard. Once, twice, Macdonald's fists fell. LeNoir's right arm hung limp by his side and he staggered back to the wall helpless. Without an instant's delay, Macdonald had him by the throat, and gripping him fiercely, began to slowly bend him backward over his knee. Then for the first time Macdonald spoke:

"LeNoir," he said solemnly, "the days of your boasting are over. You will no longer glory in your strength, for now I will break your back to you."

LeNoir tried to speak, but his voice came in horrible gurgles. His face was a ghastly greenish hue, lined with purple and swollen veins, his eyes were standing out of his head, and his breath sobbing in raucous gasps. Slowly the head went back. The crowd stood in horror-stricken silence waiting for the sickening snap. Yankee, unable to stand it any longer, stepped up to his chief, and in a most matter of fact voice drawled out, "About an inch more that way I guess'll do the trick, if he ain't double-jointed."

"Aye," said Macdonald, holding grimly on.

"Tonald"–Black Hugh's voice sounded faint but clear in the awful silence–"Tonald–you will not–be killing–him. Remember that now. I will–never–forgive you–if you will–take that–from my hands."

The cry for vengeance smote Macdonald to the heart, and recalled him to himself. He paused, threw back his locks from his eyes, then relaxing his grip, stood up.

"God preserve me!" he groaned, "what am I about?"

For some time he remained standing silent, with head down as if not quite sure of himself. He was recalled by a grip of his arm. He turned and saw his nephew, Ranald, at his side. The boy's dark face was pale with passion.

"And is that all you are going to do to him?" he demanded. Macdonald gazed at him.

"Do you not see what he has done?" he continued, pointing to his father, who was still lying propped up on some coats. "Why did you not break his back? You said you would! The brute, beast!"

He hurled out the words in hot hate. His voice pierced the noise of the room. Macdonald stood still, gazing at the fierce, dark face in solemn silence. Then he sadly shook his head.

"My lad, 'Vengeance is mine saith the Lord.' It would have pleased me well, but the hand of the Lord was laid upon me and I could not kill him."

"Then it is myself will kill him," he shrieked, springing like a wildcat at LeNoir. But his uncle wound his arms round him and held him fast. For a minute and more he struggled fiercely, crying to be set free, till recognizing the uselessness of his efforts he grew calm, and said quietly, "Let me loose, Uncle; I will be quiet." And his uncle set him free. The boy shook himself, and then standing up before LeNoir said, in a high, clear voice:

"Will you hear me, LeNoir? The day will come when I will do to you what you have done to my father, and if my father will die, then by the life of God (a common oath among the shanty-men) I will have your life for it." His voice had an unearthly shrillness in it, and LeNoir shrank back.

"Whist, whist, lad! be quate!" said his uncle; "these are not goot words." The lad heeded him not, but sank down beside his father on the floor. Black Hugh raised himself on his elbow with a grim smile on his face.

"It is a goot lad whatever, but please God he will not need to keep his word." He laid his hand in a momentary caress upon his boy's shoulder, and sank back again, saying, "Take me out of this."

Then Macdonald Bhain turned to Dan Murphy and gravely addressed him:

"Dan Murphy, it is an ungodly and cowardly work you have done this day, and the curse of God will be on you if you will not repent." Then he turned away, and with Big Mack's help bore his brother to the pointer, followed by his men, bloody, bruised, but unconquered. But before he left the room LeNoir stepped forward, and offering his hand, said, "You mak friends wit' me. You de boss bully on de reever Hottawa."

Macdonald neither answered nor looked his way, but passed out in grave silence.

Then Yankee Jim remarked to Dan Murphy, "I guess you'd better git them logs out purty mighty quick. We'll want the river in about two days." Don Murphy said not a word, but when the Glengarry men wanted the river they found it open. . . .

FURTHER READING

AVAILABLE WORKS BY CONNOR

The Man from Glengarry (Toronto: McClelland and Stewart, New Canadian Library, 1960).

Glengarry Schooldays (Toronto: McClelland and Stewart, 1965).

The Sky Pilot: A Tale of the Foothills (Lexington: University Press of Kentucky, 1970).

Ralph Connor wrote more than twenty novels, most of which are out of print. However, many are available in homes, public libraries, and second-hand book stores across Canada.

PICTURES SERIES

Canadian Authors (includes Ralph Connor) obtainable from Hilton Photo Supplies, P.O. Box 74, Chemainus, British Columbia.

Lucy M. Montgomery

Lucy M. Montgomery (1876-1942) was born on Prince Edward Island and went to Prince of Wales College and Dalhousie University. After a short stint writing for the Halifax Echo, *she went back to P.E.I. to teach school, care for an ailing grandmother and write for Canadian and American magazines.* Anne of Green Gables *(1908) was originally a short story for a Sunday School weekly. Its popularity with both children and adults brought a request from her American publisher for a sequel, and* Anne of Avonlea *(1909) was followed by four more in the series. She married the Rev. Ewen MacDonald in 1911 and went to live in southern Ontario where she wrote with less success two adult novels and* The Watchman, and Other Poems *(1917). She was awarded the O.B.E. in 1935.*

Unless the heroine in a romance figures merely as the give-away prize to the hero, her role often falls into a Cinderella pattern. Pamela marries her mistress' son, Jane Eyre marries her boss, as does Maria in *The Sound of Music*. Galatea had the most spectacular rise, starting out as a block of marble, and finishing up in the arms of her sculptor. In his epilogue to *Pygmalion*, George Bernard Shaw comments:

> The history of Eliza Doolittle, though called a romance because the transfiguration it records seems exceedingly improbable, is common enough. Such transfigurations have been achieved by hundreds of resolutely ambitious young women since Nell Gwynne set them the example by playing queens and fascinating kings in the theatre in which she began by selling oranges.

Shaw adds interest to his use of the Cinderella image by including some of the props from the fairy tale. Liza is put into a Rolls-Royce car, driven to the Embassy reception, and is taken for a princess. When she returns to Wimpole Street, a flower girl once again, "the clock on the mantelpiece strikes twelve." There is also play about

Higgins' slippers, the ring in the ashes, the "princess' " disappearance, the "hero's" search for her, and so on.

Anne of Green Gables follows the same tradition. Enter Anne, the homely unwanted orphan. Exit Anne, star pupil, star daughter, star friend. Anne is trained for her new station in life very much the same way that Eliza is–the asperity of Marilla and Higgins is softened by Matthew and Colonel Pickering. Anne, too, has her "ball scene":

> Matthew had sheepishly unfolded the dress from its paper swathings. . . . Anne took the dress and looked at it in reverent silence. Oh, how pretty it was–a lovely soft brown gloria with all the gloss of silk; a skirt with dainty frills and shirrings; a waist elaborately pintucked in the most fashionable way, with a little ruffle of filmy lace at the neck. But the sleeves–they were the crowning glory! Long elbow cuffs, and above them two beautiful puffs divided by rows of shirring and bows of brown silk ribbon. . . . and then, a pair of the daintiest little kid slippers, with beaded toes and satin bows and glistening buckles. . . . The concert came off in the evening and was a pronounced success. The little hall was crowded; all the performers did excellent well, but Anne was the bright particular star of the occasion.

Anne's friend, Diana, tells her, "When you ran off the platform after the fairy dialogue one of your roses fell out of your hair. I saw Gil pick it up and put it in his breast-pocket." Another ugly duckling has turned into a swan.

Desmond Pacey, in *Creative Writing in Canada*, reminds us that "*Anne of Green Gables* (1908) is a children's classic, and it would be silly to apply adult critical standards to it." However, children's classic or not, the novel contains a romance design common in adult fiction. For *Anne*'s significance in the field of Canadian literature, the conclusion to *Literary History of Canada* has this to say:

> At the heart of all social mythology lies what may be called, because it usually is called, a pastoral myth, the vision of a social ideal.
>
> The pastoral myth in its most common form is associated with, childhood, or with some earlier social condition–pioneer life, the small town, the *habitant* rooted to his land–that can be identified with childhood. The nostalgia for a world of peace and protection, with a spontaneous response to the nature around it, with a leisure and composure not to be found today, is particularly strong in Canada. It is overpowering in our popular literature, from *Anne of Green Gables* to Leacock's *Mariposa*, and from

Maria Chapdelaine to *Jake and the Kid*. It is present in all the fiction that deals with small towns as collections of characters in search of an author.

Mavor Moore, who was the first producer of *Anne of Green Gables* as a musical, commented once in *Maclean's* that Canadians tend to be more embarrassed over their successes than their failures. He was referring to Canadian reaction in 1969 to the success of the show in London. He felt that Canadians are, in particular, self-conscious about L. M. Montgomery, Stephen Leacock, and Mazo de la Roche, because in their view, these writers are world-famous but not sufficiently "serious" to command a place in world literature. It was not an attitude that Moore favoured.

Anne of Green Gables remains remarkably sturdy, despite criticism. When her publisher in paperback was experiencing financial difficulties, "the biggest seller on its backlist was *Anne of Green Gables*" (*Saturday Night*, June 1971). The musical has played to two world expositions and continues to draw capacity audiences each summer at the Charlottetown Festival. It has made Canadian theatre history, as a news story in the *Toronto Star*, October 20, 1971, testifies:

> Canada's very own hit musical, *Anne of Green Gables*, has made it to the theatrical big leagues–the Charlottetown Festival production opens a two-week engagement at New York's City Centre Theatre on December 21. The booking is a first in that never before has a full-scale Canadian musical with a Canadian cast been signed by a major New York theatre.

The Cinderella theme again.

AN UNFORTUNATE LILY MAID

"Of course you must be Elaine, Anne," said Diana. "I could never have the courage to float down there."

"Nor I," said Ruby Gillis with a shiver. "I don't mind floating down when there's two or three of us in the flat and we can sit up. It's fun then. But to lie down and pretend I was dead–I just couldn't. I'd die really of fright."

"Of course it would be romantic," conceded Jane Andrews. "But I know I couldn't keep still. I'd be popping up every minute or so to see where I was and if I wasn't drifting too far out. And you know, Anne, that would spoil the effect."

From: L. M. Montgomery, *Anne of Green Gables* (Toronto: Ryerson Press, 1968). Reprinted by permission of McGraw-Hill, Ryerson.

"But it's so ridiculous to have a red-headed Elaine," mourned Anne. "I'm not afraid to float down and I'd love to be Elaine. But it's ridiculous just the same. Ruby ought to be Elaine because she is so fair and has lovely long golden hair–Elaine had 'all her bright hair streaming down' you know. And Elaine was the lily maid. Now, a red-haired person cannot be a lily maid."

"Your complexion is just as fair as Ruby's," said Diana earnestly, "and your hair is ever so much darker than it used to be before you cut it."

"Oh, do you really think so?" exclaimed Anne, flushing sensitively with delight. "I've sometimes thought it was myself–but I never dared to ask anyone for fear she would tell me it wasn't. Do you think it could be called auburn now, Diana?"

"Yes, and I think it is real pretty," said Diana, looking admiringly at the short, silky curls that clustered over Anne's head and were held in place by a very jaunty black velvet ribbon and bow.

They were standing on the bank of the pond, below Orchard Slope, where a little headland fringed with birches ran out from the bank; at its tip was a small wooden platform built out into the water for the convenience of fishermen and duck hunters. Ruby and Jane were spending the midsummer afternoon with Diana, and Anne had come over to play with them.

Anne and Diana had spent most of their playtime that summer on and about the pond. Idlewild was a thing of the past, Mr. Bell having ruthlessly cut down the little circle of trees in his back pasture in the spring. Anne had sat among the stumps and wept, not without an eye to the romance of it; but she was speedily consoled, for, after all, as she and Diana said, big girls of thirteen, going on fourteen, were too old for such childish amusements as playhouses, and there were more fascinating sports to be found about the pond. It was splendid to fish for trout over the bridge and the two girls learned to row themselves about in the little flat-bottomed dory Mr. Barry kept for duck shooting.

It was Anne's idea that they dramatize Elaine. They had studied Tennyson's poem in school the preceding winter, the Superintendent of Education having prescribed it in the English course for the Prince Edward Island schools. They had analyzed and parsed it and torn it to pieces in general until it was a wonder there was any meaning at all left in it for them, but at least the fair lily maid and Lancelot and Guinevere and King Arthur had become very real people to them, and Anne was devoured by secret regret, that she had not been born in Camelot. Those days, she said, were so much more romantic than the present.

Anne's plan was hailed with enthusiasm. The girls had discovered that if the flat were pushed off from the landing-place it would drift down with the current under the bridge and finally strand itself on another headland lower down which ran out at a curve in the pond. They had often gone down like this and nothing could be more convenient for playing Elaine.

"Well, I'll be Elaine," said Anne, yielding reluctantly, for, although she would have been delighted to play the principal character, yet her artistic sense demanded fitness for it and this, she felt, her limitations made impossible. "Ruby, you must be King Arthur and Jane will be Guinevere and Diana must be Lancelot. But first you must be the brothers and the father. We can't have the old dumb servitor because there isn't room for two in the flat when one is lying down. We must pall the barge all its length in blackest samite. That old black shawl of your mother's will be just the thing, Diana."

The black shawl having been procured, Anne spread it over the flat and then lay down on the bottom, with closed eyes and hands folded over her breast.

"Oh, she does look really dead," whispered Ruby Gillis nervously, watching the still, white little face under the flickering shadows of the birches. "It makes me feel frightened, girls. Do you suppose it's really right to act like this? Mrs. Lynde says that all play-acting is abominably wicked."

"Ruby, you shouldn't talk about Mrs. Lynde," said Anne severely. "It spoils the effect because this is hundreds of years before Mrs. Lynde was born. Jane, you arrange this. It's silly for Elaine to be talking when she's dead."

Jane rose to the occasion. Cloth of gold for coverlet there was none, but an old piano scarf of yellow Japanese crêpe was an excellent substitute. A white lily was not obtainable just then, but the effect of a tall blue iris placed in one of Anne's folded hands was all that could be desired.

"Now, she's all ready," said Jane. "We must kiss her quiet brows and, Diana, you say, 'Sister, farewell for ever,' and Ruby, you say, 'Farewell, sweet sister,' both of you as sorrowfully as you possibly can. Anne, for goodness' sake smile a little. You know Elaine 'lay as though she smiled.' That's better. Now push the flat off."

The flat was accordingly pushed off, scraping roughly over an old embedded stake in the process. Diana and Jane and Ruby only waited long enough to see it caught in the current and headed for the bridge before scampering up through the woods, across the road, and down to the lower headland where, as Lancelot and Guinevere and the King, they were to be in readiness to receive the lily maid.

For a few minutes Anne, drifting slowly down, enjoyed the romance of her situation to the full. Then something happened not at all romantic. The flat began to leak. In a very few moments it was necessary for Elaine to scramble to her feet, pick up her cloth of gold coverlet and pall of blackest samite and gaze blankly at a big crack in the bottom of her barge through which the water was literally pouring. That sharp stake at the landing had torn off the strip of batting nailed to the flat. Anne did not know this, but it did not take her long to realize that she was in a dangerous plight. At this rate the flat would fill and sink long before it could drift to the lower headland. Where were the oars? Left behind at the landing!

Anne gave one gasping little scream which nobody ever heard; she was white to the lips, but she did not lose her self-possession. There was one chance—just one.

"I was horribly frightened," she told Mrs. Allan the next day, "and it seemed like years while the flat was drifting down to the bridge and the water rising in it every moment. I prayed, Mrs. Allan, most earnestly, but I didn't shut my eyes to pray, for I knew the only way God could save me was to let the flat float close enough to one of the bridge piles for me to climb up on it. You know the piles are just old tree trunks and there are lots of knots and old branch stubs on them. It was proper to pray, but I had to do my part by watching out and right well I knew it. I just said, 'Dear God, please take the flat close to a pile and I'll do the rest,' over and over again. Under such circumstances you don't think much about making a flowery prayer. But mine was answered, for the flat bumped right into a pile for a minute and I flung the scarf and the shawl over my shoulder and scrambled up on a big providential stub. And there I was, Mrs. Allan, clinging to that slippery old pile with no way of getting up or down. It was a very unromantic position, but I didn't think about that at the time. You don't think much about romance when you have just escaped from a watery grave. I said a grateful prayer at once and then I gave all my attention to holding on tight, for I knew I should probably have to depend on human aid to get back to dry land."

The flat drifted under the bridge and then promptly sank in midstream. Ruby, Jane, and Diana, already awaiting it on the lower headland, saw it disappear before their very eyes and had not a doubt but that Anne had gone down with it. For a moment they stood still, white as sheets, frozen with horror at the tragedy; then, shrieking at the tops of their voices, they started on a frantic run up through the woods, never pausing as they crossed the main road to glance the way of the bridge. Anne, clinging desperately to her precarious foothold, saw their flying forms and heard their shrieks. Help would soon come, but meanwhile her position was a very uncomfortable one.

The minutes passed by, each seeming an hour to the unfortunate lily maid. Why didn't somebody come? Where had the girls gone? Suppose they had fainted, one and all! Suppose nobody ever came! Suppose she grew so tired and cramped that she could hold on no longer! Anne looked at the wicked green depths below her, wavering with long, oily shadows, and shivered. Her imagination began to suggest all manner of gruesome possibilities to her.

Then, just as she thought she really could not endure the ache in her arms and wrists another moment, Gilbert Blythe came rowing under the bridge in Harmon Andrews' dory!

Gilbert glanced up and, much to his amazement, beheld a little white, scornful face looking down upon him with big, frightened but also scornful gray eyes.

"Anne Shirley! How on earth did you get there?" he exclaimed.

Without waiting for an answer he pulled close to the pile and extended his hand. There was no help for it; Anne, clinging to Gilbert Blythe's hand, scrambled down into the dory, where she sat, drabbled and furious, in the stern with her arms full of dripping shawl and wet crêpe. It was certainly extremely difficult to be dignified under the circumstances!

"What has happened, Anne?" asked Gilbert, taking up his oars.

"We were playing Elaine," explained Anne frigidly, without even looking at her rescuer, "and I had to drift down to Camelot in the barge–I mean the flat. The flat began to leak and I climbed out on the pile. The girls went for help. Will you be kind enough to row me to the landing?"

Gilbert obligingly rowed to the landing and Anne, disdaining assistance, sprang nimbly on shore.

"I'm very much obliged to you," she said haughtily as she turned away. But Gilbert had also sprung from the boat and now laid a detaining hand on her arm.

"Anne," he said hurriedly, "look here. Can't we be good friends? I'm awfully sorry I made fun of your hair that time. I didn't mean to vex you and I only meant it for a joke. Besides, it's so long ago. I think your hair is awfully pretty now–honest I do. Let's be friends."

For a moment Anne hesitated. She had an odd, newly awakened consciousness under all her outraged dignity that the half-shy, half-eager expression in Gilbert's hazel eyes was something that was very good to see. Her heart gave a quick, queer little beat. But the bitterness of her old grievance promptly stiffened up her wavering determination. That scene of two years before flashed back into her recollection as vividly as if it had taken place yesterday. Gilbert had called her "carrots" and had brought about her disgrace before the whole school. Her resentment, which to other and older people might be as laughable as its cause, was in no whit allayed and softened by time seemingly. She hated Gilbert Blythe! She would never forgive him!

"No," she said coldly, "I shall never be friends with you, Gilbert Blythe; and I don't want to be!"

"All right!" Gilbert sprang into his skiff with an angry colour in his cheeks. "I'll never ask you to be friends again, Anne Shirley. And I don't care either!"

He pulled away with swift defiant strokes, and Anne went up the steep, ferny little path under the maples. She held her head very high, but she was conscious of an odd feeling of regret. She almost wished she had answered Gilbert differently. Of course, he had insulted her terribly, but still–! Altogether, Anne rather thought it would be a relief to sit down and have a good cry. She was really quite unstrung, for the reaction from her fright and cramped clinging was making itself felt.

Half-way up the path she met Jane and Diana rushing back to the pond in a state narrowly removed from positive frenzy. They had found nobody at Orchard Slope, both Mr. and Mrs. Barry being away. Here Ruby Gillis had succumbed to hysterics, and was left to recover from them as best she might, while Jane and Diana flew through the Haunted Wood and across the brook to Green Gables. There they had found nobody either, for Marilla had gone to Carmody and Matthew was making hay in the back field.

"Oh, Anne," gasped Diana, fairly falling on the former's neck and weeping with relief and delight, "Oh, Anne–we thought–you were–drowned–and we felt like murderers–because we had made–you be–Elaine. And Ruby is in hysterics–oh, Anne, how did you escape?"

"I climbed up on one of the piles," explained Anne wearily, "and Gilbert Blythe came along in Mr. Andrews' dory and brought me to land."

"Oh, Anne, how splendid of him! Why it's so romantic!" said Jane, finding breath enough for utterance at last. "Of course you'll speak to him after this."

"Of course I won't," flashed Anne with a momentary return of her old spirit. "And I don't want ever to hear the word romantic again, Jane Andrews. I'm awfully sorry you were so frightened, girls. It is all my fault. I feel sure I was born under an unlucky star. Everything I do gets me or my dearest friends into a scrape. We've gone and lost your father's flat, Diana, and I have a presentiment that we'll not be allowed to row on the pond any more."

Anne's presentiment proved more trustworthy than presentiments are apt to do. Great was the consternation in the Barry and Cuthbert households when the events of the afternoon became known.

"Will you ever have any sense, Anne?" groaned Marilla.

"Oh, yes, I think I will, Marilla," returned Anne optimistically. A good cry, indulged in the grateful solitude of the east gable, had soothed her nerves and restored her to her wonted cheerfulness. "I think my prospects of becoming sensible are brighter now than ever."

"I don't see how," said Marilla.

"Well," explained Anne, "I've learned a new and valuable lesson today. Ever since I came to Green Gables I've been making mistakes, and each mistake has helped to cure me of some great shortcoming. The affair of the amethyst brooch cured me of meddling with things that didn't belong to me. The Haunted Wood mistake cured me of letting my imagination run away with me. The liniment cake mistake cured me of carelessness in cooking. Dyeing my hair cured me of vanity. I never think about my hair and nose now—at least, very seldom. And today's mistake is going to cure me of being too romantic. I have come to the conclusion that it is no use trying to be romantic in Avonlea. It was probably easy enough in towered Camelot hundreds of years ago, but romance is not appreciated now. I feel quite sure that you will soon see a great improvement in me in this respect, Marilla."

"I'm sure I hope so," said Marilla sceptically.

But Matthew, who had been sitting mutely in his corner, laid a hand on Anne's shoulder when Marilla had gone out.

"Don't give up all your romance, Anne," he whispered shyly, "a little of it is a good thing—not too much, of course—but keep a little of it, Anne, keep a little of it."

FURTHER READING

THE "AVONLEA" NOVELS
Anne of Green Gables (Toronto: Ryerson Press Paperback). Also available in Tempo Books and Penguin imprints.
Anne of Avonlea (Toronto: Ryerson Press Paperback).
Anne of the Island (Toronto: Ryerson Press Paperback).
BIOGRAPHY
Mary Quayle Innis, ed., *The Clear Spirit: Twenty Canadian Women and Their Times* (Toronto: University of Toronto Press, 1966).
THEATRE
Anne of Green Gables, a musical adapted from the novel. Performed each summer at the Charlottetown Festival, Prince Edward Island.
LITERARY SITES
Green Gables at Cavendish, Prince Edward Island, is maintained as an historic site.

A former home of Lucy Maude Montgomery at Leaskdale, Ontario, has been marked as an historic site.

The house where Lucy Maude Montgomery was born, at New London, Prince Edward Island, has been restored as an historic site by the Prince Edward Island Government.

PICTURE SERIES

Canadian Authors (includes Lucy Maude Montgomery), obtainable from: Hilton Photo Supplies, P.O. Box 74, Chemainus, British Columbia.

E. Pauline Johnson (Tekahionwake)

Emily Pauline Johnson (1862-1913) was born Tekahionwake, daughter of a Mohawk chief and an English-born Canadian girl, and brought up on her father's estate on the Six Nations Reserve near Brantford, Canada West. It was a home with more than its share of cultural amenities, and she had a good deal of her education there, from her mother who encouraged her to read the English classics and from her grandfather, Smoke Johnson, hero of Queenston Heights, who told her tales of the Mohawks. She first contributed her poems to Canadian, British and American magazines; then beginning in Toronto in 1892, made a stage career of reciting them before audiences in Canada, the United States and England. For these performances she often dressed in gorgeous native costume: buckskin dress, bear claw necklace, bracelets of wampum beads, an eagle feather in her hair and two cured scalps at her waist. For the second half of the program she might change into an evening gown with plunging neckline. As much at home reciting in the drawing rooms of London as in some poolroom in the B.C. Cariboo country, she became an internationally famous performer.

A passionate woman, she publicly proclaimed her deep pride in her Indian heritage. Much of her poetry reflected her love of nature and her romantic imagination: The Song My Paddle Sings, Legend of Qu'Appelle Valley, Lullaby of the Iroquois—*poems every school child in the next generation came to know. A few express the hurt and anger of the disinherited Indian:* Cry from an Indian Wife, The Corn Husker *and in particular,*

The Cattle Thief:

> When you pay for the land you live in,
>   we'll pay for the meat we eat.
> Give back our land and our country,
>   give back our herds of game;
> Give back the furs and the forests
>   that were ours before you came.

*In her prose writings too she strove to interpret Indian values
and explore areas of conflict between the two races, wanting
and expecting nothing less than a merging on equal terms of
the white and Indian peoples.* The Shagganappi *(1913) is a collection of boys' stories demonstrating the dignity and worth of
the Indian.* The Moccasin Maker *(1913) contains several pieces
which discover the attitudes of both white and Indian to mixed
marriage, including a biography of her mother and the revenge
tale, "As It Was in the Beginning" which has, for all its melodrama, the ring of bitter knowledge.*

*During her career she crossed Canada nineteen times. Her
stage partner from 1899 and companion until her death was
the entertainer, Walter McRaye. She stopped reciting in 1909
and settled in Vancouver, trying to live by her writing. With
the help of Chief Joe Capilano she collected and recorded the
stories of the Squamish tribe, first printed in the* Vancouver
Province, *then published as* The Legends of Vancouver *(1911).
At her death she herself became legend, honoured and loved
as a gallant woman who had declared her race, so integrating
her life and her art, and who was willing to accept as tribute
the element of conscience in the public response to her work.*

THE TWO SISTERS

You can see them as you look towards the north and the west, where
the dream hills swim into the sky amid their ever-drifting clouds of
pearl and grey. They catch the earliest hint of sunrise, they hold the
last colour of sunset. Twin mountains they are, lifting their twin
peaks above the fairest city in all Canada, and known throughout
the British Empire as "The Lions of Vancouver."

Sometimes the smoke of forest fires blurs them until they gleam
like opals in a purple atmosphere, too beautiful for words to paint.
Sometimes the slanting rains festoon scarfs of mist about their crests,
and the peaks fade into shadowy outlines, melting, melting, forever
melting into the distances. But for most days in the year the sun
circles the twin glories with a sweep of gold. The moon washes them
with a torrent of silver. Oftentimes, when the city is shrouded in
rain, the sun yellows their snows to a deep orange; but through sun
and shadow they stand immovable, smiling westward above the
waters of the restless Pacific, eastward above the superb beauty of

From: E. Pauline Johnson, *Legends of Vancouver* (Toronto: McClelland
and Stewart, 1961). Reprinted by permission of McClelland and Stewart
Limited, the Canadian Publishers.

the Capilano Canyon. But the Indian tribes do not know these peaks as "The Lions." Even the Chief, whose feet have so recently wandered to the Happy Hunting Grounds, never heard the name given them until I mentioned it to him one dreamy August day, as together we followed the trail leading to the canyon. He seemed so surprised at the name that I mentioned the reason it had been applied to them, asking him if he recalled the Landseer Lions in Trafalgar Square. Yes, he remembered those splendid sculptures, and his quick eye saw the resemblance instantly. It appeared to please him, and his fine face expressed the haunting memories of the far-away roar of Old London. But the "call of the blood" was stronger, and presently he referred to the Indian legend of those peaks—a legend that I have reason to believe is absolutely unknown to thousands of Palefaces who look upon "The Lions" daily, without the love for them that is in the Indian heart, without knowledge of the secret of "The Two Sisters." The legend was intensely fascinating as it left his lips in the quaint broken English that is never so dulcet as when it slips from an Indian tongue. His inimitable gestures, strong, graceful, comprehensive, were like a perfectly chosen frame embracing a delicate painting, and his brooding eyes were as the light in which the picture hung.

"Many thousands of years ago," he began, "there were no twin peaks like sentinels guarding the outposts of this sunset coast. They were placed there long after the first creation, when the Sagalie Tyee moulded the mountains, and patterned the mighty rivers where the salmon run, because of His love for His Indian children, and His Wisdom for their necessities. In those times there were many and mighty Indian tribes along the Pacific—in the mountain ranges, at the shores and sources of the great Fraser River. Indian law ruled the land. Indian customs prevailed. Indian beliefs were regarded. Those were the legend-making ages when great things occurred to make the traditions we repeat to our children today. Perhaps the greatest of these traditions is the story of "The Two Sisters," for they are known to us as "The Chief's Daughters," and to them we owe the Great Peace in which we live, and have lived for many countless moons. There is an ancient custom amongst the Coast tribes that when our daughters step from childhood into the great world of womanhood the occasion must be made one of extreme rejoicing. The being who possesses the possibility of someday mothering a man-child, a warrior, a brave, receives much consideration in most nations, but to us, the Sunset Tribes, she is honoured above all people. The parents usually give a great potlatch, and a feast that lasts many days. The entire tribe and the surrounding tribes are bidden to this festival. More than that, sometimes when a great Tyee celebrates for his daughter, the tribes from far up the coast, from the distant north, from inland, from the island, from the Cariboo country, are gathered as guests to the feast. During these days of rejoicing, the girl is placed in a high seat, an exalted position, for is she not marriageable? And does not marriage mean motherhood? And does not motherhood mean a vaster nation of brave sons and of gentle daughters who, in their turn, will give us sons and daughters of their own?

"But it was many thousands of years ago that a great Tyee had two daughters that grew to womanhood at the same springtime, when the first great run of salmon thronged the rivers, and the ollallie bushes were heavy with blossoms. These two daughters were young, lovable, and oh! very beautiful. Their father, the great Tyee, prepared to make a feast such as the Coast had never seen. There were to be days and days of rejoicing, the people were to come for many leagues, were to bring gifts to the girls and to receive gifts of great value from the Chief, and hospitality was to reign as long as pleasuring feet could dance, and enjoying lips could laugh, and mouths partake of the excellence of the Chief's fish, game, and ollallies.

"The only shadow on the joy of it all was war, for the tribe of the great Tyee was at war with the Upper Coast Indians, those who lived north, near what is named by the Paleface as the port of Prince Rupert. Giant war canoes slipped along the entire coast, war parties paddled up and down, war songs broke the silences of the nights, hatred, vengeance, strife, horror festered everywhere like sores on the surface of the earth. But the great Tyee, after warring for weeks, turned and laughed at the battle and the bloodshed, for he had been victor in every encounter, and he could well afford to leave the strife for a brief week and feast in his daughters' honour, nor permit any mere enemy to come between him and the traditions of his race and household. So he turned insultingly deaf ears to their war cries; he ignored with arrogant indifference their paddle dips that encroached within his own coast waters, and he prepared, as a great Tyee should, to royally entertain his tribesmen in honour of his daughters.

"But seven suns before the great feast, these two maidens came before him, hand clasped in hand.

"Oh! our father," they said, "may we speak?"

"Speak, my daughters, my girls with the eyes of April, the hearts of June" (early spring and early summer would be the more accurate Indian phrasing).

"Some day, Oh! our father, we may mother a man-child, who may grow to be just such a powerful Tyee as you are, and for this honour that may some day be ours we have come to crave a favour of you— you, Oh! our father."

"It is your privilege at this celebration to receive any favour your hearts may wish," he replied graciously, placing his fingers beneath their girlish chins. "The favour is yours before you ask it, my daughters."

"Will you, for our sakes, invite the great northern hostile tribe–the tribe you war upon–to this, our feast?" they asked fearlessly.

"To a peaceful feast, a feast in the honour of women?" he exclaimed incredulously.

"So we would desire it," they answered.

"And so shall it be," he declared. "I can deny you nothing this day, and some time you may bear sons to bless this peace you have asked, and to bless their mother's sire for granting it." Then he turned to all the young men of the tribe and commanded, "Build fires at sunset on all the coast headlands–fires of welcome. Man your canoes and face the north, greet the enemy, and tell them that I, the Tyee of the Capilanos, ask–no, command that they join me for a great feast in honour of my two daughters." And when the northern tribes got this invitation they flocked down the coast to this feast of a Great Peace. They brought their women and their children: they brought game and fish, gold and white stone beads, baskets and carven ladles, and wonderful woven blankets to lay at the feet of their now acknowledged ruler, the great Tyee. And he, in turn, gave such a potlatch that nothing but tradition can vie with it. There were long, glad days of joyousness, long pleasurable nights of dancing and camp fires, and vast quantities of food. The war canoes were emptied of their deadly weapons and filled with the daily catch of salmon. The hostile war songs ceased, and in their place were heard the soft shuffle of dancing feet, the singing voices of women, the play-games of the children of two powerful tribes which had been until now ancient enemies, for a great and lasting brotherhood was sealed between them–their war songs were ended forever.

Then the Sagalie Tyee smiled on his Indian children: "I will make these young-eyed maidens immortal," he said. In the cup of his hands he lifted the Chief's two daughters and set them forever in a high place, for they had borne two offspring–Peace and Brotherhood–each of which is now a great Tyee ruling this land.

"And on the mountain crest the Chief's daughters can be seen wrapped in the suns, the snows, the stars of all seasons, for they have stood in this high place for thousands of years, and will stand for thousands of years to come, guarding the peace of the Pacific Coast and the quiet of the Capilano Canyon."

This is the Indian legend of "The Lions of Vancouver" as I had it from one who will tell me no more the traditions of his people.

FURTHER READING

AVAILABLE WORKS BY E. PAULINE JOHNSON

Legends of Vancouver (Toronto: McClelland and Stewart, 1961). First published in 1911.

Flint and Feather: The Complete Poems of Pauline Johnson (Toronto: Musson Book Company). First published in 1912.

BIOGRAPHY

Marcus Van Steen, *Pauline Johnson* (Toronto: Musson Book Company).

RELATED MATERIAL

Norval Morriseau, *Legends of my People, the Great Ojibway* (Toronto: Ryerson Press, 1965).

Kent Gooderham, ed., *I am an Indian* (Toronto: Dent and Sons, 1969).

George Clutesi, *Potlatch* (Sidney, British Columbia: Gray's Publishing Ltd., 1969).

Ella Elizabeth Clark, ed., *Indian Legends of Canada* (Toronto: McClelland and Stewart, 1960).

LITERARY SITES

A Pauline Johnson Memorial Cairn was erected in 1922 near Siwash Rock, Stanley Park, in Vancouver.

Chiefswood, Pauline Johnson's birthplace, on the Six Nations Reserve near Brantford, Ontario, is an historic site open to the public.

PICTURE SERIES

Canadian Authors (includes E. Pauline Johnson), obtainable from: Hilton Photo Supplies, P.O. Box 74, Chemainus, British Columbia.

Charles G. D. Roberts

Charles G. D. Roberts (1860-1945) was born in New Brunswick and educated at the University of New Brunswick. In 1883 he became editor of Goldwin Smith's The Week, *one of a series of nationalist papers and journals which flourished in the post-Confederation period, then taught English at King's College, Nova Scotia, 1885-1895.* Orion, and Other Poems *(1880) and* In Divers Tones *(1886) won him recognition as a national poet. Then followed a period of twenty-eight years during which he lived in New York and England, travelled much and served in the First World War. During these expatriate years his outstanding achievement was animal fiction. He wrote some twenty volumes in this genre, including* The Kindred of the Wild *(1902),* The Watchers of the Trails *(1904),* The Haunters of Silence *(1907) and the full length biography,* Red Fox *(1905). Returning to Canada at the age of sixty-five, he engaged in a number of literary activities until his death. He was awarded the Lorne Pierce Medal in 1926, and knighted in 1935.*

ON THE ROOF OF THE WORLD

It seemed to be the very roof of the world, all naked to the outer cold, this flat vast of solitude, dimly outspread beneath the Arctic night. A line of little hills, mere knobs and hummocks, insignificant under the bitter starlight, served to emphasize the immeasurable and shelterless flatness of the surrounding expanse. Somewhere beneath the unfeatured levels the sea ended and the land began, but over all lay the monotony of ridged ice and icy, wind-scourged snow. The wind, which for weeks without a pause had torn screaming across the nakedness, had now dropped into calm; and with the calm there seemed to come in the unspeakable cold of space.

From: Charles G. D. Roberts, *Thirteen Bears* (Toronto: Ryerson Press, 1947). Reprinted by permission of McGraw-Hill Ryerson.

Suddenly a sharp noise, beginning in the dimness far to the left of the Little Hills, ran snapping past them and died off abruptly in the distance to the right. It was the ice, thickened under that terrific cold, breaking in order to readjust itself to the new pressure. There was a moment of strange muttering and grinding. Then, again, the stillness.

Yet, even here on the roof of the world, which seemed as if all the winds of eternity had swept it bare, there was life, life that clutched and clung savagely. Away to the right of the Little Hills, something moved, prowling slowly among the long ridges of the ice. It was a gaunt, white, slouching, startling shape, some seven or eight feet in length, and nearly four in height, with heavy shoulders, and a narrow, flat-browed head that hung low and swayed menacingly from side to side as it went. Had the light been anything more than the wide glimmer of stars, it would have shown that this lonely, prowling shape of white had a black-tipped muzzle, black edges to the long slit of its jaws, and little, cruel eyes with lids outlined in black. From time to time the prowler raised his head, sniffed with dilating nostrils, and questioned with strained ears the deathly silence. It was a polar bear, an old male, too restless and morose to content himself with sleeping away the terrible polar winter in a snow-blanketed hole.

From somewhere far off to seaward came across the stillness a light sound, the breaking of thin ice, the tinkle of splashings frozen as they fell. The great white bear understood that sound. He had been waiting for it. The seals were breaking their way up into their air-holes to breathe—those curious holes which form here and there in the ice-fields over moving water, as if the ocean itself had need of keeping in touch with upper air for its immeasurable breathing. At a great pace, but noiselessly as a drifting wraith of snow, the bear went towards the sound. Then suddenly he dropped flat and seemed to vanish. In reality he was crawling, crawling steadily towards the place of the air-holes. But so smooth was his movement, so furtive, and so fitted to every irregularity of the icy surface, that if the eye once lost him it might strive in vain to pick him up again.

Nearer, nearer he crept, till at last, lying motionless with his lean muzzle just over the crest of the ice-ridge, he could make out the dark shapes of the seals, vague as shadows, emerging for a few moments to sprawl upon the edge of the ice. Every few seconds one would slip into the water again, while another would awkwardly scramble forth. In that phenomenal cold it was necessary for them to take heed to the air-holes, lest these should get sealed up and leave them to drown helplessly under the leagues of solid ice-fields. These breathing-spells in the upper air, out here on the world's roof, were their moments of greatest peril. Close to the edge of the hole they sprawled; and always one or another kept anxious watch, scanning with mild, bright eyes the menacing solitude, wherein they seemed the only things alive.

About this time, from one of a group of tiny, snow-covered mounds huddled along the base of the Little Hills, emerged a man. He crawled forth on all fours from the tunnel of his doorway, and stood up and peered about him. His squat figure was clothed and hooded in furs. His little, twinkling eyes, after clearing themselves from the smoke and smart of the thick air within the igloo, could see further through the gloom than even the eyes of the bear. He noted the fall of the wind, the savage intensity of the cold, and his eyes brightened with hope. He had no fear of the cold, but he feared the hunger which was threatening the lonely village. During the long rage of the wind, the supply of food in his igloo had run low. He welcomed a cold which would close up most of the seals' breathing-holes, and force more numerous visitors to the few holes that they could keep open. For some moments he stood motionless, peering and listening as the bear had done. Suddenly he too caught that far-off light crashing of brittle ice. On that instant he turned and crawled hastily back into the hut.

A moment later he reappeared, carrying two weapons, besides the long knife stuck in his girdle. One of these was an old Hudson's Bay Company's musket. The other was a spear of spliced bone, with a steel head securely lashed to it. Powder and ball for the musket were much too precious to be expended, except in some emergency wherein the spear might fail. Without waiting for a repetition of the sounds, he started off at once unerringly in the direction whence they had come. He knew that air-hole; he could find it in the delusive gloom without the aid of landmark. For some way he went erect and in haste, though as soundlessly as the bear. Then, throwing himself flat, he followed exactly the bear's tactics, till, at last, peering cautiously over a jagged ice-ridge, he, too, could make out the quarry watchfully coming and going about the brink of the air-hole.

From this point onward the man's movements were so slow as to be almost imperceptible. But for his thick covering of furs, his skin tough as leather and reeking with oil, he would have been frozen in the midst of his journey. But the still excitement of the hunt was pumping the blood hotly through his veins. He was now within gunshot, but in that dim light his shooting would be uncertain. He preferred to worm his way nearer, and then trust to his more accustomed weapon, the spear, which he could drive half-way through the tough bulk of a walrus.

At last there remained between him and the seals but one low ridge and then a space of level floe. This was the critical point. If he could writhe his body over the crest and down the other side, he would be within safe spear-shot. He would spring to his feet and throw before the nimblest seal could gain the water. He lay absolutely still, summoning wits, nerves, and muscles alike to serve his will with their best. His eyes burned deep in his head, like smouldering coals.

Just at this moment a ghostly light waved broadly across the solitude. It paled, withdrew, wavered back and forth as shaken from a curtain in the heavens, then steadied ephemerally into an arch of glowing silver, which threw the light of a dozen moons. There were three seals out upon the ice at that moment, and they all lifted their eyes simultaneously to greet the illumination. The man irresistibly looked up; but in the same instant, remembering the hunger in the igloo, he cowered back again out of sight, trembling lest some of the seals might have caught a glimpse of his head above the ridge. Some dozen rods away, at the other side of the air-hole, the great white bear also raised his eyes towards that mysterious light, troubled at heart because he knew it was going to hamper his hunting.

For perhaps two minutes the seals were motionless, profiting by the sudden brightness to scrutinize the expanse of ice and snow in every direction. Then, quite satisfied that no danger was near, they resumed their sportive plungings while the instantly frozen waters crackled crisply about them. For all their vigilance, they had failed to detect, on the one side, a narrow, black-tipped muzzle lying flat in a cleft of the ice-ridge, or, on the other side, a bunch of greyish fur, nearly the colour of the greyish-mottled ice, which covered the head of the man from the igloo beside the Little Hills.

And now, while neither the man nor the bear, each utterly unconscious of the other, dared to stir, in a flash the still silver radiance of the aurora broke up and flamed into a riot of dancing colour. Parallel rays like the pipes of a titanic organ, reaching almost from the horizon to the zenith, hurtled madly from side to side, now elongating, now shortening abruptly, now seeming to clash against one another, but always in an ordered madness of right lines. Unearthly green palpitating into rose, and thinnest sapphire, and flame-colour, and ineffably tender violet, the dance of these cohorts of the magnetic rays went on across the stupendous arc of sky, till the man, afraid of freezing in his unnatural stillness, shrank back down the ridge, and began twisting his body, noiselessly but violently, to set his blood in motion; and the bear, trusting to the confusion of shifting lights, slipped himself over the ridge and into a convenient crevice. Under the full but bewildering glare of that celestial illumination, he had gained a good ten feet upon his human rival. The man's eyes reappeared just then at the crest of his ridge. Their piercing glance lingered, as if with suspicion, upon the crevice wherein the bear had flattened himself. Was there something unduly solid in that purple shadow in the crevice? No, a trick of the witch lights, surely. The piercing eyes returned to their eager watching of the seals.

Precious as was his ammunition, and indifferent as was his shooting with the old, big bore, Hudson's Bay musket, the man was beginning to think he would have to stake his chances on the gun. But, suddenly, as if at a handsweep of the Infinite, the great lights vanished.

For a few seconds, by the violence of the contrast, it seemed as if thick darkness had fallen upon the world.

In those few seconds, noiseless and swift as a panther, the man had run over the ridge to within a dozen paces of the seals, and paused with spear uplifted, waiting till his eyes should once more be able to see in the starlight glimmer. As he stood thus waiting, every sense, nerve, and muscle on the last strain of expectancy and readiness, he heard, or seemed to feel as much as to hear, the rush of some great bulk through the gloom. Then came a scramble, a heavy splash, a second splash, a terrible scuffling noise, and a hoarse, barking scream. The man remembered that before the light went out there had been three seals on the ice. Two he had heard escape. What had befallen the third? Fiercely, like a beast being robbed of its prey, he sprang forward a couple of paces. Then he stopped, for he could not yet see clearly enough to distinguish what was before him. His blood pounded through his veins. The cold of Eternity was flowing in upon him, here on the naked roof of the world, but he had no feeling or fear of it. All he felt was the presence of his foe, there before him, close before him, in the dark.

Then, once more, the light flooded back—the wide-flung silver radiance—as suddenly and mysteriously as it had vanished.

Close beside the air-hole, half crouching upon the body of the slain seal, with one great paw uplifted, and bloody jaws open in defiance, stood the bear, glaring at the man.

Without an instant's hesitation the man hurled his spear. It flew true. But in the same second the bear lifted his paw to ward off the blow. He was not quite quick enough, but almost. The blade struck, but not where it was aimed. It bit deep, but not to the life. With a growl of rage, the bear tore it loose and charged upon the man.

The antagonists were not more than twenty paces apart, and now a glory of coloured lights, green, red, and golden, went dancing madly over them, with a whispering, rustling sound as of stiff silk crumpled in vast folds. The man's eyes were keen and steady. In a flash both hands were out of his great fur mittens, which were tied by thongs to his sleeves. The heavy musket leaped to his shoulder, and his eye ran coolly along the barrel. There was a thunderous roar as of a little cannon. A dense cloud of smoke sprang into the air just before the muzzle of the gun.

Through the smoke a towering shape, with wide jaws and battering paws, hurled itself. The man leaped to one side, but not quite far enough. One great paw, striking blindly, smote him down; and, as he fell, the huge bulk fell half upon him, only to roll over the next instant and lie huddled and motionless upon the ice.

The man picked himself up, shook himself; and a look of half-dazed triumph went across his swarthy face as he pulled on his mittens. Then he smiled broadly, patted approvingly the old Hudson's Bay musket, turned on his heel, and sent a long, summoning cry across the ice towards the igloos at the foot of the Little Hills.

FURTHER READING

FICTION BY ROBERTS
Kings in Exile (Toronto: Ryerson Press, 1947).
Thirteen Bears (Toronto: 1947).
The Feet of the Furtive (Toronto: Ryerson Press, 1947).
Red Fox (Toronto: Ryerson Press, 1948).
The Last Barrier and Other Stories (Toronto: McClelland and Stewart, New Canadian Library, 1958).
King of Beasts and Other Stories (Toronto: Ryerson Press, 1967).
POETRY BY ROBERTS
Malcolm Ross, ed., *Poets of the Confederation* (Toronto: McClelland and Stewart, New Canadian Library, 1960).
Desmond Pacey, ed., *Selected Poems* (Toronto: Ryerson Press, 1955).
CRITICISM
W. J. Keith, *Charles G. D. Roberts* (Toronto: Copp Clark Publishers, Studies in Canadian Literature Series).
A. J. M. Smith, ed., *Masks of Poetry* (Toronto: McClelland and Stewart, 1962). Includes a critical essay on Charles G. D. Roberts.
RELATED MATERIAL
Fred Bodsworth, *Last of the Curlews* (Toronto: McClelland and Stewart, New Canadian Library, 1963).

Martha Ostenso

Norwegian-born Martha Ostenso (1900-63) lived most of her childhood in Minnesota and North Dakota before coming to live in Manitoba where her parents settled in 1915. She went to the University of Manitoba, then left Canada in 1921 to live in the United States. She won the first prize of $13,500 in a literary competition for the best first novel by a North American writer. The novel was Wild Geese, *based on a summer's experience teaching in a rural school in northern Manitoba, and it has an important place in the development of the Canadian novel.*

One fact about *Wild Geese* demands attention: it is often passionate in tone. As a matter of fact, Ostenso's first title chosen for the novel was *Passionate Flight*. In between Ellen's sessions at the organ, playing *Lead, Kindly Light*, and the days the Gares spend stacking hay in the fields, a number of strongly emotional scenes explode. There is, for instance, the terrible curse that Amelia pronounces on her own children:

> Caleb's children could wither and fall like rotten plants after frost–everything could fall into dissolution . . . they could be the sacrifice. She would bend and inure them to the land like implements. . . . She would see them dry and fade into fruitlessness and grow old before their time, but her heart would keep within itself and there would be no pity in her for the destruction of their youth.

It is in the spirit of Medea who stabs her own children to complete her vengeance on Jason. In the course of the novel, Gare brutally strikes his wife "prostrate" with "the huge cattle whip"; the love-play in Judith and Sven's first intimacy takes the form of a fierce wrestling match for supremacy in which "Judith buried her nails in the flesh over his breast, beat her knees into his loins, set her teeth in the more tender skin over the veins at his wrist." Such events reach their climax when the fire consumes Gare's flax crop, and Caleb discovers too late the truth of his own sermon, "Woe to him that is alone when he falleth."

In the face of such melodrama–and very effective melodrama too– one may question Desmond Pacey's grouping the novel, without qualification, as a "realistic study of western life," along with the novels of Stead and Grove. Ostenso makes clear that the way of life on the Gare farm is not a representation of rural economic hardship but the effect of Gare's own miser complex. His name is, after all, "gare," which is Old Norse for "covetous, greedy." Gare thinks to himself, "And there would not be a farmer in all the country around so rich as Caleb Gare. It was well that even Amelia did not know the extent of his fortune."

Although the material of *Wild Geese* may be "realistic," as a novel it is a literary structure whose shaping is basically romantic. Life-like characters and familiar setting are fused with strong emotional appeal and forceful imagery and action. There are, for example, scenes like the one after Judith has thrown the axe at her father. Now, in the Gothic romance the persecuted girl-victim is a familiar figure who suffers many indignities, a favourite among them being imprisonment in a dungeon or ruined castle. Judith experiences her nightmare in the barn:

> Presently she began to tremble uncontrollably. . . . He would be insane with rage. Murder, perhaps . . . everything going, now . . . everything closing in . . . only the land, and the cattle, and manure. . . . She lay until the diagonal shadow that fell within the door of the barn lay toward the west instead of the east; until the rope had chafed red circles about her wrists, and her hair was full of bits of dry manure.

Ostenso's point of view is circumscribed by the borders of the farm as setting, with the surrounding community swinging into perspective only as needed in the course of the plot development. The sterile human relationships make the rural setting much nearer the waste land imagery of Eliot than the pastoral ideal. The city as setting does not enter directly into the novel, but is used as a symbol of escape or fulfilment. Judith, for example, dreams of release:

> The next day was full of dreams for Judith. She stood getting chicken feed from the bag in the barn, thinking of Sven, and of the distant place where they would soon go together. . . . Soon there would be no more goodbyes. They would have a snug cottage in town, and Sven would go to his work every day, but at night they would be together again–all night. . . . It seemed that it was already true, that Caleb, and the cattle, and

the land, and sweat, and hay dust, were gone forever.

Ostenso's concern with farm is mainly spatial; it provides a stage with familiar but set limits, an area of containment for her characters' actions. The sense of farm as bodily extension of man, so basic to Grove's *Fruits of the Earth* and Stead's *Grain*, is developed in a proportion once removed from initial motivation.

Hence, Gare's obsession with his land is rooted in hatred and jealousy; the land is to him both weapon and escape. His attachment to the land is related to a process of sublimation going on within him: "While he was raptly considering the tender field of flax–now in blue flower–Amelia did not exist." Amelia is the one who has involved him "as the betrayed and cheated victim in a triangle." So he gives to the flax "a stealthy caress–more intimate than any he had ever given to woman." Nor, unlike Stead and Grove, does Ostenso present the farm in a wider social or economic context in which the unit is affected or even controlled by changes in production methods or market fluctuations.

In *Wild Geese*, the farm walls in the enactment of domestic tragedy. Ostenso pits husband against wife, father against daughter, mother against children, child against child in an atmosphere of intolerable friction generated by conflicting drives in opposition. The pattern is struggle between domination and self-fulfilment. Caleb refuses to build a new barn and house, "but Martin was a builder born, and the dream reared itself in his mind and would not down." In these collisions between differing natures–which do lie at the heart of Ostenso's realism–the quest for identity, the maintenance of human dignity, and the fulfilment of "self" are developed.

Judith thinks to herself, "She was not an animal, to be driven, and tied, and tended for the value of her plodding strength. She knew what beauty was, and love, and things in no way connected with the rude growth of the land." The main agent working against such wish-fulfilment dreams is shown to be the obsession with material gain. When thwarted, this power-drive becomes entirely destructive. Ostenso's characters, in *Wild Geese* and other novels, tend to separate themselves into two groups: those who are bonded by a common humanism, and those who represent its negation.

Martha Ostenso's presentation of experience rests on a concept of dialectical opposites: real love and mere sex; innocence and experience; the spiritual and the physical; the intellectual and the material; self-defence and aggression; involvement and isolation. These opposing forces grind themselves out within the individual, as well as between characters. Amelia thinks:

Growth–with death in its wake. She felt that in an instant her life had reached finality, that all the years behind her had been spent in a chrysalis, in a beginning. There had been no development in between–only a beginning and an end.

The sharp contrast between appearance and reality in "Woe to him that is Alone" gives the passage its rich irony.

WOE TO HIM THAT IS ALONE

Caleb finished shaving and pulled on his starched white shirt. Then he picked up the collar Amelia had laid out for him. He looked at it once and laid it down again, without a word. Amelia, stirring the porridge on the stove, prepared herself for his usual sneering comment. She was thankful Lind had gone out. But no remark came from Caleb. He left the collar where it was and passed softly into the other room.

Jude and Ellen and the boys came down one after the other and breakfast was on the table in a few minutes. Lind entered from the front doorway that looked out on the horse corral, and her silk gown billowed softly in the little breeze that came in behind her. She carried an armful of pussy willows that she had gathered in the ditch near the schoolhouse, and placed them in a basket beside the organ. Ellen gave them a glance and went into the kitchen abruptly.

"Cluttering up the house like that," she sniffed to Amelia, "Father will have something to say about her taking it on herself."

Amelia sighed. "Let him say it, then, Ellen," she replied. "Go and eat your breakfast. Tell the others to sit in. He'll not get to church if we don't eat right away."

On Sundays Caleb said grace. Meals on the other days were taken up with discussion of things on the farm. Lind and the others bowed their heads, but Judith sat upright and looked straight ahead of her. She forced herself to think of something else until Caleb had said "Amen." The thing that actually came into her mind was that he had not the Lord to thank for what they were about to receive, but her, and Martin and Ellen, Amelia, and even Charlie, whose downcast face was hiding a grin.

"I'd like to take you with me this morning, Martin," said Caleb. "It'd do you a heap o' good, gettin' out among young people for a change. But I don't want you to be ashamed o' your own father, Martin."

From: Martha Ostenso, *Wild Geese* (Toronto: McClelland and Stewart, New Canadian Library, 1961). Reprinted by permission of McClelland and Stewart Limited, the Canadian Publishers.

Martin's long countenance lifted questioningly. He did not understand Caleb's remark, and before the Teacher he dared not ask. So he fell to eating his porridge again, slowly so that he should make no uncouth sound in Lind's presence.

Everyone ate in silence. An expression of pained regret had come over Caleb's face when he spoke. Amelia knew what that meant. What he was about to say was designed to mortify her, she knew.

"No, Martin, you'll have to wait until some time when I have a clean collar to wear," he said slowly, mildly, almost humorously.

Amelia's face flamed. Her eyes darted to Lind to see if she had heard. But the Teacher went on serenely eating her breakfast.

Judith spoke up, in spite of Amelia's quick frown. "Well–I guess you'd have plenty of clean collars if you'd buy more than one a year," she snapped. "And send the stiff ones to Nykerk instead of expecting Ma to do 'em up."

"You're right, Jude. You're right," Caleb chuckled. "Guess I'm a little careless." He pushed his chair back and rose from the table. "Mind hitchin' up Lady, Charlie? You and me'll go to church anyway, collar or no collar." He turned his stooped back upon them and moved into the kitchen. Amelia followed him.

"Caleb–you're not going to church without a collar on?" she said in dismay.

He turned slowly and looked at her. "Think the Icelanders'll see what a fine wife you are, eh?" he asked softly. "Well–you go talk to Jude. See she looks to her manners. That young one is gettin' a sight too smart. Understand?" The sour grimace appeared on his face that Amelia was so used to seeing there. He ran his hand over his moustache as if to wipe the expression away. He put on his coat and went out of the house. Amelia was thankful he had not noticed the lump behind his coat collar.

She hurriedly set about clearing the table, and spoke to Judith in a low tone. "You must not cross him or be cheeky to him, Jude. You know he's getting old and can't stand it," she murmured, so that Lind should not hear.

"He's no older now than he ever was. He's always been as bad, and I'm through standin' for it," Jude replied promptly and in no low tone. "Seems to me I've just started growin' a brain enough to know how I hate him!"

"Judith!" cried Ellen, aghast. "Your own father!"

"He's not! I don't care if he is! I don't give a damn for him, and you shut up your talk!" Jude cried, wheeling upon Ellen.

"Be quiet, Jude!" Amelia said calmly. "You're crazy to go on so! Before strangers!"

Lind had discreetly slipped out the front door.

"She's been that way ever since the Teacher came. As if nothing here is good enough for her any more," Ellen said tartly.

"That's not so. The Teacher has nothing to do with it. I've stood enough of his bullying of all of us. If he doesn't get a man here soon I'm going to leave!"

"Don't talk nonsense, Judith. You have no place to go," Amelia told her.

"Haven't I? You'll see!" She went on drying the dishes then without another word. Ellen's face was a study.

Lind crept under the fence of the sheep pasture and set out across the field. The scene was painful enough without Lind's further agonizing Amelia with her presence. Distressing conflicts of this kind had become increasingly common. She felt vaguely that her coming had incited Jude to greater rebellion. Lind wondered, as she had wondered time and again since her coming to Oeland, if there were any means in her power by which she might bring a little happiness into the lives of the Gares. And then in a moment, she was overwhelmed by her helplessness against the intangible thing that held them there, slaves to the land. It extended farther back than Caleb, this power, although it worked through him. Lind found herself longing for someone of her own world to talk with, someone to whom she might escape from the oppression of the Gares.

Judith surlily attended to the milking and helped Amelia with the separator, then took out Turk, one of the colts, and proceeded to break him into the saddle. The outraged animal threw her twice, while Martin looked on with a dry smile.

"I don't need to be thrown, Martin," Jude protested when she heard his rare laugh, "but I kind o' like it."

"Aw—yes you do," Martin grinned. "So does Turk."

"Well—you see if he does it again," she retorted, jumping into the saddle once more.

Lind, who had returned from her walk, came and sat on the ground beside Martin. He moved over for her deferentially, and blushed. It was a beautiful morning, full of sunshine, and with Caleb away the atmosphere on the farmstead was almost radiant. Although there was not much change in their conduct, Lind felt a releasing of reserve among the children, and delighted in being with them. She stared at Judith on the plunging horse, her amazement at the girl's dexterity increasing every moment.

The animal reared and snorted, pawed the air with his forelegs and tossed his mane like a black cloud. He was a handsome colt, slender and glossy as black satin, with a fine blazing eye. For a half hour Jude wrestled with him, careening in mad circles about the corral, taking near somersaults as the horse's forelegs straightened under him and his rear hoofs shot into the air time after time. Her laugh rang out in peals, her eyes were full of mockery. When she came close to the bar of the corral, Lind could see that her wrists, about which the rein was tightly wound, were bleeding.

"Don't you think she ought to stop, Martin?" Lind asked anxiously.

"She wouldn't," said Martin shortly. "He's near done."

When it was over, Jude unsaddled the panting, froth-covered animal, and threw herself down beside Lind and Martin.

"Nothing like a little exercise to make you feel good," she said, wiping her wrists. Her cheeks were deep red, and little beads of moisture shone on her tilted upper lip.

"You're marvellous, Judie," Lind said admiringly, "but you did frighten me once or twice."

"Gee, it's a great day, Mart," Judith observed lightly. "Couldn't you manage to sneak the spring wagon after dinner and take us up to the Slough? I'd like to get some crocuses. The air smells full of 'em."

"He'd say you was gaddin', like as not," Martin returned dubiously, but his eyes were unwontedly bright as he leaned back on his elbows and looked on the distant horizon. "I might try, though."

Lind looked with mixed feelings from one to the other of these two Gares. The height of their desire this precious April Sunday was to go gathering crocuses, and simple as the wish was, they took it for granted that somehow it would be denied.

"He'll be back from church about now. Sorry you couldn't go, Mart?" Judith's eyes twinkled with mischief, and Martin in appreciation smiled his twisted smile. Lind sat quietly watching the two while they talked with random happiness about momentous small things.

A half hour later the rattle of a cart sounded down the road, and Martin rose quickly to unbar the gate. Presently Caleb drove in with Charlie sitting very straight and important beside him. It was the first time in his life that Charlie had gone to church, and the experience had left its mark on his face and bearing much as a physical shock might have done. Martin, in his quiet, perceiving way, looked at the boy as he got out of the gig. Caleb went on to the house, leaving the two boys to unharness.

"How'd ye like it?" Martin asked.

"I liked the singin' all right, but the rest–I dunno as it was wuth goin' for," he said with a noncommittal swagger, hands thrust in pockets. "But the singin'–yeah, it was pretty good. Everybody sung. I sung." He looked down sheepishly and kicked a pebble along the ground. "You better go next time, Mart. There was a lot o' guys there from up north way. An' some girls. I didn't talk to 'em, though–

I mean the guys. Pa said not. Said they was Swedes and like to beat a little fella like me up–huh!–I could o' licked any of 'em!'"

Martin led the horse to the corral. He saw that Lind and Jude had gone indoors. He was glad. Lind's presence was disturbing to him, he did not know why. Charlie walked thoughtfully beside him.

"Say, Mart–does Pa think he's goin' to make us all stay here after we get big?" he asked, frowning. He was an undersized lad and looked up to his brother with some respect because of his superior height. As Caleb had always made a favourite of him, and was amused by his heedlessness, he had nothing but contempt for his sisters who had been trained never to disobey their father or to speak impudently to him.

"Well, I'm big, Charlie, ain't I? I guess like as not we'll all stay," Martin replied soberly. So now Charlie was beginning to wonder, too, he thought.

Charlie was silent as they went to the house. He was only fifteen, it was true. But today he had heard singing, and had found he liked to sing, with a lot of young folks like himself or a little older. There was one boy there he would have liked to talk to. The boy had a red tie, and put collection in the plate from his own pocket.

Before dinner on Sunday it was the custom for the family to assemble in the sitting-room and hear Caleb recite the sermon that had been delivered at Yellow Post church. Although for reasons of his own he did not think it well to permit the family to go to the service, he felt that it was unbefitting a Christian to keep them from the grace of God's word.

"Will you join us in hearing the sermon, Miss Archer?" Caleb asked the Teacher when Amelia was drawing the chairs into a semi-circle in the middle of the room. His manner was his best, suave, gentle and benevolent. He had taken the Bible down from its place on the shelf above the organ, and held it a little distance away from him as he had seen the new preacher do, as if not to desecrate the book by contact with his sinfully mortal person.

Lind could not well refuse. She sat down with the others, and Ellen at the organ played "Lead, Kindly Light." Then Caleb held up a hand and intoned the Lord's prayer. His voice was miraculously soft. Suddenly Lind found herself wanting to cry out against the farce, and confront Caleb with the monstrousness of his act. But she sat silent.

Caleb opened the Bible and read:

"Again, I considered all travail, and every right work, that for this a man is envied of his neighbour. This is also vanity and vexation of spirit.

"The fool foldeth his hands together, and eateth his own flesh.

"Better is an handful in quietness, than both the hands full with travail and vexation of spirit.

"Then I returned, and I saw vanity under the sun."

Caleb paused, cleared his throat, and looked significantly at each member of the family, dwelling last upon Lind. The Teacher stirred with discomfort under the steely condemnation in the old man's eyes. His voice went on, rising to a grand sonorousness:

"There is one alone, and there is not a second; yea, he hath neither child nor brother: yet is there no end of all his labour; neither is his eye satisfied with riches; neither saith he, For whom do I labour, and bereave my soul of good? This is also vanity, yea, it is a sore travail.

"Two are better than one; because they have a good reward for their labour.

"For if they fall, the one will lift up his fellow: but woe to him that is alone when he falleth; for he hath not another to help him up.

"Again, if two lie together, then they have heat: but how can one be warm alone?

"And if one prevail against him, two shall withstand him; and a threefold cord is not quickly broken."

Caleb sternly closed the book. "So endeth the lesson," he said huskily.

The children, waiting for the end of the ordeal, had only half heard the words. But Amelia, naturally pious, had drunk them in. One phrase stuck in her mind. "The fool foldeth his hands together, and eateth his own flesh." That was what he was doing. That was what she was helping him do. Eating his own flesh, here on the land. But for her there was no alternative, no choice save which of her flesh she should eat. O God, it was unendurable! Caleb was going on—and on—the sermon—the new preacher's sermon. . . .

"So must we, who dwell in this lonely land and strive to live Christian lives on the acres the Lord hath given us, cling together for warmth and for good reward for our labour. 'Better is an handful with quietness, than both the hands full with travail and vexation of spirit.' Better live here like we are, poor but content, than to seek the world and all its vices for enlargement of our worldly wealth. That, Jude, is for you to think of, careful, and for you, Ellen and Martin, and like as not, for you, Charlie. 'For if they fall, the one will lift up his fellow: but *woe*'—hear me—'*woe* to him that is alone when he falleth.' Do they understand the lesson, Amelia?" Amelia murmured, "Yes, I think they all understand it." She could have shouted aloud, beaten his face for his hypocrisy. She could have risen and belaboured him with all her strength for his bland mis-appropriation of a noble passage from the book that had given her many an hour's comfort. But she did nothing but sit and listen attentively until he had, in a hushed voice, given the last blessing.

"This was not strictly an Easter Sunday sermon, you understand. But Reverend Blossom thought it more like for us to have a sermon that would fit in with the season, so he said. What do you think, Amelia?"

"I think it was a well-chosen sermon," said Amelia quietly.

Then they all rose and sat down at the table, while Mrs. Gare brought the food from the kitchen, and Judith, yawning with boredom, helped her.

FURTHER READING

TWO ROMANCES: PARALLELS IN IMAGERY, SETTING, AND CHARACTER
Martha Ostenso, *Wild Geese* (Toronto: McClelland and Stewart, New Canadian Library, 1961).
Emily Brontë, *Wuthering Heights* (Toronto: Ryerson Press, Airmont Classics).
TWO MANITOBA RURAL NOVELS:
ENVIRONMENT AND THE QUEST MOTIF
Martha Ostenso, *Wild Geese* (publishing details above).
Frederick Philip Grove, *Settlers of the Marsh* (Toronto: McClelland and Stewart, New Canadian Library, 1965).
OTHER FICTION BY MARTHA OSTENSO
Dark Dawn, and *Prologue to Love* are out of print, but may be available in libraries. Other fiction by the same author may be discovered in homes and second-hand book stores.

Mazo de la Roche

Mazo de la Roche (1879-1961) was born and grew up in southern rural Ontario, daughter of dry goods clerk William Roche. She began writing at the age of twenty-one, but did not publish her first novel Possession *until 1923. For a time she lived in England, where she adopted the two children of friends who had died in Italy. Unmarried, she earned a living for her family by her writing, notably the* Jalna *series. It was with* Jalna *that she won the $10,000 prize in the Atlantic Monthly competition for 1927. The C.B.C. recently turned the* Jalna *books into a T.V. serial starring Kate Reid as the redoubtable old grandmother, Adeline Whiteoak, and Paul Harding as Renny.*

WELCOME TO JALNA

The car moved slowly along the winding driveway toward the house. The driveway was so darkened by closely ranked balsams that it was like a long greenish tunnel, always cool and damp. Black squirrels flung themselves from bough to bough, their curving tails like glossy notes of interrogation. Every now and again a startled rabbit showed its downy brown hump in the long grass. So slowly the car moved, the birds scarcely ceased their jargon of song at its approach.

Piers felt horribly like a schoolboy returning after playing truant. He remembered how he had sneaked along this drive, heavy-footed, knowing he would "catch it," and how he had caught it, at Renny's efficient hands. He slumped in his seat as he thought of it. Pheasant sat stiffly erect, her hands clasped tightly between her knees. As the car stopped before the broad wooden steps that led to the porch, a small figure appeared from the shrubbery. It was Wakefield, carrying in one hand a fishing rod, and in the other a string from which dangled a solitary perch.

From: Mazo de la Roche, *Jalna* (Toronto: The Macmillan Company of Canada, 1927). Reprinted by permission of the publishers.

"Oh, hullo," he said, coming over the lawn to them. "We got your telegram. Welcome to Jalna!"

He got on to the running board and extended a small fishy hand to Pheasant.

"Don't touch him," said Piers. "He smells beastly." Wakefield accepted the rebuff cheerfully.

"I like the smell of fish myself," he said pointedly to Pheasant. "And I forgot that some people don't. Now Piers likes the smell of manure better because working with manure is his job. He's used to it. Granny says that one can get used–"

"Shut up," ordered Piers, "and tell me where the family is."

"I really don't know," answered Wakefield, flapping the dead fish against the door of the car, "because it's Saturday, you see, and a free day for me. I got Mrs. Wragge to put me up a little lunch–just a cold chop and a hard-boiled egg, and a lemon tart and a bit of cheese, and–"

"For heaven's sake," said Piers, "stop talking and stop flapping that fish against the car! Run in and see what they're doing. I'd like to see Renny alone."

"Oh, you can't do that, I'm afraid. Renny's over with Maurice this afternoon. I expect they're talking over what they will do to you two. It takes a lot of thought and talk, you see, to arrange suitable punishments. Now the other day Mr. Fennel wanted to punish me and he simply couldn't think of anything to do to me that would make a suitable impression. Already he'd tried–"

Piers interrupted, fixing Wakefield with his eye: "Go and look in the drawing-room windows. I see firelight there. Tell me who is in the room."

"All right. But you'd better hold my fish for me, because some-one might look out of the window and see me, and, now I come to think of it, Meggie told me I wasn't to go fishing to-day, and it slipped right out of my head, the way things do with me. I expect it's my weak heart."

"If I don't thrash you," said his brother, "before you're an hour older, my name isn't Piers Whiteoak. Give me the fish." He jerked the string from the little boy's hand.

"Hold it carefully, please," admonished Wakefield over his shoulder, as he lightly mounted the steps. He put his face against the pane, and stood motionless a space.

Pheasant saw that the shadows were lengthening. A cool damp breeze began to stir the shaggy grass of the lawn, and the birds ceased to sing.

Piers said: "I'm going to throw this thing away."

"Oh, no," said Pheasant, "don't throw the little fellow's fish away."

A nervous tremor ran through her, more chill than the breeze. She almost sobbed: "Ugh, I'm so nervous!"

"Poor little kid," said Piers, laying his hand over hers. His own jaws were rigid, and his throat felt as though a hand were gripping it. The family had never seemed so formidable to him. He saw them in a fierce phalanx bearing down on him, headed by Grandmother ready to browbeat–abuse him. He threw back his shoulders and drew a deep breath. Well–let them! If they were unkind to Pheasant, he would take her away. But he did not want to go away. He loved every inch of Jalna. He and Renny loved the place as none of the others did. That was the great bond between them. Piers was very proud of this fellowship of love for Jalna between him and Renny.

"Confound the kid!" he said. "What is he doing?"

"He's coming."

Wakefield descended the steps importantly.

"They're having tea in the parlor just as though it were Sunday," he announced. "A fire lighted. It looks like a plate of Sally Lunn on the table. Perhaps it's a kind of wedding feast. I think we'd better go in. I'd better put my fish away first though."

Piers relinquished the perch, and said: "I wish Renny were there."

"So do I," agreed Wakefield. "A row's ever so much better when he's in it. Gran always says he's a perfect Court for a row."

Piers and Pheasant went slowly up the steps and into the house. He drew aside the heavy curtains that hung before the double doors of the drawing-room and led her into the room that seemed very full of people.

There were Grandmother, Uncle Nicholas, Uncle Ernest, Meg, Eden, and young Finch, who was slumped on a beaded ottoman devouring seedcake. He grinned sheepishly as the two entered, then turned to stare at his grandmother, as though expecting her to lead the attack. But it was Uncle Nicholas who spoke first. He lifted his moustache from his teacup, and raised his massive head, looking rather like a sardonic walrus. He rumbled:–

"By George, this is nothing more than I expected! But you pulled the wool over Renny's eyes, you young rascal."

Meg broke in, her soft voice choked with tears:–

"Oh, you deceitful, unfeeling boy! I don't see how you can stand there and face us. And that family–Pheasant–I never spoke to you about it, Piers–I thought you'd know how I'd feel about such a marriage."

"Hold your tongues!" shouted Grandmother, who so far had only been able to make inarticulate sounds of rage. "Hold your silly tongues, and let me speak." The muscles in her face were twitching, her terrible brown eyes were burning beneath her shaggy brows. She was sitting directly in front of the fire, and her figure in its brilliant tea gown was illumined with a hellish radiance. Boney, sitting on the back of her chair, glowed like an exotic flower. His beak was sunken on his puffed breast, and he spread his feathers to the warmth in apparent oblivion to the motion of his mistress.

"Come here!" she shouted. "Come over here in front of me. Don't stand like a pair of ninnies in the doorway."

"Mamma," said Ernest, "don't excite yourself so. It's bad for you. It'll upset your insides, you know."

"My insides are better than yours," retorted his mother. "I know how to look after them."

"Come closer, so she won't have to shout at you," ordered Uncle Nicholas.

"Up to the sacrificial altar," adjured Eden, who lounged near the door. His eyes laughed up at them as they passed toward Mrs. Whiteoak's chair. Pheasant gripped Piers's coat in icy fingers. She cast an imploring look at Nicholas, who had once given her a doll and remained a kind of god in her eyes ever since, but he only stared down his nose, and crumbled the bit of cake on his saucer. If it had not been for the support of Piers's arm, she felt that she must have sunk to her knees, she trembled so.

"Now," snarled Grandmother, when she had got them before her, "aren't you ashamed of yourselves?"

"No," answered Piers, stoutly. "We've only done what lots of people do. Got married on the quiet. We knew the whole family would get on their hind feet if we told them, so we kept it to ourselves, that's all."

"And do you expect–" she struck her stick savagely on the floor–" do you expect that I shall allow you to bring that little bastard here? Do you understand what it means to Meg? Maurice was her fiancé and he got this brat–"

"Mamma!" cried Ernest.

"Easy, old lady," soothed Nicholas.

Finch exploded in sudden, hysterical laughter.

Meg raised her voice. "Don't stop her. It's true."

"Yes, what was I saying? Don't dare to stop me! This brat–this brat–he got her by a slut–"

Piers bent over her, glaring into her fierce old face.

"Stop it!" he shouted. "Stop it, I say!"

Boney was roused into a sudden passion by the hurricane about him. He thrust his beak over Grandmother's shoulder, and riveting his cruel little eyes on Piers's face, he poured forth a stream of Hindu abuse:–

"Shaitan! Shaitan ka bata! Shaitan ka butcka! Piakur! Piakur! Jab kutr!"

This was followed by a cascade of mocking, metallic laughter, while he rocked side to side on the back of Grandmother's chair.

It was too much for Pheasant. She burst into tears, hiding her face in her hands. But her sobs could not be heard for the cursing of Boney; and Finch, shaking from head to foot, added his hysterical laughter.

Goaded beyond endurance, his sunburned face crimson with rage, Piers caught the screaming bird by the throat and threw him savagely to the floor, where he lay, as gayly colored as painted fruit, uttering strange coughing sounds.

Grandmother was inarticulate. She looked as though she would choke. She tore at her cap and it fell over one ear. Then she grasped her heavy stick. Before anyone could stop her—if indeed they had wished to stop her—she had brought it with a resounding crack on to Piers's head.

"Take that," she shouted, "miserable boy!"

At the instant that the stick struck Piers's head, the door from the hall was opened and Renny came into the room, followed by Wakefield, who, behind the shelter of his brother, peered timidly yet inquisitively at the family. All faces turned toward Renny, as though his red head were a sun and they sun-gazing flowers.

"This is a pretty kettle of fish," he said.

"He's abusing Boney," wailed Grandmother. "Poor dear Boney! Oh, the young brute! Flog him, Renny! Give him a sound flogging!"

"No! No! No! No!" screamed Pheasant.

Nicholas heaved himself about in his chair, and said:—

"He deserved it. He threw the bird on the floor."

"Pick poor Boney up, Wakefield dear," said Ernest. "Pick him up and stroke him."

Except his mistress, Boney would allow no one but Wakefield to touch him. The child picked him up, stroked him, and set him on his grandmother's shoulder. Grandmother, in one of her gusts of affection, caught him to her and pressed a kiss on his mouth. "Little darling," she exclaimed. "Gran's darling! Give him a piece of cake, Meg."

Meg was crying softly behind the teapot. Wakefield went to her, and receiving no notice, took the largest piece of cake and began to devour it.

Renny had crossed to Piers's side and was staring at his head.

"His ear is bleeding," he remarked. "You shouldn't have done that, Granny."

"He was impudent to her," said Ernest.

Eden cut in: "Oh, rot! She was abusing him and the girl horribly."

Grandmother thumped the floor with her stick.

"I wasn't abusing him. I told him I wouldn't have the girl in the house. I told him she was a bastard brat, and so she is. I told him—bring me more tea—more tea—where's Philip? Philip, I want tea!" When greatly excited she often addressed her eldest son by his father's name.

"For God's sake, give her some tea," growled Nicholas. "Make it hot."

Ernest carried a cup of tea to her, and straightened her cap.

"More cake," she demanded. "Stop your sniveling, Meggie."

"Grandmother," said Meg, with melancholy dignity, "I am not sniveling. And it isn't much wonder if I do shed tears, considering the way Piers has acted."

"I've settled him," snorted Grandmother. "Settled him with my stick. Ha!"

Piers said, in a hard voice: "Now, look here, I'm going to get out. Pheasant and I don't have to stop here. We only came to see what sort of reception we'd get. Now we know, and we're going."

"Just listen to him, Renny," said Meg. "He's lost all his affection for us, and it seems only yesterday that he was a little boy like Wake."

"Heaven knows whom Wakefield will take up with," said Nicholas. "The family's running to seed."

"Will you have some tea, Renny?" asked Meg.

"No, thanks. Give the girl some. She's awfully upset."

"I don't want tea!" cried Pheasant, looking wildly at the hostile faces about her. "I want to go away! Piers, please, please, take me away!" She sank into a wide, stuffed chintz chair, drew up her knees, covered her face with her hands, and sobbed loudly.

Meg spoke with cold yet furious chagrin.

"If only he could send you home and have done with you! But here you are bound fast to him. You'd never rest till you'd got him bound fast. I know your kind."

Nicholas put in: "They don't wait till they're out of pinafores—that kind."

Eden cried: "Oh, for God's sake!"

But Piers's furious voice drowned him out.

"Not another word about her. I won't stand another word!"

Grandmother screamed: "You'll stand another crack on the head, you young whelp!" Crumbs of cake clung to the hairs on her chin. Wake regarded them, fascinated. Then he blew on them, trying to blow them off. Finch uttered hysterical croaking sounds.

"Wakefield, don't do that," ordered Uncle Ernest, "or you'll get your head slapped. Mamma, wipe your chin."

Meg said: "To think of the years that I've kept aloof from the

Vaughans! I've never spoken to Maurice since that terrible time. None of them have set foot in this house. And now his daughter–that child–the cause of all my unhappiness–brought here to live as Piers's wife."

Piers retorted: "Don't worry, Meg. We're not going to stay."

"The disgrace is here forever," she returned bitterly, "if you go to the other end of the earth." Her head rested on her hand, supported by her short plump arm. Her sweetly curved lips were drawn in at the corners, in an expression of stubborn finality. "You've finished things. I was terribly hurt at the very beginning of my life. I've tried to forget. Your bringing this girl here has renewed all the hurt. Shamed me, crushed me–I thought you loved me, Piers–"

"Oh, Lord, can't a man love his sister and another too?" exclaimed Piers, regarding her intently, with scarlet face, cut to the heart, for he loved her.

"No one who loved his sister could love the daughter of the man who had been so faithless to her."

"And besides," put in Nicholas, "you promised Renny you'd give the girl up."

"Oh, oh," cried Pheasant, sitting up in her chair. "Did you promise that, Piers?"

"No, I didn't."

Nicholas roared: "Yes, you did! Renny told me you did."

"I never promised. Be just, now, Renny! I never promised, did I?"

"No," said Renny. "He didn't promise. I told him to cut it out. I said there'd be trouble."

"Trouble–trouble–trouble," moaned Grandmother, "I've had too much trouble. If I didn't keep my appetite, I'd be dead. Give me more cake, someone. No, not that kind–devil's cake. I want devil's cake!" She took the cake that Ernest brought her, bit off a large piece, and snortled through it: "I hit the young whelp a good crack on the head!"

"Yes, Mamma," said Ernest. Then he inquired, patiently, "Must you take such large bites?"

"I drew the blood!" she cried, ignoring his question, and taking a still larger bite. "I made the lad smart for his folly."

"You ought to be ashamed, Gran," said Eden, and the family began to argue noisily as to whether she had done well or ill.

Renny stood looking from one excited face to another, feeling irritated by their noise, their ineffectuality, yet, in spite of all, bathed in an immense satisfaction. This was his family. His tribe. He was the head of his family. Chieftain of his tribe. He took a very primitive, direct, and simple pleasure in lording it over them, caring for them, being badgered, harried, and importuned by them. They were all of them dependent on him except Gran, and she was dependent,

too, for she would have died away from Jalna. And beside the fact
that he provided for them, he had the inherent quality of the chieftain. They expected him to lay down the law; they harried him till
he did. He turned his lean red face from one to the other of them
now, and prepared to lay down the law.

The heat of the room was stifling; the fire was scarcely needed;
yet now, with sudden fervor, it leaped and crackled on the hearth.
Boney, having recovered from Piers's rough handling, was crying in
a head-splitting voice, "Cake! Cake! Devil cake!"

"For God's sake, somebody give him cake," said Renny.

Little Wake snatched up a piece of cake and held it toward
Boney, but just as the parrot was at the point of taking it he jerked
it away. With flaming temper Boney tried three times, and failed to
snatch the morsel. He flapped his wings and uttered a screech that
set the blood pounding in the ears of those in the room.

It was too much for Finch. He doubled up on his footstool, laughing hysterically; the footstool slipped,–or did Eden's foot push it?–
and he was sent sprawling on the floor.

Grandmother seized her cane and struggled to get to her feet.

"Let me at them!" she screamed.

"Boys! Boys!" cried Meggie, melting into sudden laughter. This
was the sort of thing she loved–"rough-house" among the boys, and
she sitting solidly, comfortably in her chair, looking on. She laughed;
but in an instant she was lachrymose again, and averted her eyes from
the figure of Finch stretched on the floor.

Renny was bending over him. He administered three hard thumps
on the boy's bony, untidy person, and said:–

"Now, get up and behave yourself."

Finch got up, red in the face, and skulked to a corner. Nicholas
turned heavily in his chair, and regarded Piers.

"As for you," he said, "you ought to be flayed alive for what
you've done to Meggie."

"Never mind," Piers returned. "I'm getting out."

Meg looked at him scornfully. "You'd have to go a long way to
get away from scandal–I mean, to make your absence really a help
to me, to all of us."

Piers retorted: "Oh, we'll go far enough to please you. We'll go
to the States–perhaps." The "perhaps" was mumbled on a hesitating
note. The sound of his own voice announcing that he would go to a
foreign country, far from Jalna and the land he had helped to grow
things on, the horses, his brothers, had an appalling sound.

"What does he say?" asked Grandmother, roused from one of her
sudden dozes. Boney had perched on her shoulder and cuddled his
head against her long flat cheek. "What's the boy say?"

Ernest answered: "He says he'll go to the States."

"The States? A Whiteoak go to the States? A Whiteoak a Yankee? No, no, no! It would kill me. He mustn't go. Shame, shame on you, Meggie, to drive the poor boy to the States! You ought to be ashamed of yourself. Oh, those Yankees! First they take Eden's book and now they want Piers himself. Oh, don't let him go!" She burst into loud sobs.

Renny's voice was raised, but without excitement.

"Piers is not going away–anywhere. He's going to stay right here. So is Pheasant. The girl and he are married. I presume they've lived together. There's no reason on earth why she shouldn't make him a good wife–"

Meg interrupted:–

"Maurice has never forgiven me for refusing to marry him. He has made this match between his daughter and Piers to punish me. He's done it. I know he's done it."

Piers turned to her. "Maurice has known nothing about it."

"How can you know what schemes were in his head?" replied Meg. "He's simply been waiting his chance to thrust his brat into Jalna."

Piers exclaimed: "God God, Meggie! I didn't know you had such a wicked tongue."

"No back chat, please," rejoined his sister.

Renny's voice, with a vibration from the chest which the family knew foreboded an outburst if he were opposed, broke in.

"I have been talking the affair over with Maurice this afternoon. He is as upset about it as we are. As for his planning the marriage to avenge himself on you, Meg, that is ridiculous. Give the man credit for a little decency–a little sense. Why, your affair with him was twenty years ago. Do you think he's been brooding over it ever since? And he was through the War too. He's had a few things to think of besides your cruelty, Meggie!"

He smiled at her. He knew how to take her. And she liked to have her "cruelty" referred to. Her beautifully shaped lips curved a little, and she said, with almost girlish petulance:–

"What's the matter with him, then? Everyone agrees that there's something wrong with him."

"Oh, well, I don't think there is very much wrong with Maurice, but if there is, and you are responsible, you shouldn't be too hard on him, or on his child, either. I told Piers that if he went on meeting her there'd be trouble, and there has been, hasn't there? Lots of it. But I'm not going to drive him away from Jalna. I want him here– and I want my tea, terribly. Will you pour it out, Meggie?"

Silence followed his words, broken only by the snapping of the fire and Grandmother's peaceful, bubbling snores. Nicholas took out his pipe and began to fill it from his pouch. Sasha leaped from the mantelpiece to Ernest's shoulder and began to purr loudly, as though in opposition to Grandmother's snores. Wakefield opened the door of a cabinet filled with curios from India, with which he was not allowed to play, and stuck his head inside.

"Darling, don't," said Meg, gently.

Renny, the chieftain, had spoken. He had said that Piers was not to be cast out from the tribe, and the tribe had listened and accepted his words as wisdom. All the more readily because not one of them wanted to see Piers cast out, even though they must accept with him an unwelcome addition to the family. Not even Meg. In truth, Renny was more often the organ of the family than its head. They knew beforehand what he would say in a crisis, and they excited, harried, and goaded him till he said it with great passion. Then, with apparent good grace, they succumbed to his will.

Renny dropped into a chair with his cup of tea and a piece of bread and butter. His face was redder than usual, but he looked with deep satisfaction at the group about him. He had quelled the family riot. They depended on him, from savage old Gran down to delicate little Wake. They depended on him to lead them. He felt each one of them bound to him by a strong, invisible cord. He could feel the pull of the cords, drawn taut from himself to each individual in the room. To savage old Gran. To beastly young Finch. To that young fool Piers with his handerchief against his bleeding ear. To Meggie, who pictured Maurice as brooding in black melancholy all these years. Well, there was no doubt about it, Maurice was a queer devil. He had let two women make a very different man of him from what Nature had intended him to be. Renny felt the cords from himself stretching dark and strong to each member of the family. Suddenly he felt a new drawing, a fresh cord. It was between Pheasant and him. She was one of them now. His own. He looked at her, sitting upright in the big chair, her eyes swollen from crying, but eating her tea like a child. Their eyes met, and she gave a little watery pleading smile. Renny grinned at her encouragingly.

Rags had come in and Meg was ordering a fresh pot of tea.

This was the Whiteoak family as it was when Alayne Archer came into their midst from New York.

FURTHER READING

NOVELS BY MAZO DE LA ROCHE
The sixteen novels in the *Jalna* or *Whiteoak* series are available in Pan paperbacks (published by Collins Publishers, Don Mills, On-

tario). The Macmillan Company of Canada, Toronto, has many of them in hardcover; there is also a Bantam paperback of *Jalna* only. In chronological order (according to events in the series) the *Whiteoak* novels are: *The Building of Jalna, Morning at Jalna, Mary Wakefield, Young Renny, Whiteoak Heritage, The Whiteoak Brothers, Jalna, Whiteoaks, Finch's Fortune, The Master of Jalna, Whiteoak Harvest, Wakefield's Course, Return to Jalna, Renny's Daughter, Variable Winds at Jalna, Centenary at Jalna.*

Delight (Toronto: McClelland and Stewart, New Canadian Library, 1961).

BIOGRAPHY

Ringing the Changes, autobiography (Toronto: The Macmillan Company of Canada, 1957).

Ronald Hambleton, *Mazo de la Roche of Jalna* (New York: Hawthorn Books Inc., 1966).

Ronald Hambleton, *The Secret of Jalna* (Toronto: General Publishing Co., Musson Book Company).

LITERARY SITES

"Mazo de la Roche was born just plain Mazo Roche on January 15, 1879, in the big house on the south-west corner of Water St. and Prospect St. (Newmarket, Ontario) where her parents were living with her mother's family, the Daniel Lundys. The house is still there, looking out over Fairy Lake. Today it is Martin Manor Nursing Home."

Newmarket *Era*, September 8, 1971.

Mazo de la Roche's grave is in the churchyard of Sibbald's Church (St. George's Church) near Sutton, Ontario. There is a Mazo de la Roche Memorial Window in the church.

"First stop on the day-long tour was Benares, the 120 year-old home of Mr. and Mrs. Geoffrey Sayers (Mississauga, Ontario). It will be long remembered as the setting for the *Jalna* novels by Mazo de la Roche. . . . The house will eventually become a museum under the direction of the Ontario Heritage Foundation."

Toronto Daily Star, September 23, 1971.

PICTURE SERIES

Canadian Authors (includes Mazo de la Roche), obtainable from: Hilton Photo Supplies, P.O. Box 74, Chemainus, British Columbia.

AUDIO-VISUAL

Jalna, a CBC-TV series.

Stephen Leacock

English-born Stephen Leacock (1869-1944) grew up on a farm in the Lake Simcoe area of Ontario and went to Upper Canada College and the University of Toronto. For some years he was a schoolmaster at Upper Canada College, then in 1898 went to the University of Chicago for his doctorate. Returning to Canada he taught political science and economics at McGill University until retirement. He was head of the department from 1908, and was elected to the Royal Society of Canada, 1910. He wrote a number of books on political science and history, but is far better known as a humourist. Literary Lapses *(1910), containing such favourites as "My Financial Career" and "A Manual of Education," has run into some twenty editions. He wrote more than thirty volumes of humour, most of them good fun and kindly satire, but one at least sharply satirical,* Acadian Adventures of the Idle Rich *(1914).*

BASS FISHING ON LAKE SIMCOE

Among the pleasant memories of my life is the recollection of my fishing days on Ontario's Lake Simcoe with Jake Gaudaur–little excursions that extended over twenty or twenty-five years. If you don't know the name of Jake Gaudaur it only means that you were born fifty years too late. Half a century ago Jake was for several years the champion oarsman of the world–a title won on the Thames at Henley. In those days, before motor cars and aeroplanes, rowing was one of the big interests of the nations, and Jake Gaudaur was a hero to millions who had never seen him. The fact that his name was pronounced exactly as Good-Oar helped to keep it easily in mind.

From: Stephen Leacock, *Too Much College* (New York: Dodd, Mead and Company, 1945). Reprinted by permission of the publisher. Copyright 1939, by Dodd, Mead & Company, Inc. Copyright renewed 1967 by Stephen L. Leacock.

Jake was of mixed French and Indian descent but belonged in the Lake Simcoe country and English had always been his language–the kind we use up there, not the kind they use at Oxford. I can talk both, but the Lake Simcoe is easier and, for fishing, far better. It cuts out social distinction. Jake was a magnificent figure of a man: he stood nicely six feet in his stocking feet–the only way we ever measure people up there. He was broad in the shoulders, straight as a lath–and till the time when he died just short of eighty he could pick up the twenty-pound anchor of his motor-boat and throw it round like a tack-hammer. Jake–standing erect in the bow of his motorboat and looking out to the horizon, his eyes shaded with his hand–might have stood for the figure of Oshkosh, war chief of the Wisconsin Indians.

When Jake's championship days were over he came back to Canada and "kept hotel" in Sudbury. That was the thing for champions to do: in the unregenerate days of the old bar, thousands of people spent five cents on a drink just to say they had talked with Jake Gaudaur. I wish that retired professors could open up a bar. It must be a great thing to be an ex-champion or a quintuplet, and never have to work.

So Jake made his modest pile and then came back to our part of the country, the Lake Simcoe district, and set up at "the Narrows," at the top end of the lake, as a professional fisherman, taking out parties on the lake for bass fishing.

Now, who hasn't seen Lake Simcoe has never seen a lake at all. Lake Simcoe on a July morning–the water, ruffled in wavelets of a blue and green and silver, as clear as never was: the sky of the purest blue with great clouds white and woolly floating in it! Just the day for fishing–every day is, for the enthusiastic.

The lake is just right in size to be what a lake ought to be–twenty to thirty miles across in any direction–so that there's always a part of the horizon open where you can't see the land–the shore is all irregular with bays and "points" and islands and shoals, so that any roads thereabouts are away back from the water, and the shore line of trees and sand and stone looks much as Champlain saw it three hundred years ago. Over it in the summer air of July there hovers an atmosphere of unbroken peace. When I think of it I cannot but contrast it with the curse that lies over Europe where mountain lakes are scarped and galleried for guns, and every church steeple on their shores a range and target. I wish I could take Hitler and Mussolini out bass fishing on Lake Simcoe. They'd come back better men–or they'd never come back.

So here we are at ten o'clock in the morning helping Jake load the stuff out of our car into his motor-boat! Notice that–ten o'clock. None of that fool stuff about starting off at daylight. You get over that by the time you're forty. The right time to start off bass fishing is when you're good and ready to. And when I say ten o'clock, I really mean about ten-thirty. We just call it ten o'clock and when you look at your watch after you're actually started, it's always ten-thirty, or not much past it. Anyway there's no finer time in the day on the water than ten-thirty, still all the freshness of the morning and all the day in front of you–half-way between windy and calm with little ruffled waves in the sunlight, and a cool breeze, partly made by the boat itself.

As for the bass, they bite as well at any one time as at any other. The idea that they bite at daylight and don't bite after lunch is just a myth. They bite when they're ready to–the only reason they don't bite after lunch is that the fishermen are asleep till three.

Jake's boat is no "power" boat, to hit up twenty-five miles an hour. That fool stuff came to our lakes later and is out of keeping with bass fishing. Jake's in a big, roomy open boat with a front part for Jake and a big open part at the back where we sit: a broad stern seat with leather cushions and wicker armchairs on a linoleum floor. Solid comfort. No rough stuff for us: we're not sailors. And no cover to keep off the sun–who cares a darn about the sun when you're fishing?–and nothing to keep off the wind–let it come: and no protection against the rain. It won't rain. Any man who thinks it's going to rain shouldn't go fishing.

"Will it rain, Jake?"

"I don't think so, professor: not with that sky."

We've gone through that little opening dialogue, I suppose, a hundred times. That's the beauty of bass fishing: always doing the same things in the same way, with the same old jokes and the same conversation.

"I was thinking we might go out and try the big rock at McCrae's point first, professor," says Jake.

Seeing that we've never done anything else in twenty years it seems a likely thing to do.

This gives us two miles to go, down from the Narrows to the open lake and then sideways across to the first point. For me this is always the best part of the day–the cool fresh air, the anticipation better than reality, the settling into our wicker chairs and lighting up our pipes, with the stuff all properly stowed around us, the fishing gear, the lunch and the box with the soda on ice. Not that we take a drink at this time of the day. Oh, no! We're all agreed that you don't need a drink on a beautiful fine morning at ten-thirty–unless perhaps for the special reason to-day because it's such a damn fine day that you feel so good or the other–because you don't feel so good. So perhaps this morning, "Eh, what?" "Well, just a starter." "Jake, can I pass you along a horn?" "Thanks, professor, I don't mind."

There are four of us, mostly, apart from Jake, so it takes most of the time of the run to mix up and serve the drinks. I am thinking here especially of one party though really it was just like all the others. There was my brother George and George Rapley, the bank manager (a tear to his kind memory), and Charlie Janes, the railroad man of a Lake Simcoe town. George Rapley always came because he could fish, and Charlie Janes because he couldn't. You may have noticed that bank managers are always good fishermen; it's something in their profession, I think, a kind of courtesy, that gets the fish. And I am sure that everybody who goes bass fishing will agree that to make the party right you need one fellow who can't fish. In fact in any bass fishing party of friends who go out often together there is always one who is cast for the part of not knowing how to fish. No matter how often he's been out, he's not supposed to know anything about fishing and he good-naturedly accepts the role. If he loses a fish that's supposed to be because he didn't know how to land it, if we lose a fish that is supposed to be because it was impossible to land it. It's these little mutual understandings that fit life together.

So, almost before the "horn" is finished here we are bearing down on the big rock off McCrae's point. It's nearly a quarter of a mile from shore and six feet under water, but Jake steers to it like a taxi to a hotel door. The anchor goes down with a splash, our swing on it timed to throw us right over the rock! There it is! See it–big as a wagon!–and in another minute down go the baited lines trailing to go under the edge of the great rock.

This is the great moment of fishing, the first minute with the lines down–tense, exhilarating. It's always the same way–either something big happens, or nothing. Perhaps–bing! the lines are no sooner down than a bass is hooked–by Charlie Janes, of course–just like the luck of the darned fool. And while he's still hauling on it–biff! there's another one–and Jake, it seems, has quietly landed a third one when the other two were plunging round. With which there's such a period of excitement and expectation that it's nearly three-quarters of an hour before you realize that those three fish are all there are–or rather two fish: George Rapley lost his–too bad! he was playing it so beautifully. Charlie Janes, the darned old fool, flung his over the side of the boat, right slap into the ice-box.

Or else–the other alternative–the lines go down and nothing happens.

In either case we fish on and on under the rock till excitement fades into dullness, and dullness into dead certainty. That's all. At last someone says, "I guess they ain't biting here any more." Notice "They're not biting"–we never say, "They're not here." Any man who says, as I have heard some of our old guests say, "Oh, hell, there are no fish here," is not fit to be brought again. The only theory on which bass fishing can be maintained as a rational pastime is that the bass are everywhere–all the time. But they won't bite. The wind may be wrong, or the air just too damp, or too dry, or too much sun, or not enough–it's amazing how little will start a bass not biting. But the cause must always be one that can change in five minutes, or with a move of five yards. These beliefs are to a fisherman what faith is to a Christian.

"We might try out past Strawberry Island," says Jake. This means a change farther out, right out in the open water of the lake with the whole horizon of wind and wave and sun open for twenty miles all around to the south. This is not exactly a shoal. The bottom of the lake drops here from twelve feet to thirty feet of water–like the side of a hill. Jake explains it all fresh every time, and he makes each new spot seem so different and so likely that we go at each with new hope eternal. If we don't get any fish as each half-hour stop goes by, Jake tells the story of how he and I fished once and never had a bite till after sundown and then caught thirty-three bass in half an hour off McGinnis's reef. "You mind that evening, professor?" he says (to "mind" a thing is to remember it). "It was thirty-three, wasn't it?" "Thirty-four, I think, Jake," I answer, and he says, "Well, mebbe it was." We've brought those fish up a little every year.

Or else Jake tells the story of the young girl from Toledo who came up with her father and had never been fishing before and never even in a motor-boat and it was a caution how many she caught. This story, of course, conveys the idea that if inexperienced fishers, like the young lady from Toledo, can catch fish, experienced people like ourselves could hardly expect to.

Then all of a sudden, as it always seems, comes the idea of lunch– all of a sudden everybody hungry and ready for it. And does ever food taste better than out in the wind and sun in a motor-boat– salmon sandwiches, cold chicken in a salad, chunks of home-made bread, mustard pickles; all eaten partly off a plate and partly with your fingers and with bottled ale to wash it down.

People who go fishing but are not real fishermen land on shore for lunch, light a fire and, I believe, even cook the fish caught: some of them go so far as to have a game of poker or, in extreme cases of mental derangement, go for a swim. All of this to a proper fisherman is just deplorable, just lunacy. The true fisherman eats right in the boat with the lines still hanging in the water. There seems to be a sort of truce during lunch time: I never knew a bass to touch a hook till it's over. But lunch on the other hand isn't hurried. It's just eaten in the natural way. You put into your mouth all it will hold; then eat it; then start again. Eating in the open air knows no satiety, no indigestion.

The whole point is that the longest day is all too short for fishing, and no one who really loves bass fishing can bear the thought of knocking off from it even for an hour. As a matter of fact, we do take time off but we never admit it. For there always came in our fishing with Jake a drowsy part of the day when we took a sleep. Not that we ever called it that deliberately. The sleep was just a sort of accident. A little while after we'd eaten all the lunch we could hold Jake would say, "I thought we might go and try for a spell down round the corner of that shoal, just off that way a piece. You mind we was there before?" "Yes, sure, I remember it, Jake."

The place is a sort of convenient little nook among the shoals—nothing showing on top of the water; we always reckoned as if the bottom were in sight—it had the advantage that the waves couldn't reach it because of the shallows, and it was always quiet, and no fish ever came there. Jake could anchor the boat where there were just enough waves to rock the boat gently and just enough light breeze to murmur a lullaby, and with the two o'clock sun to make you pull your straw panama away over your eyes, a man seated like that in a wicker chair, with two pounds of sandwiches and six ounces of whisky in him, is as drowsy as a flower nodding on its stem, and asleep in five minutes. The lines dangle in the water; there is no conversation, no sound but the breeze and the lapping of the little waves. Up in front we could see only Jake's broad back; but there was slumber in every line of it.

It didn't matter who woke first. After about an hour anybody could straighten up and say, "By jove, I believe I was almost asleep, were you?" And the others would answer "Darn near!" and then Jake would say, as if he'd never stopped talking, "I was thinking we might go out and try the dry shoal."

This rouses us to a new search for bass, hither and thither half a mile, a mile at a time. Even then we are only covering one corner of Lake Simcoe. The lake is just big enough to seem illimitable.

Bass fishing on Lake Simcoe is not like the bass fishing you can get a hundred miles north of it, on the rivers in the bush, out of easy reach. Up there it's no come-and-go business in a day; you must stay at least two nights. You catch one hundred bass in the first day and the next day you don't even keep them, you throw them back. The third day you hate the stinking things; a bass two days dead, with its skin discoloured, would sicken even a cannibal.

Not so Lake Simcoe. There are just not enough bass, just never too many—some dead, dull days without any—they're there, but they won't bite. But even on the deadest, dullest day, always the hope of a strike.

You might wonder, if you don't know the life, why the afternoon never gets dreary, what there can be to talk about—especially among men often and always out together on the same ground. That's just ignorance. In bass fishing there are vast unsettled problems to be discussed for ever. For example, do you need to "play" a bass? or is that just a piece of damn nonsense imitated out of salmon fishing? The school to which I belong holds that "playing" a bass is just a way of losing it. What you need is a steel rod with the last section taken out and an "emergency tip" put in—making a short, firm rod about six feet long. When the bass nibbles, wait—then wait some more—then strike—with such power as to drive the hook right through his head—then shorten the line—not with a reel; that's too slow—haul it in beside the reel with your left hand and hold it firm with your right—shove the rod close to the water, if need be under the water—by that means the bass can't jump out of the water, there isn't line enough—drag him against his will till someone else holds the net—and in he comes.

Contrast this with the artistic "playing" of fish that looks so skilful —paying out line—the fish leaping the air thirty feet from the boat—and all that show stuff—only good for a picture-book!

Now can't you see that the discussion of that point alone can fill an afternoon?

Personally I am always an extremist for a short rod and rapid action—the bass right in the boat in twenty seconds. I think that in his heart Jake Gaudaur agreed with this. It's the way all Indians fish and always have. But Jake's calling demanded compromise. He favoured both sides. Rapley, like all bankers, played a fish as they play a customer with a loan, taking it in gradually.

We always knew that the afternoon was closing to evening when Jake said, "Suppose we go out and try that big rock inside McGinnis's reef: you mind, professor, the place where you caught all them bass that night—thirty-four, wasn't it?" "Yes, or thirty-five, Jake. I'm not sure: let's try it."

This sunken rock is the triumph of Jake's navigation of the lake. It's a mile from even the nearest point of land, and sunk six feet down. Beside it the big rock at McCrae's is child's play. That one you can find if you keep on looking for it. This one, never. It's all very well to say that you can do it with "bearings": any amateur yachtsman that ever wore panama pants will tell you that. But try it. Try to get bearings that are good at all hours and all lights and shadows on the shores, good in rain and good in mist, and you soon see where you are—or are not.

Jake, erect at the bow as he steers, is as straight as Oshkosh, the boat gathers speed in a curve that picks up one of the bearings and then straight as a pencil line over the water for a mile—then a stop with a reversed engine without a turn or the bearings would be lost, and there we are—right over the rock. In a clear light it's as plain as day, but on a dull day you can just make it out, a great rock sunk in a wide basin of water for the bass to get in.

Here we try our final luck. We can't leave. If the bass are there (I mean if they are biting), it's too good to leave. If we don't get a bite, we just can't leave.

We haven't realized it but the afternoon has all gone. The sun is setting behind the hills on the west side of the lake. Just before it goes its beams light up for a moment the windows of unseen farmhouses ten miles the other side of us—and then, before we know it, the sun is gone. But we can't leave. It's still broad daylight, nearly. "There's two or three hours' good fishing yet, Jake, eh?" "All of that, professor." Somehow it seems as if the day were suddenly all gone. "Have another horn, Jake?" Surely that'll hold the daylight a little, giving Jake a horn. Anyway we can't leave. The light is fading a little. A cold wind begins to move across the lake, the water seems to blacken under its touch as the boat swings to it. "The wind's kind o' gone round," says Jake. "I thought it would." It's not surprising: the wind has gone round, and the air turned chill after sundown, every evening of the sixty years I've known Lake Simcoe. But we can't leave. Charlie Janes has had a bite—or says he has—we never take Charlie's word, of course, as really good: he may have caught in a crack of rock. But Rapley thinks he had a nibble. That's better evidence. So we stay on, and, till the dark has fallen, the shores all grown dim and then vanished and the north-west wind beginning to thump the waves on the bow of the anchored boat.

"I guess, gentlemen, it's about time to pull up," says Jake. If we had caught fifteen or twenty bass he'd have said, "Boys, I guess it's about time to quit." But "gentlemen" brings us back to the cold cruel reality.

So the anchor is up and the motor-boat at its full power set for home. It's quite rough on the water now: the boat slaps into the waves and sends the spray flying clear astern to where we have our chairs huddled together, back to the wind. It's dark, too, you have to use a flashlight to open the soda for the "consolation drinks" that mark the end of the fishing. "Have a horn, Jake?" "Thanks, professor." Jake, with his oil clothes on, can't leave the wheel now: he sits there all in the spray with one hand for steering and one for the drink.

It's amazing how a lake like Lake Simcoe can change–a few hours ago a halcyon paradise, still and calm–and now with the night the wind gathering over it–"Oh, well, Jake knows the way," and anyway it's only three miles till we'll be in shelter of the Narrows!–Whew! that was a corker, that wave! "Here, put these newspapers behind your back, Charlie, they'll keep off the spray."

Just enough of this to give one a slight feeling of night and mimic danger–and then in no great time, for the distance is short, we round into the shelter of the Narrows with just a mile of water, smoother and smoother, to run. All different it looks from the morning; what you see now is just lights–a perplexing galaxy of lights, white and green and red here and there on the unseen shore–and great flares of moving white light that must be the motors on the highway.

"What's the red light away up, Jake?"

"That's the one above the railway bridge." We always ask Jake this and when he answers we know we are close in. The water suddenly is quite smooth, a current running with us–the summer cottages and docks come in sight, with "young fellers" and girls in canoes and the sound of a radio somewhere discussing war in Europe.

We're back in the world again, landed at Jake's dock with a little crowd of loafers and boys standing round to see "how many fish Jake got,"–not us, *Jake*. We unload the boat and take a look at the string of fish. "Let's see that big one that Rapley caught, eh?" But where is it? Surely it can't be this small dirty-looking flabby thing–I'm afraid it is.

We divide the fish. Jake won't take any. We try to work them off on one another. Fishermen want *fishing*, never fish–and end by slinging them into the car all in one box. "Well, we certainly had a fine day, good night, Jake." And another fishing day has gone–now never to return.

I can only repeat, in tribute to a fine memory, "Good night, Jake."

FURTHER READING

WORKS BY STEPHEN LEACOCK AVAILABLE IN THE NEW CANADIAN LIBRARY SERIES, MCCLELLAND AND STEWART, TORONTO

Literary Lapses, Arcadian Adventures with the Idle Rich, Sunshine Sketches of a Little Town, My Discovery of England, Nonsense Novels, Moonbeams from a Larger Lunacy, Behind the Beyond, Frenzied Fiction, Further Foolishness, My Remarkable Uncle, Short Circuits, Last Leaves, Winnowed Wisdom.

BIOGRAPHY AND CRITICISM

Feast of Stephen, an anthology of some of the less familiar writings of Stephen Leacock, with a critical introduction by Robertson Davies (Toronto: McClelland and Stewart, 1970).

Robertson Davies, *Stephen Leacock* (Toronto: McClelland and Stewart, Canadian Writers Series, 1970).

Elizabeth Kimball, *The Man in the Panama Hat: Reminiscences of my Uncle, Stephen Leacock* (Toronto: McClelland and Stewart, 1970).

D. M. Legate, *Stephen Leacock* (Toronto: Doubleday Publishers, 1970).

A. J. M. Smith, ed., *Masks of Fiction* (Toronto: McClelland and Stewart, New Canadian Library, 1961).

Leacock, Canadian Jackdaws Series (collections of exhibits) (Toronto: Clarke Irwin Publishers).

LITERARY SITES

Leacock's summer home at Old Brewery Bay on Lake Couchiching is now the Stephen Leacock Memorial Home, Orillia, Ontario.

The churchyard of St. George's Church, Jackson's Point, Ontario, where Stephen Leacock is buried, is an historic site.

PICTURE SERIES

Canadian Authors, (includes Stephen Leacock), obtainable from: Hilton Photo Supplies, P.O. Box 74, Chemainus, British Columbia.

Emily Carr

Emily Carr (1871-1945) was born in Victoria, B.C. and as a young girl studied art in San Francisco. Later she studied in England and France. But aside from these brief sojourns she spent the whole of her life in western Canada, learning it, and particularly learning about the Indians, whom she respected and loved: travelling on fish boats to Indian villages along the B.C. coast, living with the people while she sketched and painted. Now-famous paintings such as "Indian Church," "D'Sonoqua" and "Indian Village, Alert Bay" were the product of these years. But her art met with no response; met rather with hostility. She was reduced to financial straits and had to give up her painting to run a boarding house. It was not until 1927 that her art began to win recognition. When her health failed around 1940 she turned to writing. Klee Wyck (1941), winner of the Governor-General's Award, is a collection of pieces about Indian places and people, written at various times during her painting trips.

THE STARE

Millie's stare was the biggest thing in the hut. It dimmed for a moment as we stood in its way—but in us it had no interest. The moment we moved from its path it tightened again—this tense, living stare glowing in the sunken eyes of a sick Indian child.

All the life that remained in the emaciated, shrivelled little creature was concentrated in that stare. It burned a path for itself right across the sea to the horizon, burning with longing focused upon the return of her father's whaling-boat.

The missionary bent over the child.

"Millie!"

Millie's eyes lifted grudgingly, then hastened back to their watching.

Turning to the old crone who took the place of a mother who was dead and cared for the little girl, the missionary asked, "How is she, Granny?"

"I t'ink 'spose boat no come quick, Milly die plitty soon now."

"Is there no word of the boats?"

"No, maybe all Injun-man dead. Whale fishin' heap, heap bad for make die."

They brought the child food. She struggled to force down enough to keep the life in her till her father came. Squatted on her mat on the earth floor, her chin resting on the sharp knees and circled by her sticks of arms, she sat from dawn till dark, watching. When light was gone the stare fought its way, helped by Millie's ears, listening, listening out into black night.

It was in the early morning that the whaling-boats came home. When the mist lifted, Millie saw eight specks out on the horizon. Taut, motionless, uttering no word, she watched them grow.

"The boats are coming!" The cry rang through the village. Women left their bannock-baking, their basket-weaving and hurried to the shore. The old crone who tended Millie hobbled to the beach with the rest.

"The boats are coming!" Old men warming their stiff bodies in the sun shaded dull eyes with their hands to look far out to sea, groaning for joy that their sons were safe.

"The boats are coming!" Quick ears of children heard the cry in the school-house and, squeezing from their desks without leave, pattered down to the shore. The missionary followed. It was the event of the year, this return of the whaling-boats.

Millie's father was the first to land. His eyes searched among the people.

"My child?"

His feet followed the women's pointing fingers. Racing up the bank, his bulk filled the doorway of the hut. The stare enveloped him, Millie swayed towards him. Her arms fell down. The heavy plaits of her hair swung forward. Brittle with long watching, the stare had snapped.

FURTHER READING

BOOKS BY EMILY CARR

Klee Wyck (Toronto: Clarke Irwin Paperback, 1965). First published 1941.

The Book of Small (Toronto: Clarke Irwin Paperback, 1966). First published 1942.

The House of All Sorts (Toronto: Oxford University Press). First published 1946.

Hundreds and Thousands: The Journals of Emily Carr (Toronto: Clarke Irwin, 1966).

BIOGRAPHY

Edythe Hembroff-Schleicher, *M.E., A Portrayal of Emily Carr* (Toronto: Clarke Irwin, 1969).

EMILY CARR: PAINTER

Emily Carr, her Paintings and Sketches, published for the National Gallery of Canada, and the Art Gallery of Ontario (Toronto: Oxford University Press, 1945).

PICTURE SERIES

Canadian Authors (includes Emily Carr), obtainable from: Hilton Photo Supplies, P.O. Box 74, Chemainus, British Columbia.

LITERARY SITE

The house in which Emily Carr lived for many years has been established as an Emily Carr Memorial in Victoria, British Columbia.

Frederick Philip Grove

Frederick Philip Grove (1879-1948) was born Felix Paul Greve at Radomno on the Polish-Russian border, his parents having stopped there in the course of a journey. He grew up in Hamburg, Germany, where his father was employed in the collections department of the city transport company. He studied classical philology at Bonn, then studied in Rome and Munich. He was married in 1902 and earned his living by translating and free-lance writing. In 1909 or 1910 he came to Canada.

*These facts, lately discovered by the literary detective work of Douglas Spettigue (*Queen's Quarterly, *Spring 1972, pp. 1, 2), supersede those given in earlier biographies and based on accounts related by Grove himself in his autobiographical novel* A Search for America *(1927) and in his autobiography* In Search of Myself. *Grove's own story is that he was born into a wealthy family of Swedish landowners, that his childhood home was "Castle Thurow" near Lund in Sweden, and that he spent his youth travelling about Europe with his mother. He concluded his account by stating that he was left penniless when his father died bankrupt, and that he spent some twenty years wandering in North America before settling in Manitoba.*

At this point the stories converge. He took a post as a school teacher in rural Manitoba, the scene of many of his short stories and novels. He married Catherine Wiens, herself a teacher, in 1915. After many years of struggle with ill health and poverty, he succeeded in publishing his writing. He won the Lorne Pierce Medal in 1934; was elected to the Royal Society in 1941. In Search of Myself *(1946) won the Governor-General's Award. Based on the fictions about his early years which he had sustained throughout his life, it remains a profoundly moving record of a spiritual odyssey.*

THE DESERT

Alice left the west-bound train at Medicine Hat and, placing her suitcase of black-enamelled duck on the platform, looked about her.

The sunken valley in which the city stands seemed somehow to indicate the natural level of things. Was it not the level at which she had been travelling in coming from the east? Up there, at the height of the hill-tops, she knew, stretched a plain probably no more than a few hundred feet higher than the floor of the valley; yet it seemed vastly nearer the sun and open to the winds of the mountains which reached into the clouds.

She smiled wistfully to herself and revisualized a thousand things at once: things which had happened only a few days ago and things which had happened in the faraway past. Many threads–the threads that made the woof of her life–were gathering into the tangled knot of the present. Half an hour ago she had played with the idea of going on, of not alighting from the train before it reached Banff. At Banff he was waiting for her; he would meet this very train. He knew of all her perplexities. She liked him; she loved him. If she did not go on to join him, her failure to do so would be tantamount to telling him that she loved something else more than him. Only a few minutes before she had reached Medicine Hat, she had suddenly understood what it meant that he was waiting for her at Banff. It meant exactly the same thing; he, too, loved something else more than he loved her; that something was his career. In an impulse of rebellion she had alighted.

Standing on the long platform of the open station, she frowned as she thought of that. She knew that at this very moment her trunk was being unloaded from the baggage van. Remaining, going on–that was the question of the moment. These few minutes while the train waited were a tragic crisis in her life. She was subject to conflicting impulses. If she took a few quick steps and secured a ticket, six or eight hours travelling would reunite her with him; if she stood still, she would have to let things take their course.

All about her now people were boarding the train; others were rushing into the refreshment rooms and returning with sandwiches, cones of ice cream, lunches done up in cardboard boxes. By a sort of second sight she seemed to see herself standing there, undecided, the battlefield of conflicting impulses. She wondered which one would carry the day.

The minutes sped. There was a sudden change in the tempo of the movements about her. The conductor had come forth from the station building, watch in hand. At the front of the train, the baggage truck was being pulled away from the van. On that van her trunk reposed. Perhaps there was still time.

From: Frederick Philip Grove, *Tales from the Margin* (Toronto: Ryerson Press, 1971). Reprinted by permission of McGraw-Hill Ryerson.

But no. "All aboard!" The chaotic movements about her crystallized into a sort of order. Knots of people divided themselves into those who mounted the steps of the cars, turning back when they had reached their platforms, and those who were to remain behind and whose faces now were raised.

A little nervously, Alice shrugged her shoulders. In the corners of her clear, grey eyes stood tears. She picked her suitcase up, turned to the station building, went to the wicket, and drew a pad of telegraph blanks to herself, holding her pencil poised. What was she to tell him? To come? What would he say? What think? That, after all, she wanted to eat her cake and have it, too? Or that she wanted to make herself precious by withholding herself?

This thing lay deeper than that; and it could not be expressed in a few words. Besides, she had told him before. It was useless to hint at it again. He must either divine it or he must misinterpret her.

Yet, unless she helped him, she could not help herself. She might be sowing regret for the rest of her life. Him she understood only too well because she understood herself. Well, then, he must understand her in the same way. If he did not, perhaps she was merely misunderstanding him?

A slight jerk of her well-shaped head, a motion backward–these seemed somehow to help her in making up her mind. She put the pencil down. At the same moment she became aware of the fact that behind the glass of the wicket a young man had been waiting and watching her, ready to receive her completed message. She smiled apologetically, nodded, and said, "I've changed my mind, thank you!" And, after having checked her suitcase at the parcel room, she issued quickly from the building into the street.

Within an hour she had had a lunch, made a number of purchases, and had engaged a car at one of the numerous garages of the little city. In this car, driven by a grimy young mechanic, she made the rounds from the station to the various stores to pick up her baggage and her parcels, some of which were bulky and heavy. When she had checked the last item on her list, she said to the driver before she re-entered the car, "That's all. We can go now." It was two o'clock in the afternoon.

A few minutes later the car began, from the northwest corner of the city, a steady climb along the steep slope of the river-valley. Then came a turn and a twist in the road, through a ravine, and they were on the plateau of eastern Alberta. Ahead of them loomed the smoke-stacks of the brick-kilns of Redcliff. The car soon left them behind; and when they had crossed the track to the north there remained no trace of industrial activities. They were in what the eastern Albertans call "the desert."

The road led alternately north and west for from ten to twenty miles on each leg of the journey. And at the same time it swung up and down, incessantly, over bare, treeless hills which, near their tops, were stony and rough. Everywhere the soil was covered with the sparse grass of the dry country which did not entirely hide the grey-yellow clay.

Again Alice re-experienced the prevailing impression of her childhood, that she was here on the roof of the world, nearer to sun and stars than anywhere else in this country except perhaps on a mountain-top. Even the air seemed strangely rarefied; and the sun burned down with unimpeded heat. Was this beauty? She could not tell. But she felt at home in it. This country had borne her. The woods and valleys, the closely settled districts, the towns and cities were alien to her. In them she had always felt as if in exile. Here was her home. Life might be poor and monotonous; it might pass close to the no-man's land of death and extinction; but it was life in a familiar atmosphere, her atmosphere!

Here and there she saw the remains of abandoned irrigation ditches —how prematurely old they looked, prehistoric, like the ruins of Cyclopean earthworks. She almost rejoiced in these ruins. Had man prevailed when he tried to change this country of soil and sky into human settlements, he would have spoiled it for her. It would be what the irrigation district beyond Brooks was now: the home of a race different from her own. Yes, for more than ten years she had lived in exile; she had come home.

They went on for two hours after they had left the first straight northwest stretch of the road, driving fast. Twice they passed through little towns, Suffield and Alderson; then they were suddenly in a more familiar neighbourhood.

It was after four o'clock when Alice bent forward to give the driver some directions. He slowed down. They left the main road and made several turns; and then they were on a trail along which, at almost regular intervals, stood abandoned homesteads. Alice felt as if her heart were rising into her throat. She knew that these people had all left. Especially when, on the crest of a hill, she looked through the upper windows of a house right into the sky beyond–the house was unroofed–she felt that she was undertaking what was, after all, beyond her human power. Little panicky waves ran through her.

Then they topped a sharp ridge with steep flanks; and suddenly the next hill, a dome-shaped expanse, higher than all the others, showed her the familiar buildings among which she had spent her childhood. Nearest the road stood the house, painted a pale, washed-out green, with dark patches scattered irregularly over its straight wall. These were the boards that had been nailed in front of the windows after the death of her parents.

The long struggle between the easy life in the great city and her homesickness was at last decided; she was coming to live here, definitely, for the rest of her life! Intensely that thought held her; and poignantly another thought pierced it. She was thirty-two; and she had just now thrown away the prospect of another sort of happiness, a warm, human companionship the offer of which had come to her late in life and had been received by her with a sober sort of joy, making her forget for a moment what had always been in her veins, the longing for the landscape in which she had grown up.

They shot up the hill, which, though higher, was of gentler approach than most over which they had come. Again it seemed to her as if, in that climb, they were being lifted above the abodes of other men. To their left, the line-fence had sprung up, in good condition. In this dry country posts did not rot; nor was wire purloined by those in need of it from any place not known to be definitely and finally abandoned; for of such there were plenty.

"This is the place," Alice said.

"Eh?" the driver asked in astonishment.

"Just stop at the gate. I'll open it."

The direction was obeyed; and, Alice having alighted, the car swung into the yard, to come to a stop in front of the nailed-up door. The driver sat and stared blankly.

Alice, in sudden nervous haste, took her suitcase from the seat, put it on the ground, and produced a hammer. "I'll try to open the door," she said. "I'd like you to put the baggage inside."

This galvanized the driver into activity. He vaulted out of his seat, took the hammer from her, and began tearing the boards down.

Then Alice unlocked the door and entered the dark hall. The floor creaked; she breathed air that had not been renewed for years and years.

"If you'd be kind enough to put the boxes and the trunk in here, I'll be all right," said Alice.

"Are you going to stay here alone? Aren't you afraid?"

Alice laughed. "What is there to be afraid of?"

"Well . . ." And then, "Would you like me to open a window or two?"

"If it isn't imposing upon you." Seeing his readiness, she pointed out two windows to him, one in the parlour, piercing the south wall, and one in the kitchen which formed a lean-to in the west.

Soon the light penetrated the dark interior. In the parlour, the ordinary furniture of a little-used room was covered with huge sheets of packing paper. The smell of moth-balls was strong. In the kitchen the bare table, the range, the sink, the cabinet were covered with a fine sandy dust to the depth of an eighth of an inch. Alice meanwhile explored odd corners of the ground-floor, for only now had a number

of difficulties occurred to her. When she had first thought of returning she had, in spite of her better knowledge, instinctively pictured
the place as surrounded by neighbours. The neighbours had pulled
up their stakes to a man. Yet, when she had opened the gate, she had
noticed one place, perhaps two miles north, from the house of which
smoke was rising into the clear blue of the summer afternoon.

One of these difficulties was fuel; the other water. As for fuel, the
back-shed contained a not inconsiderable quantity of coal. As for
water, she would have to see. Just then the driver entered.

"Thanks", said Alice. "I believe I have everything except water.
There's a well in the back yard. I found the old rope and pail. Do
you know whether it will be safe to use the water?"

"When was it used last?"

"Ten years ago."

The driver laughed. "Should be cleaned out first, I suppose."

"Well", she said, a little helplessly, "I'll walk over to the Watsons'
place."

"How far's that?"

"Two miles."

"Have you any vessel? I'll take the bus and drive over."

"Oh, would you? I found a cream-can. I wonder whether it's
clean?"

Having been tightly closed it was clean, though the air imprisoned
in it had a peculiar smell. "I'll rinse it", said the driver.

Alice picked up courage again. The man was hardly gone when,
in exaggerated haste, she divested herself, in the hall, of her travelling suit and, having taken a housedress from her suitcase, donned it,
watching the road meanwhile. Then, fetching rope and pail, she went
to the well and drew a pail of water. It smelt "sloughy." But she
took it to the house, got soap, and began the work of cleaning the
kitchen. The car returned and the young fellow carried the cream-can
into the house.

"Fellow said he'd be over to-night and give you a hand."

"Thanks," Alice replied, "I think I can manage now." And she
dried her hands in order to pay him. Then she stood for a moment,
pensive. "I wonder", she asked, "would you be kind enough to send
a wire for me?"

"Sure."

She found a piece of paper and wrote. It was no message, just the
township and range of her location, signed by her name, Alice Whitney, and addressed to Dr. Thomas Ashmole, Banff.

Five minutes later she stood in the door, looking after the car as
it sped south, on its way back to the city.

By evening she had got things in the house into such shape that, as she said to herself, she could "camp." Kitchen and parlour were clean. In the latter stood a large chesterfield which she could use for her bed. She felt now that she could face the night. Through the door suddenly she saw a man on horseback coming from the north. It was Mr. Watson.

He was forty years old, stout, sunburnt, massive; about his neck he wore a red bandana handkerchief; a grey moustache adorned his unsmiling face. As he reached the gate, he greeted her as though she had been absent for only a few days. But he looked her up and down.

"You are the only one left, Mr. Watson?" asked Alice.

"The only one this side of town. That's five miles."

"But why?"

"They won't learn. They think they can farm here and find they can't."

"They won't take to sheep? Is that it?"

"They hate sheep, they say. They leave and give up. Anything I can do?"

"Hardly to-night," Alice said. "I was wondering whether you'd take the boards down from my windows. There's no hurry, of course. Any time."

"To-morrow morning?"

"Very good. And if you'd be kind enough to let me know when you go to town so I can get supplies. Till I get a horse of my own."

"Sure. Going to stay?"

"For some time at least."

"Still teaching?"

"I have been till day before yesterday."

Mr. Watson sat and looked around without moving. Then he said, "Well, if I can't do anything, I'll be moving."

"Much obliged for coming over", said Alice and smiled.

In the light of the sinking sun Alice, having put on a light coat, went westward across the yard with its long, low sheds, its small horse-stable, and its sheep-run, and out on the open prairie beyond. Yes, she thought, this is that sparse, hard grass! The light, powdery soil under and between the tufts felt to the foot like the matted dust of unaired and unswept subterranean quarters. Here and there, embedded in it, lay huge granitic boulders. For more than ten years this soil had not been trodden upon; yet it looked as if it had been stirred by the small, hoofed feet of thousands upon thousands of animals, though nothing had touched it but the wind of the plains.

The sun for a moment lay on the horizon, heatless, rayless, the colour of a blushing rose. In the whole vault of the sky there was not a wisp of cloud. All around, the horizon was even with the hill on which she stood. This bare and apparently cheerless landscape was exalted. When she stood still, she seemed to see and almost feel how the earth was swinging eastward. The sun was suspended over the edge of the world, hanging over a bottomless abyss into which all living things had to plunge sooner or later—an unknown beyond.

Then, a moment later, the sun, half hidden by the edge of the world, was no more than a rose-coloured spot, and in another minute the whole world grew grey. This was a moment filled with an intense emotional content almost painful. "Here I lie", the landscape seemed to say, "indifferent to the seasons. Summer or winter—to me they are both alike. They come and they go; and I remember them as though I do not distinguish between them, for there is nothing to distinguish them by. There is no past and no future; there is only a present; a present that changes and yet remains ever itself."

But it did not remain itself. Time flew. Within half an hour the first stars leapt out of the firmament and the landscape lost its apathy. During this darkening of the night which delayed, yet, when it came, seemed more sudden than elsewhere, the hills were raised towards the firmament as though by an inner urge, lifting themselves higher and higher till they aspired like altars, upward. The smoke from what there might be of human habitations rose like the incense from sacrifices; the light of the stars streamed down to meet that incense and the thought of man.

Alice let these varying moods enter her being, as if through the pores of her skin. When the cosmic night reached its fervour, she shivered and turned. To her right, on the very summit of the dome, she saw a grey granite boulder half embedded in the soil. It looked like a sheep crouched down for the night. She approached and sat upon it, huddling there to preserve the heat of her body in the air, which was rapidly cooling.

Her thought now became concrete: she considered her past life. How she had grown up here with the regret that she was a girl and not a boy; how her parents had worked and planned, with that in-defeasible confidence in the power of education to perform miracles for their children; how they had sent her two brothers to school in the city and later to college, denying themselves the most common comforts in order to give them what they had not had themselves; how the war had broken out, her brothers enlisting, and how they had both been killed in action; how, then, the parents had transferred to her that longing to give their children all possible advantages, send-ing her to the city; how she had become a teacher; how the parents had died of typhoid here in the wilderness; and how, after their death, too late for them to know and be proud of it, she had taken her place in the work of the world as the principal of one of the large schools in Winnipeg. After that she had gone on, in perpetual homesickness for the scene of her childhood: for this next-to barren prairie of the west, living in exile, but still doing what her parents would have wished her to do. And then she had met Thomas–not in passion, but in something which had seemed deeper and greater: in a liking and a love as between brother and sister. But he had lived in the city; and, being unable to face the prospect of a lifetime there where the days went by like fever-pulses, apparently filled with life, in reality, empty, she had never consented to be his. Till, a few days ago, he had broken through her restraint and had told her that he must now do one of two things, either make her his own or leave her and try to free himself from her bond.

The train which she had left at Medicine Hat was at Banff now; and so probably was her wire. What message would he read out of it?

As she sat on that stone, till late into the night, in fact, till a half-waned moon rose in the east as if to meet the projecting eminence of the world on which she was sitting, she called for him with her soul, with all the powers of her heart. She had been unable to go to him because it would have meant the surrender of her own true life; but she wanted him to come to her; she wanted it more fervently than she had ever wanted anything before except to live out her natural life on this spot of the world which, in the pale, bluish radiance of the moon, she embraced with her half-unseeing look.

During the days that followed, she put the house into order, till it would have been clear to any casual observer that whoever lived there meant to stay. On Wednesday she went along with the Watson children, who drove daily to town, where they attended school. At the local "Sales and Feed Stable" she bought a horse and buggy and drove herself home.

The train from the west passed through Alderson late at night. And, though she tried to persuade herself that she expected nothing whatever, invariably in the morning, when she went about her work in the house, she stopped from time to time at one of the windows looking south, over the trail that connected her with the rest of the world.

Meanwhile Mr. Watson had opened all her windows for her; he had cleaned the well, and hauled a few loads of hay to the yard. She had written a well-known breeder of sheep and awaited the foundation of her future flocks. When they arrived she hired two men in town to drive them out to her place. On her way home, she felt for the first time that house and yard resumed the air of a settled homestead which had never been abandoned. You could not see from the road that the downstairs floors in the house were warped, so that, in walking over them, she sometimes had the sensation of going up a hill; and the next moment felt her strides lengthened by a corresponding downward slope; nor could you tell that, upstairs, the boards having shrunk, the floors rattled when they were crossed.

That night, naturally, all her thoughts were confined to the welfare of the flock, which was scattered over the huge west slope of the dome on which the house stood. For several hours she had to lift water from the well and pour it into the trough which reached through the yard-fence into the pasture beyond. Already she was planning improvements. She would install a pump. She would replace the barbed wire of the line fence by woven wire, which would turn the coyotes. She would improve the native pasture by sowing the seeds of such grasses as had been proved to flourish under these arid conditions. While she gave herself over to these thoughts, she was half aware that she did so, partly at least, in order to keep another thought submerged: the thought of what apparently she had lost.

For that she had lost that other thing which life seemed to have promised her, it now seemed impossible to doubt. He had not come; he had not written. There was only one explanation: he had taken her message to mean a definite "no." That settled it, did it not? Was it not her own well-considered doing? But when she reached her house, she sat for a while in the dark parlour and wept.

The weeks went by; a regular routine had become established. The fifty-odd sheep were beginning to feel at home; already they knew her. She rose very early in the morning and did her housework. Then, putting on a wide-brimmed hat to protect her from the glaring summer sun, she went for a walk of inspection over the half-section of land that was hers. She knew by this time that the half-section adjoining hers in the south had been "proved up" before it had been abandoned, and was for sale at a ridiculously low price. Already she included it in her walk; for she planned its purchase. When she had done so, she returned along the high ridge next to the dome.

Another few weeks went by; and the end of August came. There had been one or two short rains, but on the whole the weather had been dry. Alice tried to persuade herself that, with the expected increase in her flock next spring, the sheep would be better off for a doubled area to graze over. The truth was that she began to find her life just a little empty, in spite of the fact that meanwhile her books had arrived. In Winnipeg, another had stepped into the place which she had given up. To that city, no doubt, Thomas Ashmole had returned; for there was no reason any longer why he should stay away. Defiantly she told herself she had found what she had been looking for; that already—and this was no more than the truth—she had recovered zest in the trivial things of her life: the joy of mere walking and stretching her limbs; that all she needed was a widening of her activities, so that she could feel that what she was doing was worth while.

She wrote at last to the owners of that half-section adjoining hers. She would secure the land and then, perhaps, double her flock that very fall. All the time, however, she was half-conscious that this was a mere illusion, the same illusion from which the hurry and fever of city life sprang. But she could not help herself. The letter had gone off to Calgary, and she felt committed.

It was a week before the answer came. The people regretted that the land had just changed hands. Whether the new owner intended to live on it or not, they could not tell. If Miss Whitney wished to write herself . . . The name of the purchaser was Dr. Thomas Ashmole.

Her heart missed a beat, and she felt herself blushing all over. Then she laughed—a curious laugh, almost shamefaced, in spite of the fact that she was all alone, standing by the gate of her yard where she had met the Watson children on their way home from school.

What did it mean? Well, what could it mean except one thing? Namely, that her great wish was coming true after all? That she could live in her native element and yet not remain alone?

That night, for the first time in weeks, she went to the summit of the dome behind her yard and watched the sun set and the night rise over the hills; strange to say, it no longer seemed to her that these bare, barren hills lay apathetically waiting for summer or winter, indifferent to their succession. If the hills remembered the seasons, this one would be distinguished from all the others because a human being had gone over them, happy at heart.

As often happens in life, no waiting was needed now. Once the fret and fever were gone, events moved fast enough. That very night Alice was, towards morning, awakened by the hum of a passing car, and when, a few hours later, she rose to begin her morning's work, and went out for a moment to take the air, she saw, to her astonishment, a tent pitched on the land north of hers, and behind it the car which she had heard passing. It was land which had fallen back to the crown, the former settlers having left before they had proved up. There was only one explanation: it had been homesteaded again, by new settlers; and apparently, since the car looked to be of a good make and new, they came supplied with what they needed till they could get established.

Alice went back into the house and prepared her breakfast. After that she would have to pump water for an hour or so. Meanwhile she wondered. Yes, it would be a little less lonely. Once or twice, during the last few weeks, she had felt oppressed with the solitude of the hills, and she had walked over to the Watson farm. There, she had found relief by listening to the complaints and troubles of others. It was Mr. Watson who, throughout the long years, had held on to the homestead, slowly and by dint of many privations forging through to success. Mrs. Watson would long since have given up and joined the trek to the city; she hated the barren hills. Alice, in looking at the man, had seen that in his eyes which betrayed to her that, like herself, he was susceptible to that sort of almost incomprehensible beauty which, for man, or for some men, attaches to the grandeur of wide, desolate spaces. Perhaps she could be useful to these new settlers in cautioning them against the mistakes made by the first generation that had tried to make a stand against the frugal soil!

With such thoughts in mind, consciously focusing her attention on the new neighbours to the north rather than on the hypothetical one to the south, she made ready to do her morning's work at the pump. But she had not been at work very long, in the first rays of the rising sun–rays which at this height seemed to come almost from below– when she saw the figure of a man emerging from the tent. He was tall, clad in military breeches and army-shirt, with a wide-brimmed felt hat on his head. He looked about, surveying the landscape. Then, just as she had caught sight of him he, over the intervening valley of half-a-mile or so, caught sight of her and lifted his hand in greeting.

The handle of the pump sank from her hands. The man was Thomas Ashmole!

For a moment she felt faint. Then, as a day ago, she blushed from head to foot. Like an automaton she walked down the north slope of the dome to meet him. Two fences intervened, those of the winter run of the sheep which connected with the sheds. Through these she stepped with still mechanical motions. And then they met at her line-fence.

He looked at her with his peculiar smile. She felt alternately hot and cold.

"Unexpected?" he asked. "I have acquired a section and a half of land in this district. That is, I am homesteading this quarter and pre-empting the one to the west. I have bought the quarters east and west of yours and the half to the south. They told me at Calgary, at the land-titles office, that a man needs two sections for a thousand sheep; and that nothing less than a thousand pays in this country. So I made up my mind to take the plunge."

"Two sections?" Alice asked. "You said you had only one and a half."

"True," he replied. "I counted your half-section in. I thought you might by this time be willing to sell. Or, considering what passed between us at our last interview, to give it to me or to loan it, at least."

"Thomas . . .", she began, but could not proceed.

"I know," Thomas Ashmole nodded, leaning an elbow on a fence-post. "I didn't write. I'll tell you why. When you failed to come, I made up my mind to forget. I had your wire. But I was not going to be stampeded. I was going to find out whether I could live without you. I found I could not. So I did what I have done. I interpreted your wire to mean that if I cared to come and to stay, I should find you willing. Will you tell me whether I was right?"

FURTHER READING

WORKS BY GROVE

Over Prairie Trails (Toronto: McClelland and Stewart, New Canadian Library, 1957). First published 1922.

Settlers of the Marsh (Toronto: McClelland and Stewart, New Canadian Library, 1965). First published 1925.

A Search for America (Toronto: McClelland and Stewart, New Canadian Library, 1971). First published 1927.

Fruits of the Earth (Toronto: McClelland and Stewart, New Canadian Library, 1965). First published 1933.

The Master of the Mill (Toronto: McClelland and Stewart, New Canadian Library, 1961). First published 1944.

Tales from the Margin (Toronto: Ryerson Press, 1971).

CRITICISM

Ronald Sutherland, *Frederick Philip Grove* (Toronto: McClelland and Stewart, Canadian Writers Series, 1969).

Desmond Pacey, ed., *Frederick Philip Grove* (Toronto: Ryerson Press, Critical Views on Canadian Writers Series).

Douglas Spettigue, *Frederick Philip Grove* (Toronto: Copp Clark Publishers, Studies in Canadian Literature Series).

A. J. M. Smith, ed., *Masks of Fiction* (Toronto: McClelland and Stewart, New Canadian Library, 1961). Grove is one of the authors whose work is discussed.

PICTURE SERIES

Canadian Authors (includes Frederick Philip Grove), obtainable from: Hilton Photo Supplies, P.O. Box 74, Chemainus, British Columbia.

Malcolm Lowry

Malcolm Lowry (1909-1957) was born and grew up in England, and studied classics and English at Cambridge, though not until he had worked his way to China by freighter and travelled for a few years. Under the Volcano (1947), his major novel, was set in Mexico where he lived for several years before coming to British Columbia in 1939. Living in a beach shack at Dollarton on Burrard Inlet, he found a refuge from the realities he couldn't cope with, and a focus for his development as a writer. The stories in Hear Us O Lord from Heaven Thy Dwelling Place *were written at Dollarton, the Eridanus of "Present Estate of Pompeii," and* Under the Volcano *was completed there after much revision. When the beach squatters came under threat of eviction, he and his wife Marjorie Bonner Lowry returned to England in 1954.* Hear Us O Lord *won the Governor-General's Award for 1961.*

PRESENT ESTATE OF POMPEII

In thunder, at noon, in a leaden twilight, just outside the Pompeii station, a man said to them:

"Come to my Restaurant Vesuvius. The other restaurant is broken . . . in the bombardment," he added.

Inside the restaurant during the thunderstorm, there was one moment of pure happiness within the dark inner room when it started to rain. "Now thank God I don't have to see the ruins," Roderick thought. And he watched, through the window, the dove in its little rainbeaten house, with just its feet peeping out, and then, the next moment, not a finger's breadth away, the same dove on the windowsill.

This happiness was spoilt for him by the proprietor's continued insistence on what he was going to eat—when he was perfectly content, after an antipasto, with bread and wine: moreover now the rain had stopped he knew he damned well had to see the ruins.

Still he could have sat with his wife forever in that dark deserted inner room of the Restaurant Vesuvius.

Yes, it was wonderful in the restaurant here at Pompeii, with the train whistling by on one side, and the thunder crashing around Vesuvius on the other: with the rain—liquid syllables of its epilogue—the pigeon, the girl standing under the garden trellis singing, and washing dishes in the rainwater, and Tansy happy, if impatient, he wanted never to go out, to leave this scene. But when the full bottle of vino rosso was depleted by as much as one glass his spirits correspondingly sank, and almost for a moment he did not care whether he stayed or left. He cared all right though: he wanted to stay.

If only that rich flagon of hope would stay too, undiminished with them! Or if one could only go on looking at it as if it were some symbolic vessel of an unevictable happiness!

Roderick McGregor Fairhaven sat listening to his wife describe the scenes from the train yesterday (not this train, which was the Circumvesuviana, but the Rapido, the Rome-Naples Express), how fast it went, past the magnificent Claudian aqueducts, a station, Torricola—och aye, it was a rapido indeed, he thought, as once more in memory, bang: and they flashed through Divino Amore. (No stop for Divine Love.) And the white oxen and high tension lines, the lupine and hayricks, the bellflowers and yellow mullein, the haystacks like leaning towers of Pisa, a lone hawk fluttering along the telegraph wires, the rich black soil—Tansy had seen and recorded everything, down to the wildflowers whose name she didn't know: "Lilac and gold, like a Persian carpet." The precipitous, hilly country, and now on the narrow coastal plain, the feeling of the shape of Italy: "like a razor-backed hog." Suddenly rain, and the castellated cities on the hilltops, a few dark tunnels, and beyond in the fields, in brilliant sunshine again, the men winnowing, the black chaff blowing from the wheat. And there had been nothing so beautiful, Tansy was saying, as the vermilion poppies blowing among the delicate tufted ivory-colored wheat. And then Formia, a dull station stop, but with a Naples-like town way off in the distance. They'd looked out of the window at more castellated towns built on gray rock, a blaze of poppies by a ruined wall, a flock of white geese waddling toward a pond where dark gray cows lay submerged like hippopotami. And "You should have seen them, I thought they were hippopotami," Tansy said, though now there were a flock of goats, rust-red, black and cream-colored, being herded up a steep hill by a skinny little boy with bare feet and bare chest and bright blue trousers. And the signs: *Vini Pregiati–Ristoro–Cola-zioni Calde* . . . What did one want to look at ruins for? Why shouldn't one prefer the Restaurant Vesuvius to Pompeii, to Vesuvius itself for that matter? Roderick was now, in so far as he was listening, but delighted to hear her talk, vicariously enjoying the train trip in a way he hadn't at all in the howling electric train itself. Another brief stop: Villa Literno. And the sign: *E Proibito Attraversare I Binario*. These were the kind of things he'd planned to jot down for his students–but it was Tansy who turned out to be memorizing them. And as they approached Naples he thought, there is an anonymity in movement. But when the train stops, voices are louder, more searching it seems, it is time to take stock. To him of whom stock is being taken these are bad moments . . . And there was an anonymity too in sitting still, in the dark restaurant at Pompeii, listening to one's wife talk so entrancingly. And he didn't want her to stop. Naples had been ruin enough in this year of 1948, and sad enough to have driven Boccaccio himself–Giovanni della Tranquillità indeed–right back to Florence without even having paid a visit to Virgil's tomb–

"Pompeii," Tansy was reading aloud from her guidebook–as now thank God it started to rain again–"an old Oscan town dating from the sixth century B.C., which had adopted the Greek culture, lay in the rich and fertile campania felix close to the sea, possessing moreover a busy harbour . . ."

"I know . . . it exported fish sauce and millstones . . . But I was thinking–" Roderick brought out his pipe–"that I've read little about the malaise of travelers, even the sense of tragedy that must come over them sometimes at their lack of relation to their environment."

"–what?"

"The traveler has worked long hours and exchanged good money for this. And what is this? This, pre-eminently, is where you don't belong. Is it some great ruin that brings upon you this migraine of alienation–and almost inescapably these days there seems a ruin of some kind involved–but it is also something that slips through the hands of your mind, as it were, and that, seen without seeing, you can make nothing of: and behind you, thousands of miles away, it is as if you could hear your own real life plunging to its doom."

"Oh for God's sake, Roddy–!"

Roderick leaned over and replenished their wine glasses, at the same time catching sight of his reflection in a flawed mirror in which also appeared the rain barrel and the rain-dripping trellis in the garden and the dove and the girl washing dishes, where behind the word *Cinzano* and to one side of a card stuck in the frame which stated enigmatically *26-27 Luglio Pellegrinaggio a Taranto (in Autopull-*

man) he saw himself: beaming, merry, spectacled, stocky, strong, reflective, and grave, forceful yet shy, brave and timid at once, and above all patient, impatient only with impatience and intolerance, the liberal-minded and progressive Scotch-Canadian schoolmaster: he absolutely refused to credit himself the gloomy train of thought that had just been his, and indeed his mien contradicted it.

". . . the eruption began on August twenty-fourth in the early afternoon with the emission of vast quantities of vapor, mostly steam, which rushed high into the air in a vertical shaft and terminated in a canopy of cloud . . ."

Watching his wife, admiring her, touched by her enthusiasm, a great feeling of tenderness for her overcame him. And then it seemed to him for a moment that this was not unlike tenderness for himself. In fact half watching himself watch his life in the mirror he could almost imagine he saw the brightness and generosity of his soul flashing off his glasses.

"Roddy, it does look a bit brighter, doesn't it? Well, if it doesn't stop we'll just go in the rain!"

And now, as the time drew closer to leave it, the Restaurant Vesuvius was already beginning to be invested with a certain nostalgia. And after another glass of wine he took delight in reflecting how something in the very depths of his wife's being seemed to respond to a moving fluctuant exciting scene: Tansy, pretty, a bit wild, delightful, enthusiastic, was a born traveler, and he often wondered if her true environment was not simply this moving ever changing background—he reached in his pocket for some matches and a news clipping fluttered out.

"Is that Dad's latest news report flying away?" Tansy said.

Roderick's father-in-law, who was a boatbuilder in British Columbia, near Vancouver, scarcely ever wrote his daughter at all and his correspondence with Roderick consisted of clippings from newspapers. Sometimes bits would be marked, sometimes not; very occasionally there would be half a page with some comment, in red carpenter's pencil. The enclosure Roderick had received at the American Express in Naples this morning was rather more fulsome, and consisted of half a page, mostly given over to advertisements for consolidated brokers, limited petroleum companies and drilling companies, and crowned by the gigantic headline: OIL! OIL! OIL! Subsidiary headlines appeared: BRITISH COLUMBIA RIDING HUGE INDUSTRIAL BOOM, OIL GAS ALUMINUM SPEARHEADING COLOSSAL INDUSTRIAL SURGE $BILLION PROGRAM.

At first Roderick thought this was an ironic reference to their own small speculation, which had so astonishingly paid off. Then he saw the item the old man had marked: a small "filler" which apparently had nothing to do with British Columbia at all and ran:

SCARED TO DEATH

In Arizona, a 1,000-acre forest of junipers suddenly withered and died. Foresters are unable to explain it, but the Indians say the trees died of fear but they are not in agreement as to what caused the fright.

Eridanus. Now, in July, the forest, behind the pretty shacks built on stilts grouped around the bay with his father-in-law's boat-building shed in the middle, would be in full bright leaf, celestially green and sunfilled, the winding path leading you through scent of mushrooms and ferns and dark firs to airy spaces where golden light sifted down through vine-leaved maples and young swaying hazel trees. Tansy's rocky ten-foot garden would be blooming with foxgloves and wild geranium, marigolds and nasturtiums and sweet alyssum, fireweed and hawks-beard would have sprung up on the bank, the sea (between visits of oil tankers to the refinery over the bay), cold, salt and pure, would be glittering in the sun and wind below the porch, and beyond, the mountains, still with high patches of snow, would rise to heaven in a turquoise haze. The wild cherry and dogwood blossoms would be gone now, the huckleberries and the blueberries would be ripe. Every day the mink would emerge from the hollow tree where he lived with his family and prance and dart secretively along the beach, or swim, only a tiny vicious sleek brown head, importantly by. The fishermen would all have sailed north to Active Pass or Prince Rupert, and save at week ends there'd be nobody there at all save the Wildernesses and perhaps the Llewellyns and his father-in-law. And that was where he should be now—not in Paris or Naples or Rome, in Eridanus, reading, correcting papers and taking notes in the long summer twilight, chatting with Tansy's father or drifting down the inlet in their rowboat, or taking Tansy and Peggy on a picnic—watching the constellations; mens sano in corpore sano. Sailing boats would sweep downstream or tack across the bay, and at night the lights of the little ferryboat would move silently down the swift dark stream among the reflections of the stars. And at night, when Peggy was asleep, he and Tansy would argue, have a moonlight swim, talk some more over a pot of tea about *Time, Life*, Thomas Mann, Communism, the *Partisan Review*, the sthenic confusion of technological advance, the responsibilities of education, Peggy's future, Gurko's *Angry Decade*–

"In 79 A.D. the catastrophe occurred. For thirty-six hours Vesuvius poured down upon the town a rain of pumice stone followed by a rain of ashes and boiling water which mixture formed into a mass that covered the earth with a layer several yards thick. The survivors returned after days of terror."

Suddenly Roderick remembered an evening last summer, remembered it with such intensity and longing he stared about him a moment as if seeking some escape from the Restaurant Vesuvius. A baby seal had come swimming up on the beach a few afternoons before, he and Sigbjorn Wilderness had picked it up, fearing it might be threatened or starve without its mother, and they'd kept it for several days in their bathtub. This particular day they'd taken the seal for a swim and suddenly, in a flash, it slipped away and was gone. They'd swum after it hopelessly, they walked along the beach, searching, and his father-in-law, who rightly considered the whole procedure puerile in the extreme, had annoyed him slightly by choosing this moment to mumble to them at length a story about a mermaid he claimed to remember some fishermen's having once picked up at Port Roderick in the Isle of Man and also put in a bathtub. (According to him they had boiled some eggs for the poor monster, but while they were doing this the mermaid escaped and he recalled distinctly that when they returned from searching for it along the beach, all the water had boiled out of the saucepan.) Because a killer whale–and not merely a killer whale but a white killer whale, an albino, the first seen in nineteen years–had been sighted from the control tower of the Second Narrows Bridge swimming their way into the inlet (one of a school, but it was the Melvillean qualification that had supplied the menace) they were anxious about the seal, cursed themselves for picking it up at all, questioning too the humane paradox of the whole thing since the seal was the greatest enemy of their friends the fishermen, and Roderick and Tansy had ended up sitting on the Wildernesses' porch and talking . . . Sometime later on –it must have been nearly midnight for it was dark–Fairhaven had gone back to his shack to get an ill-translated collection of ancient belles-lettres published in the nineties, and a damned stupid book too–Lamartine, Volney, God knows who–he for some reason wanted to read from in answer to something Wilderness had said. And it was this walk through the woods and back that he particularly remembered now: the stillness in the forest, the absolute peace, the stars sparkling and blazing through the trees (high on a cedar his flashlight gleamed on the four watching shining timorous curious eyes of two raccoons), the stillness, the peace, but also the sense of hurt, the anxiety because of the renewed talk that evening of the possibility of the railroad's coming through, or that the forest would be slaughtered to make way for auto camps or a subsection, so that their troubles had seemed all at once, or once again, like those of country folk in a novel by George Eliot, or Finnish pioneers in the sixties (or, as Primrose Wilderness had remarked bitterly, Canadians or human beings of almost any period): and the sense too of something else topsy-turvily all the wrong way; Roderick stood quietly on his porch a moment, listening to the conversation of the tide coming in, bringing distantly, shadowily, more luminously, an oil tanker with it. To him, standing on his porch, holding his book and flashlight, it was as if Eridanus had suddenly become, like ancient Rome, a theater of prodigies, real and imaginary. As though the white whale hadn't been enough, the four o'clock news report from Vancouver heard over the Wilderness radio had related this in renewed reports from "several accredited sources" of the famous "flying saucers" of that period which had been witnessed that very afternoon from several different points traveling over Eridanus itself, and a sworn statement by the Chief of Police "now released for the first time to the public, that he had, while fishing with his son beyond Eridanus Port the previous Sunday, seen, cavorting there, a sea serpent." Good God! This was all hilariously, horribly funny, and Roderick could laugh again thinking about it now. But the truth was he wasn't really amused: these things taken together with his other deeper anxieties, agitated him with that kind of dark conviction of the monstrous and threatening in everything sometimes begotten by a hangover. And unable to fit these matters comfortably into the filing cabinet of a civilized mind it was as if willy-nilly he'd begun to think with the archaic mind of his remote ancestors instead, and the result was alarming to a degree. More alarming still was that with his civilized mind he had calmly taken what might prove a threat to the whole world with far less seriousness than he took a rumored threat to his home. Roderick saw that the tanker had stolen silently right past the refinery without his noticing it:

> Frère Jacques!
> Frère Jacques!
> Dormez-vous?
> Dormez-vous?

went the engines, if you listened carefully . . .

And now, with an appalling chain-rattling, smiting and dither of bells, hubbub of winches, submarine churning of propellers, and orders sounding as if they were spoken half a cable's length away, though she was two miles distant, and besides by now nearly invisible, all these noises traveling over the water with the speed of a slingshot, she dropped anchor: a few final orders floated across the inlet, then silence. Roderick stood gazing at the oil refinery, "all lit up," as Wilderness had put it, "like a battleship on the Admiral's birthday . . ." But if the oil tanker had seemed, for an inexplicable moment, to threaten the refinery, the refinery, with its hard brilliant impersonal electric glitter, seemed at this instant suddenly to threaten him. In a day of prodigies, the refinery, though as an anything but absurd one, now also took its place in the series. As if he had never seen the place before at night, or as if it had just materialized, electrified with impersonal foreboding, it seemed now a sinister omen.

The light was on in his father-in-law's house next door, and he could see the old boatbuilder through the window, sitting in the warm soft golden light of his oil lamp that cast gentle shadows over the hammers and frows and adzes, the tools all sharp and oiled and lovingly cared for, smoking his pipe, but with his three other pipes ready filled for the morning beside him on the table, sitting under the oil lamp with his spectacles on, reading the *History of the Isle of Man–*

"The ruins are open to visitors daily, free of charge, from nine to seventeen o'clock. At the entrance, and even at the station, Italian, French, German and English-speaking guides (tariff!) press their services on the tourists."

"God damn it, yes, what?" Fairhaven sighed, smiling at Tansy.

"The time required for a conducted round is from one and a half to two hours, but to view the place properly, four or five hours are necessary. Visitors are not allowed to take food in with them. Do you know, when I was a very little girl, my mother had a stereopticon," Tansy said, "with pictures of Pompeii. Really it was my grandmother's."

"Hoot toot!"

"Oh, I wonder if it'll look like those pictures! I remember them perfectly . . . You haven't heard a word I said."

"Och yes . . . they're going to rain ashes and boiling water on us, and we can't take any food in," Roderick said. "But what about wine?"

–"All kind of different bird here," said the guide, "snail, rabbit, ibis, butterfly, zoology, botanic, snail, rabbit, lizard, eagle, snake, mouse."

There was no one else in the city of Pompeii (which at first sight had looked to him a bit like the ruins of Liverpool on a Sunday afternoon: or supposing it to have suffered another, latter-day catastrophe since the Great Fire of 1886, Vancouver itself–a few stock exchange pillars, factory chimneys, the remnants of the Bank of Montreal), just the guide; and Roderick, while returning Tansy's glance of mocking wide-eyed pleasure at this mysterious statement, knew he'd done his best to avoid him.

It was not precisely because he, Roderick, was mean, Roderick felt, nor was it precisely because there happened to be few things more natively loathsome to him than the whole business of bargaining and tipping, no, he'd avoided the guide out of a kind of ridiculous fear. For he'd so signally failed to make himself understood on this trip, often, as just now at the Restaurant Vesuvius, in the most elementary commerce, that the failure was beginning to strike at his amour propre. And so, rather than spoil matters at the outset by making a fool of himself, he liked rather to wander, to drift alone with Tansy, letting this sense of the strange and utter meaninglessness, to him, of his surroundings, be absorbed in that of their happiness just of being together, which certainly was real, in her happiness at being in Europe–just as he would have liked to let it be absorbed wandering with her now around Pompeii. Moreover at such times he had some opportunity for imagining that he (as he damned well should be, as he really wanted to be) was the cicerone: Tansy was too intelligent to be deceived, but she was also too kind to appear undeceived; but in any case the ruse would actually work, and romance be begotten or preserved in the shape of a sort of mutual astral body of inattention outside which Tansy's own intelligence and delighted personal response no doubt operated independently, yet out of which, as if it were a godlike cloud, Roderick could imagine his most banal utterance sounding useful and informative, such as just now, he had planned to say something like, "Temple of Vespasian," or "Doric and Corinthian," or even "Bulwer Lytton."

But the guide had been waiting for them, sitting between two ruinations, and in the twinkling of an eye they were in his clutches. And as a matter of fact he half remembered Tansy saying that you couldn't escape those clutches, you were legally bound to take a guide. He'd left the bargaining this time entirely up to Tansy, even though carried on in English. But Tansy was fortunately too caught up in her delight at the immediate situation to perceive Roderick's shame which had not, however, inspired in him any antipathy to the guide himself, who vaguely reminded Roderick of his eldest brother. He was a swarthy, swift-moving, eagle-nosed fellow, ot medium height, with a flashing eye, threadbare clothes, and a military walk.

"Pompeii was a school of immorality. No hypocrite life like ours," he was announcing thoughtfully as he marched along a little ahead of them. "Blue mountains, blue sky, blue sea, and a white marble city."

The Fairhavens smiled. The mountains and sky were indeed blue, now the thunderstorm had rolled away, and could one have seen it from this point, no doubt the Bay of Naples would have appeared blue too. But there was something extraordinarily eerie about the way the guide had said this to them, Roderick thought, as they followed him through the truncated and darkened stumps of the inundated and exhumed city, adding, proudly smiling to Tansy, "Si, I am Pompeiian!" as though to him this old Cuernavaca-cum-Acapulco of the Romans, and manufacturer of fish sauce and millstones, were not a heap of ruins but were still here, gleaming, alive, peopled and thriving, and with the sea, now withdrawn miles away, at their very doorstep; "After Pompeii was destroyed," he went on rapidly, but still thoughtfully, glancing up a moment at Vesuvius, "Christians make-a the strong propaganda. They say their God have destroyed Pompeii for its wickedness. Now Pompeiians they say: Pompeii is immoral town? If that were-a so, Vesuvius must-a come every day to punish us."

Roderick smiled, liking the guide, and he also looked again at Vesuvius which, now clear, with its conventional plume of smoke, seemed too far away and insignificant to have done much damage anyhow. Still, out of fairness to the volcano it seemed proper to note that its physical insignificance must be largely due to the damage it had done, Roderick went on to say to Tansy.

Alas, poor old Vesuvius had really waged a war of attrition on itself in the last century. No longer did the fire-spouting mountain wax and grow taller on the sacrifice of those beneath him, all the territory it had demolished of late years had been at its own expense, every explosion and inundation it had sent forth had decreased its own stature until now, having literally blasted its own cone off, it appeared little more than a distant hill. Vesuvius was Paricutin in reverse. Though it might still, even now at this moment, be working up more fury, perhaps the god that wished to be believed in should be wary too often of speaking through fire, of giving too many direct signs of his presence.

Actually, he was frightened of Vesuvius, in so far as he could bring himself to think of it at all. All of which caused him to remember that Tansy and he had climbed it only the day before yesterday in the company—"visiting their old stamping ground," Tansy said—of some Greeks. And he certainly would not have cared to belittle it then, Roderick thought, crossing himself as they passed the Temple of Venus and went on into the Forum. The cinders got into their shoes, the guides, with their staffs, shrouded in fog and resembling black magicians, had urged them on with loud cries toward the top, where Tansy lamented it was not now possible to descend, like Lamartine, into the crater because a recent earthquake had caused great clefts in the path down into the noisome and shattered abyss. Roderick had, by placing it in the earth, lit a cigarette to bring him luck.

It was difficult to keep up with the guide who now seemed to wear a somewhat different appearance, perhaps because his complete air of belonging, even of ownership, had begun to invest him with a curious and different dignity: he had, or had now, the aspect to Roderick of a stout, prosperous and jovial businessman, quite carefully dressed, in conservative business clothes: dark gray striped coat, light gray flannel trousers, dark gray tie, white shirt. His coat, from whose pocket papers protruded, was too tight over his stomach, the sleeves drew up on his shirt, while the trousers were frayed: this had given the effect of shabbiness. But at the same time he had this hearty soldierly quality about him, and this swift military walk of Roderick's brother, a walk which carried him, and Tansy with him, often quite far ahead of Roderick's measured pace. They crossed the Forum obliquely and disappeared ahead of him amid some huge blackened pillars.

"You see, Temple of Augustus," he was saying when Roderick overtook them. "You see? Acorn and Laurel: force and power. The Romans say, 'Each moment of love lost is a moment of happiness spoiled . . .' The Romans say, 'Life is a very long-a dream with open eyes,'" he greeted Roderick, "'when eyes closed all-a finished, all is-a dust . . .' Lovers just like-a beasts . . . They spend life in honey, sweet life." "He means bees," Tansy explained to Roderick, turning to him conspiratorially. "Beasts, bees . . . Acorn, laurel, butchers, fish beefmarket. Ventilation from sea, breeze come inside, to smell out."

"Ah yes," said Roderick . . . "Der Triumphbogen der Nero."

"What, darling?"

"The Arco di Nerone. Only I thought it sounded better in German."

"Si. Arco di Nerone . . . The Romans say: 'Life is a series of formalities, too seriously taken,'" the guide assured them, turning around. He possessed an admirable name: Signor Salacci.

And there was no doubt about it, Roderick thought again, this town, that both was and was not here, was obviously very real and complete to the excellent Signor Salacci: he saw it all. And moreover he was utterly adjusted to it. In a far realer sense than an actor lives in his scene Signor Salacci lived here, in Pompeii. Meantime these arches and temples and markets created and uncreated themselves before Roderick's eyes so that he almost began to see them with the guide's eyes. What was strange was this tragic–tragic because almost successful–effort at performance. It looked sometimes as though the Romans here had made all their dreams come true in terms of convenience, wicked and good alike. Vesuvius had long since destroyed Pompeii's old inhabitants, but there seemed an immortality about the conveniences, which was a disturbing thought.

"Pompeii may have been beautifully proportioned, but it was not, so far as I know, a town singular in its era for any remarkable nobility of conception," he said. "On the other hand—"

"If you compare it with Bumble, Saskatchewan—"

"But what seems most remarkable to me is that no one has attempted to draw a moral from this relative survival of Pompeii, when so much breath has been wasted on the divine judgment of its destruction. Of the two the survival seems the more sinister . . . Compared with St. Malo or parts of Rotterdam it's a triumph. In fact alongside of what's left of Naples it seems to me to have a positive civic grace."

The junipers that died of fear . . . Ruins, ruins, ruins—

—The first night they arrived in Naples they had taken a cab and driven for an hour behind the sidestepping horse along the promenade. What was left of this great city of stupendous history where Virgil had written the Aeneid and which was once the extreme western point of the Greek world? No doubt much had survived. Yet to him it had appeared, where it was not simply a heap of gray rubble, like a second-rate seaside resort, with ugly soulless buildings and mediocre swimming, on the northwest coast of England. Surely, he'd thought, as he held Tansy's hand in the clopping and side-slipping cab, he could invest it with more excitement than that for her.

That night they wandered through the incredibly steep dark back streets of the Neapolitan slums, past the shrines, the niches, the children setting up Catherine wheels, up the long smelly wonderful stairways between houses, past the bedsteads set right on the street, the sailors lurchingly carrying the girls' bags—the Rembrandt Supper at Emmaus around every corner. From a high top window of a narrow tall building a basket was lowered, little by little, and at the bottom filled with wine, and bread and fruit, and, jerkingly, withdrawn. And that was what travel was supposed to be, thought Roderick, like that basket that is lowered down into the past, and is brought back again, safely through one's window, filled with the spiritual nourishment of one's voyaging. And that, he profoundly hoped, would be what it was for Tansy . . . Here were the poor, here were the ruins, but the great difference between these man-made ruins and the ruins of Pompeii was that the ruins for the most part had not been found worth preserving or had been carried away . . . Life itself was something like the desolation that comes to one eternally wading through the poem of *The Waste Land* without understanding it. Awestruck by his callousness, his ignorance, his lack of time, his fear that there will be no time to build anything beautiful, fear of eviction, of ejection, man no longer belongs to or understands the world he has created.

Man had become a raven staring at a ruined heronry. Well, let him deduce his own ravenhood from it if he could.

They came to the Casa dei Vettii, or the Domus Vettorium, the most famous house in Pompeii, which partly accounted for their guide's haste; Pompeii closed at five and they had a late start.

Signor Salacci produced a key, unlocked a door, and they entered: "You want lady-wife to see pictures? Only marrieds can see," he explained. "Each house a little town: garden; theater: vomitory, to vomit, and a love room inside."

"And to the right of the entrance is a Priapus," observed Roderick, reading from the guidebook, "only shown by request. However, Tansy," he continued, "here 'one has the best possible picture of a Pompeiian noble's house since the beautiful paintings and marble decorations have been left as they were in the peristyle which has been furnished with plants. One portion of the house has been provided with a roof and windows so as to protect the surprisingly well-preserved and most wonderfully executed murals depicting mythological scenes. There is a kitchen containing cooking utensils, and adjoining a locked private cabinet (obscene paintings) which belonged to the master of the house and here too is a statue of Priapus intended as part of the fountain . . .' I hope," Roderick added, "this is not what your mother showed you on the stereopticon."

"Basin for goldfish," the guide was saying. "Peacocks and dogs. Put phosphorus on stone. White columns and a blue sky. Difficult to believe . . . original . . ." Signor Salacci sighed.

"You mean–?"

"Water jets and flying birds and phosphorus in the pavement," sang Signor Salacci, "and the walls lacquered red and then waxed, with Afrika leopard, and an erotic frieze–"

"They had torches burning so that the inside of this room was in red light to make everyone excited," Tansy was explaining to Roderick, who'd been standing at a little distance. "But in contrast to this the garden was all in white marble, with cool fountains playing and open to the moonlight."

"Usually gave these orgy feasts to the full moon," the guide mused nostalgically.

"And during these orgy feasts?"

"Slaves had to pray for them–" they had arrived at a shrine to the household gods, the Lares and Penates (how would their old kettle be, their stove, Tansy's copper pans?)–"for bachelors had," he said devoutly, "too much to do bachelor."

The guide was now opening the padlock on an oblong wooden cover, that he folded back to reveal, momentarily, an oblong framed picture, about eighteen inches long, and a foot wide, evidently of some kind of unusual Cyrano de Bergerac, painted (and from all appearances quite recently subtly improved upon in Marseilles) in black, ocher and red, of a Cyrano engaged in weighing, it seemed at first sight, upon a sort of Safeway scale, his nose, which emitted curious carmine sparkles: "Where there is money, there is art, there is taste, there is intelligence, there is perdition, there is fight–that is Pompeii!" glowed Signor Salacci, turning the key in the padlock again upon this jealously preserved and athletic relic.

"I always heard there was a reproduction of the Screw of Archimedes in Pompeii," Roderick observed. "But I thought he worked it with his feet."

"But I don't understand about the windows, Rod," Tansy was giggling, perhaps to conceal her embarrassment, or her embarrassment at evincing before the guide that she was one in whom a natural innocence and decency were combined with a restrained yet wholeheartedly Rabelaisian appreciation.

"Well, it's just as he said, Tansy dear. There aren't any bloody windows, or rather there weren't. Just as the walls weren't marble, but covered with stucco imitation of marble facing. They're simply paintings of windows to give the impression you're looking through a real window." Roderick filled his pipe. "Of course according to Swedenborg the real sunrise is an imitation too . . . The technique seems vaguely literary in origin."

"You've got to admit it has certain advantages of privacy–"

"Och aye . . . In short, with certain obvious reservations it's much the same bastard-mansard ye olde Wigwamme Inne Cockington Moosejaw and Damnation-in-the-Wold–"

"What did you say, Rod?"

"I said, do you remember the man who wanted to pebbledash Gerald's house? Or perhaps I was thinking of those sheets of fabric on Percy's garage that are painted to look like red brick."

"First wine, everyone will be drunk, and afterwards brothel," announced Signor Salacci, locking Casa dei Vettii behind them and with the air of an indulgent host in the middle of a debauch proposing further delights.

They left the house and drifted off at a great pace through the sunshine down the Vico dei Vettii, and after casting a glance down the Strada dei Vesuvio in the direction of the mountain, turned into Strada Stabiana.

"It was a silly place to put a volcano," said Roderick as now, passing the Casa di Cavio Rufo on their right, they arrived at a crossroads made by the intersection of the Strada degli Augustali with the Strada Stabiana.

They turned right again into a narrow, rough, and extremely crooked and winding street that had the appearance of going on forever.

"Vico de Lupanare. Wine woman and song street," crowed the guide triumphantly. "First wine, and afterwards brothel," he repeated. "Bread and woman, the first element in life, symbolic . . . All symbolic . . . wait! One entrance–bachelors downstairs; marrieds, priests and the shamefuls upstairs."

There are, unless you happened to be Toulouse-Lautrec, few things in life less profitable than going to a brothel, unless, Roderick reflected, it was going to a ruined brothel. This was a whole street of ruined brothels. The houses had been built of stone but it was necessary to use considerable imagination to people them, least of all with delights. To him they resembled at first rather a series of disjasked ovens, or, if one could imagine pigpens made of brick, pigpens, but with shelves and niches, so that they seemed to have been made to accommodate the consummations of some race of voluptuous dwarfs.

"Roderick, do look, honey, here are the mills where the flour was ground!–and the ovens, see, there's even a petrified loaf of bread!"

"Si, first bread, then wine, then women on this-a street," Signor Salacci was nodding importantly. "First elements of life, all symbolic!"

Roderick was aware now of a certain blasé obtuseness. Still, a whole street of dead brothels, that had so miraculously survived–relatively–the wrath of God–that was perhaps something to stimulate the lower reaches of the mind after all! Or if not, the ruined pharmacist's, which the guide was pointing out so conveniently placed on the corner, might have indeed. It was abundantly clear too, that once again, so far as Signor Salacci was concerned, these places not merely existed, but were, for him, doing a lively, if ghostly, trade. Particularly their guide seemed pleased by the Cyranesque-priapic trade emblem that, set from time to time amidst the cobbles, indicated waggishly the direction in which even now the phantom bachelors of Pompeii were perhaps proceeding to their grisly quarters downstairs where, once ensconced, past them an eternal ascending procession of marrieds, priests and shamefuls floated on their way to be vampired and counter-whored upstairs. Signor Salacci's romantic attachment touched and delighted Roderick. He was making the afternoon a success. It was not even impossible–Roderick saw him once brushing away what might have been a tear–some great grief, some romance, survived, for him, here.

Nonetheless Roderick found himself suddenly hating this street with an inexplicable virulence. How he loathed Pompeii! His mouth positively watered with his hatred. Roderick was almost prancing. It seemed to him now that it was as though, by some perverse grace, out of the total inundation of some Pacific North-western city, had been preserved a bit of the station hotel, a section of the gasworks, the skeletal remains of four or five palatial cinemas, as many bars and several public urinals, a fragment of marketplace together with the building that once housed the Star Laundries, what was left of several fine industrialists' homes (obscene paintings), a football stadium, the Church of the Four Square Gospel, a broken statue of Bobbie Burns, and finally the remains of the brothels in Chinatown which, though the mayor and police force had labored to have them removed right up to the time of the catastrophe, had nonetheless survived five thousand nine hundred and ninety-nine generations whereupon it was concluded, probably rightly, that the city was one of the seven wonders of the world, as it now stood, but wrongly that anything worthwhile had been there in the first place, with the exceptions of the mountains. The guide had just said too that even the noise of traffic had been so deafening in Pompeii that during certain hours they'd had to put a stop to it altogether, as one could well imagine on the stone paved streets–God how one must have longed to get away! And then he remembered that Pompeii was not a city at all, it was only a small town, by the, by the–

–Roderick had found his book among a collection of old *American Mercurys* that must have been there since he'd built the house, and started back; but when he came out on his porch he stopped: the beauty of the scene was phenomenal, terrifying, ominous and yet oddly reassuring at once. The moon had come out and now it shone high in a sky of fleece, in which were patches of sky the color of dark blue serge, twinkling with brilliant stars. The tide was at high slack, the water so calm and still the whole heavens were reflected as in a dark mirror. Then he realized that it was not the moonlight or even the inlet that gave the scene its new, unique beauty, but precisely the oil refinery itself, or more precisely still, the industrial counterpoint, the flickering red pyre of the burning oil waste. Now over the water (so still he could hear the Wildernesses talking softly together two hundred yards away) came the slow warning bell of a freight train chiming on the rail over Port Boden as for a continual vespers, now closer, now receding, now Byzantine in its timbre, as it vibrated in the water, now dolorous like Oaxaquenian bells, now a blue sound, now as it approached, fuller, more globular, then fading, but always as if some country sound heard long ago that might have inspired a Wordsworth or Coleridge to describe church bells borne over the fields to some wandering lovers at evening. But whereas the moonlight washed the color out of everything, replacing it by luminousness, providing illumination without color, the flaming burning vermilion oil waste below the moon to the right halfway up the opposite bank made the most extraordinary lurid color, enormously real, as it were, bad: as the bell continued to chime intermittently along the rail, the continual vespers not receding, or drowned by an occasional mournful whistle and distant clunking of wheels on iron, Roderick thought how different Eridanus would look from the refinery side. What would they see? Nothing at all, perhaps only the oil lamp in his father-in-law's house and the illumined open windows of the Wildernesses', nothing else, probably not even the Wildernesses' pier which looked so magnificent in the moonlight, striking down into its reflection with its geometrically beautiful cross-braces, just the shadowy bulk of his father-in-law's shed, perhaps, and then the dark bulk of the forest, and the mountains rising above; they wouldn't see even the shapes of the shacks, or perhaps that there was a bay at all; the whole perhaps inseparable from its own shadow.

The Wildernesses' cat debouched itself from his father-in-law's house and followed him, bounding up the steps and along the trail, leading him back to the Wildernesses, stopping for him to catch up, then leaping on again. Once he stopped to pet the creature which suddenly seemed to him like some curious aspect or affection of eternity and for some reason, standing there in the forest, it had struck him as strange that cats must have looked and behaved exactly the same in, say, not merely Volney's but Dr. Johnson's day. Meanwhile with his flashlight he sought one of the passages from Volney's *Ruin of Empires* that he'd recalled and wanted to read: "Where are the ramparts of Nineveh, those walls of Babylon, those palaces of Persepolis, those temples of Balbec and Jerusalem—" It was absolutely the most obvious kind of dithyrambic tripe, but considering when it was written might be, so he felt at that moment anyhow, interesting in his discourse with Wilderness, to compare with Toynbee. "—the temples are fallen, the palaces overthrown, the ports filled up, the cities destroyed, and the earth, stripped of its inhabitants, has become a place of sepulchres. Great God! Whence proceed such fatal revolutions? What causes have so changed the fortunes of those countries? Wherefore are so many cities destroyed . . . where are those brilliant creations of industry . . .?"

Going through the forest that night with the bounding and whirling cat all at once it had seemed to him, as if he stood outside time altogether, that in some way these cities of Volney's had not been exactly destroyed, that the ancient populations had been reproduced and perpetuated, or rather that the whole damned thing was happening now, at this moment, continually repeating itself, that continually those empires and cities were being created and destroyed and created again as it were before his eyes: then again he began to think that, far more mysterious than any of the questions Volney posed, was the fact that people still found it necessary to ask them, or answer them with unsatisfactory explanations. Had Toynbee really said anything new? Had Volney in his day? With his flashlight, while the cat impatiently sharpened its claws on a tree, he had recourse to the forgotten Volney once more. "Individuals will feel that private happiness is allied to the public good." Well, that seemed a point worth discussing at any rate: but what was the public good? What was private happiness?

"In Germany, England, red light," Signor Salacci was saying. "Roman better idea. Cock outside."

Well, St. Malo was wiped out, Naples defaced, but a cock in the street outside an antique Pompeiian brothel still survived. Well, why not?

"Aesculapius snakes outside, a doctor . . ." the guide went on. "The chemist and public bathwash . . . Soldiers, students, cheapest prices. Just before the war, in Mussolini time, they had just like this. Regular price is fifteen lire. For students and soldiers half price seven-fifty–but cheap is always dangerous . . . Chemist and public bathwash," he pointed down the Vico dei Lupanare. "In southern Italy is plenty clap. Seventy per cent of people have-a the clap but now is American penicillin–whissht, in a few days!–so nobody know percentage."

Roderick purred . . . Man, excellent in wit, had discovered how to cure clap in twenty-four hours. Without resource he meets nothing that must come! So with his resource therefore he saw, in this marvelous discovery, the possibility of catching a different kind of clap every day for the next seventy-two days, perhaps on the seventy-third an absolutely unique kind.

"Wine street, woman street, and public bathwash," the guide was intoning in somber, almost biblical tones . . . "In Pompeii you pay advance. Many men come. Etrangers. Strangers, and sailors, you understand. No speak-a the Latin. But Romans make it easy. In every room is painted different position and man pick-a what he want. Ah, wine woman and song street! Wait," he added, raising an admonitory finger as Roderick seemed about to say something. "All street symbolic. All anchored east and west, north and south. Except crooked street, wine street and woman street . . . A man drunk can-a say, 'I don't know where I am. I don't-a know where I was.' So streets are straight except for curved, so he can't say I don't know where I was. Si," he said, as now they walked on down the circumambient Vico dei Lupanare toward the Strada dell' Abbondanza. "So streets are straight except for curved so he can't-a say I don't know where I was." He shook his head.

–Roderick's last memory of Eridanus was of a colossal fire: the *Salinas* meekly unloading crude oil at the refinery, innocent rakish smokestacks aft, and then bang, and up went the wharf, sirens wailing as though it were suddenly the lunch hour; then the tanker backing out silently into the inlet, or rather pulling, breaking her mooring lines, and the flames on the tanker apparently subdued as a mushroom of smoke went up on its extending columnar stalk a thousand feet into the air from the refinery: bang, bang, watching the fire from the Wildernesses' pier, for it looked like a major and terrifying disaster to the whole waterfront, his knees trembling so hard that he couldn't hold the binoculars still: bang, and the *Salinas* now motionless right opposite, and the fire getting worse, the noise of crackling, roaring, and the two-toned moaning rockets of sound of sirens, whirring diminuendo, and then, after half an hour or so, the arrival of the magnificent turreted fireboat, neighing like a horse, from the town, like a urinating dinosaur, a monitor, a medieval but supermodern fantasy, a creation of Leonardo da Vinci–and the disaster averted–unless the oil on the ebbing tide should catch fire: and the trellis work of the oil company pier clearly silhouetted against the smoke and steam: the planes flying overhead trying to photograph it for the newspapers: and the *Salinas* that seemed to have no one aboard slowly, slowly and silently steaming guiltily down and away to Port Boden: and then the excitement over, and then all afternoon the maniacal aspect of the sky, the sun like a fiery hub to a gigantic black-disked wheel tired by a rainbow, and the stink of fried oil drifting over the water, and in the evening the curious sightseers rowing over to the hissing wharf: and then to see, the next morning, though the wharf seemed half destroyed, by God, the *Salinas*, with a guilty expression, sneaking slowly and silently back to the refinery from Port Boden: the cottage on the opposite green bank slowly sliding aft of the bridge, aft of the mainmast, aft of the funnel, as with her fire-scarred paintwork to starboard she now silently soundlessly and slowly and wearing that guilty expression approached the refinery again, on which wreckage a single hose was still playing like a distant flickering white line, the *Salinas* now wearing an expression like a drunk with a hangover approaching at early morning the pub from which she has been thrown out the previous night, the necessary flag pretended to fly on the stunted foremast like a ragged tie tied with trembling hand, and the American flag at the stern as if her shirt tail were hanging out drooping aft in the windless gloomy air of seven bells in the morning, obviously half wanting to give the refinery a wide berth, but just as obviously having to pass it (and as obviously wanting to stop in), invested as it was for her with her abhorrence and like some subdued roguish Don Quixote–because of excesses there, which she did not know or could not remember but in any case would probably be blamed for, tip-toeing past the refinery, but next moment–and by God she had guts, she had character to brave the irate and weary oiltender this morning–as large as life, as if propped on elbow against the ravaged and wrecked bar of the refinery, in exactly the same place as the day before . . . "As I was saying, fellow, when we were so rudely interrupted . . ." And that evening, hours and hours later, with a shameless but unmistakably rakish raffish list to starboard toward the wharf, in exactly the same place, as if talking her head off. And then–so much for symbols and presciences of disaster!–the next morning dawning blue and clean and fresh, with white horses running past the refinery wharf, that now looked completely undamaged, and the *Salinas* gone, to be plunging innocently somewhere in the blue Pacific her hangover washed away and the fire gone, and the smell and noise and sirens gone, and the fresh green of the forest, the blowing blue and white smoke of saw-mills against the green hills, and the maniacal sky gone and the mountains high and the sea blue and cold and clean and an innocent sun over all . . .

"Where there is-a too much religion, is perdition–white, red light and a cock outside," the guide mused, discovering another horizontal emblem in the pavement outside the ex-respectable lupanar. "For-malities!" He regarded this dislocated and unusual signpost–perhaps the great-grandfather of all signposts–a moment. "Friend ask–" he began. "But how to find this-a house? Friend say: go to fountain thirty paces on left pavement is cock pointing. Friend go . . ." He gestured significantly, as if having gone. "Why for this? He goes in. Very nice, very clean, separate rooms for love and fine garden where walk around first to get excited . . ." Signor Salacci was tired and sat down for a moment on a ruined wall. The abomination of desola-tion sitting in the unholy place. "Very dirty streets," he added as now they started to move on once more. "Contrasts," he said musingly, "in everything. Roman Empire start-a in Pompeii to-a going down . . . old marbles a-broken," he said sadly. He pointed to a lone bust, sad in the brilliant sunshine. "A facsimile of Apollo–exactly the same size but–" he hissed and made a long expression–"with a lady-face, because the Greeks make everything so sweet and gentle, but the Romans make everything like this: "–he drew down a growth of savage air from his chin–"with beards."

"Roman exaggerations is," he continued after a while, "each exaggeration in life is defeat, and therefore downfalls . . . You see," he said, pointing out an example of this phenomenon, "Lime is-a stronger than stone, stones worn out, lime still good. Attention, gentlemen, the curve!" He guided their steps around a pre-Roman Doric column. "In Italian we laugh and we say, 'Attention, gentle-ment, the curve.' A pun," he explained. "Curva also mean lost woman . . ." They approached a heap of rubble. "Americans drop bombs here . . . Americans will drop bomb anywhere," he lamented delightedly. "Students walking in garden." The Fairhavens looked around but they didn't see them. "Greek theatre, soldier barrack, night theater, pine trees," he hummed. "Where is too much religion is perdition," he added; "white, red light, and a cock outside. Formalities! See, modern plumbing." And Roderick reflected, looking at the twisted pieces of big lead pipes, that once upon a time it was true, the Romans did have modern plumbing.

Until a man has built (or helped to build—for he had helped the Wildernesses build their house) a house with his own hands, Roderick thought, he may feel a sense of inferiority before such things as Greek columns. But if he happens to have helped build so much as a summer shack upon the beach he will not feel inferiority, even if he does not understand in the aggregate the entire meaning of a Doric temple. The baseless shaft, the capital, and the lower fascia, that would connect the columns, at least become clear. The shaft was analogous to the cedar piles that they had sunk into the hardpan. Capitals they had achieved without meaning to, solely because it would turn out that a pile had unintentionally been sunk too deep for the stringer and the post to be square, so between the stringer and the post they would insert a block. The wooden stringer, say a two- or three-inch plank, corresponded to the lower fascia, though if one had been completely successful the stringer would rest directly upon the post: thus, the capital, as something deliberate, perhaps had no function, and was the result of an original disharmony, when people built with wood; someone had decided, perhaps on some occasion when a mistake on one side had been balanced by a similar mistake on the other, that it was an aesthetic improvement. These curious thoughts occurred to Roderick as, bent over his camera, he was trying to get Tansy and the guide, who were having a conversation over by the Temple of Apollo, into focus, for the light from the slowly westering sun was good now and the ruins were full of interesting, if pretty obvious, shadows. Ridiculous and far-fetched though it might sound, what he had been thinking gave Roderick, finally, a certain kinship with the builders of Pompeii . . . But these Pompeiians— what had they built for? What was this instinct that made man herd together like partridges, like sardines in tomato paste, this cowardly dependence on the presence of others?

Suddenly he thought he knew what was wrong. This—in Pompeii, in Naples—this had happened to him, to Roderick McGregor Fairhaven, the visitor from Ultima Thule. What it amounted to was a feeling that there was not going to be time. Did you want to harrow yourself looking at what had been only temporarily spared, at what was finally doomed? And Roderick could not help but wonder whether man too was not beginning to stand, in some profound inexplicable sense, fundamentally in some such imperfect or dislocated relation to his environment as he. Man once stood at the center of the universe, as Elizabethan poets stood at the center of the world.– But the difference between the man-made ruins and the ruins of Pompeii was that the man-made ones had not for the most part been found worth preserving, or had been carried away. Had some precious part of man been carried away with the ruins? Partly it was as if man built with ruin in view . . . See Naples and die!

"Thank you, Tansy dear," Roderick said, clicking the shutter. "Now may I take one of you alone, Signor?"

"Si," the guide said, evidently finishing something he'd been saying to Tansy. "Si, I am Pompeiian."

And suddenly laughing as if to please them, the guide, that perfectly adjusted man, made a Roman salute, and Roderick snapped him standing there–right arm upraised, so that it drew his coat very tight under his arms, and the papers stood out of his pockets– between the pillars of the demolished Temple of Apollo.

"We thank you very much indeed for everything, Signor," Roderick said, winding the film forward and replacing the camera in his pocket.

They were about to leave Pompeii by the Porta Marina and Signor Salacci said to them: "The gate is built like a funnel, for a ventilation, to suck up fresh air from the sea, blowing up to the mountain and ventilate town–street banked very straight to the right. So when it rains, water runs to right, you walk dry on left.

"Slaves and animals on one side," he reminded them as they shook hands at the portal. "People on the other."

They all stood looking back over the ancient town toward Vesuvius and Roderick asked:

"And when do you think there's going to be another eruption, Signor?"

"Ah . . ." Signor Salacci wagged his head somberly. And then as he regarded the mountain a look of enormous pride came over his face. "But yesterday," he said, "yesterday she give-a the beeg-a shake!"

FURTHER READING

WORKS BY MALCOLM LOWRY
Ultramarine (Toronto: Clarke Irwin, 1963).
Under the Volcano (Philadelphia: J. B. Lippincott Company, 1947).

Also available in Signet paperback and Penguin edition.

Hear Us O Lord from Heaven Thy Dwelling Place (Philadelphia: J. B. Lippincott Company, 1961).

Earle Birney and Marjorie Lowry, eds., *Selected Poems of Malcolm Lowry* (San Francisco: City Lights Books, 261 Columbus Avenue, Pocket Poets Series). May also be ordered through any university book store.

Earle Birney and Marjorie Lowry, eds., *Lunar Caustic* (London: Jonathan Cape). May be ordered through Clarke Irwin Publishers, Toronto.

Dark as the Grave Wherein my Friend is Laid (Toronto: General Publishing Company).

October Ferry to Gabriola (Toronto: Nelson, Foster and Scott).

CRITICISM

William H. New, *Malcolm Lowry* (Toronto: McClelland and Stewart, Canadian Writers Series, 1972).

George Woodcock, ed., *Malcolm Lowry: The Man and his Work* (Vancouver: University of British Columbia Press, 1971).

George Woodcock, *Odysseus Ever Returning* (Toronto: McClelland and Stewart, New Canadian Library, 1970). Lowry's work is discussed.

A. J. M. Smith, ed., *Masks of Fiction* (Toronto: McClelland and Stewart, New Canadian Library, 1961). Lowry's work is discussed.

Anthony Kilgallin, *Malcolm Lowry* (Toronto: Copp Clark Publishers, Studies in Canadian Literature Series).

Harvey Breit and Marjorie Lowry, eds., *Malcolm Lowry (1909-1957): Selected Letters* (Toronto: McClelland and Stewart, 1965).

Part Two

Hugh MacLennan

Hugh MacLennan (1907-) was born in Glace Bay, Cape Breton, not only a fourth generation Canadian and Nova Scotian, but a fourth generation Cape Bretoner. The family moved to Halifax when he was seven years old. Graduating in classics from Dalhousie, he went to Oxford as a Rhodes Scholar in 1929, then continued his classical studies at Princeton for his Ph.D. Returning to Canada in 1935 he embarked on his dual career of writer and teacher, winning recognition as a foremost Canadian writer with the publication of his first novel, Barometer Rising *(1941). He won the Lorne Pierce Medal in 1952 and has several times won the Governor-General's Award. He was elected to the Royal Society of Canada in 1953 and made a Companion of the Order of Canada in 1967. He lives in Montreal where he has been for many years a teacher in the English Department of McGill University.*

THE HALIFAX EXPLOSION, 1917

eight-fifteen o'clock

Jim and Mary Fraser ate breakfast together in sunlight so bright it dazzled their eyes, for their breakfast nook overlooked the Basin, which now angled the reflected beams of the sun directly at them. After eating they watched Jean set out up the forest path with the maid for her morning's outing. Then they put on their hats and coats and went down the road to the station to catch the local train into town.

The unwonted brilliance of the day and the quietness of the air delighted Mary, and she began to speak of returning home for a lighter coat. "It's almost like Indian summer," she said.

From: Hugh MacLennan, *Barometer Rising* (Toronto: McClelland and Stewart, New Canadian Library, 1958). Reprinted by permission of McClelland and Stewart Limited, the Canadian Publishers.

Jim looked at the treetops, motionless in the still air, and then he sniffed loudly. "There's east in that wind."

"Nonsense, there isn't any wind at all."

They were still arguing good-naturedly when they boarded the train for Halifax.

There was now only one vessel moving north toward the upper harbour, the French munition ship *Mont Blanc*. An ugly craft of little more than three thousand tons, she was indistinguishable from thousands of similar vessels which came and went during these days. She was inward bound, heading for Bedford Basin to await convoy. Moving very slowly, she had crawled through the opened submarine net and now was on her way up the Stream, past the breakwater, George's Island, and then the South End docks. She had been laded a week ago in New York with a cargo consigned to a French port, but only her crew, the Admiralty authorities, and the captain of the British cruiser in port to command the convoy, knew what her main cargo was.

Men on the motionless ships in the Stream watched her pass and showed no interest. The previous day they had all received orders not to move until further notification, but none had been told they were giving sea-room to a floating bomb.

The cruiser's captain came on deck to watch the *Mont Blanc* pass and estimate the speed she would be able to produce. He was about the only person in the vicinity of Halifax to take any overt notice of her passage up the harbour.

The *Mont Blanc* moved so slowly that her bow seemed to push rather than cut the water as she crept past the cruiser. The pilot was proceeding cautiously and the cruiser's captain observed this with satisfaction. What was not so satisfactory to him was the manner in which the cargo was stowed. Her foredeck was piled with metal canisters, one on top of the other, held down with guy ropes and braced at the sides by an improvised skeleton of planks. The canisters and visible parts of the deck glistened patchily with oil. The afterdeck was clear and some sailors in dungarees were lounging there out of the wind.

"I wonder what she's got in *those things?*" the captain muttered to his Number One. "Petrol?"

"More likely lubricating oil, I should think, sir."

"I doubt it. She's not a tanker, after all. Might be benzol from the colour of it. How much speed would you say she's got in her?"

"Ten knots at the most, I'd say."

"Doubt if it's even that. I wish they'd realize that a munition ship ought to be faster than the general run of ships. I can't have a cargo like that keeping station with the rest of them. She's got to cruise on the fringe, and she needs about three extra knots to do it."

But the *Mont Blanc* glided on up the harbour with little sound or evidence of motion except for a ripple at the bows and a thin wake. She was low in the water and slightly down by the head. A very sloppily-laded ship, the cruiser's captain decided. She passed awkwardly onward, the pilot pulling her out to the exact centre of the channel as the harbour narrowed. The tricolour flapped feebly from her stern as she floated in, and as she reached the entrance to the Narrows, bells sounded in the engine-room calling for a still further reduction in speed.

eight-forty o'clock

The *Mont Blanc* was now in the Narrows and a detail of men went into her chains to unship the anchor. It would be dropped as soon as she reached her appointed station in the Basin. A hundred yards to port were the Shipyards and another hundred yards off the port bow was the blunt contour of Richmond Bluff; to starboard the shore sloped gently into a barren of spruce scrub. During the two minutes it took the *Mont Blanc* to glide through this strait, most of Bedford Basin and nearly all its flotilla of anchored freighters were hidden from her behind the rise of Richmond Bluff.

Around the projection of this hill, less than fifty fathoms off the port bow of the incoming *Mont Blanc*, another vessel suddenly appeared heading for the open sea. She flew the Norwegian flag, and to the startled pilot of the munitioner the name *Imo* was plainly visible beside the hawse. She was moving at half-speed and listing gently to port as she made the sharp turn out of the Basin to strike the channel of the Narrows. And so listing, with white water surging away from her fore-foot, she swept across the path of the *Mont Blanc*, exposing a gaunt flank labelled in giant letters BELGIAN RELIEF. Then she straightened, and pointed her bow directly at the fore-quarter of the munitioner. Only at that moment did the men on *Imo*'s bridge appear to realize that another vessel stood directly in their path.

Staccato orders broke from the bridge of the *Mont Blanc* as the two ships moved toward a single point. Bells jangled, and megaphoned shouts came from both bridges. The ships sheered in the same direction, then sheered back again. With a violent shock, the bow of the *Imo* struck the plates of the *Mont Blanc* and went grinding a third of the way through the deck and the forward hold. A shower of sparks splashed out from the screaming metal. The canisters on the deck of the *Mont Blanc* broke loose from their bindings and some of them tumbled and burst open. Then the vessels heeled away with engines reversed and the water boiling out from their screws as the propellers braked them to a standstill. They sprawled sideways across the Narrows, the *Mont Blanc* veering in toward the Halifax shore, the *Imo* spinning about with steerageway lost entirely. Finally she drifted toward the opposite shore.

For a fraction of a second there was intense silence. Then smoke appeared out of the shattered deck of the *Mont Blanc*, followed by a racing film of flame. The men on the bridge looked at each other. Scattered shouts broke from the stern, and the engine-room bells jangled again. Orders were half-drowned by a scream of rusty metal as some sailors amidships followed their own inclination and twisted the davits around to lower a boat. The scurry of feet grew louder as more sailors began to pour out through the hatches onto the deck. An officer ran forward with a hose, but before he could connect it his men were ready to abandon ship.

The film of flame raced and whitened, then it became deeper like an opaque and fulminant liquid, then swept over the canisters of benzol and increased to a roaring tide of heat. Black smoke billowed and rolled and engulfed the ship, which began to drift with the out-going tide and swing in toward the graving-dock of the Shipyards. The first trembled and leaped in a body at the bridge, driving the captain and pilot aft, and there they stood helplessly while the tarry smoke surrounded them in greasy folds and the metal of the deck began to glow under their feet. Both men glanced downward. Underneath that metal lay leashed an incalculable energy, and the bonds which checked it were melting with every second the thermometers mounted in the hold. A half-million pounds of trinitrotoluol and twenty-three hundred tons of picric acid lay there in the darkness under the plates, while the fire above and below the deck converted the hollow shell of the vessel into a bake-oven.

If the captain had wished to scuttle the ship at that moment it would have been impossible to do so, for the heat between decks would have roasted alive any man who tried to reach the sea-cocks. By this time the entire crew was in the lifeboat. The officers followed, and the boat was rowed frantically toward the wooded slope opposite Halifax. There, by lying flat among the trees, the sailors hoped they would have a chance when their ship blew up. By the time they had beached the boat, the fore-deck of the *Mont Blanc* was a shaking rampart of fire, and black smoke pouring from it screened the Halifax waterfront from their eyes. The sailors broke and ran for the shelter of the woods.

By this time men were running out of dock sheds and warehouses and offices along the entire waterfront to watch the burning ship. None of them knew she was a gigantic bomb. She had now come so close to the Shipyards that she menaced the graving-dock. Fire launches cut out from a pier farther south and headed for the Narrows. Signal flags fluttered from the Dockyard and the yardarms of ships lying in the Stream, some of which were already weighing anchor. The captain of the British cruiser piped all hands and called for volunteers to scuttle the *Mont Blanc*; a few minutes later the cruiser's launch was on its way to the Narrows with two officers and a number of ratings. By the time they reached the burning ship her plates were so hot that the seawater lapping the plimsoll line was simmering.

The *Mont Blanc* had become the centre of a static tableau. Her plates began to glow red and the swollen air inside her hold heated the cargo rapidly toward the detonation point. Launches from the harbour fire department surrounded her like midges and the water from their hoses arched up with infinite delicacy as they curved into the rolling smoke. The *Imo*, futile and forgotten, was still trying to claw her way off the farther shore.

Twenty minutes after the collision there was no one along the entire waterfront who was unaware that a ship was on fire in the harbour. The jetties and docks near the Narrows were crowded with people watching the show, and yet no warning of danger was given. At that particular moment there was no adequate centralized authority in Halifax to give a warning, and the few people who knew the nature of the *Mont Blanc*'s cargo had no means of notifying the town or spreading the alarm, and no comfort beyond the thought that trinitrotoluol can stand an almost unlimited heat provided there is no fulminate or explosive gas to detonate it.

Bells in the town struck the hour of nine, and by this time nearly all normal activity along the waterfront had been suspended. A tug had managed to grapple the *Mont Blanc* and was towing her with imperceptible movement away from the Shipyards back into the channel of the Narrows. Bluejackets from the cruiser had found the bosun's ladder left by the fleeing crew, and with flesh shrinking from the heat, were going over the side. Fire launches surrounded her. There was a static concentration, an intense expectancy in the faces of the firemen playing the hoses, a rhythmic reverberation in the beat of the flames, a gush from the hose-nozzles and a steady hiss of scalding water. Everything else for miles around seemed motionless and silent.

Then a needle of flaming gas, thin as the mast and of a brilliance unbelievably intense, shot through the deck of the *Mont Blanc* near the funnel and flashed more than two hundred feet toward the sky. The firemen were thrown back and their hoses jumped suddenly out of control and slashed the air with S-shaped designs. There were a few helpless shouts. Then all movement and life about the ship were encompassed in a sound beyond hearing as the *Mont Blanc* opened up.

nine-five o'clock

Three forces were simultaneously created by the energy of the exploding ship: an earthquake, an air-concussion, and a tidal wave. These forces rushed away from the Narrows with a velocity varying in accordance with the nature of the medium in which they worked. It took only a few seconds for the earthquake to spend itself and three minutes for the air-expansions to slow down to a gale. The tidal wave travelled for hours before the last traces of it were swallowed in the open Atlantic.

When the shock struck the earth, the rigid ironstone and granite base of Halifax peninsula rocked and reverberated, pavements split and houses swayed as the earth trembled. Sixty miles away in the town of Truro windows broke and glass fell to the ground, tingling in the stillness of the streets. But the ironstone was solid and when the shock had passed, it resumed its immobility.

The pressure of the exploding chemicals smashed against the town with the rigidity and force of driving steel. Solid and unbreathable, the forced wall of air struck against Fort Needham and Richmond Bluff and shaved them clean, smashed with one gigantic blow the North End of Halifax and destroyed it, telescoping houses or lifting them from their foundations, snapping trees and lampposts, and twisting iron rails into writhing, metal snakes; breaking buildings and sweeping the fragments of their wreckage for hundreds of yards in its course. It advanced two miles southward, shattering every flimsy house in its path, and within thirty seconds encountered the long, shield-like slope of the Citadel which rose before it.

Then, for the first time since it was fortified, the Citadel was able to defend at least a part of the town. The air-wall smote it, and was deflected in three directions. Thus some of its violence shot skyward at a twenty-degree angle and spent itself in space. The rest had to pour around the roots of the hill before closing in on the town for another rush forward. A minute after the detonation, the pressure was advancing through the South End. But now its power was diminished, and its velocity was barely twice that of a tornado. Trees tossed and doors broke inward, windows split into driving arrows of glass which buried themselves deep in interior walls. Here the houses, after swaying and cracking, were still on their foundations when the pressure had passed.

Underneath the keel of the *Mont Blanc* the water opened and the harbour bottom was deepened twenty feet along the channel of the Narrows. And then the displaced waters began to drive outward, rising against the towns and lifting ships and wreckage over the sides of the docks. It boiled over the shores and climbed the hill as far as the third cross-street, carrying with it the wreckage of small boats, fragments of fish, and somewhere, lost in thousands of tons of hissing brine, the bodies of men. The wave moved in a gigantic bore down the Stream to the sea, rolling some ships under and lifting others high on its crest, while anchor-chains cracked like guns as the violent thrust snapped them. Less than ten minutes after the detonation, it boiled over the breakwater off the park and advanced on McNab's Island, where it burst with a roar greater than a winter storm. And then the central volume of the wave rolled on to sea, high and arching and white at the top, its back glossy like the plumage of a bird. Hours later it lifted under the keel of a steamer far out in the Atlantic and the captain, feeling his vessel heave, thought he had struck a floating mine.

But long before this, the explosion had become manifest in new forms over Halifax. More than two thousand tons of red hot steel, splintered fragments of the *Mont Blanc*, fell like meteors from the sky into which they had been hurled a few seconds before. The ship's anchor soared over the peninsula and descended through a roof on the other side of the North-west Arm three miles away. For a few seconds the harbour was dotted white with a maze of splashes, and the decks of raddled ships rang with reverberations and clangs as fragments struck them.

Over the North End of Halifax, immediately after the passage of the first pressure, the tormented air was laced with tongues of flame which roared and exploded out of the atmosphere, lashing downward like a myriad blow-torches as millions of cubic feet of gas took fire and exploded. The atmosphere went white-hot. It grew mottled, then fell to the streets like a crimson curtain. Almost before the last fragments of steel had ceased to fall, the wreckage of the wooden houses in the North End had begun to burn. And if there were any ruins which failed to ignite from falling flames, they began to burn from the fires in their own stoves, onto which they had collapsed.

Over this part of the town, rising in the shape of a typhoon from the Narrows and extending five miles into the sky, was poised a cloud formed by the exhausted gases. It hung still for many minutes, white, glossy as an ermine's back, serenely aloof. It cast its shadow over twenty miles of forest land behind Bedford Basin.

nine-ten o'clock

The locomotive was still panting. Little puffs of dust spurted out from the piles of rubble and broken glass about its wheels and fell in a powder on Jim Fraser's face as he lay on his back. What had a few minutes before been a dirty roof of glass was now a pall of smoke dissolving into open sky. Sunlight shot through breaches in the brick and cement wall of the station like searchlights cutting paths through darkness, and the dust of shattered mortar danced in it.

He heard a groan and tried to move. Instantly an agony racked him as though a saw had been drawn across the bones of his spine. He tried to lift his hands but they were helpless. There was a film over his eyes and he shook his head to clear it away. Where was Mary? It was going to snow tonight, it was going to be a very cold winter. What had happened? The shock of concussion and the unbearable noise of the station falling—and that heavy glass roof, thousands of spikes and arrows of glass hurtling nearly seventy feet to the platforms!

The film momentarily cleared from his eyes and he saw bubbles of blood breaking and forming and breaking again. They were directly in front of him. They came from his own mouth. What was that triangle beyond? The square on the hypoteneuse of a right-angle triangle equals the sum of the squares on the other two sides. He tried to lift his hand again and saw another bubble break. He was wet through. Where did the apex of that triangle end? That glass triangle with the smoke smudge on its face?

The locomotive continued to pant and stir the dust. It was easier to remember now where he was. He had been passing the driver's cab heading for the news-stand at the end of the platform and Mary had been hoping he would not buy a paper because she hated hearing the war news.

"Mary—what the devil has happened?"

Silence, except for the panting of the engine, except for a queer sound somewhere in his own chest. Silence; the sort of silence that is all a man's own when he is falling asleep and hears the street noises of a strange city pass the window of his hotel.

The film cleared from his eyes again. The triangle of glass was an arrow and its apex was buried in the lung beside his heart. What a way to die, bleeding to death in North Street Station beside an idle locomotive!

He twisted his head and the pain nearly blinded him, but he saw Mary and knew that her eyes were closed and her face composed under a film of dust. Her hat was over one ear and the feather on its side flicked back and forth under the impact of the engine's exhaust. He heard a faintly hoarse sound which seemed to be his own voice calling her name, something stirred beside him and he saw her head waver through the haze, then turn over and settle like a cut flower on its stalk. Somewhere nearby a large sheet of broken glass toppled over with a puny, tinkling sound.

These things Jim Fraser perceived with a peculiar and distant curiosity before his vision darkened and all perception ceased. The locomotive continued to pant and blow dust over his face. And at the same time billions of motes of pulverized mortar began to float down through the sunbeams and settle over all the human beings who had been in the North Street Station when it crumbled.

FURTHER READING

WORKS BY HUGH MACLENNAN

Barometer Rising (Toronto: McClelland and Stewart, New Canadian Library). First published 1941.

Two Solitudes (Toronto: The Macmillan Company of Canada, Laurentian Library). First published 1945.

The Precipice (Popular Library paperback). First published 1948.

Each Man's Son (Toronto: McClelland and Stewart, New Canadian Library). First published 1951.

The Watch that Ends the Night (Signet Classic Paperback). First published 1959.

The Return of the Sphinx (Toronto: The Macmillan Company of Canada, Laurentian Library). First published 1967.

CRITICISM

Alex Lucas, *Hugh MacLennan* (Toronto: McClelland and Stewart, Canadian Writers Series, 1970).

George Woodcock, *Hugh MacLennan* (Toronto: Copp Clark Publishers, Studies in Canadian Literature Series).

Peter Buitenhuis, *Hugh MacLennan* (Toronto: Forum House Publishing Company, Writers and their Works Series). Sold through Coles Book Stores.

Robert H. Cockburn, *The Novels of Hugh MacLennan* (Montreal: Harvest House).

George Woodcock, *Odysseus Ever Returning* (Toronto: McClelland and Stewart, New Canadian Library, 1970). MacLennan's work is discussed.

A. J. M. Smith, ed., *Masks of Fiction* (Toronto: McClelland and Stewart, New Canadian Library, 1961).

AUDIO-TAPES

Canadian Writers on Tape (includes Hugh MacLennan), obtainable from: OISE, Publications Sales, 102 Bloor St. West, Toronto.

COMPARATIVE STUDY: THE HALIFAX EXPLOSION

Hugh MacLennan, *Barometer Rising* (publishing details above).

Michael Bird, *The Town that Died* (Toronto: Ryerson Press).
Thomas Raddall, *At the Tide's Turn and Other Stories* (Toronto: McClelland and Stewart, New Canadian Library, 1959).
PICTURE SERIES
Canadian Authors (includes Hugh MacLennan), obtainable from: Hilton Photo Supplies, P.O. Box 74, Chemainus, British Columbia.

Sinclair Ross

Sinclair Ross (1908-) was born near Prince Albert, Saskatche-
wan. He started working for the Royal Bank of Canada in 1924
and, being transferred from one town to another, came to know
well the prairie communities he writes about. He retired from
the bank in 1968 and at that time was planning to leave Canada
and live in Greece. He has written a number of fine short
stories, many of them published in Queen's Quarterly. *His*
highly-praised first novel, As for Me and My House *(1941) tells*
the story of a minister and his wife whose lives wither in the
arid spiritual wasteland of a little prairie town during the
'thirties.

Wednesday evening, October 18

THERE'S AN OLD MAN DYING . . .

There's an old man dying on the other side of town. This is the
second night Philip has been away to sit with him.

Last night, after he was gone, I began to think about Judith. On
his way out he said he might be late, and it isn't like him to spend
many hours at a deathbed. The thought struck me that perhaps he
had arranged to meet her somewhere. There was a strong, bitter
wind. I went from window to window, came back and sat beside the
stove a while, stared out into the night again.

It was starting to snow. I could see the flakes spinning like white,
angry flies against the pale light of the corner lamp. I turned away
at last and went to the piano–started to read, started to sew. I kept
saying to myself how wrong and foolish it was to be suspicious this
way, and all the time sat tense, pinched, my head a little forward, my
eyes fixed staring on the lamp.

From: Sinclair Ross, *As for Me and My House* (Toronto: McClelland
and Stewart, New Canadian Library, 1957). Reprinted by permission of
McClelland and Stewart, the Canadian Publishers.

There was a listening, pressing emptiness through the house. It began to hover round me, to dim the room, at last to merge with the yellow lamp flame like a haze. And then on the smooth expanse of it as on a screen my dread began to live and shape itself. I saw them meet. I saw her white face. Over and over. And I couldn't stand it. I paced, shook up the fire–paced, paced–and then I put my hat and coat on, and went outside.

There was no one to see me, but I crept down side streets, in and out of shadows like a fugitive. El Greco started following, and I cuffed him back. When finally I reached the old man's cottage I circled it, crawled through the fence, and at last gathered courage to cross the yard. Then, hugging the walls, I stole from window to window, trying to get a glimpse inside. But the blinds were all drawn. I fancied that I heard voices, but couldn't be sure for the whistle of the wind. A shadow passed the window once where I was standing, but I knew that the old man had a woman looking after him. I came home again, and waited beside the stove. The emptiness returned. I saw them together–over and over–her white face–heard her little laugh–and then it flashed on me why not pay a visit to Mrs. Wilson where Judith was working. I'd know then at least whether she were at home.

She had gone out on an errand for Mrs. Wilson to one of the neighbors. I stayed nearly an hour, waiting for her; then instead of coming home, I flattened myself against an old shed that stands on a strip of vacant ground beside the Wilson house.

I couldn't return to face the uncertainty, the yellow, lamplit emptiness. I had to see her–see the door close after her. Not that it would tell me anything–she might be alone, and still just have come from him–but though I knew that, still I huddled there.

It was colder. The snow was thickening. An automobile swung down from Main Street, revealing me for a moment in its funnel of glare. Then the night was darker than ever, like a slate, and again my dread began to write and shape itself.

It must have been another hour before she came. When at last I reached home Philip was already there. I was inside, shivering beside the stove, when I saw him. He had come to his study door, and was watching me. There was a cold stare like metal in his eyes, and a faint, half-smiling curl to his lips that made me stammer to explain myself, "It was so lonely here by myself–I went out. I went over to see Mrs. Wilson. She's not very well–expecting her baby almost any day."

His eyes shifted to my numb blue hands, then to my shoulders and arms, where there were still tight-packed little wrinkles of snow to tell him how long I had been out of doors. "With Mrs. Wilson–all evening." He spoke in a thin voice. His eyes came back to my face hard and unrelenting. "It was kind of you."

He turned into his study, and on a sharp sudden impulse I ran to him. "No"–I caught his hand and made him look at me. "You mustn't think that–what you're thinking. I haven't seen Paul to-night –I wasn't with him–you must believe me."

"Paul?" He was still cold and hard. "Who mentioned Paul? I thought it was Mrs. Wilson, going to have her baby?"

"I was lying–you know. I haven't seen anyone tonight. Just Mrs. Wilson for a few minutes. It was the wind, and the empty house–I couldn't sit listening to it any longer. I went out and walked up the railroad track. But it's such a cold night to go walking–I thought you wouldn't believe me–and that's the only reason that I lied."

He drew a chair up to the stove and made me sit down. I don't know whether he believed me or not. His mouth softened a little. A look came into his eyes as if he were sorry for me. But he said nothing, and after a minute went back to his study.

And all for nothing. I learned from Mrs. Bird today that he and the doctor were both with the old man till half-past ten–and when I got back it was a quarter to eleven. Tonight while he's there again I'm being sensible, thinking sanely, staying safe beside the fire. But I'm hoping just the same that the old man doesn't last to take him out another night.

FURTHER READING

NOVELS BY SINCLAIR ROSS
As for Me and My House (Toronto: McClelland and Stewart, New Canadian Library, 1957). First published 1941.
The Well (Toronto: The Macmillan Company of Canada). First published 1958.
A Whir of Gold (Toronto: McClelland and Stewart, 1971).
SHORT STORIES BY SINCLAIR ROSS
The Lamp at Noon and Other Stories (Toronto: McClelland and Stewart, New Canadian Library, 1968).
CRITICISM
R. Chambers, *Ernest Buckler and Sinclair Ross* (Toronto: Copp Clark Publishers, Studies in Canadian Literature Series).
AUDIO-VISUAL
Canadian Writers on Tape (includes Sinclair Ross), obtainable from: OISE, 102 Bloor St. West, Toronto.

"*As for Me and My House* is about to be made into a movie by Milne Pearson Productions, with Kate Reid playing Mrs. Bentley. Graeme Gibson is doing the script."
Toronto Daily Star, November 13, 1970.

RELATED FICTION

W. O. Mitchell, *Who Has Seen the Wind* (Toronto: The Macmillan Company of Canada, 1947).

PICTURE SERIES

Canadian Authors (includes Sinclair Ross), obtainable from: Hilton Photo Supplies, P.O. Box 74, Chemainus, British Columbia.

Gabrielle Roy

Gabrielle Roy (1909-) now lives and works in Quebec City. But she was born in the French-Canadian community of St. Boniface, Manitoba, where her father was colonization agent for the federal government, and spent the first twenty-nine years of her life in rural Manitoba. For a time she was a schoolteacher, then considered making the theatre her career and went to England to study dramatics. But on her return she became a free-lance journalist in Montreal. Her first novel, Bonheur d'Occasion *(1945), for which she won the Governor-General's Award and the Prix Fémina (France, 1947), is based on her knowledge of the lives of Montreal slum dwellers. She was elected to the Royal Society of Canada in 1947, the first woman to be so honoured, and was made a Companion of the Order of Canada in 1967, the year that award was established.*

WHAT ARE YOU DOING TONIGHT?

Where was the young man who had given her so many admiring glances yesterday? Florentine found herself watching out for him eagerly, although the memory of his bantering tone was still fresh in her mind. The noon-hour rush was in full swing.

The fever of the store communicated itself to her in a kind of irritation, mingled with a vague feeling that some day all this seething activity would come to a stop, and her purpose in life would become plain. It never occurred to her that she might meet her fate elsewhere than here, enveloped in the pungent aroma of caramel, between the tall mirrors pasted over with strips of paper announcing the day's menu, and to the crackling report of the cash register, a sound like the very expression of her frantic hopes. For her this

From: Gabrielle Roy, *The Tin Flute* (Toronto: McClelland and Stewart, New Canadian Library, 1969). Reprinted by permission of McClelland and Stewart, the Canadian Publishers.

place summed up the pinched, hurried, restless character of her whole life in Saint-Henri.

Her glance slipped past the five or six diners she was serving toward the front of the store–the restaurant was in the rear of the five-and-ten–and in the play of light on the nickeled panels, the glass and the tinware, her peevish smile attached itself aimlessly to sparkling objects here and there.

Her duties as waitress permitted her no leisure in which to dwell on the memory of what had happened yesterday, but in fleeting moments the face of the unknown youth came back to her again and again. Neither the clatter of the dishes, however, nor the shrill voices of the other waitresses as they called out their orders, could rouse her completely from her reverie, which from time to time sent little tremors over her face.

Suddenly she felt disconcerted, almost abashed. While she had been watching out for him among the crowd at the swinging doors of the store, the young stranger had seated himself at the counter and was calling her impatiently. She moved toward him, pouting. It was annoying to have him take her by surprise just as she was trying to remember his features and the tone of his voice.

"What's your name?" he snapped.

More than the question itself, his mocking, almost insolent manner put her back up.

"You'd like to know, wouldn't you?" she answered scornfully, but without finality, not as if she wanted to silence him. On the contrary, her tone invited a reply.

"Come now," he urged, with a smile. "My name's Jean. Jean Lévesque. And to start with, I know yours is Florentine. . . . It's Florentine here, Florentine there . . . Florentine's in a bad temper today; you can't get a smile out of her. You see I know your first name. I like it, too."

Then he changed his tone imperceptibly and gave her a rather stern look.

"But you're Mademoiselle who? Won't you tell me?" he insisted with feigned seriousness.

As he moved his face closer she could read all the impudence in his eyes. Today for the first time she noticed his firm willful jaw, the insufferable mockery in his dark eyes, and she was furious with herself. What a fool she was to have bothered about a fellow like that! She drew herself up so sharply that her little amber necklace rattled.

"Next you'll be asking me where I live and what I'm doing tonight," she said. "I know your kind!"

"My kind! What kind?" he mocked, pretending to look over his shoulder to see if there were someone behind him.

"Oh, you!" she burst out in vexation.

And yet that common, almost vulgar touch placed the young man on her own level, and displeased her less than his usual language and behavior, which, she felt dimly, put a distance between them. The smile returned to her face, a petulant, provocative smile.

"Okay," she said. "What'll you have today?"

But he continued to stare at her impudently.

"I hadn't got around to asking you what you're doing to-night," he answered. "I wasn't in that much of a hurry. Usually it takes me at least three days more to get to that point. But as long as you give me a lead . . ."

He threw himself back in his revolving chair and spun around from side to side, his eyes narrowing as he examined her.

"Well, Florentine, what are you doing tonight?"

He saw at once that his question had upset her. She caught her lower lip in her teeth to keep it from trembling. Then with a businesslike air she pulled a paper napkin from the container, unfolded it, and spread it out in front of the young man.

She had a thin, delicate, almost childish face. As she struggled to get a grip on herself the small blue veins in her temples swelled and throbbed, and the skin of her cheeks, smooth, and fine-textured as silk, was drawn toward the almost transparent wings of her nose. Her mouth quivered from time to time. But Jean was particularly struck by the expression in her eyes. Under the high arch of her plucked and penciled eyebrows, her lowered lids concealed all but a glint of bronze, but he could see that the eyes were watchful, and yet extraordinarily eager. Then the eyelids fluttered open and the whole pupil became visible, full of a sudden iridescence. A mass of light brown hair fell over her shoulders.

In observing her thus intently the young man had no definite purpose in mind. She surprised him more than she attracted him. He had not planned his last words: "What are you doing tonight?" They had sprung to his lips without his being aware of it; he had tossed them out as one might test the depth of a pool with a pebble. However, the result encouraged him to go on. Would I be ashamed to go out with her? he wondered. And then the idea of restraining himself for such a reason, considering how little he cared for the girl, annoyed him and put him on his mettle. With his elbows on the counter and his eyes glued on Florentine, he waited patiently for her next move, as if they were playing a cruel game.

She stiffened under this brutal examination, and he saw her more clearly. Catching her reflection in the mirror against the wall, he was startled to see how thin she was. She had pulled the belt of her green uniform about her waist as far as it would go, but her clothes still hung loosely on her slender body. The young man had a sudden insight into the narrow life of such a girl afloat in the turbulent eddy of Saint-Henri. Like all the girls of her type, she had probably been scorched by the meager little fires of fictitious love in the pages of cheap novels.

His voice became sharp, incisive.

"Do you come from around here, from Saint-Henri?" he asked.

She twitched her shoulders, and gave him a rueful smile by way of response.

"Me too," he added with mocking condescension. "So we can be friends. No?"

He noticed that her hands were shaking, hands as fragile as those of a child; he saw her collarbones sticking out above the opening of her blouse.

After a moment she leaned sideways against the counter before him, trying to hide her uneasiness under a sulky air, but he no longer saw her as she was. He saw her in his mind's eye all primped up, ready to go out in the evening, her cheeks plastered with rouge to conceal her pallor, cheap jewelry rattling all over her skinny person, wearing a silly little hat, perhaps a veil, her eyes glittering with makeup, a flighty girl, bent on making herself attractive to him, Jean Lévesque. The thought went through him like a gust of wind.

"Then you'll come to the movies with me tonight?"

He was aware of her hesitation. If he had taken the trouble to state his invitation more politely, in all likelihood she would have agreed immediately. But that was how he wanted it; hard and straight, since he was inviting her in spite of himself, against his will.

"All right then. It's a date," he said. "Now bring me your famous special."

Whereupon he pulled a book out of the pocket of his overcoat, which was lying on the seat beside him, opened it, and immediately became absorbed.

A flush spread over Florentine's cheeks. She hated him for his power to disturb her deeply one moment and put her out of his mind the next, dropping her as if she did not interest him in the slightest degree. And yet it was he who had made all the advances in the last few days. She had not taken the first step. It was he who had aroused her from the torpor in which she had taken refuge from the disappointments of her daily life, it was he who had awakened her from the deep trance where suffering could not touch her, where she was alone with her undefined hopes. It was he who had given form to those hopes, now clear, sharp, tormenting as desire.

As she looked at him her heart contracted. She found him very attractive. To her he seemed the well-dressed young man, unlike the others she waited on at the store, dull salesmen or workmen with greasy sleeves and collars. He was a cut above the silly youths she ran across at the neighborhood cafés, juke-box joints where she and Pauline and Marguerite went dancing in the evening, or idled the hours away in a booth, nibbling chocolate and giggling at the boys as they came in. Yes, he was different from anyone she had ever met in the course of her timid, uneventful life. She liked the way his thick black hair bristled up from his forehead; at times she had to suppress an impulse to seize his wild thatch with both hands.

She had marked him out the first time he had come to the five-and-ten, and had schemed to wait on him. Now she longed both to run away from him and defy him at the same time, to prove that he meant nothing to her. Some fine day he'll try to make a date with me, she had said to herself with a strange sense of power in the hollow of her chest. And then she wondered: Will I take him up?

The other girls, Louise, Pauline, Marguerite, all except Eveline, who acted as manager, were always teasing each other about making dates with young men at the lunch hour. Pauline claimed that you ran no risk if the fellow called for you at home and took you to the movies. Then you had plenty of time to look him over and decide whether you wanted to continue seeing him. Louise had even become engaged to a young soldier she had first met at the restaurant. Ever since the war began the new recruits had shown considerable eagerness to form attachments before they went off to training camp. Friendships sprang up quickly and under altogether novel conditions, some of them ending in marriage.

Florentine dared not follow her thought through to the end. Even while reading, the young man wore a quizzical expression at the corners of his mouth that baffled her.

I'll show him, she thought, pursing her lips. I'll show him that I don't give a rap for him. But curiosity to see what he was reading overcame her momentary vexation. She leaned boldly over the open book. It was a trigonometry textbook. The queer shapes of the triangles and the polygons, the heavy black print of the equations, all of it totally incomprehensible to her, made her smile inwardly.

"No wonder you're so fresh," she said, "when you read stuff like that!"

And tripping over to the order phone she called out in a shrill, affected voice: "One thirty-cent special!"

Her piercing tone carried all over the restaurant, and Jean Lévesque felt the blood rush to his face. His eyes flamed darkly for a moment with resentment. Then pulling his book closer, he bent over it again, his face in his strong brown hands.

New customers were crowding around the counter in the usual noon-time rush: a few workmen from nearby factories, store clerks from Notre-Dame Street in white collars and felt hats, two Sisters of Mercy in gray cloaks, a taxi driver, and several housewives breaking up a shopping tour with a cup of hot coffee or a plate of fish and chips. The five waitresses were on the go constantly, colliding with each other as they darted about. Sometimes a spoon fell to the tiled floor with a hard, ringing sound. A girl would pick it up in passing, toss it into the sink with a grumble, and tear off with lowered head leaning forward to gain speed. They were always in one another's way. Their brisk staccato steps, the rustle of their starched blouses, the click of the toaster when the toast popped out, the purr of the coffeepots on the electric plates, the buzzing of the kitchen phone, all these made a sustained clatter, a vibration as of summer, distilling vanilla flavors and sugary scents. One could hear too the stifled rumble of the malted-milk shakers, like the interminable murmur of flies caught in glue, then the tinkle of a coin on the counter, and the ring of the cash register from time to time, like a period. Although the swinging glass doors at the entrance to the store were covered with frost in fantastic patterns, here, in the rear, the heat was tropical.

Marguerite, a big fat girl whose naturally rosy cheeks seemed to be smarting from cold even in this hot-box, had charge of the ice cream. She would lift the lid of the cooler, plunge the scoop into the cream and empty the contents into a large glass dish. Then she would squeeze a bit of whipped cream out of a pastry bag like toothpaste from a tube. Over this went a spoonful of marshmallow, caramel or some other syrup, the whole surmounted with half a maraschino cherry of an alluring red. In a twinkling the fifteen-cent sundae special, a favorite with the customers, appeared on the table, like a cool fountain on a burning summer day. Marguerite would pick up a coin, deposit it in the cash register, and return to create another sundae special. The procedure never varied, but Marguerite took as much care and innocent pleasure in building her masterpiece the tenth time as the first. Of peasant stock, she had only recently come to stay with relatives in the city, and she had not yet lost her illusions about the cheap glitter of the quarter. Nor was she surfeited with the wonders or the sugary smells of the restaurant. The animation, the flirtations going on about her continually, the atmosphere of pursuit and recoil, of halfhearted compliance, of temptation and daring, all this amused and delighted her, without troubling her deeply. "Florentine's boy-friend," as she designated Jean Lévesque, had made a great impression on her. And as Florentine went by, carrying a plate loaded with food, she could not help making her usual remark, with a hearty, kindly laugh:

"Your boy-friend's giving you the eye, eh?"

And licking her moist lips, which always seemed to taste of marshmallow, she added:

"I think he's smart, Florentine, and a good-looker, too. He'll come around soon."

Florentine gave her a smile of disdain. Marguerite was such a fool. To her, life was a perpetual round of sundaes, at the end of which each one of the girls, without half trying, without lifting a little finger, would find herself engaged, married, in her wedding dress, with a little bouquet in her hand. As she approached Jean Lévesque, nevertheless, Florentine had the not unpleasant thought that the young man must really have shown her some special attention since a girl as dumb as Marguerite had noticed it and could tease her about it. But what a funny way to pay attention to a girl, she thought with a start, her face clouding over.

She placed the food in front of Jean Lévesque and waited for him to speak to her. But absorbed in his reading, he only murmured "Thank you," without raising his eyes; then, absent-mindedly, he took his fork and began to eat, while she lingered, irresolute, finding his silence even harder to bear than his odd way of talking. At least when he spoke to her she had the pleasure of a retort. She walked slowly back to the other end of the counter to watch the hot dogs on the grill. All of a sudden she felt unutterably weary and depressed. Her body drooped against the edge of the sink.

God, how tired she was of this job! Waiting on rough men who made insulting advances, or else others, like Jean Lévesque, who made sport of her. Waiting on people, always waiting on people! And forever smiling, when her feet felt as if she were walking on a bed of hot coals! Smiling when her aching legs were about to give way with exhaustion! Smiling no matter how enraged and miserable she might be!

In repose her face took on a look of stupefaction. For the moment, despite her heavy make-up, the image of the old woman she would become was superimposed on her childish features. By the set of her lips one could foresee the wrinkles into which the fine modeling of her cheeks would dissolve. All youth, confidence, vivacity seemed to have fled from her listless, shrunken eyes, leaving a vacuum. But it was not only the mature woman that appeared portentously in Florentine's face; even more shocking were the marks of inherited debility and deep poverty that she bore. These seemed to rise from the depths of her somber pupils and spread like a veil over the naked, unmasked face.

All this passed in less than a minute. Abruptly Florentine straightened up, and the smile returned of itself to her rouged lips, as if it responded not to her will, but to some powerful reflex, the natural ally of her challenge to life. Of all the confused thoughts that had run through her mind, she retained only one, a conviction as clear and sharp as her congealed smile, that she must immediately stake everything she still had to offer, all her physical charm, on one wild chance of happiness. As she leaned over the counter to pick up some dirty dishes, she caught a glimpse of Jean Lévesque's profile, and it came to her with the force of a staggering blow, that whether she wished it or not, she could no longer be indifferent to him. She had never been so ready to hate him. Save for his name, which she had just learned, she knew nothing about him. Louise, who was a little better informed, said that he was employed at a foundry as an electrical machinist. From Louise too she had heard that Jean never went out with girls, an item that had intrigued her. It was a pleasing thought.

She glanced down the length of the counter. Out of the corner of her eye she could see a row of faces bent over plates, mouths open, jaws chewing, greasy lips–a sight that usually infuriated her–and then, at the end of the table, the square shoulders of her young man in his well-cut brown suit. One of his hands cupped his face; his brown skin was drawn tight over his cheeks; his teeth were clenched. Fine lines spread fanwise from his chin to his temples. Young as he appeared, light furrows were already drawn on his stubborn brow. And his eyes, whether skimming over nearby objects or studying his book, were hard and brilliant.

Florentine stole up on him and observed him minutely through half-closed lids. His suit was made of English cloth, unlike the stuff to be found in the neighborhood stores. It seemed to her that his clothing indicated a special character, an almost privileged kind of existence. Not that the youth dressed with studied elegance; on the contrary, he affected a certain carelessness. His tie was knotted loosely, his hands still bore slight traces of grease, he wore no hat in any weather, and his hair was thick and unmanageable from exposure to sun and rain and heavy frost. But it was just this negligence in small details that lent importance to the expensive things he wore: the wrist watch whose dial flashed with every gesture, the heavy silk scarf draped about his neck, the fine leather gloves sticking out of his pocket. Florentine had the feeling that if she leaned over him she would catch the very essence of the big city, with its well-dressed, well-fed, contented people on their rounds of pleasure. She visualized St. Catherine Street in Montreal, the windows of the big department stores, the fashionable crowd on Saturday evening, the florists' displays, the revolving doors of the restaurants, their tables almost flush with the street behind glittering plate glass, the brightly lit theater lobbies, with their long passages beyond the cashier's cage leading up between walls of mirrors, past polished rails and potted plants, up, up toward the screen where the most beautiful pictures in the world are shown: all that she most longed for, admired, envied, swam before her eyes. Surely this boy knew how to have a good time on Saturday night! As for her, when did she ever have a good time? On rare occasions, to be sure, she had gone out with young men, but only to a cheap movie in the neighborhood, or to some run-down dance-hall on the outskirts of town. In return for such paltry entertainment they always tried to get their money's worth in kisses, and thus she could not even enjoy the movie because she would be so busy holding them off. Her few trips over to the west side of the city with some other girls had not proved enjoyable. On the contrary, she had been angry and ashamed to be seen in a group of chattering females. Every passing couple had caught her eye and increased her resentment. The city was made for couples, not for four or five silly girls with their arms interlaced, strolling up St. Catherine Street, stopping at every shop window to admire things they would never own.

But the city beckoned to her now through Jean Lévesque. Because of this stranger how brilliant were the lights, how gay the crowd! Even the spring no longer seemed so far away; the stunted trees of Saint-Henri seemed about to turn green! But for the extreme constraint she felt in his presence, she would have cried out: "Let's be friends; we are made for each other!" And again she felt an absurd impulse to bury her hands in his tousled hair. Never before had she met anyone who bore so many visible marks of success. He might be nothing but a machinist at this moment, but she was confident that he would be prosperous in the future, a future with which a strong instinct urged her to ally herself.

She came to, from far away, and asked him in the tough accent she assumed for the customers:

"Well, do you want dessert?"

Jean raised his head, squared his broad shoulders and gave her a glance of mingled impatience and mischief.

"No. But you . . . you haven't told me yet if I'm to be the lucky guy tonight. You've had ten minutes to think it over; what have you decided? Are you coming to the movies with me, yes or no?"

He saw Florentine's green pupils light up with impotent rage, but quickly she lowered her eyes. When she replied, her voice was both angry and mournful, yet with a conciliatory undertone.

"Why should I go to the movies with you? I don't know you! How should I know who you are?"

He chuckled. It was obvious that she was fishing for information about him.

"Come now," he said. "You'll find that out gradually, if you've a mind to."

Dismayed less by his evasion than by his detachment, Florentine thought to herself in some shame: He wants me to do all the talking. Maybe he only wants to make fun of me. And she herself broke into a forced laugh.

But his attention had turned from her. He seemed to be listening to sounds out in the street. A moment later Florentine heard the distant beating of drums. A crowd was gathering in front of the store windows. Salesgirls who were unoccupied hurried to the street side of their counters. Although Canada had declared war against Germany six months before, military parades were still a novelty in the Saint-Henri quarter.

A platoon filed past the five-and-ten. Florentine leaned forward to see with breathless, almost childish interest, as the soldiers swung by, lusty fellows, stalwart in their heavy khaki coats, their arms stiff under a light powdering of snow. She whirled around to look at Jean, as if to have him witness the girlish delight in her face, but his expression was so hostile, so scornful, that she shrugged her shoulders and left him, eager not to miss anything of the show going on in the street. The latest recruits were moving into her line of vision; they were in civilian clothes, some in light suits, others wearing shabby fall coats, torn and patched, pierced by the bitter wind. She knew by sight some of these young men marching behind the soldiers. Like her own brother, like her father, they had long been on relief. And suddenly, mingled with her consciousness of the exciting and inscrutable elements of the military pageant, she had a vague intuition that desperate poverty had found its final solution in war. As in a dream she recalled the depression years when she alone of her entire family had been able to bring any money home. And even before that, when her mother had gone out to work by the day. A vivid picture of Rose-Anna passed before her eyes, making her wretched as usual. For a moment she saw these men marching by in their tatterdemalion rags through the eyes of her mother. But her mind could not long retain an idea with dreary associations. Such as it was, the parade was a distraction, a break in the monotony of her long hours at the store. Her eyes wide, her cheeks flushed under the rouge, she turned again to Jean Lévesque, and remarked coolly, almost lightheartedly: "It's crazy, don't you think?"

Far from smiling at her sally, as she had hoped, he eyed her with such animosity that she felt a flicker of joy, almost of vengeance, as she thought: "Why he's a crazy fool too!" And it gave her a spark of satisfaction to have judged him so severely in her mind.

He meanwhile was rubbing his hand over his face as if to wipe out unpleasant thoughts, or perhaps simply to hide a sardonic smile, and then, catching the girl's eye, he pressed her once more:

"What's your name? Tell me your name."

"Florentine Lacasse," she answered drily, already sobered after her little victory, and angry because she could not wriggle out of his clutches.

"Florentine Lacasse," he murmured, as he felt for change in his trouser pocket. "Very well, Florentine Lacasse, until you find a soldier boy to suit your taste, you can always meet me tonight in front of the Cartier Theater. Eight o'clock, if that's all right with you," he added, almost in jest.

Florentine made no move. Disappointed though she was, the temptation was great. She thought it over. This was not the kind of date she had hoped for. However, they were showing *Bitter Sweet* at the Cartier. Yesterday Marguerite had told her the story; it was thrilling. Florentine felt more and more comforted as she remembered her new hat and the perfume she had just bought, and thought of what a handsome couple they would make, she and Jean, since they were both about the same height. People would look at them twice as they walked down the street. She went so far as to imagine the gossip that would be spread on her account. The idea of being a subject for gossip tickled her. What did she care what stupid people thought! She pictured herself after the movie in a smart restaurant, alone with her young man in a booth, while soft music was wafted to them from the automatic phonograph. There she would be sure of her power and her charm. There she would make this insolent boy eat out of her hand. She would lead him on to offer one invitation after another. A dreamy, artless smile began to play about her mouth just as Jean rose and threw a half-dollar on the table.

"Keep the change," he said coldly. "And use it to eat some solid food. You're much too skinny."

A nasty retort rose to her lips. She was deeply hurt, more by her secret subjection to him than anything else, and would have thrown the coin back at him, but that Jean was already slipping into his overcoat.

"You hate me, don't you?" he murmured. "You hate it here, you hate everything," he continued relentlessly, as if he could see clear through to the very core of her, a waste land where nothing grew but bitterness and dissent.

Then off he went with quick strides, his shoulders swinging with determination and nervous energy. It was unnecessary for him to elbow his way through the crowd; a path opened at his approach. As she watched him leave, Florentine had almost a presentiment that she would never see him again if she did not keep the appointment. She had a blind conviction that this stranger knew her, instinctively, better than she knew herself. He came to her darting lightning, and in an instant she had discerned a thousand aspects of her life that had hitherto been obscure. Now that he had gone she seemed to be sinking back again into ignorance of her own thoughts. A deep uneasiness took possession of her. I won't go, I won't go, he'll see if I go, she said to herself, digging her nails into her palms. But just then she caught Eveline's watchful eye, and repressed a giggle. Marguerite pushed past her, carrying a sundae, and whispered:

"It wouldn't get me down if he made eyes at me, that guy. He's just my type!"

And Florentine's anger subsided, making way for the agreeable sensation of being envied. Never in her life had any object, or friendship, or experience acquired value for her save through the eyes of others.

FURTHER READING

WORKS BY GABRIELLE ROY

Bonheur d'Occasion (Montréal: Société des Editions Pascal, 1945). English translation–*The Tin Flute* (Toronto: McClelland and Stewart, New Canadian Library, 1969).

La Petite Poule d'eau (Montréal: Beauchemin, 1950). English translation–*Where Nests the Water Hen* (Toronto: McClelland and Stewart, New Canadian Library, 1961).

Alexandre Chenevert (Montréal: Beauchemin, 1954). English translation–*The Cashier* (Toronto: McClelland and Stewart, New Canadian Library, 1963).

Rue Deschambault (Montréal: Beauchemin, 1955). English translation–*Street of Riches* (Toronto: McClelland and Stewart, New Canadian Library, 1957).

La Route d'Altamount (Montréal: Editions HMH, 1966). English translation–*The Road Past Altamount* (Toronto: McClelland and Stewart, 1966).

La Rivière sans Repos (Montréal: Beauchemin, 1970).
English translation–*Windflower* (Toronto: McClelland and Stewart, 1970).

CRITICISM

Phyllis Grosskurth, *Gabrielle Roy* (Toronto: Forum House Publishing Company). Sold through Coles Book Stores.

Ethel Wilson

Ethel Wilson (1890-), née Bryant, was born in South Africa of English parents. Orphaned at an early age, she came to Vancouver as a school girl to live with her mother's family, the Malkins, recently emigrated from Staffordshire and establishing themselves as leaders of that frontier community. The Innocent Traveller *(1949) is a biography, thinly disguised as fiction, of that family, centering around one of its members, the irrepressible Eliza Phillips Edge, the Topaz Edgeworth of the novel. Ethel Wilson taught school until her marriage in 1920. Her first short story, "I Just Love Dogs," appeared in the* New Statesman *and was included in O'Brien's* Best Short Stories of 1937. *She was fifty-seven when her first novel,* Hetty Dorval *(1947) was published, and in the next nine years she produced four more. She received the Lorne Pierce Medal in 1964 and an Order of Canada Medal of Service in 1970.*

WEDNESDAY

If there was one person more than another that Mort liked seeing, it was Eddie Hansen. They had worked together at a logging camp up Jervis Inlet when jobs were scarce in Vancouver and Mort could get no work in town; and they had got drunk together more than once when Eddie had come down to Vancouver, and if there was one person more than another that Myrtle couldn't stand the sight of, it was Eddie Hansen.

Eddie Hansen was tall and fair and pleasant-looking and slow moving, with a quizzical look caused by a dropped eyelid, and as he moved among other men he was almost head and shoulders above them. He was a powerfully built logger, a high rigger, and was well

Adapted from: Ethel Wilson, *The Equations of Love* (Toronto: The Macmillan Company of Canada, 1952). Reprinted by permission of the publisher.

known and well liked up and down the coast, and he got good money. When he was on his job which was now at a big logging camp at Knight Inlet, he never drank, but when he came to town as he did two or three times a year, then he drank.

Eddie was technically and legally a widower. Actually he never thought of himself as a widower at all. He was no widower. The word widower carries a dominant overtone of loss. Eddie had nothing to do with loss. He had forgotten what his wife Signe had looked like and he did not care; he never liked Signe anyway and he had forgotten her. He did not care for women except sometimes. Then he forgot them again. But he had a lot of friends up and down the coast and in Vancouver. He liked Mortimer Johnson, and sometimes he dropped Mort a letter which read like a telegram without the word Stop in it.

"DEAR MORT:

Well how are you Mort may bee Ile be down by fridy boat if I doent get tite on the bot Ile go to Olys place and if I do get tite I gess Ile go to the same old place ware I all ways went you no Mort well so long and Ile be seeing you dont you forget it Mort and oblidge

EDDIE H."

Eddie had sent Mort a note of that kind when he came down at the New Year's which Myrtle remembered with so much resentment and which she unwisely cast up at Mort whenever she sniffed one sniff on him. But this time, when Eddie was to land in Vancouver on the very Tuesday that Mort went to work at little Horse Dunkerley's, Eddie sent Mort no letter because he remembered how that wife of Mort's gave him hell last New Year's, and if he saw Mort, well and good; and if he didn't, it was too bad.

This time Eddie began to drink on the boat coming down from Knight Inlet. He had a certain brash charm and he became very funny. But many people who had laughed with him and encouraged him at the beginning of the trip wished later on that they had never given Eddie any encouragement at all, because by the time they were halfway down the coast Eddie had become far too friendly and had adopted them completely, still being funny, but tiresome now; his charm had palled and was not charm any more; and towards the end of the journey, by evening, as the boat steamed below the golden lights of the beautiful Lions' Gate Bridge and entered the harbour of Vancouver, Eddie was beginning to be hostile, and resented the less warm attitude of all his dear friends on the boat. When the boat at last docked it was all right, because people got away from Eddie, and, safe in the immunity of shore and darkness, they walked quickly into the night as if Eddie no longer existed. The brush-off.

It took Eddie some time and argument to find his suitcase. His suitcase contained his store clothes to wear in Vancouver, if he ever got sobered up enough to put them on. He had a suit of very bright blue which he had chosen from amongst some other more conservative suits of clothes at the Army and Navy Stores, and an overcoat with a velvet collar which he had bought at a second-hand store on Cordova Street. When Eddie was sober and wore his overcoat with a velvet collar he did not look like a high rigger, bold and strong, magnificent among men, a rollicking Paul Bunyan of the Canadian woods, which he was; but like an imitation deacon, which he was not.

Eddie found his own suitcase and picked it up and stumbled along in the lighted dark in the rear of the smartly stepping crowd off the boat who so soon vanished out of his sight intent on their own business, weighed down, too, with hand baggage or packs. He knew that he was rather but not quite tight, and this decided him not to go to Mount Pleasant and stay with his friends Mr. and Mrs. Ole Almquist to whom he was always welcome when sober, but to go along Powell Street to the Regal Rooms where he often stayed and where he knew a guy who knew a guy who could get him some bottles of good rye any time he wanted.

Eddie reached the Regal Rooms all right, and met there a couple of friends, and after they had slapped each other largely upon the shoulders they went on to make a night of it, and so it was that in the early morning they all helped each other to bed, aided by the proprietor, and they all slept in their clothes.

Eddie's friends Mr. and Mrs. Almquist, who had been notified by Eddie of his probable arrival, looked at each other at about eleven o'clock, and Mrs. Almquist said to her husband, "Well, Ole, I guess Eddie's done it again," and they waited no longer, but turned out the lights and went to bed. Mrs. Almquist lay awake for a while, regretting that such a nice fellow as Eddie should be so dumb, and then she went to sleep.

It was in the early afternoon of Wednesday that Eddie woke up and thought he'd better get up and put on his good blue suit and go out somewhere. He didn't feel so good and thought that perhaps Herman might not be feeling so good either, and first of all he'd better go and find Hermy and what about a little drink. So he took a bottle and went to find Hermy's room which was on another floor, and when he got there he found that Hermy had got up and gone out. He felt affronted and deceived by this action of Hermy's and so he had a little drink. He then remembered his blue suit and started back to his room. But because of his condition, he did not go back to his own room, all the rooms being very much alike, but went into another room, had another drink, lay down on the bed and went to sleep again.

When he woke up late in the afternoon he pulled himself together once more and thought again of his bright blue suit. He got up and went again to his suitcase, but the suitcase was not there. Who had taken his suitcase? Eddie became very angry. It was a shame that a guy could not leave his room for two minutes without having his suitcase stolen off of him. As he stood looking down at where his suitcase was not, the thought came spinning into his head, righted itself, and straightened itself up and stated that perhaps he had never brought his suitcase to the Regal Rooms at all, but had left it on the dock. So he started down the stairs which heaved up and down at him and at last he reached the door. All this time he was talking to himself or somebody.

When poor Eddie (who three days ago was so fine and strong and knowledgeable and sober, shinning skilfully up the great firs and monumental cedars on the sloping shores of Knight Inlet) began to progress along Powell Street towards the docks, he found the going hard. He addressed the passers-by, but they, silent as fishes, swam noiselessly past and vanished. He spoke to them loudly, greeting them, telling them what he thought of them for passing him silently like fishes, and telling them that he had lost his suitcase. They did not care and continued to swim past him past him swimming past him. He beckoned and waved to them but they, suddenly multiplying to three or four apiece and then vanishing, neither saw nor heard him. They saw and heard him all right, but found it more convenient to appear blind and deaf to Eddie Hansen. As Eddie weaved along he discovered that one side of the pavement of Powell Street was no good. That was, really, the curb side. The other side was good and there was something hard which responded to you by holding you up. That was a house or a shop. So tall Eddie travelled along, leaning against this something solid from time to time, and it was as he took his ease against The Fishermen's Book Shop and harangued the shadows that slid by him without caring that he had lost his suitcase, that he saw as in a wavering cloud the good face of his friend Mort Johnson.

Eddie lunged out awkwardly and seized Mort strongly by some part of him and a great gladness filled him, and before he told Mort about going down to the dock to find his suitcase, he pumped Mort's arm up and down and told him again and again how fine it was to

see him; and Morty was just as glad to see old Eddie, his big friend
and high rigger, Paul Bunyan of Jervis Inlet, good old Eddie, drunk
or sober.

Morty felt some kind of protective feeling for Eddie drunk. He had
never come across Eddie drunk before. He had got drunk with Eddie,
which was quite a different thing, and did not engender a protective
feeling. But now Morty, sober, with a fellow-feeling for Eddie (high-
rigger, swell fellow, good old Eddie) drunk, shepherded and steered
and protected Eddie although he had no confidence that they would
ever find the suitcase on the dock–but, just to oblige, he did this;
and it was a good thing he'd happened along, because by the time
they reached the dock it was quite dark and the rain made the visi-
bility very bad and goodness knows what would have happened to
Eddie the old fool crossing the street if Morty hadn't been along to
take care of him. Mort, I wish you to understand, was very very kind
to Eddie, and almost gentle with him, if anyone can be gentle with
a high-rigger who measures over six feet and is drunk.

By the time they reached the place at which you turn off to go
down to the dock–and their progress had been slow–the street lights
were all on, and there is nothing like street lights for announcing the
arrival of night. It was unquestionably night. A light shone in an
office where the Company's dock watchman was on duty. But as
the watchman had gone into the lavatory for a moment, he could not
and did not see the wavering arguing figures of two men, one tall
and one shorter, cross the beam of light that fell from his window
upon the wooden planking of the dock. He did not see the two men
advance onto the dock. If he had, he would have gone out and
shouted Hey at them, and found out what they were doing there, and
turned them back if he could. But as he was in the washroom, no
one saw Eddie and Mort walk together along the dock in the direction of a faint high light at the end of the dock, both of them fairly
contented, yes, very contented in their own mutual company. It did
not occur to Morty to be nervous of Eddie's safety on a dock when
he was drunk, because Mort knew, if he had happened to think of
it but he didn't that Eddie had teetered about on half the docks and
wharves of the logging camps of the coast of British Columbia and
had never fallen in yet and never would. So Morty did not accompany Eddie on to the dock with any idea of protecting him from
falling in–trust Eddie–but for the pleasure of being with him and
because when they did not find the suitcase–and they would not–
then Morty would go with Eddie back to the Regal Rooms and see
him to bed. And next day he would go back and visit with him. He
really did not think of Myrtle at all, and anyway he literally had his

hands full, clutching hold of two hundred and forty pounds of old Eddie.

Eddie, whose head was clearing a little, had a lot to tell Mort about the fellows they both knew who used to be up at Jervis Inlet and especially about a very very funny guy called Mike Jerkin who was now with Eddie at Knight Inlet who had a stammer which he used to exploit when he got in wrong with people and whom Eddie could take off to the King's taste; and Eddie broke away from Mort and acted out Mike Jerkin the time the moose got into the cook-house. By this time they had reached the end of the dark and meagrely lighted wharf and had for a moment forgotten about the suitcase because of Eddie telling in a very drunken way—but still funny—about what Mike Jerkin said to the moose, when Eddie took a lunge in his story and stepped off the dark wharf into the dark night and fell with a tremendous splash into the dark water which closed over him and only a dirty spangly light moved on the surface of the water, although there were signs of commotion beneath.

Everything in the world narrows down now with horrid immediacy and intensity to only Eddie struggling alone down there in the dark and churning up the spangly water and clawing the empty water in panic haste because he cannot swim, and only Mort crouched alone up there in the dark . . . in the sky it seems . . . his arms extended, looking down into the high tide water under the dim light at the place where Eddie churns his way up to the surface of the water. Everything in the world vanishes, gives way, all laughing and story give way to Mortimer's terror as, crouched with his arms extended as if frozen there, he sees the dark agitation of the water with its dirty spangled light and then he sees the white face of Eddie, staring, unrecognizable in its surprised fear, rise for a moment above the indifferent moving water. And at the sight of this white patch of face turning, choking, shouting, covered again, sinking again Mort is vicariously in Eddie there; he is Eddie, struggling there. And he moves, and is released, and shouts, and does not know that he shouts and shouts and looks wildly around and runs wildly around and comes back for anything. Is that a rope yes it is a coiled rope. And he throws the end of the rope and it misses, and he leans far down and takes a good purchase on it and throws it again to poor old Eddie Mort Eddie who is going to drown sure if Mort doesn't do something quickly but I don't have to jump in do I Myrtle do I Eddie no no I don't have to jump in do I: and he sees again the ghastly face above the water. And the rope because it is not attached and has no purchase runs smoothly out and falls into the sea, and so because Mort has no real purchase, he falls into the sea, and

Eddie who is strong, and is dying, and does not wish to die, seizes hold of Mort, and the empty water slides through Mort's fingers, and he seizes Eddie and they fight there, choking, grappling, the two good friends, in the dark water . . .

. . . but have to live and is drowning me God God what a fool blasted fool me Myrtle kitchen me Myrtle bedroom I mighta been there now little white house what white house Myrt God fool Eddie . . . bitterness despair anguish dreadful tearing anguish. And the water suffocated his eyes and blinded his lungs and Eddie held him tangled with hands and arms and legs and the agony grew and grew and at last diminished and ceased and Mort and Eddie in their loosening embrace sank uselessly down through the dark water and became both of them drowned men.

Woe for Mort. Woe for Mort's angel speeding away with an inaudible cry.

FURTHER READING

WORKS BY ETHEL WILSON
Hetty Dorval (Toronto: The Macmillan Company of Canada, Laurentian Library).
The Equations of Love (Toronto: The Macmillan Company of Canada).
Swamp Angel (Toronto: McClelland and Stewart, New Canadian Library, 1962).
Love and Salt Water (Toronto: The Macmillan Company of Canada).
Mrs. Golightly and Other Stories (Toronto: The Macmillan Company of Canada).
CRITICISM
A. J. M. Smith, ed., *Masks of Fiction* (Toronto: McClelland and Stewart, New Canadian Library, 1961). Ethel Wilson's work is discussed.
Desmond Pacey, *Ethel Wilson* (New York: Twayne Publishers, 1967).

Robertson Davies

Robertson Davies (1913-) was born in Thamesville, Ontario, and educated at Upper Canada College, Queen's University and Oxford. After working with the Old Vic Repertory Company in England, acting, directing, stage managing, teaching, he returned to Canada in 1940 to become literary editor of Saturday Night, *then editor and publisher of the* Peterborough Examiner. *His Marchbanks books of essays, witty and satirical thrusts at aspects of Canadian society, were based on syndicated newspaper columns of these years. In the late 'forties and 'fifties he emerged as a leading Canadian playwright. A prolific writer, he was at the same time beginning his career as a novelist, winning the Leacock Medal for Humour with* Leaven of Malice *(1954), and the Lorne Pierce Medal in 1961. He has been teaching English at the University of Toronto since 1960, and has been Master of Massey College since 1962.*

LOUISA'S LAST AT HOME

It was appropriate that Mrs. Bridgetower's funeral fell on a Thursday, for that had always been her At Home day. As she had dominated her drawing-room, so she dominated St. Nicholas' Cathedral on this frosty 23rd of December. She had planned her funeral, as she had planned all her social duties and observances, with care.

Of course the Prayer Book sets the form of an Anglican funeral, and Mrs. Bridgetower had no quarrel with that. Every social occasion has its framework; it is in enriching that framework with detail that the exceptional hostess rises above the mediocrity. Not two hours after her physician had pronounced her dead, her lawyer, Mr. Matthew Snelgrove, had put a fat letter in the hands of her

From: Robertson Davies, *A Mixture of Frailties* (Toronto: The Macmillan Company of Canada, Laurentian Library, 1958). Reprinted by permission of the publisher.

son Solomon, on the envelope of which was written in her firm, large hand, *Directions for My Funeral.*

Poor Solly, thought her daughter-in-law Veronica, what a time he has had! The most difficult job of all had been getting, at short notice, a coffin which was as nearly as possible a mate to that in which the late Professor Bridgetower had been buried sixteen years before. Mrs. Bridgetower had supplied the number and specifications of that model, but styles in coffins change, so it was only by great exertions that a similar one had been found in time. And as Mrs. Bridgetower had said that she did not wish to lie in a vault, and as the frost was already in the ground, arrangements had to be made to dig her grave with the aid of blow-torches and pneumatic drills. There had been no difficulty in persuading her oldest friend, Miss Laura Pottinger, to arrange the flowers in the church—"dear Puss has always had unexceptionable taste in such matters"—but Miss Pottinger had been so swollen with grief and self-importance that she had quarrelled with everyone and struck at an undertaker's assistant with her walking-stick. Luckily Veronica had been able to spare Solly most of the dealings with Miss Puss. And Veronica had addressed the two hundred cards of invitation herself, for Mrs. Bridgetower, while insisting on a private funeral, had left a long list of those whom she wished to be present at it. She had also specified the gown in which she was to be buried, and as it would no longer go over her great bulk at the time of her death, Veronica had personally altered it and put it on the corpse—a task which she had not relished. Veronica also had dressed Mrs. Bridgetower's hair and delicately painted her face, for the *Directions* had said that this should be done, but were firm that no male undertaker should do it; Miss Puss had stood at her elbow during that macabre hour, offering advice and fretful comment. Veronica had done everything possible to spare her husband, who now sat beside her, pale and worried, not with grief but with fear that something might yet go wrong.

It was not the service which was troubling him. That was under way and out of his hands. It was the funeral tea which was to follow the return from the graveyard which was on his mind. That was certain to be an ordeal, for all the funeral guests were bidden, and most of them were certain to come. He had attempted, that morning, to remove his mother's accustomed chair from the drawing-room, fearing that the sight of it might distress some of her old friends. But the oldest of these, Miss Puss Pottinger, had caught him in the act, and berated him for heartlessness. Louisa's chair, she said through angry tears, must stay where it had always been; she, Miss Puss, would not permit this relic of a great and fragrant spirit to be banished to an upstairs room on the very day of the funeral. And to make sure that no one committed unwitting sacrilege by sitting in it, she would herself lay one of the funeral wreaths–the cushion of white roses from the Imperial Order, Daughters of the Empire–on the seat. So the chair remained, a shrine and, for Solly, a portent of the ordeal which was yet to come.

The service was running according to schedule. A full choir had been specified in the *Directions*, and as full a choir as could be mustered on a week-day was present. Because the schools had closed for the Christmas holidays, eighteen of the Cathedral's twenty boys had been secured; eight of the singing-men had been able to come. Forty dollars for the men and thirty-six for the boys; well, Mother had wanted it. They had sung Samuel Sebastian Wesley's *Man That is Born* and had followed it with Purcell's *Thou Knowest, Lord*. Luckily in these two selections Mother's taste had agreed with that of the Cathedral organist, Humphrey Cobbler. The hazard was yet to come.

This hazard was Mrs. Bridgetower's personal contribution to the funeral service. She had attended many funerals in her time, and had been unfavourably impressed by the fact that what the Prayer Book had to say about death seemed to apply chiefly to men. A feminist of a dignified sort all her life, she felt that the funeral service lacked the feminine touch, and she had arranged for this to be supplied at her own burial. She had specified that a certain piece of music be sung, and that it be sung by a female voice. She admired, she said in her last letter to her son, the fine choir of men and boys which Mr. Cobbler had made so great an adornment of St. Nicholas', but at her funeral she wanted a woman to sing *My Task*, E. L. Ashford's lovely setting of Maude Louise Ray's dear and inspiring poem.

The Dean had not liked the idea, but he did not go so far as to forbid it. He knew that he would have to brave Miss Puss if he did so. But Humphrey Cobbler had hooted. Cobbler was a personal friend of Solly's and he had spoken with great freedom. "Music is like wine, Bridgetower," he had said, "the less people know about it, the sweeter they like it. You can't have that sickening musical bonbon at your Mum's funeral. It'll disgrace us all." But after prolonged argument he had succumbed. He had even undertaken to find a woman to sing.

She was about to sing now. The Dean, rather sneakily in Solly's opinion, was uttering a disclaimer.

"At this point," he said, "there will be sung some verses which were dear to our deceased sister, and which she specifically requested should be given utterance at this service." Then he seated himself in his stall, looking as much as possible as if he were someone else, somewhere else, and deaf.

It's not really the poem that's biting him, thought Solly, angrily. It's the idea of the poem applied to Mother. Well, she wanted it, and here it is. To hell with them all.

The singer was by the organ console, with Cobbler, and thus could not be seen by the mourners in the nave. Pure, sweet and clear, her voice made itself heard.

> To love someone more dearly ev'ry day;
> To help a wand'ring child to find his way;
> To ponder o'er a noble thought, and pray;
> And smile when ev'ning falls–
> This is my task.

That was how she thought of herself, mused Veronica. Probably it didn't seem as sticky to her as it does to us. And Oh, that last six months! Was that what she called smiling when evening falls? But I tried; I really did try. I slaved for her as I never slaved for my own mother. I did all I could to make her feel our marriage was a good thing for Solly. Did I ever pierce through to her heart? I hope so. I pray so. I want to think kindly of her.

A very little wintry sun struck through one of the Cathedral windows. The calm, silvery voice, somewhat hollow and echoing under the dome, continued.

To follow truth as blind men long for light–Veronica cast a sidelong glance at her husband. Silently, he was weeping. He truly loved his mother, in spite of everything, she thought. How I wish I thought that his mother had loved him.

The funeral tea was even more of an ordeal than Solly had foreseen. Such a function is not easily managed, and his mother's two old servants had been quick to declare that they were unable to attempt it. They were too broken up, they said. They were not so broken up, however, that they were incapable of giving a lot of trouble to the caterer who had been engaged for the work. They thought poorly of his suggestion that three kinds of sandwiches and three kinds of little cakes, supplemented by fruitcake, would be enough. The relatives from Montreal, the Hansens, would expect cold meat, they said; and as it was so near Christmas ordinary fruitcake would not suffice; Christmas cake would be looked for. Madam had never been one to skimp. When old Ethel, the cook, remembered that Thursday had always been Madam's At Home day, she had a fresh bout of grief, and declared that she would, after all, prepare the funeral tea herself, if it killed her. Solly had been unable to meet this situation and it was Veronica who, at last, made an uneasy peace between Ethel the cook, Doris the housemaid, and the caterer.

The caterer had his own, highly professional attitude toward funeral teas. What about drinks? he said. Sherry would be wanted for the women who never drank anything except at funerals, and there were always a few Old Country people who expected port–especially if there was cold meat. But most of the mourners would want hard liquor, and they would want it as soon as they got into the house. These winter funerals were murder; everybody was half perished by the time they got back from the graveyard. Solly would have to get the liquor himself; the caterer's banquet license did not cover funerals. He would, of course, supply all the glasses and mixings. He advised Solly to get a good friend to act as barman; it wouldn't do to have a professional barman at such an affair. Looked too calculated. Similarly, the icing which said Merry Christmas would have to be removed from the tops of the fruitcakes. Looked too cheerful.

Obediently, Solly procured and hauled a hundred and fifty dollars' worth of assorted liquors from the Government purveyor on the day before the funeral. But his acquaintance among skilled mixers of drinks was small, and in the end he had to ask the Cathedral organist, Humphrey Cobbler, to help him.

Was Solly grieving for his mother, when he wept during the singing of *My Task*? Yes, he was. But he was also grieving because Veronica had had such a rotten time of it during the past three days. He was worrying that there would not be enough to eat at the funeral tea. He was worrying for fear there would be too much to eat, and that the funeral baked-meats would coldly furnish forth his own table for days to come. He was worrying that Cobbler, triumphant behind the drinks-table, would fail to behave himself. He was worrying for fear the Hansen relatives would hang around all evening, discussing family affairs, as is the custom of families at funerals, instead of decently taking the seven o'clock train back to Montreal. He was hoping that he could live through the next few hours, get one decent drink for himself, and go to bed.

Solly and Veronica rode to the graveyard in an undertaker's limousine with Uncle George Hansen, Mrs. Bridgetower's brother, and Uncle George's American wife. But as soon as the burial was over they hurried to where Solly had left their small car earlier in the day, and rushed with irreverent haste back to the house, to be on hand to greet the mourners when they came ravening for liquor, food and warm fires.

"Do you think they'll all come?" said Veronica, as they rounded the graveyard gate.

"Very likely. Did you ever see such a mob? I didn't think more than a hundred would go to the cemetery, but it looks as if they all went. Have we got enough stuff, do you suppose?"

"I can't tell. I've never had anything to do with one of these things before."

"Nor have I. Ronny, in case I go out of my head before this tea thing is over, I want to tell you now that you've been wonderful about it all. In a week or so we'll go for a holiday, and forget about it."

When they entered the house it looked cheerful, even festive. Fires burned in the drawing-room, dining-room and in the library, where Cobbler stood ready behind an improvised bar. There was some giggling and scurrying as Solly and his wife came in, and Ethel and Doris were seen making for the kitchen.

"Just been putting the girls right with a strong **sherry-and-gin,**" said Cobbler. "They're badly shaken up. Needed bracing. Now, what can I give you?"

"Small ryes," said Solly. "And for heaven's sake use discretion, Humphrey."

"You know me," said Cobbler, slopping out the rye with a generous hand.

"I do," said Solly, "That's why I'm worried. Don't play the fool for the next couple of hours. That's all I ask."

"You wound me," said the organist, and made an attempt to look dignified. But his blue suit was too small, his collar was frayed, and his tie was working toward his left ear. His curly black hair stood out from his head in a mop, and his black eyes gleamed unnervingly. "You suggest that I lack a sense of propriety. I make no protest; I desire only to be left to My Task." He winked raffishly at Veronica.

He's our oldest friend as a married couple, thought she, and a heart of gold. If only he were not so utterly impossible! She smiled at him.

"Please, Humphrey," said she.

He winked again, tossed a lump of sugar in the air and caught it in his mouth. "Trust me," he said.

What else can we do? thought Veronica.

The mourners had begun to arrive, and Solly went to greet them. There was congestion at the door, for most of the guests paused to take off their overshoes and rubbers, and those who had none were scraping the graveyard clay from their feet. It was half an hour before the last had climbed the stairs, left wraps, taken a turn at the water-closet, descended the stairs and received a drink from Cobbler.

They had the air, festive but subdued, which is common to funeral teas. The grim business at the graveside done, they were prepared to make new, tentative contact with life. They greeted Solly with half-smiles, inviting him to smile in return. Beyond his orbit conversation buzzed, and there was a little subdued laughter. They had all, in some measure, admired or even liked his mother, but her death at seventy-one had surprised nobody and such grief as they felt for her had already been satisfied at the funeral. Dean Jevon Knapp, of St. Nicholas', bustled up to Solly; he had left his cassock and surplice upstairs, and had put on the warm dry shoes which Mrs. Knapp always took to funerals for him, in a special bag; he had his gaiters on, and was holding a large Scotch and soda.

"I have always thought this one of the loveliest rooms in Salterton," said he.

But Solly was not allowed to answer. Miss Puss Pottinger, great friend and unappeased mourner of the deceased, popped up beside him.

"It is as dear Louisa would have wished it to be," she said, in an aggressive but unsteady voice. "Thursday was always her At Home day, you know, Mr. Dean."

"First Thursdays, I thought," said the Dean; "this is a third Thursday."

"Be it what it may," said Miss Puss, losing control of face and voice, "I shall think of this as dear Louisa's–last–At Home."

"I'm very sorry," said the Dean. "I had not meant to distress you. Will you accept a sip–?" He held out his glass.

Miss Pottinger wrestled with herself, and spoke in a whisper. "No," said she. "Sherry. I think I could take a little sherry."

The Dean bore her away, and she was shortly seen sipping a glass of dark brown sherry in which Cobbler, unseen, had put a generous dollop of brandy.

Solly was at once engaged in conversation by his Uncle George Hansen and Uncle George's wife. This lady was an American, and as she had lived in Canada a mere thirty-five years, still found the local customs curious, and never failed to say so.

"This seems to me more like England than at home," she said now.

"Mother was very conservative," said Solly.

"The whole of Salterton is very conservative," said Uncle George; "I just met old Puss Pottinger mumbling about At Homes; thought she was dead years ago. This must be one of the last places in the British Empire where anybody has an At Home day."

"Mother was certainly one of the last in Salterton to have one," said Solly.

"Aha? Well, this is a nice old house. You and your wife going to keep it up?"

"I haven't had time to think about that yet."

"No, I suppose not. But of course you'll be pretty well fixed, now?"

"I really don't know, sir."

"Sure to be. Your mother was a rich woman. You'll get everything. She certainly won't leave anything to me; I know that. Ha ha! She was a wonder with money, even as a girl. 'Louie, you're tighter than the bark to a tree,' I used to say to her. Did your father leave much?"

"He died very suddenly, you know, sir. His will was an old one, made before I was born. Everything went to mother, of course."

"Aha? Well, it all comes to the same thing now, eh?"

"Solly, do you realize I'd never met your wife until this afternoon?" said Uncle George's wife. "Louise never breathed a word about your marriage until she wrote to us weeks afterward. The girl was a Catholic, wasn't she?"

"No, Aunt Gussie. Her mother was a Catholic, but Veronica was brought up a freethinker by her father. Mother and her father had never agreed, and I'm afraid my marriage was rather a shock to her. I'll get Veronica now."

"Why do you keep calling her Veronica?" said Uncle George. "Louie wrote that her name was Pearl."

"It still is," said Solly. "But it is also Veronica, and that is what she likes me to call her. Her father is Professor Vambrace, you know."

"Oh God, that old bastard," said Uncle George, and was kicked on the ankle by his wife. "Gussie, what are you kicking me for?"

At this moment a Hansen cousin, leaning on a stick, approached and interrupted.

"Let's see, George, now Louisa's gone you're the oldest Hansen stock, aren't you?"

"I'm sixty-nine," said Uncle George; "you're older than that, surely, Jim?"

"Sixty-eight," said Jim, with a smirk.

"You look older," said Uncle George, unpleasantly.

"You would, too, if you'd been where I was on the Somme," said Cousin Jim, with the conscious virtue of one who has earned the right to be nasty on the field of battle.

"You people certainly like it hot in Canada," said Aunt Gussie. And she was justified, for the steam heat and three open fires had made the crowded rooms oppressive.

"I'll see what I can do," said Solly and crept away. He ran upstairs and sought refuge in the one place he could think of which might be inviolable by his mother's relatives. As he entered his bathroom from his dressingroom his wife slipped furtively in from the bedroom. They locked both doors and sat down to rest on the edge of the tub.

"They're beginning to fight about who's the oldest stock," said Solly.

"I've met rather too many people who've hinted that our marriage killed your mother," said Veronica. "I thought a breather would do me good."

"Mother must have written fifty letters about that."

"Don't worry about it now, Solly."

"How is Humphrey doing?"

"I haven't heard any complaints. Do people always soak like this at funerals?"

"How should I know? I've never given a funeral tea before."

When Solly and his wife went downstairs again they found that most of the guests had turned their attention from drink to food, save for a half-dozen diehards who hung around the bar. The mourners were, in the main, elderly people who were unaccustomed to fresh air in the afternoon, and the visit to the cemetery had given them an appetite. The caterer directed operations from the kitchen, and his four waitresses hurried to and fro with laden platters. Ethel and Doris, ranking as mourners, pretended to be passing food, but were in reality engaged in long and regretful conversations with family friends, one or two of whom were unethically sounding them out about the chances of their changing employment, now that Mrs. Bridgetower was gone. (After all, what would a young man with an able-bodied wife want with two servants?) Miss Puss had been expected to pour the tea, a position of special honour, but she gave it up after over-filling three cups in succession, and seemed to be utterly unnerved; little Mrs. Knapp took on this demanding job, and was relieved after a hundred cups or so by Mrs. Swithin Shillito. The fake beams of the dining-room ceiling seemed lower and more oppressive than ever as the mourners crowded themselves into the room, consuming ham, turkey, sandwiches, cheese, Christmas cake and tartlets with increasing gusto. Those who were wedged near the table obligingly passed plates of food over the heads of the crowd to others who could not get near the supplies. The respectful hush had completely vanished, laughter and even guffaws were heard, and if it had not been a funeral tea the party would have been called a rousing success.

The mourners had returned from the graveyard at four o'clock, and it was six before any of them thought of going home. It was the general stirring of the Montreal Hansens, who had a train to catch, which finally broke up the party.

"Good-bye, Solly, and a Merry Christmas!" roared Uncle George, who had returned to the bar immediately after finishing a hearty tea. His wife kicked him on the ankle again, and he straightened his face. "Well, as merry as possible under the circumstances," he added, and plunged into the scramble for rubbers which was going on in the hall. Cousin Jim was sitting on the stairs, while a small, patient wife struggled to put on and zip up his overshoes. "Take care of my bad leg," he said, in a testy voice, to anyone who came near. It was some time before all the Hansens had gone. Several of them trailed back into the drawing-room, in full outdoor kit, to wring Solly's hand, or to kiss him on the cheek. But at last they went, and the Saltertonians began to struggle for coats and overshoes.

Mr. Matthew Snelgrove, solicitor and long-time friend of Mrs. Bridgetower, approached Solly conspiratorially. He was a tall old man, stiff and crane-like, with beetling brows.

"Will tomorrow, at three o'clock, suit you?" he said.

"For what, Mr. Snelgrove?"

"The will," said Mr. Snelgrove. "We must read and discuss the will."

"But is that necessary? I thought nobody read wills now. Can't we meet at your office some day next week and discuss it?"

"I think that your Mother would have wished her will to be read in the presence of all her executors."

"All her executors? Are there others? I thought that probably you and myself—"

"There are two executors beside yourself, and it is not a simple will. Not simple at all. I think you should know its contents as soon as possible."

"Well—if you say so."

"I think it would be best. I shall inform the others. Here, then, at three?"

"As you please."

Solly had no time to reflect on this arrangement, for several people were waiting to say good-bye. Dean Knapp and his wife approached last, each holding an arm of Miss Puss Pottinger, who wore the rumpled appearance of one who has been put into her outside clothes by hands other than her own. One foot was not completely down into her overshoe, and she lurched as she walked.

"We shall see Miss Pottinger home," said the Dean, smiling but keeping a jailor's grip on Auntie Puss.

"Solly, dear boy," cried that lady, and breaking free from the Dean she flung herself upon Solly's bosom, weeping and scrabbling at his coat. It became clear that she wanted to kiss him. He stooped and suffered this, damp and rheumy as it was; then, taking her by the shoulders, he passed her back to Mrs. Knapp. With a loud hiccup Auntie Puss collapsed, and almost bore the Dean's wife to the floor. When she had been picked up, she was led away, sobbing and murmuring, "Poor Louisa's last At Home—shall never forget—" They were the last to go.

"Well, well, well," said Cobbler, strolling in from the hall, when he had helped the Dean to drag Auntie Puss down a rather icy walk, and boost her into a car; "quite overcome with grief. Sad."

"She was drunk," said Solly. "What on earth did you give her?"

"The poor old soul was badly in need of bracing," said Cobbler. "I gave her a sherry with a touch of brandy in it, and it did the trick. But would she let well alone? She would not. She kept coming back. Was I to refuse her? I tried her once without the brandy, but she passed back her glass and said, 'This isn't the same.' Well–she had seven. I couldn't put her on the Indian list; she'd have made a scene. Whatever she feels like tomorrow, I am pure as the driven snow. Never say No to a woman; my lifelong principle."

He was helping Veronica to clear up the mess. Paper napkins were everywhere. Dirty plates covered the top of the piano. Cake had been ground into the carpet. The pillow of white roses in Mrs. Bridgetower's chair had been pushed under it by the callous Cousin Jim, who wanted to sit down and had no feeling for symbolism.

"For heaven's sake leave that," said Solly. "Let Ethel and Doris cope with it."

"'Fraid the girls are a bit overcome," said Cobbler. "They told me they were good for nothing but bed. Odd phrase, considering everything."

"Humphrey, what did you do?" said Veronica.

"Me? Not a thing. Just my duty, as I saw it. People kept asking for drinks and I obliged them. Really, Solly, those Hansen relatives of yours are something special. Hollow legs, every one of them."

"Was there enough?"

"Just managed. Do you know that there were two hundred and forty-seven souls here, and not one of them was a teetotaller? I always count; it's automatic with me. I count the house at every Cathedral service; the Dean likes to know how he's pulling. I consider that the affair was a credit to your late Mum, but we nearly ran out of swipes. It was a close thing."

He sat down at the grand piano, and sang with great expression, to the tune of the popular ballad *Homing*–

> All things get drunk at eventide;
>   The birds go pickled to their snoozing;
> Heaven's creatures share a mighty thirst–
>   Boozing–Bo-o-o-zing.

"Humphrey, stop it!" said Veronica. "If you must do something, will you get me a drink? I'm completely done up."

Cobbler got them all drinks, and while Solly and Veronica sat by the fire, trying to forget the trials and miseries of the past few days, he played Bach choral preludes on the old piano, to heal their wounded spirits.

FURTHER READING

FICTION BY ROBERTSON DAVIES
The "Salterton" Trilogy (setting: presumably Kingston, Ontario):
Tempest-Tost (Toronto: Clarke Irwin Paperback). First published 1951.
Leaven of Malice (Toronto: Clarke Irwin Paperback). First published 1954.
A Mixture of Frailties (Toronto: The Macmillan Company of Canada, Laurentian Library). First published 1958.

Fifth Business (Toronto: The Macmillan Company of Canada, 1970). Also available in Signet Paperback.
ESSAYS BY ROBERTSON DAVIES
The Diary of Samuel Marchbanks (Toronto: Clarke Irwin Paperback, 1966). First published 1947.
The Table Talk of Samuel Marchbanks (Toronto: Clarke Irwin Paperback). First published 1949.
Marchbanks' Almanack (Toronto: McClelland and Stewart, New Canadian Library, 1967).
PLAYS BY ROBERTSON DAVIES
At My Heart's Core and *Overlaid* (Toronto: Clarke Irwin Paperback).
Four Favourite Plays (Toronto: Clarke Irwin Paperback).
CRITICISM
A. J. M. Smith, ed., *Masks of Fiction* (Toronto: McClelland and Stewart, New Canadian Library, 1961). Robertson Davies' work is discussed.

Marie-Claire Blais

Marie-Claire Blais (1939-) has been quoted as saying that she wrote about monsters "because they are alone and unloved. They are incapable of love. That is the tragedy of life. To be unloved and unable to love." She was scarcely twenty-years old at the time, and had just published her first novel, La Belle Bête *(1959). It was an immediate success, going through two editions (5,000 copies) in six weeks. Since then she has continued to write about the tragedies of the warped and unlovely, stories of disease, brutality and death.*

The eldest of five children in a Quebec City working-class family (her father is an electrician), she took a job as a typist at the age of fifteen. At night she wrote, turning out masses of manuscript. Later she got some financial help from a Guggenheim Fellowship and went to live in the United States, choosing to live in a small cottage in Cape Cod with other artists nearby. She imposes a strict work discipline on herself, enjoying her isolation and living for her writing by which she now supports herself.

PATRICE

One night Patrice walked into his mother's room to say good night, at the hour when Louise usually wandered dreamily between the mirror and the window, pulling the combs from her hair. But this time Louise was not there. The gold cane had been left across the open covers of the bed and a man's glove lay in the middle of the sheets. Lanz's silk handkerchiefs hung everywhere, each with a different scent. Though he did not know why, Patrice took fright. Suddenly the room no longer offered the velvet warmth, the arms that

From: Marie-Claire Blais, *Mad Shadows* (Toronto: McClelland and Stewart, New Canadian Library, 1971). Reprinted by permission of McClelland and Stewart, the Canadian Publishers.

opened and closed and embraced. He looked around in despair, no longer finding any security. The gold cane reminded him of Lanz and of his walk that afternoon, and also Lanz's beard, and Lanz's eyes which he feared. Patrice hardly even dared sit on the edge of the bed. He felt as though he were being crushed by the walls. Everything was different. He stood there without moving, uneasy and bewildered, engulfed by a hostile presence.

He felt a bitter need to beg for mercy, but his own feelings were as confusing to him as his soul.

Next door, on a farm which belonged to a large, happy family, a party was being given, and Patrice could hear the singing. It filled him with melancholy. For a moment he forgot the gold cane and the silk handkerchiefs and even the glove that belonged to old Lanz. He leaned close to the damp shutters, letting his sadness merge with the evening shadows. Over there, girls and boys were dancing, kissing, and shouting songs of youth. Patrice listened and marveled, his mind drowned deeper than ever in troubled waters.

He had never known any human beings except his mother, his fly-by-night tutors, and Isabelle-Marie. Other people only admired him as they passed. They never looked back to find out what they had seen. Then, too, Louise protected him from everyone else in order to strengthen her own hold upon him. This was not hard for her to do.

Alone in his room, Patrice danced and imitated, for he always imitated everything, the gestures of the young couples. He danced and laughed as he danced, feeling an urge for speed throb within him. Isabelle-Marie would have loved to dance like this, but Isabelle-Marie was ashamed and worked in the fields where no one could see her, talking to the animals who would never insult and wound her, the way people did. Confused, Patrice closed the shutters against this night that sang like cicadas, and his gaze again took in the unmade bed, the white sheets, the glove . . . and Lanz's hateful cane. He felt a strange contempt, half-masculine, half-childish, and his dilated nostrils made his mask of pride into a mask of rebellion.

He looked for Louise's hair which to him was a soft cloth on which he could dry his tears of woe. He saw a tall man in the mirror: himself. He touched the glass with the tip of his fingernail and smiled, but was not satisfied. He went back to the bed. Louise would say, 'Come here, let me take those leaves out of your hair,' or 'How you have grown, Patrice!' but this evening she was silent. Everything was silent. Patrice knelt on the floor with his head buried in the sheets and sobbed like a starving child. He cried and cried, and the sight of this fair adolescent with his shoulders trembling, convulsed by despair, was pitiful.

Louise and Lanz came into the room.

Louise blanched beneath her make-up and the mark on her cheek seemed redder.

"Help me, Lanz. Patrice is feverish. He's sick again. I can tell."

Lanz obeyed and sponged Patrice's brow but the poor idiot clung all the harder to Louise, weeping on his mother's neck.

"What is the matter? Tell me . . ." murmured Louise.

He did not answer. Suddenly he rose to his feet and started to run away but Lanz kept him back with one bare hand, holding his other gloved hand behind his back.

"Are you in pain, Patrice?"

Patrice looked back with an expression that disturbed Lanz . . . Lanz, who never paid attention to anything but himself and his world of dolls. Isabelle-Marie had often asked herself how a creature as egotistical as Lanz could be capable of any normal emotions. But now he felt naked under Patrice's stare. "What could such an expression mean?" he wondered. "Has he any intelligence, or is he unhappy because he has none?"

Then, smoothing his eyebrows, he announced in a worldly tone of voice, "Patrice, we have something to tell you. Louise and I are going to be married. Does this make you smile? Look, Louise, he is smiling. He isn't sick at all."

He was right. Patrice was smiling, for he did not understand. Louise clasped him to her bosom and praised him. She laughed, and her cheeks glowed.

"Bring the glasses and we'll all drink together!"

"Isabelle-Marie, where are you, Isabelle-Marie?"

Patrice was left alone in the room. A tear fell on his pouting lips.

"Isabelle-Marie, you must celebrate with us. I am almost your father now."

"Drink to us, Isabelle-Marie!" said Louise; then, more tenderly, "Patrice, why are you biting your nails?"

Patrice lifted his glass and struck it mechanically against Lanz's in a gesture that meant nothing to him.

"Why are you always so quiet, Patrice?"

"He has nothing to say," snapped Isabelle-Marie. She, too, looked glum.

No one heard her. She was not quite so frightening this evening. She had tied a white scarf over her black dress and had used a little lipstick. She too was listening to the wild music which came from the farm next door.

"Isabelle-Marie, what are you thinking about?"

"Isabelle-Marie, bring some more wine."

Her body stiffened.

She thought of the approaching marriage of this pair of dolls, a male doll and a female doll. She would have to live in the midst of this depravity—the artificial depravity of faces in the movies. How sad, she thought, they have no souls.

Far off in her childhood, she could see her father, the austere peasant, the maker of bread. When he tilled the virgin loins of the earth, he was penetrating to the heart of God. In his soul, honesty mingled with instinct, just as good wine mellowed his complexion.

Isabelle-Marie remembered her father's enormous boots, which smelled of wheat and loam.

"Why, Isabelle-Marie, you are all pink! Something has finally turned you into a young girl . . . Is it the wine?"

Isabelle-Marie did not hear her mother. Louise was confusing her various roles; first she abandoned Patrice for her lover and then Lanz for Patrice. She laughed, enjoying these two beautiful heads, and sometimes Patrice nuzzled his forehead against her shoulder while Lanz amused himself elsewhere. He amused himself everywhere . . . he, Lanz! . . . so strangely fresh and youthful. He laughed, and his laughter was the graceful, congealed laughter of marionettes. That was all there was to Lanz. He was elegant; even his laughter was elegant.

And so the dolls met and were united, without needing to know one another. Patrice stood by, sparkling with innocence.

Overcome, quivering with the same anguish as that day on the train, Isabelle-Marie left the room.

FURTHER READING

WORKS BY MARIE-CLAIRE BLAIS

La Belle Bête (Québec: Institut Littéraire, 1959).

English translation—*Mad Shadows* (Toronto: McClelland and Stewart, New Canadian Library, 1971).

Tête Blanche (Québec: Institut Littéraire, 1960).

English translation—*Tête-Blanche* (Toronto: McClelland and Stewart, 1961).

Le Jour est Noir (Montréal: Editions du Jour, 1962).

English translation—*The Day is Dark* (New York: Farrar, Straus and Giroux, 1967).

Les Voyageurs Sacrés (Montréal: Editions HMH, 1969).

English translation—*Three Travelers*, published with, *The Day is Dark* (publishing details above).

Une Saison dans la Vie d'Emmanuel (Montréal: Editions du Jour, 1968).

English translation–*A Season in the Life of Emmanuel* (New York: Farrar, Straus and Giroux, 1966).

Manuscrits de Pauline Archange (Montréal: Editions du Jour, 1968).

English translation–*The Manuscripts of Pauline Archange* (New York: Farrar, Straus and Giroux, 1970).

CRITICISM

Philip Stratford, *Marie-Claire Blais: Canadian Writers and their Works* (Toronto: Forum House Publishing Company). Sold through Coles Book Stores.

Thomas Raddall

English-born Thomas Raddall (1903-) came to Halifax in 1913. He was first a coastguard and ships' wireless operator, a career he began when he was only fifteen; then bookkeeper-turned accountant for a Nova Scotia paper mill. He quit this job in 1938 to become a full-time writer and has since become recognized for historical romances, short stories and novels chronicling the life of Nova Scotia, past and present. Of particular interest is the well-documented and fast-moving His Majesty's Yankees *(1942). Raddall has three times won the Governor-General's Award for fiction, as well as the Lorne Pierce Medal (1956) and an Order of Canada Medal of Service (1970). He was elected to the Royal Society of Canada in 1949.*

Statistics tell us that the average Canadian family moves once every four years. Little wonder then that the journey is one of the favourite themes in Canadian literature. Five separate chapters in *Literary History of Canada* deal with books on Canadian exploration and travel. Very often the theme is combined with another recurring image, that of the hostile landscape. Take for example Alan Sullivan's well-known short story, *The Essence of a Man*, or Frederick Philip Grove's story, *Snow*. Novels begin with the end of a journey, as in *Anne of Green Gables*, or end with the beginning of a journey, as in *A Jest of God*.

The semi-nomadic quality of Canadian life is reflected in this preoccupation with travel, but there is more to it than that. The road becomes a metaphor through whose image is expressed the idea of quest. This metaphor is explicit in the Canadian film, *Going Down the Road*–the road is to lead the two young men from personal stagnation to a life of excitement and opportunity. Road and adventure become synonymous.

In *The Wedding Gift*, the heroine–and it is, after all, Kezia's story –is sent on her way by forces she strongly resents but which she is helpless to defy:

. . . her dreams were full of forbidding faces–Mr. Barclay's, Mrs. Barclay's, Mr. Hathaway's; especially Mr. Hathaway's. Out of a confused darkness Mr. Hathaway's hard acquisitive gaze searched her shrinking flesh like a cold wind.

But the journey which is meant to fix her bonds permanently, Kezia turns into a means for freeing herself. By using her native or acquired ingenuity, she succeeds in frustrating the plans of her antagonists. The landscape which more often figures in Canadian literature as a hostile agent, in this situation becomes an ally. At first the weather fails her:

> Kezia had prayed for snow, storms of snow, to bury the trail and keep anyone from crossing the cape to Bristol Creek. But now they were setting out from Harper's Farm, with Harper's big brown horse, and all Kezia's prayers had gone for naught.

But the wind whistles up "from the invisible sea" and brings the snowstorm which saves her. Not only does it force the two young people to seek shelter together, but the horse runs off, startled by "some snow" that "fell off a branch." The snowstorm literally drives the two travellers into each others' arms.

The forced marriage, imposed by parents on their unwilling young, is a popular subject for romance. Its popularity is no doubt related to the satisfaction felt by the reader in observing the success which meets the young lovers' efforts to outwit their parents. Shakespeare contains many variations on the theme. "See to beguile the old folks/ How the young folk lay their heads together," says the December suitor, Gremio, in *The Taming of the Shrew*.

In pursuing the romantic theme in *The Wedding Gift*, Raddall makes clear that the marriage agreement between Kezia and Mr. Mears is not based on mere expediency, but on affection. From their first meeting, the two show concern for each others' welfare. The preacher announces that he will walk, "and the young woman can ride." Kezia offers him the use of her woollen shawl. When Kezia kisses his cheek, "it seemed a very natural thing to do."

Neither is impressive in appearance: Mr. Mears is "a pallid young man," and Kezia, "a colourless little creature." Both have been managed by others: Mr. Mears has been "sent out from England by Lady Huntingdon's Connexion," and Kezia is handed over to Mr. Hathaway very much like a piece of merchandise in Mr. Barclay's business dealings. But the preacher is "firm," at least on the point of travel by land, and Kezia soon displays her resourcefulness. Each characterization is consistent with events–the apparent change in character is convincing, if not expected. The two characters find themselves in a situation which demands adaptability, and we can only presume that the potential for strength has always been present in them. The surprise ending, which shows that Kezia has been telling the truth, but not the whole truth, reinforces her sturdy declaration, that she is "not going to Mr. Hathaway." The significance of the wedding gift remains hidden to the end, although it is mentioned equivocally earlier in the story:

> Beneath her arm she clutched the small bundle which contained all she had in the world—two flannel nightgowns, a shift of linen, three pairs of stout wool stockings—and of course Mr. Barclay's wedding gift for Mr. Hathaway.

The Wedding Gift contains the elements of surprise, romance, nostalgia, and colour which we associate with historical fiction.

THE WEDDING GIFT

Nova Scotia, in 1794. Winter. Snow on the ground. Two feet of it in the woods, less by the shore, except in drifts against Port Marriott's barns and fences; but enough to set sleigh bells ringing through the town, enough to require a multitude of paths and burrows from doors to streets, to carpet the wharves and the decks of the shipping, and to trim the ships' yards with tippets of ermine. Enough to require fires roaring in the town's chimneys, and blue wood smoke hanging low over the roof tops in the still December air. Enough to squeal under foot in the trodden places and to muffle the step everywhere else. Enough for the hunters, whose snowshoes now could overtake the floundering moose and caribou. Even enough for the always-complaining loggers, whose ox sleds now could haul their cut from every part of the woods. But not enough, not nearly enough snow for Miss Kezia Barnes, who was going to Bristol Creek to marry Mr. Hathaway.

Kezia did not want to marry Mr. Hathaway. Indeed she had told Mr. and Mrs. Barclay in a tearful voice that she didn't want to marry anybody. But Mr. Barclay had taken snuff and said, "Ha! Humph!" in the severe tone he used when he was displeased; and Mrs. Barclay had sniffed and said it was a very good match for her, and revolved the cold blue eyes in her fat moon face, and said Kezia must not be a little fool.

There were two ways of going to Bristol Creek. One was by sea,

From: Thomas Raddall, *At the Tide's Turn and Other Stories* (Toronto: McClelland and Stewart, New Canadian Library, 1959). Reprinted by permission of McClelland and Stewart Limited, the Canadian Publishers.

in one of the fishing-sloops. But the preacher objected to that. He was a pallid young man lately sent out from England by Lady Huntingdon's Connexion, and seasick five weeks on the way. He held Mr. Barclay in some awe, for Mr. Barclay had the best pew in the meeting-house and was the chief pillar of godliness in Port Marriott. But young Mr. Mears was firm on this point. He would go by road, he said, or not at all. Mr. Barclay had retorted "Ha! Humph!" The road was twenty miles of horse path through the woods, now deep in snow. Also the path began at Harper's Farm on the far side of the harbour, and Harper had but one horse.

"I shall walk," declared the preacher calmly, "and the young woman can ride."

Kezia had prayed for snow, storms of snow, to bury the trail and keep anyone from crossing the cape to Bristol Creek. But now they were setting out from Harper's Farm, with Harper's big brown horse, and all Kezia's prayers had gone for naught. Like any anxious lover, busy Mr. Hathaway had sent Black Sam overland on foot to find out what delayed his wedding, and now Sam's day-old tracks marked for Kezia the road to marriage.

She was a meek little thing, as became an orphan brought up as house-help in the Barclay home; but now she looked at the preacher and saw how young and helpless he looked so far from his native Yorkshire, and how ill-clad for this bitter trans-Atlantic weather, and she spoke up.

"You'd better take my shawl, sir. I don't need it. I've got Miss Julia's old riding-cloak. And we'll go ride-and-tie."

"Ride and what?" murmured Mr. Mears.

"I'll ride a mile or so, then I'll get down and tie the horse to a tree and walk on. When you come up to the horse, you mount and ride a mile or so, passing me on the way, and you tie him and walk on. Like that. Ride-and-tie, ride-and-tie. The horse gets a rest between."

Young Mr. Mears nodded and took the proffered shawl absently. It was a black thing that matched his sober broadcloth coat and small-clothes, his black woollen stockings and his round black hat. At Mr. Barclay's suggestion he had borrowed a pair of moose-hide moccasins for the journey. As he walked, a prayerbrook in his coat-skirts bumped the back of his legs.

At the top of the ridge above Harper's pasture, where the narrow path led off through gloomy hemlock woods, Kezia paused for a last look back across the harbour. In the morning sunlight the white roofs of the little lonely town resembled a tidal wave flung up by the sea and frozen as it broke against the dark pine forest to the west. Kezia sighed, and young Mr. Mears was surprised to see tears in her eyes.

She rode off ahead. The saddle was a man's, of course, awkward to ride modestly, woman-fashion. As soon as she was out of the preacher's sight she rucked her skirts and slid a leg over to the other stirrup. That was better. There was a pleasant sensation of freedom about it, too. For a moment she forgot that she was going to Bristol Creek, in finery second-hand from the Barclay girls, in a new linen shift and drawers that she had sewn herself in the light of the kitchen candles, in white cotton stockings and a bonnet and shoes from Mr. Barclay's store, to marry Mr. Hathaway.

The Barclays had done well for her from the time when, a skinny weeping creature of fourteen, she was taken into the Barclay household and, as Mrs. Barclay so often said, "treated more like one of my own than a bond-girl from the poorhouse." She had first choice of the clothing cast off by Miss Julia and Miss Clara. She was permitted to sit in the same room, and learn what she could, when the schoolmaster came to give private lessons to the Barclay girls. She waited on table, of course, and helped in the kitchen, and made beds, and dusted and scrubbed. But then she had been taught to spin and sew and to knit. And she was permitted, indeed encouraged, to sit with the Barclays in the meeting-house, at the convenient end of the pew, where she could worship the Barclays' God and assist with the Barclay wraps at the beginning and end of the service. And now, to complete her rewards, she had been granted the hand of a rejected Barclay suitor.

Mr. Hathaway was Barclay's agent at Bristol Creek, where he sold rum and gunpowder and corn meal and such things to the fishermen and hunters, and bought split cod—fresh, pickled or dry—and ran a small sawmill, and cut and shipped firewood by schooner to Port Marriott, and managed a farm, all for a salary of fifty pounds, Halifax currency, per year. Hathaway was a most capable fellow, Mr. Barclay often acknowledged. But when after fifteen capable years he came seeking a wife, and cast a sheep's eye first at Miss Julia, and then at Miss Clara, Mrs. Barclay observed with a sniff that Hathaway was looking a bit high.

So he was. The older daughter of Port Marriott's most prosperous merchant was even then receiving polite attentions from Mr. Gamage, the new collector of customs, and a connection of the Halifax Gamages, as Mrs. Barclay was fond of pointing out. And Miss Clara was going to Halifax in the spring to learn the gentle art of playing the pianoforte, and incidentally to display her charms to the naval and military gentlemen who thronged the Halifax drawing-rooms. The dear girls laughed behind their hands whenever long solemn Mr. Hathaway came to town aboard one of the Barclay vessels and called at the big house under the elms. Mrs. Barclay bridled at Hathaway's presumption, but shrewd Mr. Barclay narrowed his little black eyes and took snuff and said, "Ha! Humph!"

It was plain to Mr. Barclay that an emergency had arisen. Hathaway was a good man–in his place; and Hathaway must be kept content there, to go on making profit for Mr. Barclay at a cost of only fifty pounds a year. 'Twas a pity Hathaway couldn't satisfy himself with one of the fishermen's girls at the Creek, but there 'twas. If Hathaway had set his mind on a town miss, then a town miss he must have; but she must be the right kind, the sort who would content herself and Hathaway at Bristol Creek and not go nagging the man to remove and try his capabilities elsewhere. At once Mr. Barclay thought of Kezia–dear little Kezzie. A colourless little creature but quiet and well-mannered and pious, and only twenty-two.

Mr. Hathaway was nearly forty and far from handsome, and he had a rather cold, seeking way about him–useful in business of course –that rubbed women the wrong way. Privately Mr. Barclay thought Hathaway lucky to get Kezia. But it was a nice match for the girl, better than anything she could have expected. He impressed that upon her and introduced the suitor from Bristol Creek. Mr. Hathaway spent two or three evenings courting Kezia in the kitchen–Kezia in a quite good gown of Miss Clara's gazing out at the November moon on the snow, murmuring now and again in the tones of someone in a rather dismal trance, while the kitchen help listened behind one door and the Barclay girls giggled behind another.

The decision, reached mainly by the Barclays, was that Mr. Hathaway should come to Port Marriott aboard the packet schooner on December twenty-third, to be married in the Barclay parlour and then take his bride home for Christmas. But an unforeseen circumstance had changed all this. The circumstance was a ship, "from Mogador in Barbary" as Mr. Barclay wrote afterwards in the salvage claim, driven off her course by gales and wrecked at the very entrance to Bristol Creek. She was a valuable wreck, laden with such queer things as goatskins in pickle, almonds, wormseed, pomegranate skins and gum arabic, and capable Mr. Hathaway had lost no time in salvage for the benefit of his employer.

As a result he could not come to Port Marriott for a wedding or anything else. A storm might blow up at any time and demolish this fat prize. He dispatched a note by Black Sam, urging Mr. Barclay to send Kezia and the preacher by return. It was not the orthodox note of an impatient sweetheart, but it said that he had moved into his new house by the Creek and found it "extream empty lacking a woman," and it suggested delicately that while his days were full, the nights were dull.

Kezia was no judge of distance. She rode for what she considered a reasonable time and then slid off and tied the brown horse to a maple tree beside the path. She had brought a couple of lamp wicks to tie about her shoes, to keep them from coming off in the snow, and she set out afoot in the big splayed tracks of Black Sam. The soft snow came almost to her knees in places and she lifted her skirts high. The path was no wider than the span of a man's arms, cut out with axes years before. She stumbled over a concealed stump from time to time, and the huckleberry bushes dragged at her cloak, but the effort warmed her. It had been cold, sitting on the horse with the wind blowing up her legs.

After a time the preacher overtook her, riding awkwardly and holding the reins in a nervous grip. The stirrups were too short for his long black-stockinged legs. He called out cheerfully as he passed, "Are you all right, Miss?" She nodded, standing aside with her back to a tree. When he disappeared ahead, with a last flutter of black shawl tassels in the wind, she picked up her skirts and went on. The path climbed and dropped monotonously over a succession of wooded ridges. Here and there in a hollow she heard water running, and the creak of frosty poles underfoot, and knew she was crossing a small stream, and once the trail ran across a wide swamp on half-rotten corduroy, windswept and bare of snow.

She found the horse tethered clumsily not far ahead, and the tracks of the preacher going on. She had to lead the horse to a stump so she could mount, and when she passed Mr. Mears again she called out, "Please, sir, next time leave the horse by a stump or a rock so I can get on." In his quaint old-country accent he murmured, "I'm very sorry," and gazed down at the snow. She forgot she was riding astride until she had passed him, and then she flushed, and gave the indignant horse a cut of the switch. Next time she remembered and swung her right leg back where it should be, and tucked the skirts modestly about her ankles; but young Mr. Mears looked down at the snow anyway, and after that she did not trouble to shift when she overtook him.

The ridges became steeper, and the streams roared under the ice and snow in the swales. They emerged upon the high tableland between Port Marriott and Bristol Creek, a gusty wilderness of young hardwood scrub struggling up amongst the grey snags of an old forest fire, and now that they were out of the gloomy softwoods they could see a stretch of sky. It was blue-grey and forbidding, and the wind whistling up from the invisible sea felt raw on the cheek. At their next meeting Kezia said, "It's going to snow."

She had no knowledge of the trail but she guessed that they were not much more than halfway across the cape. On this high barren the track was no longer straight and clear, it meandered amongst the meagre hardwood clumps where the path-makers had not bothered to cut, and only Black Sam's footprints really marked it for her unaccustomed eyes. The preacher nodded vaguely at her remark.

The woods, like everything else about his chosen mission field, were new and very interesting, and he could not understand the alarm in her voice. He looked confidently at Black Sam's tracks.

Kezia tied the horse farther on and began her spell of walking. Her shoes were solid things, the kind of shoes Mr. Barclay invoiced as "a Common Strong sort, for women, Five Shillings"; but the snow worked into them and melted and saturated the leather. Her feet were numb every time she slid down from the horse and it took several minutes of stumbling through the snow to bring back an aching warmth. Beneath her arm she clutched the small bundle which contained all she had in the world–two flannel nightgowns, a shift of linen, three pairs of stout wool stockings–and of course Mr. Barclay's wedding gift for Mr. Hathaway.

Now as she plunged along she felt the first sting of snow on her face and, looking up, saw the stuff borne on the wind in small hard pellets that fell amongst the bare hardwoods and set up a whisper everywhere. When Mr. Mears rode up to her the snow was thick in their faces, like flung salt.

"It's a nor'easter!" she cried up to him. She knew the meaning of snow from the sea. She had been born in a fishing-village down the coast.

"Yes," mumbled the preacher, and drew a fold of the shawl about his face. He disappeared. She struggled on, gasping, and after what seemed a tremendous journey came upon him standing alone and bewildered, looking off somewhere to the right.

"The horse!" he shouted. "I got off him, and before I could fasten the reins some snow fell off a branch–startled him, you know–and he ran off, over that way." He gestured with a mittened hand. "I must fetch him back," he added confusedly.

"No!" Kezia cried. "Don't you try. You'd only get lost. So would I. Oh, dear! This is awful. We'll have to go on, the best we can."

He was doubtful. The horse tracks looked very plain. But Kezia was looking at Black Sam's tracks, and tugging his arm. He gave in, and they struggled along for half an hour or so. Then the last trace of the old footprints vanished.

"What shall we do now?" the preacher asked, astonished.

"I don't know," whispered Kezia, and leaned against a dead pine stub in an attitude of weariness and indifference that dismayed him.

"We must keep moving, my dear, mustn't we? I mean, we can't stay here."

"Can't stay here," she echoed.

"Down there–a hollow, I think. I see some hemlock trees, or are they pines?–I'm never quite sure. Shelter, anyway."

"Shelter," muttered Kezia.

He took her by the hand and like a pair of lost children they dragged their steps into the deep snow of the hollow. The trees were tall spruces, a thick bunch in a ravine, where they had escaped the old fire. A stream thundered amongst them somewhere. There was no wind in this place, only the fine snow whirling thickly down between the trees like a sediment from the storm overhead.

"Look!" cried Mr. Mears. A hut loomed out of the whiteness before them, a small structure of moss-chinked logs with a roof of poles and birch-bark. It had an abandoned look. Long streamers of moss hung out between the logs. On the roof shreds of birch-bark wavered gently in the drifting snow. The door stood half open and a thin drift of snow lay along the split pole floor. Instinctively Kezia went to the stone hearth. There were old ashes sodden with rain down the chimney and now frozen to a cake.

"Have you got flint and steel?" she asked. She saw in his eyes something dazed and forlorn. He shook his head, and she was filled with a sudden anger, not so much at him as at Mr. Barclay and that–that Hathaway, and all the rest of menkind. They ruled the world and made such a sorry mess of it. In a small fury she began to rummage about the hut.

There was a crude bed of poles and brushwood by the fireplace–brushwood so old that only a few brown needles clung to the twigs. A rough bench whittled from a pine log, with round birch sticks for legs. A broken earthenware pot in a corner. In another some ash-wood frames such as trappers used for stretching skins. Nothing else. The single window was covered with a stretched moose-bladder, cracked and dry-rotten, but it still let in daylight while keeping out the snow.

She scooped up the snow from the floor with her mittened hands, throwing it outside, and closed the door carefully, dropping the bar into place, as if she could shut out and bar the cold in such a fashion. The air inside was frigid. Their breath hung visible in the dim light from the window. Young Mr. Mears dropped on his wet knees and began to pray in a loud voice. His face was pinched with cold and his teeth rattled as he prayed. He was a pitiable object.

"Prayers won't keep you warm," said Kezia crossly.

He looked up, amazed at the change in her. She had seemed such a meek little thing. Kezia was surprised at herself, and surprisingly she went on, "You'd far better take off those wet moccasins and stockings and shake the snow out of your clothes." She set the example, vigorously shaking out her skirts and Miss Julia's cloak, and she turned her small back on him and took off her own shoes and stockings, and pulled on dry stockings from her bundle. She threw him a pair.

"Put those on."

He looked at them and at his large feet, hopelessly.

"I'm afraid they wouldn't go on."

She tossed him one of her flannel nightgowns. "Then take off your stockings and wrap your feet and legs in that."

He obeyed, in an embarrassed silence. She rolled her eyes upward, for his modesty's sake, and saw a bundle on one of the low rafters–the late owner's bedding, stowed away from mice. She stood on the bench and pulled down three bearskins, marred with bullet holes. A rank and musty smell arose in the cold. She considered the find gravely.

"You take them," Mr. Mears said gallantly. "I shall be quite all right."

"You'll be dead by morning, and so shall I," she answered vigorously, "if you don't do what I say. We've got to roll up in these."

"Together?" he cried in horror.

"Of course! To keep each other warm. It's the only way."

She spread the skins on the floor, hair uppermost, one overlapping another, and dragged the flustered young man beside her, clutched him in her arms, and rolled with him, over, and over again, so that they became a single shapeless heap in the corner farthest from the draft between door and chimney.

"Put your arms around me," commanded the new Kezia, and he obeyed.

"Now," she said, "you can pray. God helps those that help themselves."

He prayed aloud for a long time, and privately called upon heaven to witness the purity of his thoughts in this strange and shocking situation. He said "Amen" at last; and "Amen," echoed Kezia, piously.

They lay silent for a long time, breathing on each other's necks and hearing their own hearts–poor Mr. Mears' fluttering in an agitated way, Kezia's as steady as a clock. A delicious warmth crept over them. They relaxed in each other's arms. Outside, the storm hissed in the spruce tops and set up an occasional cold moan in the cracked clay chimney. The downswirling snow brushed softly against the bladder pane.

"I'm warm now," murmured Kezia. "Are you?"

"Yes. How long must we stay like this?"

"Till the storm's over, of course. Tomorrow, probably. Nor'easters usually blow themselves out in a day and a night, 'specially when they come up sharp, like this one. Are you hungry?"

"No."

"Abigail–that's the black cook at Barclay's–gave me bread and cheese in a handkerchief. I've got it in my bundle. Mr. Barclay thought we ought to reach Bristol Creek by suppertime, but Nabby said I must have a bite to eat on the road. She's a good kind thing, old Nabby. Sure you're not hungry?"

"Quite. I feel somewhat fatigued but not hungry."

"Then we'll eat the bread and cheese for breakfast. Have you got a watch?"

"No, I'm sorry. They cost such a lot of money. In Lady Huntingdon's Connexion we–"

"Oh well, it doesn't matter. It must be about four o'clock–the light's getting dim. Of course, the dark comes very quick in a snowstorm."

"Dark," echoed young Mr. Mears drowsily. Kezia's hair, washed last night for the wedding journey, smelled pleasant so close to his face. It reminded him of something. He went to sleep dreaming of his mother, with his face snug in the curve of Kezia's neck and shoulder, and smiling, and muttering words that Kezia could not catch. After a time she kissed his cheek. It seemed a very natural thing to do.

Soon she was dozing herself, and dreaming, too; but her dreams were full of forbidding faces–Mr. Barclay's, Mrs. Barclay's, Mr. Hathaway's; especially Mr. Hathaway's. Out of a confused darkness Mr. Hathaway's hard acquisitive gaze searched her shrinking flesh like a cold wind. Then she was shuddering by the kitchen fire at Barclay's, accepting Mr. Hathaway's courtship and wishing she was dead. In the midst of that sickening wooing she wakened sharply.

It was quite dark in the hut. Mr. Mears was breathing quietly against her throat. But there was a sound of heavy steps outside, muffled in the snow and somehow felt rather than heard. She shook the young man and he wakened with a start, clutching her convulsively.

"Sh-h-h!" she warned. "Something's moving outside." She felt him stiffen.

"Bears?" he whispered.

Silly! thought Kezia. People from the old country could think of nothing but bears in the woods. Besides, bears holed up in the winter. A caribou, perhaps. More likely a moose. Caribou moved inland before this, to the wide mossy bogs up the river, away from the coastal storms. Again the sound.

"There!" hissed the preacher. Their hearts beat rapidly together.

"The door–you fastened it, didn't you?"

"Yes," she said. Suddenly she knew.

"Unroll, quick!" she cried. "No, not this way–your way."

They unrolled, ludicrously, and the girl scambled up and ran across the floor in the stockinged feet, and fumbled with the rotten door-bar. Mr. Mears attempted to follow but he tripped over the nightgown still wound about his feet, and fell with a crash. He was up again in a moment, catching up the clumsy wooden bench for a weapon, his bare feet slapping on the icy floor. He tried to shoulder her aside, crying, "Stand back! Leave it to me!" and waving the bench uncertainly in the darkness.

She laughed excitedly. "Silly!" she said. "It's the horse." She flung the door open. In the queer ghostly murk of a night filled with snow they beheld a large dark shape. The shape whinnied softly and thrust a long face into the doorway. Mr. Mears dropped the bench, astonished.

"He got over his fright and followed us here somehow," Kezia said, and laughed again. She put her arms about the snowy head and laid her face against it.

"Good horse! Oh, good, good horse!"

"What are you going to do?" the preacher murmured over her shoulder. After the warmth of their nest in the furs they were shivering in this icy atmosphere.

"Bring him in, of course. We can't leave him out in the storm." She caught the bridle and urged the horse inside with expert clucking sounds. The animal hesitated, but fear of the storm and a desire for shelter and company decided him. In he came, tramping ponderously on the split-pole floor. The preacher closed and barred the door.

"And now?" he asked.

"Back to the furs. Quick! It's awful cold."

Rolled in the furs once more, their arms went about each other instinctively, and the young man's face found the comfortable nook against Kezia's soft throat. But sleep was difficult after that. The horse whinnied gently from time to time, and stamped about the floor. The decayed poles crackled dangerously under his hoofs whenever he moved, and Kezia trembled, thinking he might break through and frighten himself, and flounder about till he tumbled the crazy hut about their heads. She called out to him, "Steady, boy! Steady!"

It was a long night. The pole floor made its irregularities felt through the thickness of fur; and because there seemed nowhere to put their arms but about each other the flesh became cramped, and spread its protest along the bones. They were stiff and sore when the first light of morning stained the window. They unrolled and stood up thankfully, and tramped up and down the floor, threshing their arms in an effort to fight off the gripping cold. Kezia undid her bundle in a corner and brought forth Nabby's bread and cheese, and they ate it sitting together on the edge of the brushwood bed with the skins about their shoulders. Outside the snow had ceased.

"We must set off at once," the preacher said. "Mr. Hathaway will be anxious."

Kezia was silent. She did not move, and he looked at her curiously. She appeared very fresh, considering the hardships of the previous day and the night. He passed a hand over his cheeks and thought how unclean he must appear in her eyes, with this stubble on his pale face.

"Mr. Hathaway–" he began again.

"I'm not going to Mr. Hathaway," Kezia said quietly.

"But–the wedding!"

"There'll be no wedding. I don't want to marry Mr. Hathaway. 'Twas Mr. Hathaway's idea, and Mr. and Mrs. Barclay's. They wanted me to marry him."

"What will the Barclays say, my dear?"

She shrugged. "I've been their bond-girl ever since I was fourteen, but I'm not a slave like poor black Nabby, to be handed over, body and soul, whenever it suits."

"Your soul belongs to God," said Mr. Mears devoutly.

"And my body belongs to me."

He was a little shocked at this outspokenness but he said gently, "Of course. To give oneself in marriage without true affection would be an offense in the sight of heaven. But what will Mr. Hathaway say?"

"Well, to begin with, he'll ask where I spent the night, and I'll have to tell the truth. I'll have to say I bundled with you in a hut in the woods."

"Bundled?"

"A custom the people brought with them from Connecticut when they came to settle in Nova Scotia. Poor folk still do it. Sweethearts, I mean. It saves fire and candles when you're courting on a winter evening. It's harmless–they keep their clothes on, you see, like you and me–but Mr. Barclay and the other Methody people are terrible set against it. Mr. Barclay got old Mr. Mings–he's the Methody preacher that died last year–to make a sermon against it. Mr. Mings said bundling was an invention of the devil."

"Then if you go back to Mr. Barclay–"

"He'll ask me the same question and I'll have to give him the same answer. I couldn't tell a lie, could I?" She turned a pair of round blue eyes and met his embarrassed gaze.

"No! No, you mustn't lie. Whatever shall we do?" he murmured in a dazed voice. Again she was silent, looking modestly down her small nose.

"It's so very strange," he floundered. "This country–there are so many things I don't know, so many things to learn. You–I–we shall have to tell the truth, of course. Doubtless I can find a place in the Lord's service somewhere else, but what about you, poor girl?"

"I heard say the people at Scrod Harbour want a preacher."

"But–the tale would follow me, wouldn't it, my dear? This–er–bundling with a young woman?"

"'Twouldn't matter if the young woman was your wife."

"Eh?" His mouth fell open. He was like an astonished child, for all his preacher's clothes and the new beard on his jaws.

"I'm a good girl," Kezia said, inspecting her foot. "I can read and write, and know all the tunes in the psalter. And–and you need someone to look after you."

He considered the truth of that. Then he murmured uncertainly, "We'd be very poor, my dear. The Connexion gives some support, but of course–"

"I've always been poor," Kezia said. She sat very still but her cold fingers writhed in her lap.

He did something then that made her want to cry. He took hold of her hands and bowed his head and kissed them.

"It's strange–I don't even know your name, my dear."

"It's Kezia–Kezia Barnes."

He said quietly, "You're a brave girl, Kezia Barnes, and I shall try to be a good husband to you. Shall we go?"

"Hadn't you better kiss me, first?" Kezia said faintly.

He put his lips awkwardly to hers; and then, as if the taste of her clean mouth itself provided strength and purpose, he kissed her again, and firmly. She threw her arms about his neck.

"Oh, Mr. Mears!"

How little he knew about everything! He hadn't even known enough to wear two or three pairs of stockings inside those roomy moccasins, nor to carry a pair of dry ones. Yesterday's wet stockings were lying like sticks on the frosty floor. She showed him how to knead the hard-frozen moccasins into softness, and while he worked at the stiff leather she tore up one of her wedding bed-shirts and wound the flannel strips about his legs and feet. It looked very queer when she had finished, and they both laughed.

They were chilled to the bone when they set off, Kezia on the horse and the preacher walking ahead, holding the reins. When they regained the slope where they had lost the path, Kezia said, "The sun rises somewhere between east and southeast, this time of year. Keep it on your left shoulder a while. That will take us back toward Port Marriott."

When they came to the green timber she told him to shift the sun to his left eye.

"Have you changed your mind?" he asked cheerfully. The exercise had warmed him.

"No, but the sun moves across the sky."

"Ah! What a wise little head it is!"

They came over a ridge of mixed hemlock and hardwood and looked upon a long swale, and again where it entered the dark mass of the pines beyond.

"Praise the Lord!" said Mr. Mears.

When at last they stood in the trail, Kezia slid down from the horse.

"No!" Mr. Mears protested.

"Ride-and-tie," she said firmly. "That's the way we came, and that's the way we'll go. Besides I want to get warm."

He climbed up clumsily and smiled down at her.

"What shall we do when we get to Port Marriott, my dear?"

"Get the New Light preacher to marry us, and catch the packet for Scrod Harbour."

He nodded and gave a pull at his broad hat brim. She thought of everything. A splendid helpmeet for the world's wilderness. He saw it all very humbly now as a dispensation of Providence.

Kezia watched him out of sight. Then, swiftly, she undid her bundle and took out the thing that had lain there (and on her conscience) through the night–the tinderbox–Mr. Barclay's wedding gift to Mr. Hathaway. She flung it into the woods and walked on, skirts lifted, in the track of the horse, humming a psalm tune to the silent trees and the snow.

FURTHER READING

SELECTED WORKS BY THOMAS RADDALL

At the Tide's Turn and Other Stories (Toronto: McClelland and Stewart, New Canadian Library, 1959).

The Nymph and the Lamp (Toronto: McClelland and Stewart, New Canadian Library, 1963).

Footsteps on Old Floors (New York: Doubleday Publishers, 1968). May be ordered through Doubleday Publishers, Toronto.

The Pied Piper of Dipper Creek (Toronto: McClelland and Stewart, 1948).

Wings of Night (Toronto: Doubleday Publishers).

RELATED MATERIAL

Helen Creighton, ed., *Songs and Ballads from Nova Scotia* (Toronto: General Publishing Company).

PICTURE SERIES

Canadian Authors (includes Thomas Raddall), obtainable from: Hilton Photo Supplies, P.O. Box 74, Chemainus, British Columbia.

Mordecai Richler

Mordecai Richler (1931-) was born in Montreal and lived on St. Urbain, one of the streets of the Jewish ghetto and the psychological milieu for much of his writing. He began attending Sir George Williams University, but dropped out and went to Europe for two years when he was nineteen. Returning to Canada in 1952, he was a news editor for the CBC for a short while, then went to England where he has since lived most of the time, a full-time writer of film scripts, short stories, novels, criticism and pungent, often derogatory, comment about Canada. His first novel, The Acrobats, *was published in 1954. He won the Governor-General's Award for both* Cocksure, *a satirical novel, and* Hunting Tigers under Glass, *a collection of journalistic pieces, in 1968, and again for* St. Urbain's Horseman *in 1971.*

THE MARCH OF THE FLETCHER'S CADETS

Lance-corporal Boxenbaum led with a bang bang bang on his big white drum and Litvak tripped Cohen, Pinsky blew on his bugle, and the Fletcher's Cadets wheeled left, reet, left, reet, out of Fletcher's Field, led by their Commander-in-chief, that snappy five-footer, W. E. James (that's "Jew" spelt backwards, as he told each new gym class). Left, reet, left, reet, powdery snow crunching underfoot, Ginsburg out of step once more and Hornstein unable to beat his drum right because of the ten-on-each Mr. Coldwell had applied before the parade. Turning smartly right down Esplanade Avenue they were at once joined and embarrassed on either side by a following of younger brothers on sleighs, little sisters with running noses, and grinning delivery boys stopping to make snowballs.

"Hey, look out there General Montgomery, here comes your mother to blow your nose."

From: Mordecai Richler, *The Apprenticeship of Duddy Kravitz* (Toronto: McClelland and Stewart, New Canadian Library, 1969). Reprinted by permission of McClelland and Stewart Limited, the Canadian Publishers.

"Lefty! Hey, Lefty! Maw says you gotta come right home to sift the ashes after the parade. No playing pool she says. She's afraid the pipes will burst."

Tara-boom, tara-*boom*, tara-BOOM-BOOM-BOOM, past the Jewish Old People's Home where on the balcony above, bedecked with shawls and rugs, a stain of yellowing expressionless faces, women with little beards and men with sucked-in mouths, fussy nurses with thick legs and grandfathers whose sons had little time, a shrunken little woman who had survived a pogrom and two husbands and three strokes, and two followers of Rabbi Brott the Miracle Maker, watched squinting against the fierce wintry sun.

"Jewish children in uniform?"

"Why not?"

"It's not nice. For a Jewish boy a uniform is not so nice."

Skinny, lumpy-faced Boxenbaum took it out on the big white drum and Sergeant Grepsy Segal, who could burp or break wind at will, sang,

> BULLSHIT, that's all the band could play,
> BULLSHIT, it makes the grass grow green.

Mendelsohn hopped to get back into step and Archie Rosen, the FFHS Cadet Corps Quartermaster who sold dyed uniforms at $8.00 each, told Naturman the one about the rabbi and the priest and the bunch of grapes. "Fun-*ny*," Naturman said. Commander-in-chief W. E. James, straight as a ramrod, veteran of the Somme, a swagger stock held tight in his hand, his royal blue uniform pressed to a cutting edge and his brass buttons polished perfect, felt a lump in his throat as the corps bugles blowing approached the red brick armoury of the Canadian Grenadier Guards. "Eyes . . . RIGHT," he called, saluting stiffly.

Duddy Kravitz like the rest turned to salute the Union Jack and the pursuing gang of kid brothers and sisters took up the chant,

> Here come the Fletcher's Cadets,
> smoking cigarettes,
> the cigarettes are lousy
> and so are the Fletcher's Cadets.

Crunch, crunch, crunch-crunch-crunch, over the powdery snow ears near frozen stiff the FFHS Cadet Corps marched past the Jewish Library, where a poster announced,

Wednesday Night
ON BEING A JEWISH POET
IN MONTREAL WEST
A Talk by H. I. Zimmerman, B.A.
Refreshments

and smack over the spot where in 1933 a car with a Michigan licence plate had machine-gunned to death the Boy Wonder's uncle. They stopped in front of the YMHA to mark time while the driver of a KIK KOLA truck that had slid in a No. 97 street-car began to fight with the conductor.

"Hip, hip," W. E. James called. "Hup-Hip-Hip."

A bunch of YMHA boys came out to watch.

"There's Arnie. Hey, Arnie! Where's your gun? Wha'?"

"Hey, Sir! Mr. James! You know what you can do with that stick?"

"Boxenbaum. Hey! You'll get a rupture if you carry that drum any further."

"Hip, Hip," W. E. James called. "Hip-Hip-Hip."

Geiger blew on his bugle and Sivak goosed Kravitz. A snowball knocked off Sergeant Heller's cap, Pinsky caught a frozen horse-bun on the cheek, and Mel Brucker lowered his eyes when they passed his father's store. Monstrous icicles ran from the broken second floor windows of his home into the muck of stiff burnt dry goods and charred wood below. The fire had happened last night. Mel had expected it because that afternoon his father had said cheerfully, "You're sleeping at grandmaw's tonight," and each time Mel and his brother were asked to sleep at grandmaw's it meant another fire, another store.

"Hip. Hip. Hip, hip, hip."

To the right Boxenbaum's father and another picketer walked up and down blowing on their hands before the Nu-Oxford Shoe Factory, and to the left there was Harry's War Assets Store with a sign outside that read, IF YOU HAVEN'T GOT TIME TO DROP IN–SMILE WHEN YOU WALK PAST. Tara-boom, tara-*boom*, tara-BOOM-BOOM-BOOM, past the Hollywood Barbershop where they removed blackheads for 50 cents around the corner of Clark where Charna Felder lived, the FFHS Cadet Corps came crunch-crunch-crunch. Tansky started on his drum, Rubin dropped an icicle down Mort Heimer's back, and the cadets wheeled left, reet, left, reet, into St. Urbain Street. A gathering of old grads and slackers stepped out of the Laurier Billiard Hall, attracted by the martial music.

"Hey, Sir. Mr. James! Is it true you were a pastry cook in the first war?"

"We hear you were wounded grating latkas."

"There's Stanley. Hey, Stan! Jeez, he's an officer or something. STAN! It's O.K. about Friday night but Rita says Irv's too short for her. Can you bring Syd instead? Stan! STAN?"

Over the intersection where Gordie Wiser had burnt the Union Jack after many others had trampled and spat on it the day Ernest Bevin announced his Palestine policy, past the house where the Boy

Wonder had been born, stopping to mark time at the corner where their fathers and elder brothers armed with baseball bats had fought the frogs during the conscription riots, the boys came marching. A little slower, though, Boxenbaum puffing as he pounded his drum and thirteen or thirty-five others feeling the frost in their toes. The sun went, darkness came quick as a traffic light change, and the snow began to gleam purple. Tansky felt an ache in his stomach as they slogged past his house and Captain Bercovitch remembered there'd be boiled beef and potatoes for supper but he'd have to pick up the laundry first.

"Hip. HIP. Hip, hip, hip."

To the right the AZA Club House and to the left the poky Polish synagogue where old man Zabitsky searched the black windy street and saw the cadets coming towards him.

"Label. Label, come here."

"I can't, zeyda, it's a parade."

"A parade. *Narishkeit.* We're short one man for prayers."

"But zeyda, please."

"No buts, no please. Rosenberg has to say kaddish."

Led by the arm, drum and all, Lionel Zabitsky was pulled from the parade.

"Hey, Sir. A casualty."

"Chic-*ken!*"

Past Moe's warmly lit Cigar Store where you could get a lean on rye for 15 cents and three more cadets defected. Pinsky blew his bugle faint-heartedly and Boxenbaum gave the drum a little bang. Wheeling right and back again up Clark Street five more cadets disappeared into the darkness.

"Hip. Hip. HIP, HIP, HIP."

One of the deserters ran into his father, who was on his way home from work.

"Would you like a hotdog and a coke before we go home?"

"Sure."

"O.K., but you mustn't say anything to Maw."

Together they watched the out-of-step FFHS Cadet Corps fade under the just starting fall of big lazy snowflakes.

"It's too cold for a parade. You kids could catch pneumonia out in this weather without scarves or rubbers."

"Mr. James says that in the first world war sometimes they'd march for thirty miles without stop through rain and mud that was knee-deep."

"Is that what I pay school fees for?"

FURTHER READING

SELECTED WORKS BY MORDECAI RICHLER

Son of a Smaller Hero (Toronto: McClelland and Stewart, New Canadian Library, 1965). First published in 1955.

The Apprenticeship of Duddy Kravitz (Toronto: McClelland and Stewart, New Canadian Library, 1969). First published 1959.

The Incomparable Atuk (Toronto: McClelland and Stewart, New Canadian Library, 1963).

Cocksure (Toronto: McClelland and Stewart, 1968). Also available in Bantam Pocketbooks.

The Street (Toronto: McClelland and Stewart, 1969).

Hunting Tigers Under Glass (Toronto: McClelland and Stewart, 1969).

St. Urbain's Horseman (Toronto: McClelland and Stewart, 1971).

CRITICISM

George Woodcock, *Mordecai Richler* (Toronto: McClelland and Stewart, Canadian Writers Series, 1970).

Mordecai Richler, Canadian Writers and Critics Series. (Toronto: Coles Publishing House).

G. David Sheps, *Mordecai Richler* (Toronto: Ryerson Press, Critical Views on Canadian Writers Series).

AUDIO-TAPE

Canadian Writers on Tape (available on both reel tape and cassettes, and includes Mordecai Richler), obtainable from: Publications Sales OISE, 102 Bloor St. West, Toronto.

Brian Moore

Brian Moore (1921-) was born in Belfast, Northern Ireland, of Catholic parents. He attended a Jesuit college, but left in 1940 without graduating. During the war he served with the British Ministry of War Transport in North Africa. At the end of the war he was with the UNRRA mission in Warsaw, then worked as a free-lance correspondent in Europe. He came to Canada in 1948 and became a Canadian citizen. He was a newspaperman for the Montreal Gazette *and wrote his first two novels in this country,* The Lonely Passion of Judith Hearne *(1955) and* The Feast of Lupercal *(1957) and most of the third,* The Luck of Ginger Coffey *(1960) which he finished in New York on a Guggenheim Fellowship. He did not return to Canada, but continued to live in New York, then in California where he now has his home.*

J. F. COFFEY, JOURNALIST

The tavern described by Mr. Hickey was unnamed. Above its door was an electric sign: *Verres Stérilisés–Sterilized Glasses,* a sign which no one read but which conveyed to the passing eye that here was a place to drink, a place which shut late or never, a place unlikely to be well-frequented. This last was its deception, Coffey found. Forgotten, faded, off the main streets, in a downtown limbo where property owners allowed buildings to live out a feeble charade of occupation until the glorious day when all would be expropriated in a city slum clearance drive, the tavern, instead of dying, had burgeoned in a new and steady prosperity. As Coffey pushed open its doors he was met by a beer stench and a blast of shouted talk. Two waiters in long white aprons, each balancing a tray containing a dozen full glasses of draught beer, whirled in and out among the

From: Brian Moore, *The Luck of Ginger Coffey* (Toronto: McClelland and Stewart, New Canadian Library, 1972). Reprinted by permission of McClelland and Stewart Limited, the Canadian Publishers.

scarred wooden tables, answering thirsty signals. Slowly Coffey moved up the room, searching for the man with a crutch. The customers put him in mind of old Wild West films: they wore fur caps, peaked caps, toques. They wore logging boots, cattle boots, flying boots. They talked in roars, but they numbered also their solitaries. These sat alone at smaller tables, staring at the full and empty bottles in front of them as though studying the moves in some intricate game.

No one heeded Coffey as he moved on. At the far end of the room a huge jukebox, filled with moving colours and shifting lights, brooded in silence amid the roar of voices. Near it, disfigured with initials, an empty phone booth; symbol of the wives and worries the tavern's customers bought beer to forget. Coffey paused by the phone. What if she were sitting in the duplex this minute, already sorry for what she'd said? She could be. Yes, she might be.

He went into the booth and shut the door on the noise. He dialled and Paulie answered.

"Oh, it's you, Daddy."

"Is your mother home yet?"

"She was in but she went out again."

"Where?"

"She didn't say, Daddy."

"And she left you all alone, Pet?"

"Oh, that's all right, Daddy. I'm going to supper at a girl friend's house and her mother's giving me a lift home in their car."

"Oh."

"I must go now, Daddy. I'm late already."

"Wait a minute, Pet. Did Mummy tell you I've got a job?"

"No."

"Well, I have. A–an editing job on a newspaper. Isn't that good?"

"Yes, Daddy."

"Well–well, tell your mother I phoned her, will you, Apple?"

"Okay, Daddy."

"And listen, Apple–don't be too late getting home, will you?"

But Paulie had already hung up. Who the blazes was selfish–he or a woman who would go out of the house and leave her little girl all alone? Suffering J! Ah well–let's have a beer. Where's this man I'm supposed to meet? Fox with a crutch.

He came out of the phone booth and stood solitary among the shouting drinkers searching for the cripple's sign. On the top of a radiator by the far wall, he saw an aluminium cane with a rubber-covered elbow grip. Near-by, sticking out into the aisle, a built-up boot. Its owner was a tall, vaguely professional man with fairish hair and a grey stubbled chin. Coffey went over.

"Mr. Fox?"

The cripple ignored him. "First million," he said to his companions. "That's the caste mark. As long as they made it long enough ago for people to forget what it was made in, they become one of Canada's first families."

One of the men at the table, a bald, sweating person in a navy blue shirt and a vermilion tie, looked up, saw Coffey. "Fu-Fox," he said. "Wu-wanted."

"Oh." The cripple sprawled backwards in his chair, letting his gaze travel slowly from Coffey's brown suède boots to the tiny Tyrolean hat. "New man, eh?"

"Yes. How did you know?"

"How did I know? Hear that, Harry?"

Both Fox and the stammerer were seized with a laughing fit. Fox cleared glasses and bottles from in front of him in a rash sweep of his arm, laying his laughing face on the beer-wet table top. He was, Coffey realized, half seas over.

"Sit down," said a third reader, pulling out a chair for Coffey. He was very old, strangely dressed in a duck-billed fawn cap, fawn windbreaker and high, elastic-sided boots. A feathery white goatee grew precariously on his caved-in jaws and as he reached forward to shake hands, Coffey was put in mind of the recruiting poster's Uncle Sam. "My name's Billy Davis," he said. "And this here is Kenny."

Kenny was little more than a boy. His face, tortured by eczema, looked up at Coffey in a lost, posed smile. His right hand clutched the neck of a beer bottle. He sat primly on the edge of the chair.

"Drink up, Paddy," Fox said, signalling a waiter. "You're behind."

A waiter came and Fox paid for four glasses of draught beer which he at once lined up in front of Coffey. His companion, Harry, seemed to consider this a further occasion for laughter. "Now, Paddy," Fox said. "Let's see you sink these. Go ahead."

"Thanks very much," Coffey said. "That's very decent of you. My next treat, I hope?"

"Drink!" Fox shouted. "One, two three, four. Go ahead."

Lord knows, Coffey liked a wet as well as the next man. But there was something lunatic about this. He began on the first beer. Bald Harry's upper lip dripped sweat. The boy widened his fixed smile a fraction, in encouragement. The old man nodded his goatlike chin. Glass empty, Coffey put it down and reached for a second.

"Good man," Fox said. "Away you go. One swallow."

It took two swallows.

"Number three, now," Fox said.

But as he raised the third glass to his lips, Coffey paused. Wasn't this daft? What was he doing, drinking himself stocious for a clatter of strangers?

"What's up?" Fox said.

"Nothing. Only that it's against nature, guzzling like this. What's the rush?"

Fox and Harry exchanged glances. "A good question, Paddy," Fox said. "And it answers mine. Booze is not your problem, right?"

They must be joking. It must be some sort of joke, this chat?

"Never mind him," the girlish boy said. "Say, that's a dandy over-coat you have. Sharp." He touched Coffey's sleeve.

"Wu-women?" Harry said. "Du-do you think that's his pu-problem, Foxey?"

"Why must I have a problem?" Coffey said. "What are you talk-ing about?"

"Every proofreader has," Fox said. "All ye who enter here. Look at Kenny." He leaned over as he spoke and put his arm around the boy's shoulders. "You know what Kenny's problem is, I suppose?"

"Shut up," the boy said. "Lousy gimp."

"Hostility to the father figure," Fox shouted. "Classic!"

Feathery fingers plucked at Coffey's wrist. The old man thrust his Uncle Sam visage close. His mouth opened, showing gaps of gums policed by ancient dental survivors. "Could be money," he said. "That's everybody's problem, am I right, fellow?"

"That's right," Coffey said, uneasily jovial. "It's the root of all evil, they tell me."

"Wrong!" Fox shouted. "Why, money is not evil, Paddy my boy. Money is the Canadian way to immortality."

"Cu-Christ, here he gu-goes again," Harry said.

"Quiet now," Fox shouted. "I have to explain the facts of life to our immigrant brother. Do you want to be remembered, Paddy? Of course you do. Then you must bear in mind that in this great country of ours the surest way to immortality is to have a hospital wing called after you. Or better still, a bridge. We're just a clutch of little Ozymandiases in this great land. Nobody here but us builders. This is Canada's century, they tell us. Not America's, mind you. Not even Russia's. The twentieth century belongs to Canada. And if it does, then you had better know our values. Remember that in this fair city of Montreal the owner of a department store is a more important citizen than any judge of the Superior Court. Never forget that, Paddy boy. Money is the root of all good here. One nation, indivis-ible, under Mammon, that's our heritage. Now drink up."

Coffey reached for his fourth glass of beer. Might as well. She didn't bloody well love him any more so what did it matter if he got drunk. Today was enough to drive any man to drink.

"Tonight, Coffey, you will become a proofreader. You will read all the news. War in China, peace in our time. Mere finger exercises. Later, Coffey, if you show promise, we may let you read something more important. The Quebec Social Notes, for instance. Of the Governor-General's speech to the Crippled Deaf Mute Division of the United Sons of Scotland. And if you continue to show promise– if you make no mistake, allow no errors typographic or orthographic to slip into print, then we may even let you read an advertisement. And some day, you may become a senior man, a man who reads only advertisements. Because, Coffey, news is cheap. Here today and gone tomorrow. But advertisements cost money. They count. So you must get them right, do you hear? Compree?"

"Compree," Coffey said, raising his hand to signal the waiter.

The old man nodded and smiled. "It's money that counts, all right," he said. "Ten men run this country, did you know that? Ten big finenceers. And did you know there's a book tells you who they are and how they made it. You'll want to read that book, being a New Canadian. Yes, you will. You can borrow my copy, if you like."

Yes, Coffey said, he must dip into that some time. He paid for another round of beers.

"Are you just pu-passing through?" Harry asked him. "Or du-do you pu-plan to stay for a while?"

Coffey took a long pull of his beer. "Passing through," he said. "Matter of fact, I'm just in the proofroom so's I can pick up the Tribune style. MacGregor's going to make me a reporter."

As he said this, he saw Fox screw up his left eye in a large drunken wink. Harry collapsed in a fresh rush of laughter. The old man shook his head. "Big finenceers," he mumbled. "Scab labour, that's what we are."

"But–but what's the matter?" Coffey asked. "I mean, what's funny about it?"

Again Fox winked at the others. "Nothing funny," he said. "I just hope you succeed, that's all."

Coffey stared at their knowing faces. What did they mean? Had he been tricked? "Look, fellows," he said. "Tell me, I want to know. Do you think he will make me a reporter?"

"Stranger things have happened," Fox said. "Drink up."

"Big finenceers," the old man mumbled. "I remember one time–"

But Coffey no longer listened. He sat dumb, drowsy with beer, the glasses multiplying in front of him, the style book forgotten in his pocket. Were they making a joke of him? Was MacGregor trick-ing him, what was going on? Was it for this he had travelled across half a frozen continent and the whole Atlantic ocean? To finish up as a galley slave among the lame, the odd, the halt, the old?

"Money," Fox was saying. "Oh, let me tell you, you can be a four-letter bastard all your life but never mind. If you die with enough in the bank, the Tribune will write you a fine editorial eulogy–"

Had he been wrong to bet his all on Canada? Would he have been better to stick in those dead end jobs at home, plodding along, day in and day out, until he dropped?–listen to these fellows–they seem to think Canada is the back of beyond–

"Nu-nother depression," Harry said. "You just wu-watch it. They sneeze in the States and we get pneumonia here."

Was that true? Was it a backwater, like the land he had fled? Had he made the mistake of his life, landing himself up here among these people, either mugs like old Gerry, or full of gloomy prophecies like these fellows? Bloody Canada! Bloody Canadians!

"Just a poor clutch of Arctic-bound sods–" Fox was saying.

For if Veronica was going to leave him, then hadn't this been the greatest mistake ever?

"Greatest mistake this country ever made was not joining the United States–" Fox said.

–There was always Paulie. I've got a job, Pet, he'd told her. Yes, Daddy. Daddies are supposed to get jobs. Not very great to have a job, is it? Not this job. Yes, if he lost Veronica, he would lose Paulie too. And would have no one.

"Drink up," Fox said. "Last call, boys."

"Must phone," he said, standing up. "Just a moment."

Because, ah, Vera didn't mean it, did she? She was just upset, she would say she was sorry now. Never mind, dear, he'd say. My fault. I love you, Kitten. I love you too, Ginger. Yes . . . she'd be over it now–

He dialled. "Vera?"

"It's me. Paulie."

"Oh, Paulie," Coffey said, closing his eyes, leaning his forehead against the cool glass of the booth. "Is your mother there, Pet?"

"I told you she went out."

"Out?"

"Daddy, are you drinking?"

"No, no, that's a way to speak to your Daddy! Listen, Apple. Give her a message. Tell her to phone me. All right?"

"Where?"

"The Tribune. It's a newspaper. All right?"

"Okay. I'll leave a note for her," Paulie said.

"Listen–Paulie?"

"What is it?" Paulie asked crossly.

"Paulie . . . You don't think I'm selfish, do you? I mean–listen, Apple. You're still my own little Apple, hmm?"

"Oh, stop it, Daddy!"

"Not cross at me . . . I mean . . . listen, Pet. I mean Paulie . . . Daddy's not bad, is he? Mmm? . . . Paulie?"

–Dizzy, all that beer in a hurry, but that pane of glass was so cool against his forehead–

"Listen, Pet . . . won't be home. Want to speak to Mummy . . . tell her . . . Apple . . . Tell her, Daddy's sorry–"

Fox banged on the door of the booth. "Saddle up," he shouted. "Come on galley slave. Hitler's Legion rides again."

"Paulie–Paulie?"

Brr-brr-brr-brr, the phone went. He shovelled the receiver back on to its cradle, and looked at it dully. No, Paulie didn't care . . .

He stepped out of the booth and stumbled. "I'm drunk," he said. "I'm plootered."

"Never mind," Fox said. "So are we all, all honourable men. Take his arm there. Hurry! Hurry!"

Into the men's wash-room behind the composing-room, Old Billy Davis led Coffey, fumbling drunk. Stood him beside the basins, took hold of Coffey's jaws, forcing them open as though he would administer a pill, but instead darted his finger into Coffey's mouth, pulled it out again and forced Coffey's head down towards the wash-basin. Then waited, placid and fragile in his fawn windbreaker, as his victim, hands gripping the basin, retched wildly, flooding the bowl.

"Once more?"

"No . . . no." Coffey moaned, coughing until the tears came.

"Better now? All right. Follow me."

Out of the men's locker-room in a trembling run, past the compositors' lockers, through the lanes of Linotype machines to the row of steel desks. Hands reached past, claiming galleys, shuffling copy, spiking galleys, busy, everyone busy, no voices heard above the chattering mumble of machines. Drained, but still ill, Coffey made a cradle of his arms and rested his head on the dirty steel desk top. J. F. Coffey, Editor, J. F. Coffey, Journalist. In a weak moment he felt the tears come: she did not love him; she hated him and why shouldn't she, rotten with drink, he was, great drunken lump, J. F. Coffey, journalist, plootered his first night on the job. Ah God! He hated this great lump, blowing into his thick red moustache, self-pitying fool . . .

"Hey, hey," Fox said, shaking him. "Wake up, Paddy. Hitler's coming. Here you are." A half-finished galley appeared in front of Coffey's face. And just in time.

Mr. MacGregor was coming through. Bony old arms hanging naked from shirt sleeves, blue vein pumping in his pale forehead, fanatic eye, starved for trouble. As he swept out on his nightly visitation, office boys, delinquent deskmen, guilty reporters, all avoided his eye, practised the immobility of small animals as a hawk moves over a forest. But on the instant MacGregor entered the composing-room, some of the ferocity drained from his walk. Here, old battles had been fought, old forts abandoned. Here, the enemy was in full command, camped permanently within MacGregor's walls. Strikes, scabs, shutouts; all had failed. Hedged around by clause and contract, the managing editor was forbidden to lay a finger on one stick of type, denied the right to speak one word of direct command. The composing-room foreman waited his nightly sortie with the amused contempt of a Roman general dealing with the chieftain of a small hill tribe. Here, each night, MacGregor relived his defeat.

And so, as was his custom, his impotence sought its revenge. Alone in that union camp, the proofreaders were still his servants. "Who let this pass?" he shouted, shaking a galley high above the dirty steel desks. "Who let this pass?"

Fox raised his grey stubbled chin, took the galley, consulted the pencilled initials. "Day man," he said.

"Jesus Christ! Got this name wrong, see? Friend of the publisher. Jesus Christ!"

Fox looked at the ceiling as though engaged in mental arithmetic. His fellow workers read proofs with awful intensity. "Not our shift, sir," Fox said. "And we're late, sir. Still short of men."

"I gave you a new man tonight. Where is he? New man—aye—let's see—"

As he spoke, MacGregor ran around the desks and snatched up the half-finished galley. "Well, Coffey, let's see your wurrk?" He spread the galley on the desk top, scanning it, block-reading not for sense but for typographical errors. Years of practice gave him an unerring eye for flaw, but tonight, he saw no flaw. Four errors on the galley, four caught, so far. A new man? He did not believe it. He turned on Fox. "These aren't his marks. They're yours."

It was a guess, but once he had made it, MacGregor snatched some of Fox's galleys off the spike and compared. "Aye, these are your marks," he said in triumph. "Coffey?"

"Yes, sir."

"Show me your other galleys."

Behind his high desk, the composing-room foreman had been watching. He saw the new man's face, red, confused, turn upwards towards his tormentor. Poor sod. The foreman stepped down from his desk, approached, stopping MacGregor in mid-shriek. "Your men are behind here, Mr. Mac," he said. "All this talk is holding up the work. You're short-staffed here, as usual. And we're late."

"We're doing our best, damn ye!"

But MacGregor turned away, spiked the galleys and made off without another word, fearful of a new defeat, a new infestation of mediators, arbitrators, international representatives and similar union incubi and succubi. The foreman winked at Coffey's bewildered face and returned to his desk. The linotypers, prim and efficient on their little stools, smiled as at an old and favourite joke and–monks performing a rite of exorcism–the proofreaders downed galleys and intoned a short chant of MacGregorian abuse. Then, the obscenities observed, Fox leaned across the desk and fed Coffey his first galley of the night. "All right," he said. "Coast's clear. Do your best."

At ten the bell rang for supper break. At ten-fifteen it rang again and they went on to work until one. Sober now, Coffey found that he could do the job. Soon he was reading galleys only seconds slower than old Billy and half as quick as Fox. He was surprised, and pleased, because, all his life, do you see, he had been in jobs whose only purpose seemed to convince some higher-up that you were worth the money he was paying you. But in this job, you read your galley and made your corrections and if you looked across the room, you could see the make-up men going on with the next step in the process. Within an hour or two, a newspaper would come off the press and tomorrow morning, people would buy it, would read it over breakfast. You made something. There was no coming the old soldier, either. You signed your initials at the foot of each galley and if you let something slip, it could be traced back to you.

It was a new and satisfying feeling.

And so, at one in the morning, when Coffey rode home on the bus, a newly-printed newspaper on his lap, he had, by his habitual processes of ratiocination, convinced himself that the day was not a defeat but a victory. A little victory. He had a job; he was working alongside a bunch of Canadians in a far-off country, pulling his weight with the best of them. As for Vera, she would be over her bad temper by now. He would make a cup of cocoa for her, bring her into the kitchen and tell her all about this evening. He would kiss her and they would say they were sorry, both of them. Hardworking Ginger. Not selfish, no. Doing the best he could.

FURTHER READING

WORKS BY BRIAN MOORE

The Lonely Passion of Judith Hearne (Toronto: McClelland and Stewart, New Canadian Library, 1964).

The Luck of Ginger Coffey (Toronto: McClelland and Stewart, New Canadian Library, 1972).

The Emperor of Ice Cream (Toronto: McClelland and Stewart, 1965). Also available in Bantam paperback.

Fergus (Toronto: McClelland and Stewart, 1970).
The Revolution Script (Toronto: McClelland and Stewart, 1971).
Catholics (Toronto: McClelland and Stewart, 1972).
CRITICISM
George Woodcock, *Odysseus Ever Returning* (Toronto: McClelland and Stewart, New Canadian Library, 1970).
Hallvard Dahlie, *Brian Moore* (Toronto: Copp Clark Publishers, Studies in Canadian Literature Series).

Morley Callaghan

Morley Callaghan (1903-) was born in Toronto, went to St. Michael's College and studied law at Osgoode Hall. He was called to the bar in 1928, but did not practice. His first novel Strange Fugitive *was published that year, and the following year his first book of short stories,* A Native Argosy. *He spent eight months in Paris where he profited by the friendship of F. Scott Fitzgerald and Ernest Hemingway, whom he had met in Toronto when they were both working for the* Toronto Daily Star. *After the publication of his second book of stories,* Now that April's here *(1936), the* New York Times *commented, "If there's a better short story writer in the world, we don't know where he is." In his novels, beginning with* Such is My Beloved *(1934) he reflects the influence of the French Catholic philosopher, Jacques Maritain, with whom he had established a warm rapport. He was offered the Order of Canada Medal of Service in 1967, but refused it, feeling he had suffered critical neglect in Canada. But he won the Governor-General's Award for* The Loved and the Lost *(1951), the Lorne Pierce Medal (1960), the $15,000 Molson Prize (1969), and $50,000 from the Royal Bank of Canada (1971) in recognition of his work. He lives in Toronto where he is a well-known radio and T.V. personality.*

BOXING MATCH WITH HEMINGWAY

Ernest and his boxing! After the events I'm relating had occurred, Ernest back in the States could say to Josephine Herbst, "But my writing is nothing. My boxing is everything." When Miss Herbst told this to me I laughed, but was full of wonder. That a great artist like Ernest could have such a view of himself seemed incredible. Yet in

From: Morley Callaghan, *That Summer in Paris* (Toronto: The Macmillan Company of Canada, 1963). Reprinted by permission of the publisher.

the strange dark depths of his being he had to pretend to believe it. For the sake of the peace of their own souls most men live by pretending to believe in something they secretly know isn't true. It seems to be a dreadful necessity. It keeps life going on. We agree especially to pretend to believe in things that can never be known. Each civilization seems to have derived some creative energy from an agreement upon the necessity of a general pretending. Why it was necessary for Ernest to pretend to believe that his boxing was the root of his whole life, I don't know. It is true some men are much better at pretending than others. It's a built-in gift. The game for them takes on a reality that shapes their whole lives.

I had discovered that Ernest's attitude to his boxing was related to the source of his power as an imaginative writer. His imaginative work had such a literal touch that a whole generation came to believe he was only telling what he, himself, had seen happen, or what had actually happened to him. His readers made him his own hero. As he grew older it must have had tragic disadvantages for him. Now it seems to me that he shared with Sherwood Anderson, at least in this matter of his boxing, a matter of vital importance to his whole view of himself, a strange trick of the imagination–the built-in gift.

The night my wife and I went to dine with Anderson in the Washington Mews, where he was staying, we all sat around a long table after dinner, drinking and talking till two in the morning. We talked about many things. Hemingway's name came into the conversation. Next day I was meeting Max Perkins. As soon as he saw me he said, "I hear you had an interesting evening with Sherwood last night. I hear you made a splendid defense of Hemingway's Catholicism." Defend it! A look of indignant consternation must have come on my face. "Why, I never mentioned it. Why–" Taking my arm, Perkins said urgently, "Now just a minute. Before you go any further, please let me explain something to you. Don't let this spoil Sherwood for you. It's happened with others. You must understand Sherwood wasn't really lying . . ." Surely I would understand that Anderson, a story-teller, couldn't help going on with a story. From past experience with Anderson, Perkins knew what had happened. Last night after we had gone home, Anderson, lying awake, would have wished he had raised the subject of Hemingway's Catholicism; in his imagination he had heard himself raise certain questions; he had heard me answer; absorbed in his dream he had supplied a brilliant defense for me. In this extension of the real conversation, the thing that should have happened, would have happened; in his imagination it would have belonged completely to the small thing that did happen, and so it had truth for him.

Now Hemingway in his turn loved boxing. Every chance he got

he must have boxed with someone, and he had all the lingo, he had hung around gyms, he had watched fighters at work. Something within him drove him to want to be expert at every occupation he touched. In those days he liked telling a man how to do things, but not by way of boasting or arrogance–it was almost as if he had to feel he had a sense of professionalism about every field of human behavior that interested him. To this day I know you will find some Broadway columnist, or some gym instructor in New York, who will assure the world he had seen Hemingway working out like a pro, or taking a punch at someone. The truth was that we were two amateur boxers. The difference between us was that he had given time and imagination to boxing; I had actually worked out a lot with good fast college boxers.

In Paris there were scoffers, envious men, always belittling Ernest, who would whisper that his physical roughness was all a bluff. It was utter nonsense. He was a big rough tough clumsy unscientific man. In a small bar, or in an alley, where he could have cornered me in a rough-and-tumble brawl, he might have broken my back, he was so much bigger. But with gloves on and in a space big enough for me to move around, I could be confident. My wife remembers how, when I came home, she would complain that my shoulders were black and blue. Laughing, I would explain that she should feel thankful; the shoulder welts and bruises meant Ernest had always missed my jaw or nose or mouth. She worried about the day coming when I would walk in with welts on my jaw or cheeks rather than my shoulders.

One dark cloudy afternoon I had called for Ernest and when we came out to the street, a soft rain had begun to fall. It was one of those lovely soft early-summer Paris rains. I was coatless; Ernest had brought a raincoat. We could have got a taxi, but the rain now was so gentle and the air so soft he said, "Let's walk." Taking one arm of the raincoat, he held that side of the coat out wide like a tent over me, his arm like a tent pole, and we loafed along. We talked. No big talk. Just gossip. It was like times at home at college when I might have called for an old friend and decided to walk with him in the rain because I liked being with him and felt sure of him.

That day, and for the first time, he did something that astonished me. At the American Club, we had undressed and got down to the business of boxing. By this time, knowing his style, I had worked out a routine. Moving in and out, I had to make him lead at me. He knew what I was doing. His brown eyes always on me, he waited for a chance to nail me solidly. When he finally threw his long left, I slipped it and then stepped in and caught him on the mouth with my own left. He knew by the book he should catch me with his right.

It must have been exasperating to him that my left was always beating him to the punch. His mouth began to bleed. It had happened before. It wasn't important. His tongue kept curling along his lip, wiping off blood. Again he got hit on the lip, yet his eyes held mine as he swallowed the blood. But his mouth kept on bleeding. He loudly sucked in all the blood. He waited, watching me, and took another punch on the mouth. Then as I went to slip in again, he stiffened. Suddenly he spat at me; he spat a mouthful of blood; he spat in my face. My gym shirt too was spattered with blood.

I was so shocked I dropped my gloves. My face must have gone white, for I was shaken and didn't know what to do. It is a terrible insult for a man to spit at another man. We stared at each other. "That's what the bullfighters do when they're wounded. It's a way of showing contempt," he said solemnly.

My sense of outrage was weakened by my bewilderment when he suddenly smiled. Apparently he felt as friendly as ever. I tried to laugh. But we had to stop boxing so I could wipe off the blood. I didn't even complain, for I saw that he had more complete goodwill for me than ever. But I was wondering out of what strange nocturnal depths of his mind had come the barbarous gesture. What other wild gesture might he make in some dark moment in his life to satisfy himself, or put himself in a certain light, following, or trying to follow, some view he had of himself? But here he was, so sweet and likeable again, so much at ease with me. I tried to tell myself he had put it just right; he had yielded to his boyish weakness for amusing and theatrical gestures. The whole thing could have been pure theatre.

As we sat down to talk before we dressed he seemed to be full of lighthearted enthusiasm. Standing up, he regarded me with a professional eye. "You're really a light heavyweight," he insisted. "It's the way you're built. I thought at first it was just fat on you." I assented to this rather reluctantly, knowing I was twenty-five pounds overweight, simply potbellied and secretly ashamed of it. I liked eating. Then he told me he had written to Max Perkins, trying to describe the fun we had been having and my peculiar boxing style.

He suggested we go up to the Falstaff, off Montparnasse, an oak-paneled English bar presided over by Jimmy, a friend of his, an Englishman who had been a pro lightweight fighter. At that hour hardly anyone else was in the bar. Behind the bar Jimmy now looked like an amiable roly-poly host. Just a day or two ago I had been asking Jimmy what Lady Duff, the Lady Brett of The Sun Also Rises, was really like. Leaning across the bar, Jimmy had said confidentially, "You won't tell Hemingway, will you? No? Well, she was one of those horsey English girls with her hair cut short and the

English manner. Hemingway thought she had class. He used to go dancing with her over on the Right Bank. I could never see what he saw in her."

But now Jimmy, observing the bag with the boxing gloves Ernest was carrying, and our scrubbed, wet-haired look, the look of men who have been exercising then showering, grinned knowingly. "You've been boxing, eh?" Smiling happily, Ernest touched his swollen lip, rolling it back to show it to Jimmy, the old fighter. I remember Ernest's line: "As long as Morley can keep cutting my mouth he'll always remain my good friend." We all laughed. Yet Ernest did look remarkably happy. His cut and swollen mouth seemed to make him feel jolly and talkative. He told how good Jimmy had been in the ring. He insisted Jimmy have a drink with us. And the strange part of it was that in spite of the fact that Ernest had spat his blood on my face, I felt closer than ever to him.

But the look on his face as he spat at me must have stayed in my head. Of course I had to explain to Loretto the cause of the blood marks on my gym shirt. We wondered at the source of his unbridled impulse, so primitive and insulting. Supposing it had enraged me and caused us to part forever? Had such a thought ever entered his head?

Late one night we were at the Sélect, six or seven of us around two tables, and a pretty woman named Mary Bryant, whom I had never met before and who had been the wife of William Bullitt, the the U.S. Ambassador to Moscow, told a story about Hemingway. She had had a Turkish boy as a protégé. This boy was an expert knife thrower. The boy had been with her one time when she had told Hemingway he could throw a knife at twenty paces and pin an object, a man's hand for example, to a door. Getting up suddenly, Hemingway had gone over to the door, and thrust out his hand. "Come on, show me. Come on," he challenged the boy. "Pin my hand to the door." The story may or may not have been true. I had been rejecting all stories about Ernest that made him a strange dark primitive nocturnal figure. Yet now I seemed to know from what had happened between us that any time he faced a situation from which he ought to recoil protestingly or normally, he might start to play around with the destructive idea, testing his own courage in his imagination. In those days, as I said before, it seemed to me he could make the imagined challenging fear become so real, it might become unbearable. And he would act. Somehow these thoughts seem to tie up with that picture I had of him spitting the blood at me with such theatrical scorn, and then, knowing he shouldn't have done it, laughing.

At the Sélect that night, after hearing the story about the Turkish boy, I laughed with the others. Ernest did a lot of things that were merely imaginative gestures, I said. But they were only gestures. And I told about him spitting a mouthful of blood all over me when we were boxing, and how it hadn't altered our relationship at all. It was the only time I had talked about any incident in our boxing matches. Later on it became important to me to recall this one occasion. But the Quarter in those days, crowded as it was at certain hours with tourists, was a very small, backbiting, gossipy little neighborhood.

FURTHER READING

WORKS BY MORLEY CALLAGHAN

Strange Fugitive (Edmonton: Hurtig Publishers, 1970). First published 1928.

Such is my Beloved (Toronto: McClelland and Stewart, New Canadian Library, 1957). First published 1934.

They Shall Inherit the Earth (Toronto: McClelland and Stewart, New Canadian Library, 1962). First published 1935.

More Joy in Heaven (Toronto: McClelland and Stewart, New Canadian Library, 1960). First published 1937.

The Loved and the Lost (Toronto: The Macmillan Company of Canada, Laurentian Library, 1970). First published 1951.

Morley Callaghan's Stories (Toronto: The Macmillan Company of Canada, Laurentian Library, 1967). First published 1959.

The Many Colored Coat (Toronto: The Macmillan Company of Canada, 1960).

A Passion in Rome (Toronto: The Macmillan Company of Canada, 1961). Also available in Dell paperback.

That Summer in Paris (Toronto: The Macmillan Company of Canada, 1963).

RELATED WORKS

Ernest Hemingway, *A Moveable Feast* (Bantam Paperback, 1965).

John Glassco, *Memoirs of Montparnasse* (Toronto: Oxford University Press, 1970).

CRITICISM

George Woodcock, *Odysseus Ever Returning* (Toronto: McClelland and Stewart, New Canadian Library, 1970).

A. J. M. Smith, ed., *Masks of Fiction* (Toronto: McClelland and Stewart, New Canadian Library, 1961).

Victor Hoar, *Morley Callaghan* (Toronto: Copp Clark Publishers, Studies in Canadian Literature Series).

Morley Callaghan (Toronto: Coles Publishing Company, Canadian Writers and Critics Series).

Leonard Cohen

Leonard Cohen (1934-), was born into a prosperous Jewish family in Montreal, and grew up in the suburb of Westmount. He majored in English at McGill, graduating in 1955. He attempted first the family clothing business, then law at Columbia, but abandoned both to live and write on the small Greek Island of Hydra. During this time he supported himself on the proceeds from his writing and a small inheritance of $750 a year, supplemented by Canada Council Grants in 1960 and 1961 and the Quebec Prize for Literature in 1964. He has gained an international reputation as a novelist, poet and, more recently, composer and singer of folk songs. He won the Governor-General's Award for Selected Poems, 1956-68, *but turned it down with this explanation: "Much in me strives for this honour but the poems themselves forbid it absolutely." His strict artistic code has not, however, hindered his emergence as an international pop star and flamboyant leader of the youth culture.*

GONE FOR GOOD

Still Breavman and Krantz often used to drive through the whole night. They'd listen to pop tunes on the local stations or classics from the United States. They'd head north to the Laurentians or east to the Townships.

Breavman imagined the car they were in as seen from above. A small black pellet hurtling across the face of the earth. Free as a meteor and maybe as doomed.

They fled past fields of blue snow. The icy crust kept a stroke of moonlight the way rippled water does. The heater was going full blast. They had nowhere to be in the morning, only lectures and that

From: Leonard Cohen, *The Favourite Game* (Toronto: McClelland and Stewart, New Canadian Library, 1970). Reprinted by permission of McClelland and Stewart, the Canadian Publishers.

didn't count. Everything above the snow was black–trees, shacks, whole villages.

Moving at that speed they were not bound to anything. They could sample all the possibilities. They flashed by trees that took a hundred years to grow. They tore through towns where men lived their whole lives. They knew the land was old, the mountains the most ancient on earth. They covered it all at eighty miles an hour.

There was something disdainful in their speed, disdainful of the eons it took the mountains to smooth out, of the generations of muscle which had cleared the fields, of the labour which had gone into the modern road they rolled on. They were aware of the disdain. The barbarians must have ridden Roman highways with the same feeling. We have the power now. Who cares what went before?

And there was something frightened in their speed. Back in the city their families were growing like vines. Mistresses were teaching a sadness no longer lyrical but claustrophobic. The adult community was insisting that they choose an ugly particular from the range of beautiful generalities. They were flying from their majority, from the real bar mitzvah, the real initiation, the real and vicious circumcision which society was hovering to inflict through limits and dull routine.

They spoke gently to the French girls in the diners where they stopped. They were so pathetic, false-toothed and frail. They'd forget them in the next twenty miles. What were they doing behind the arborite counters? Dreaming of Montreal neon?

The highway was empty. They were the only two in flight, and that knowledge made them deeper friends than ever. It elated Breavman. He'd say, "Krantz, all they'll ever find of us is a streak of oil on the garage floor without even rainbows in it." Lately Krantz had been very silent, but Breavman was certain he was thinking the same things. Everyone they knew or who loved them was sleeping miles behind the exhaust. If the radio music was rock-and-roll, they understood the longing of it; if it was Handel, they understood the majesty.

At some point in these rides Breavman would proposition himself like this: Breavman, you're eligible for many diverse experiences in this best of all possible worlds. There are many beautiful poems which you will write and be praised for, many desolate days when you won't be able to lay pen to paper. There will be many heights of emotion, intense sunsets, exalting insights, creative pain, and many murderous plateaus of indifference where you won't even own your personal despair. There will be many good hands of power you can play with ruthlessness or benevolence, many vast skies to lie under and congratulate yourself on humility, many galley rides of suffocating slavery. This is what waits for you.

Now, Breavman, here is the proposition: Let us suppose that you could spend the rest of your life exactly as you are at this very minute, in this car hurtling toward brush country, at this precise stop on the road beside a row of white guideposts, always going past these posts at eighty, this jukebox song of rejection pumping, this particular sky of clouds and stars, your mind including this immediate cross-section of memory—which would you choose? Fifty more years of this car ride, or fifty more of achievement and failure?

And Breavman never hesitated in his choice.

Let it go on as it is right now. Let the speed never diminish. Let the snow remain. Let me never be removed from this partnership with my friend. Let us never find different things to do. Let us never evaluate one another. Let the moon stay on one side of the road. Let the girls be a gold blur in my mind, like the haze of the moon, or the neon glow above the city. Let the compounded electric guitar keep throbbing under the declaration:

> *When I lost my baby*
> *I almost lost my mind.*

Let the edges of the hills be just about to brighten. Let the trees never fuzz with leaves. Let the black towns sleep in one long night like Lesbia's lover. Let the monks in the half-built monasteries remain on there in the 4 A.M. Latin prayer. Let Pat Boone stand on the highest rung of the Hit Parade and tell all the factory night shifts:

> *I went to see a gypsy*
> *And had my fortune read.*

Let snow always dignify the auto graveyards on the road to Ayer's Cliff. Let the nailed shacks of apple vendors never show polished apples and hints of cider.

But let me remember what I remember of orchards. Let me keep my tenth of a second's worth of fantasy and recollection, showing all the layers like a geologist's sample. Let the Caddie or the VW run like a charm, let it go like a bomb, let it blast. Let the tune make the commercial wait forever:

> *Well I can tell you people,*
> *The news was not so good.*

The news is great. The news is sad but it's in a song so it's not so bad. Pat is doing all my poems for me. He's got lines to a million people. It's all I wanted to say. He's distilled the sorrow, glorified it in an echo chamber. I don't need my typewriter. It's not the piece of luggage I suddenly remembered I forgot. No pencils, ball-pens, pad. I don't even want to draw in the mist on the windshield. I can make up sagas in my head all the way to Baffin Island but I don't have to write them down. Pat, you've snitched my job, but you're such a good guy, old-time American success, naïve big winner, that it's okay. The PR men have convinced me that you are a humble kid. I can't resent you. My only criticism is: be more desperate, try and sound more agonized or we'll have to get a Negro to replace you:

> *She said your baby has quit you,*
> *This time she's gone for good.*

Don't let the guitars slow down like locomotive wheels. Don't let the man at CKVL tell me what I've just been listening to. Sweet sounds, reject me not. Let the words go on like the landscape we're never driving out of:

> *gone for good*

Oh, let the last syllable endure. This is the tenth of a second I've traded all the presidencies for. The telephone poles are playing intricate games of Cat's Cradle with the rushing wires. The snow is piled like the Red Sea on either side of our fenders. We're not expected and we're not missed. We put all our money in the gas tank, we're fat as camels in the Sahara. The hurtling car, the trees, the moon and its light on the fields of snow, the resigned grinding chords of the tune–everything is poised in perfection for the quick freeze, the eternal case in the astral museum.

> *ood*

So long, mister, mistress, rabbi, doctor. 'By. Don't forget your salesman's bag of adventure samples. My friend and I we'll stay right here–on our side of the speed limit. Won't we, Krantz, won't we, Krantz, won't we, Krantz?

"Want to stop for a hamburger?" says Krantz as though he were musing on an abstract theory.

"Now or one of these days?"

FURTHER READING

NOVELS BY LEONARD COHEN

The Favourite Game (Toronto: McClelland and Stewart, New Canadian Library, 1970). First published 1963.

Beautiful Losers (Toronto: McClelland and Stewart, 1966). Also available in Bantam paperback.

POETRY BY LEONARD COHEN

The following have all been published by McClelland and Stewart, Toronto:

Flowers for Hitler, 1964
Let Us Compare Mythologies, 1966
The Spice Box of Earth, 1961
Selected Poems, 1956-1968
Parasites of Heaven, 1966

CRITICISM

Michael Ondaatje, *Leonard Cohen* (Toronto: McClelland and Stewart, Canadian Writers Series, 1970).

Gary Geddes, *Leonard Cohen* (Toronto: Copp Clark Publishers).

George Woodcock, *Odysseus Ever Returning* (Toronto: McClelland and Stewart, New Canadian Library, 1970).

RECORDINGS BY LEONARD COHEN

Leonard Cohen
Songs from a Room
Leonard Cohen: Songs of Love and Hate
The above are produced by Columbia Records.
Canadian Poets, 2 records which include Leonard Cohen reading seven of his poems. Obtainable from: CBC, Box 500, Terminal A, Toronto.

RELATED STUDY

Jack Kerouac, *On the Road* (Signet Paperback).

Hugh Garner

Hugh Garner (1913-) was born in England, and came to Canada as a child. The family lived in Toronto in the slum district he described with such fidelity in Cabbagetown, *his novel about the depression years. During the 'thirties he was already establishing a reputation as a short story writer, contributing to* Canadian Forum, 1936-37. *He joined the Mackenzie-Papineau Battalion and fought in the Spanish Civil War in 1937. In the Second World War he joined the army, then served in the navy on convoy duty in the Atlantic. After the war he wrote prolifically, contributing short stories and humorous essays to popular magazines such as* Chatelaine, Liberty *and the* Star Weekly *as well as to* Northern Review, Queen's Quarterly, Tamarack Review *and the CBC. He received the Governor-General's Award for* Hugh Garner's Best Stories *(1963). To date he has also written five novels, three of them published between 1968 and 1970.*

E EQUALS MC SQUARED

There were two guys standing at the inspection bench when I came back from the water fountain. A short Bulgarian we called Joe had an angle bracket with holes at each end. I picked it up, glanced at the layout on the greasy blueprint, and measured the diameters and positions of the holes with my scale. Most of the operators liked to bring their work to the counter, especially the first ones off the press, for it gave them a short break away from their machines.

"Is good?" Joe asked.

"Sure. You've got a tolerance a mile wide on this," I told him.

I filled out a "first off" tag and attached it to the inspected part.

In those days, just after the war, Malloy-Harrison was swamped with orders for self-propelled combines, and the plant was humming three shifts a day, six days a week. Every shift another trainload of the big red reaper-threshers came off the assembly lines and began their journey to West Germany, Ireland, Turkey, South Africa, and a dozen other countries you'd hardly even heard of. We had a good union and a closed shop, and you could make fifty bucks a week without overtime. Changing shifts every week was murder, though, and nobody really liked working for Malloy-Harrison, but the money was better than most places, and the whole world needed farm machinery.

Matt Colby, one of the gang-press operators, placed a long piece of T-stock on the metal counter top.

"Give me a first off on this, Eric," he said.

"What do you think of the heat, Matt?"

He shook his head wearily. "It's hotter'n the hubs a'hell in here," he answered. "I don't know how those guys on the forges can stand it."

"I hear two of them collapsed on the four-to-twelve shift," I told him. "The forge foreman can't get some of them to take the salt tablets."

Matt gave a cynical laugh. "I guess they think anything Malloy-Harrison gives for free has a catch in it," he said.

His length of T-stock was punched with a complicated series of holes, not counting the ones drilled in the machine-shop. The part would become a movable component of the combine when it was finished, and it was pretty tricky. There could be no guesswork on it—all the holes had to be scaled, and calipered too.

Matt was stripped to the waist, as most of the operators were during this July heatwave. Except for some oil streaks on his chest and back his skin was a dead white beneath the dim naked lights hung high in the vault-like chamber the punch press shared with the forges. He wore a faded tattoo on his upper arm: a small warship with the name H.M.C.S. *Burnaby* beneath it.

"This heat hasn't let up since last Thursday," he said as I inspected the piece. "One of my kids has got pneumonia, and this heat is hard on him. The heat's worse than cold when you've got pneumonia."

When I looked up I saw that his thoughts were a thousand miles from the farm implement plant. I felt sorry for all the guys whose marriages kept them stuck in a crummy job like this. Alex Bellamy, the chief inspector, used to say that our part of the factory had been built to change the swords of 1812 into ploughshares, and I think he was right. Most of the other departments were housed in modern buildings, but management seemed to think that this rickety old hole was good enough for unskilled forge and press operators.

The pressmen were looked down on by the machinists, moulders, pattern-makers–and even by the jerks on sub-assembly. In the cafeteria, a quarter of a mile from our little corner of hell, some of the smart-alecs greeted us by folding a couple of fingers into a fist, as if they'd been amputated. We didn't have to joke about such things; there were enough guys in our department minus fingers and hands to turn the joke sour.

Matt said, "Connolly, the guy that was working my press on the four-to-twelve, quit the job tonight. The time-study people have raised production on this part to three hundred and forty a shift, and he couldn't punch more than two-eighty-five. If I didn't have a family and a mortgage I'd quit this lousy job myself."

I didn't answer him but concentrated on the inspection. The tolerances were pretty fine, and McKillup, the punch-press foreman, was sure to check the piece himself.

"That stinking gang press slips too," Matt went on. "I shoulda told the superintendent when I come off shift yesterday mornin'. I told McKillup about it, but that rat-faced clown is too worried about his production figures. He told me I'm not workin' the foot-pedal right." I looked up, and his mouth had tightened nervously. "It's dangerous. I think that's the real reason Connolly quit."

I attached a tag to his piece of stock. "This piece is good, Matt," I said. "Take it easy, and don't worry about production–or McKillup either."

He picked up the piece from the counter, and I watched him as he threaded his way down the aisle towards the room across the alley where the three gang presses were housed.

It was nearly one-thirty before Larry Stepanich, the other inspector, came down the aisle, dodging a speeding forklift being driven by a young truck-jockey from final assembly. The echoing noise joined with the heat to frazzle your nerve ends–the clump-thud-swish of half a hundred presses, the fiery roar of the forges, and the bell-like clang of steel parts boxes as they were moved from beside the machines. From overhead the ancient shafts and belts moaned and rattled, and threatened to bring down the roof.

"All the presses running, Step?" I asked my partner as he came around the counter.

"The die-setters are working on eighteen, nineteen, and thirty-seven," he said. "Only one of the gang presses is operating."

"I know. I gave a first off to Matt Colby."

Step pulled a bottle of Coke from the lukewarm water in the washbowl, and knocked off its top against the steel edge of the inspection bench. He was wearing a once-white undershirt and army fatigue pants. A paperback book peeked from a pocket of his oily fatigues. He tilted his head back and drained the bottle at a gulp.

I picked up my gloves, and shoved my scale and calipers into the back pocket of my dungarees. As I reached for my clipboard Step said, "Did you hear about McKillup?"

"No."

"You know about the new specifications for those lengths of one-eighth spring stock?"

I nodded, and pointed to the note clipped to my board.

"The drawing calls for a length of twelve and three-sixteenths, but engineering asked for a change in length during the day shift, and old Ernie is shearing them to eleven and three-sixteenths."

Ernie Colby was Matt's father, a union steward who had operated a shearing press for thirty years.

"What happened?" I asked, smiling in anticipation.

"Everybody knew about the change in length but McKillup. You know how he'd like a chance to hurt old Ernie." Step began to laugh. "That dopey foreman. He didn't bother to check with me, but just picked up a handful of the shortened stock, and the blueprint, and stormed off to his office."

"Go on," I said.

"He called up the chief inspector first, but Alex hung up on him. Then McKillup, hotter'n a two-dollar pistol by now, called up the department superintendent."

"Old Walters himself? In the middle of the night!"

"Sure." We both laughed. "Walters chewed him out for not knowing that the specifications had been changed, and for waking him up at a quarter to one in the morning."

"I'd sure like to have seen his face."

"The timekeeper told me he just kept opening and shutting his mouth but nothing came out."

After we stopped laughing, Step pulled his book from his pocket and sat down on our only stool. Step was pretty bright. He had graduated from technical high, and was going to university in the fall to take an engineering course. I liked him, but his choice of reading material used to bug me.

"What's the name of the book?" I asked him.

He held it up. It was something called "Breakthroughs in Scientific Thought."

"You really like that kind of stuff, Step?"

"This is very good," he said, slapping the book against his knee. "Imagine a guy like Albert Einstein sitting down and just thinking that E equalled MC squared. It baffles the mind."

"It baffles mine how you can read stuff like that," I said as I headed around the counter.

"Watch out for McKillup, he's really on the warpath now," Step shouted after me.

I gave a fleeting thought or two to E equalling MC squared, but I forgot about it by the time I reached my first press. Bobby Earle pulled a bar strut from his machine and handed it to me.

"You tryin' out for the bowling team, Eric?" he asked.

"Sure thing. You?"

"May as well. Run-offs are on Thursday night," he said.

I distributed tags to all the machines but those that were being set up, marking the press and part numbers, and the time, on my inspection sheet. I finished in the big room before I looked at my watch. It was almost three o'clock.

"Hi, Eric!" shouted Pete Adams, one of the forge operators, from where he was standing at the drinking fountain.

I crossed the grime-slippery floor and watched him gargle a mouthful of water before spitting it into the floor drain. He was soaking wet, and the drops of sweat were quicksilver against his black skin as they gathered to run down his body in rivulets. He was wearing shoes and socks, and a pair of jockey shorts.

I told him about McKillup, but he disliked the foreman as much as the rest of us, and he didn't laugh.

He sluiced some water down his glistening chest. "The guy who said Negroes could stand the heat sure never worked a forge press this weather," he remarked.

"You taking your salt pills, Pete?" I asked him.

"Man, I'm eatin' them like popcorn," he answered laughing.

"I'll see you, Pete," I said as I hurried away from the terrible heat from the forges.

When I reached the yard between the big press room and the smaller one holding the gang presses, I paused in the unbelievable quiet and coolness and lit a cigarette. There was a breeze blowing across the railroad yards, and a switch engine was moving a string of flat-cars from a company siding. Each car carried three big red-painted combines, all wedged and strapped securely for their trip to a seaport or out west. Seeing the finished product, like this, was the only time that the punch-press department seemed to make any sense.

"Is that what you're being paid for?" a familiar voice snarled in my ear.

Without looking around I knew it was McKillup. I wiped the sweat from my throat with the backs of my cotton gloves. The foreman had no jurisdiction over the inspectors, even if he could make trouble by reporting you.

"I see you guys haven't put no hold tags on the parts coming from the gang press."

I turned to him then. "I gave Colby a first off at the beginning of the shift," I said. "I'm just on my way to the gang press now."

He leaned his mean unsweated face into mine and said, "Colby spoiled the last twenty pieces. You ever heard of torn and cracked walls in a punched hole?"

"Sure."

"Then take a look at this." He shoved a length of T-stock into my hands.

I carried it over to the lighted doorway of the shop and glanced down at it. It was a mess, the only good holes along its entire length being those drilled in the machine-shop. Those made by the gang press were uneven and oblique, their edges ringed with sunbursts of tiny cracks.

"You think they can countersink them holes?" McKillup asked.

I shook my head.

"Colby's lucky I didn't fire him on the spot," the foreman said.

There was something phony about his generosity towards Ernie Colby's son, and I thought I knew what it was.

"You having the bull-gang fix that press?" I asked him. "I know Colby reported to you that it was slipping."

"That's no business of the inspectors. If you and that bohunk partner of yours had checked the gang press as you're supposed to, Colby mightn't have spoiled so many pieces."

He was a real nice guy. I threw the long piece of T-stock back to him, and he had to grab it fast to keep it from dropping on his toes.

When I reached the gang-press room I couldn't see Colby's press, which was hidden from the doorway by the other giant machines. Except for a dim sound of hammering the room was unnaturally quiet. The big hydraulic presses stood silent, their terrible punch-toothed maws waiting for a foot on their treadles to make them close with a room-shaking bite. The mere sight of their size and power made me hate to enter the place, and I was always happy to leave the room again when my job was finished.

A long hoarse hoot of the factory whistle announced the lunch break, and I dropped my clipboard and gloves onto the table of the nearest machine and scooted up the passageway towards the cafeteria. This time I'd be lucky and beat the mob to the cafeteria queue.

I ate a lunch of meat pie, mashed and gravy with Larry Stepanich,

Pete Adams, and another forge operator called Morgan. We all got quite a bang over the story about McKillup calling up Walters, the super. Step asked Pete Adams how his other job was coming, and Pete smiled and shrugged. Adams was a jazz pianist who hadn't got it made yet, and he played piano in a downtown restaurant at the dinner hour. He didn't swing his shifts, but worked a steady grave-yard.

Morgan nodded his head in the direction of a table across the room. We looked over to where old Ernie Colby was eating his homemade sandwiches. He was with a couple of his cronies from the machine-shop.

"Those three old geezers have worked here since they invented the gang plough," Morgan said.

"Even before that," added Step.

"Man, what a horrible way to die!" Pete exclaimed, his black face splitting with a burst of laughter.

Both Pete and Step were working for Malloy-Harrison with an end in view. I guess I was too, but right then I didn't know what it was. The idea of working all my life at the plant, like Ernie Colby had done, scared me. The deadly sameness of the work, and conditions that even the union hadn't been able to change, made me despise people like Ernie. Running a shearing press for thirty years had made him an unthinking part of his machine.

I wondered why he had ever got his son a job in the place. In a few years Matt Colby would be just like his father, held to his press not by love or loyalty but by a lethargy that wouldn't let him quit. I realized I had to get away myself, before a steady pay envelope conned me out of whatever ambitions were in the back of my mind.

"Why didn't Matt come up here tonight?" Step asked.

I told him about meeting McKillup, and about the spoiled pieces from the gang press.

"I knew that machine was slipping. When are they going to fix it?"

"It's being fixed right now. I could hear the bull-gang hammering in there just as the lunch whistle blew."

The tables were clearing, and a noisy gang from sub-assembly were shoving and skylarking their way through the door, when the alarm bell began to ring. The three short rings showed it was an accident, and the two longs and a short which followed gave the location.

"It's the paint shop," Pete said. "One of those monkeys musta sprayed the foreman."

My laugh died on my lips as Morgan said, "It's the press room. The gang-press room."

The meat pie turned a flip in my stomach as I thought of the men of the bull-gang–any accident in the gang press was sure to be a bad one.

We all left our paper cups and sandwich papers and hurried out of the cafeteria.

There was a small crowd clustered in the gang-press doorway, and somebody mentioned that the doctor and the safety director had been called on the phone. I shouldered my way in and picked up my clipboard and gloves from where I'd thrown them when the lunch whistle went. There were whispered voices at the back end of the room, and I made my way between the presses and the wall.

The body was hanging out from the clenched lips of the press, its feet suspended in the air. It looked like a messy doll hanging over the edge of a shelf. The machine was clamped across it near the shoulders, leaving one limp and lifeless arm hanging down beside the body. Through the seeping blood that dripped inexorably to the floor I saw a tattooed ship on the hanging arm. Three or four men stood in a white-faced group apart from the machine, keeping their eyes on me so they wouldn't have to look at the other. I turned away sickened, and got out of the place fast.

Back at the inspection bench Step said, "It's a breach of company and union regulations for an operator to fix his own machine."

"I know it is."

"McKillup will deny that he ordered Colby to fix it himself. You can bet he's already filled out a breakdown report to the millwrights."

"Sure."

Step said, "When they told old Ernie that Matt was dead, he didn't say anything . . . or want to go see him . . . or anything. He just shut off his press, took off his apron, and walked to the time clocks. He seemed incapable of any feelings at all, as if the last thirty years had crushed them completely. You'd have thought . . . happening to his own son . . ." He picked up his clipboard and hurried from the inspection bench.

As Step had said he would, the foreman denied having ordered Matt Colby to make the repairs on the machine, and he had a time-stamped breakdown report to the millwrights to back up his lie. The verdict of the coroner's jury was accidental death, and all that happened was a rash of safety posters for a while. Matt's widow was given a compensation pension, and neither the union nor the company pressed for a further investigation.

The terrible accident to McKillup happened near the end of the summer, on the four-to-twelve shift. The usual absenteeism at that time of year, and some breakdown in the decrepit machinery, had put the department behind. The foreman was worried about his production figures, and he was all over the floor cursing and ranting at the operators. Sub-assembly was running short of parts, the most important being some quarter-inch strapping, a reaper cutter-bar we called the BF-204. The piece had to be sheared and punched before going to the forge to be extruded, and only old Ernie Colby's press was set up to do the job. The day-shift assembly had caught up, and even with a lift truck hurrying the parts to the forge we were falling behind.

Larry Stepanich, who was doing the floor inspection, told me that McKillup had ordered old Ernie to feed two pieces at a time into his machine.

The old man had stared at him for a minute. "It'll ruin the dies," he told the foreman. "She's on'y set up to take one piece at a punch."

"I know that, but we can't shut down the sub-assembly," McKillup said, anger and panic fighting for his voice.

The old man shrugged. "I ain't goin' to take the responsibility though," he said.

McKillup called Step over as a witness, and ordered the old man to feed the pieces two at a time. Ernie did as he was ordered, with only a shake of his head to show his disapproval.

Step said that the machine nearly tore itself from its bed, but it sheared the pieces all right. By seven-thirty we had caught up with the sub-assembly. Then the press jammed.

Ernie wasted several minutes fooling around with it, but finally found the foreman and got him to call the bull-gang. McKillup ranted and raged, for he found that the millwrights were busy in the machine-shop and it would be another hour before they could come down to fix the shearing press. When the lunch whistle blew, old Ernie followed the rest of us to the cafeteria, leaving the foreman staring angrily at the shut-down press.

We had only just begun our lunch when the alarm bell rang, so the only ones who got up were the first-aid men. By the time I got back to the punch-press department McKillup had been rushed to the hospital and the mess had all been cleared up. The die-setters were setting up two other machines to punch and shear the BF-204 parts. By half-past ten we had caught up once more with sub-assembly.

There was an investigation about McKillup's accident, and some talk about a missing cam from the gear box of the shearing press. Ernie Colby was questioned but he told the safety committee that he knew nothing about a cam, and that he'd reported the breakdown to the foreman as soon as he'd been able to find him. The board decided that McKillup had been negligent, and the walls broke out once more in a display of safety slogans.

On his final shift before he left the job to go to university, I asked Larry Stepanich, "What will McKillup do, now that he has no arms and gets no compensation?"

"The company will give him a watchman's job or something, I guess."

"It's funny how that cam came to be missing from the gear box. The head of the machine was sure to fall if anybody reached inside and moved the gears."

He nodded.

"Do you think the cam was taken out on purpose, Step?"

"The board didn't seem to think so. Anyhow, McKillup wasn't supposed to try to clear the machine himself."

"I guess nobody'll ever know how it happened."

Step gave me a long look. "It works for more things than relativity," he said. And, seeing my bewilderment, added, "Remember, Eric? The night Matt was killed, E equals MC squared?"

I didn't know what he was talking about. "What do those letters stand for anyway?"

"Well, in this case MC could stand for Matt Colby, if you wanted them to."

It was long after I too had left the plant that I found what the letters really stood for. Einstein's equation might mean one thing to science, but to me it will always mean Matt Colby's death, and the awful retribution to the foreman. It ties them both together neatly, squaring off one with the other, and pointing to the relative factor E, which could mean Ernie. I don't know whether I really believe that or not— it's a theory, that's all.

A short time ago I was driving past the main gate of the Malloy-Harrison plant, and I noticed McKillup tending the gates. One uniform sleeve was empty, and the other ended above one of those steel mechanical hands. The sight of him brought it all back to me, but I'd just as soon forget it if I could.

FURTHER READING

NOVELS BY HUGH GARNER
The following have all been published by Simon and Schuster of Canada, Toronto, and are all in paperback.

Storm Below, first published 1949.

Cabbagetown, first published 1950, and revised in 1968.

Silence on the Shore, first published 1962.

The Sin Sniper, first published 1970.

A Nice Place to Visit, first published 1970.

SHORT STORIES BY HUGH GARNER

Hugh Garner's Best Stories (Toronto: Simon and Schuster of Canada, 1963).

Violation of the Virgins: Stories by Hugh Garner (Toronto: McGraw-Hill Ryerson, 1971).

AUDIO

Canadian Writers on Tape (includes Hugh Garner), obtainable from: Publications Sales, OISE, 102 Bloor St. West, Toronto.

Farley Mowat

Farley Mowat (1921-), son of the well-known Canadian librarian, Angus Mowat, was born in Belleville, Ontario, but spent part of his childhood in Saskatchewan. He served in the Second World War, then lived in the Arctic for two years before returning to the University of Toronto to graduate in 1949. In his first book, People of the Deer *(1952), he tackled the problem of the ecology of the Barren Lands of Canada long before the environment had become of general concern. He has written on a wide range of subjects: Norse communities in Greenland and North America, histories of sea rescues, humorous personal reminiscences, adventure stories for children, including* Lost in the Barrens *(1956) which won a Governor-General's Award. He has also edited narratives of Arctic explorers.*

GOOD OLD UNCLE ALBERT

As I grew more completely attuned to their daily round of family life I found it increasingly difficult to maintain an impersonal attitude toward the wolves. No matter how hard I tried to regard them with scientific objectivity, I could not resist the impact of their individual personalities. Because he reminded me irresistibly of a Royal Gentleman for whom I worked as a simple soldier during the war, I found myself calling the father of the family George, even though in my notebooks, he was austerely identified only as Wolf "A."

George was a massive and eminently regal beast whose coat was silver-white. He was about a third larger than his mate, but he hardly needed this extra bulk to emphasize his air of masterful certainty. George had presence. His dignity was unassailable, yet he was by no means aloof. Conscientious to a fault, thoughtful of others, and af-

From: Farley Mowat, *Never Cry Wolf* (Toronto: McClelland and Stewart, 1963). Reprinted by permission of McClelland and Stewart, the Canadian Publishers.

fectionate within reasonable bounds, he was the kind of father whose idealized image appears in many wistful books of human family reminiscences, but whose real prototype has seldom paced the earth upon two legs. George was, in brief, the kind of father every son longs to acknowledge as his own.

His wife was equally memorable. A slim, almost pure-white wolf with a thick ruff around her face, and wide-spaced, slightly slanted eyes, she seemed the picture of a minx. Beautiful, ebullient, passionate to a degree, and devilish when the mood was on her, she hardly looked like the epitome of motherhood; yet there could have been no better mother anywhere. I found myself calling her Angeline, although I have never been able to trace the origin of that name in the murky depths of my own subconscious. I respected and liked George very much, but I became deeply fond of Angeline, and still live in hopes that I can somewhere find a human female who embodies all her virtues.

Angeline and George seemed as devoted a mated pair as one could hope to find. As far as I could tell they never quarrelled, and the delight with which they greeted each other after even a short absence was obviously unfeigned. They were extremely affectionate with one another, but, alas, the many pages in my notebook which had been hopefully reserved for detailed comments on the sexual behavior and activities of wolves remained obstinately blank as far as George and Angeline were concerned.

Distressing as it was to my expectations, I discovered that physical lovemaking enters into the lives of a pair of mated wolves only during a period of two or three weeks early in the spring, usually in March. Virgin females, (and they are all virginal until their second year) then mate; but unlike dogs, who have adopted many of the habits of their human owners, wolf bitches mate with only a single male, and mate for life.

Whereas the phrase "till death us do part" is one of the more amusing mockeries in the nuptial arrangements of a large proportion of the human race, with wolves it is a simple fact. Wolves are also strict monogamists; and although I do not necessarily consider this an admirable trait, it does make the reputation for unbridled promiscuity which we have bestowed on the wolf somewhat hypocritical.

While it was not possible for me to know with exact certainty how long George and Angeline had been mated, I was later able to discover from Mike that they had been together for at least five years–or the equivalent of thirty years in terms of the relative longevity of wolves and men. Mike and the Eskimos recognized the wolves in their area as familiar individuals, and the Eskimos (but not Mike) held the wolves in such high regard that they would not have thought of killing them or doing them an injury. Thus not only were George, Angeline and other members of the family well known to the Eskimos, but the site of their den had been known for some forty or fifty years, during which time generations of wolves had raised families there.

One factor concerning the organization of the family mystified me very much at first. During my early visit to the den I had seen *three* adult wolves; and during the first few days of observing the den I had again glimpsed the odd-wolf-out several times. He posed a major conundrum, for while I could accept the idea of a contented domestic group consisting of mated male and female and a bevy of pups, I had not yet progressed far enough into the wolf world to be able to explain, or to accept, the apparent existence of an eternal triangle.

Whoever the third wolf was, he was definitely a character. He was smaller than George, not so lithe and vigorous, and with a gray overcast to his otherwise white coat. He became "Uncle Albert" to me after the first time I saw him with the pups.

The sixth morning of my vigil had dawned bright and sunny, and Angeline and the pups took advantage of the good weather. Hardly was the sun risen (at three A.M.) when they all left the den and adjourned to a nearby sandy knoll. Here the pups worked over their mother with an enthusiasm which would certainly have driven any human female into hysterics. They were hungry; but they were also full to the ears with hellery. Two of them did their best to chew off Angeline's tail, worrying it and fighting over it until I thought I could actually see her fur flying like spindrift; while the other two did what they could to remove her ears.

Angeline stood it with noble stoicism for about an hour and then, sadly disheveled, she attempted to protect herself by sitting on her tail and tucking her mauled head down between her legs. This was a fruitless effort. The pups went for her feet, one to each paw, and I was treated to the spectacle of the demon killer of the wilds trying desperately to cover her paws, her tail, and her head at one and the same instant.

Eventually she gave it up. Harassed beyond endurance she leaped away from her brood and raced to the top of a high sand ridge behind the den. The four pups rolled cheerfully off in pursuit, but before they could reach her she gave vent to a most peculiar cry.

The whole question of wolf communications was to intrigue me more and more as time went on, but on this occasion I was still laboring under the delusion that complex communications among animals other than man did not exist. I could make nothing definite of Angeline's high-pitched and yearning whine-cum-howl. I did, however, detect a plaintive quality in it which made my sympathies go out to her.

I was not alone. Within seconds of her *cri-de-coeur*, and before the mob of pups could reach her, a savior appeared.

It was the third wolf. He had been sleeping in a bed hollowed in the sand at the southern end of the esker where it dipped down to disappear beneath the waters of the bay. I had not known he was there until I saw his head come up. He jumped to his feet, shook himself, and trotted straight toward the den—intercepting the pups as they prepared to scale the last slope to reach their mother.

I watched, fascinated, as he used his shoulder to bowl the leading pup over on its back and send it skidding down the lower slope toward the den. Having broken the charge, he then nipped another pup lightly on its fat behind; then he shepherded the lot of them back to what I later came to recognize as the playground area.

I hesitate to put human words into a wolf's mouth, but the effect of what followed was crystal clear. "If it's a workout you kids want," he might have said, "then I'm your wolf!"

And so he was. For the next hour he played with the pups with as much energy as if he were still one himself. The games were varied, but many of them were quite recognizable. Tag was the standby, and Albert was always "it." Leaping, rolling and weaving amongst the pups, he never left the area of the nursery knoll, while at the same time leading the youngsters such a chase that they eventually gave up.

Albert looked them over for a moment and then, after a quick glance toward the crest where Angeline was now lying in a state of peaceful relaxation, he flung himself in among the tired pups, sprawled on his back, and invited mayhem. They were game. One by one they roused and went into battle. They were really roused this time, and no holds were barred—by them, at any rate.

Some of them tried to choke the life out of Albert, although their small teeth, sharp as they were, could never have penetrated his heavy ruff. One of them, in an excess of infantile sadism, turned its back on him and pawed a shower of sand into his face. The others took to leaping as high into the air as their bowed little legs would propel them; coming down with a satisfying thump on Albert's vulnerable belly. In between jumps they tried to chew the life out of whatever vulnerable parts came to tooth.

I began to wonder how much he could stand. Evidently he could stand a lot, for not until the pups were totally exhausted and had collapsed into complete somnolence did he get to his feet, careful not to step on the small, sprawled forms, and disengage himself. Even then he did not return to the comfort of his own bed (which he had undoubtedly earned after a night of hard hunting) but settled himself instead on the edge of the nursery knoll, where he began wolf-napping, taking a quick look at the pups every few minutes to make sure they were still safely near at hand.

His true relationship to the rest of the family was still uncertain; but as far as I was concerned he had become, and would remain, "good old Uncle Albert."

FURTHER READING

SELECTED WORKS BY FARLEY MOWAT

People of the Deer (Toronto: McClelland and Stewart, 1965).

The Dog Who Wouldn't Be (Toronto: McClelland and Stewart). Also available in Pyramid Willow pocket book.

The Grey Seas Under (Toronto: McClelland and Stewart).

The Serpent's Coil (Toronto: McClelland and Stewart).

Never Cry Wolf (Toronto: McClelland and Stewart, 1963). Also available in Dell paperback.

The Boat Who Wouldn't Float (Toronto: McClelland and Stewart, 1969).

Sibir (Toronto: McClelland and Stewart, 1970).

RELATED MATERIAL

David Walker, *Where the High Winds Blow* (Toronto: Book Society of Canada, 1960).

FILMS

Death of a Legend, one hour documentary by the National Film Board on myths about wolves, filmed by Bill Mason.

PICTURE SERIES

Canadian Authors (includes Farley Mowat), obtainable from: Hilton Photo Supplies, P.O. Box 74, Chemainus, British Columbia.

Margaret Laurence

Margaret Laurence (1926-), née Wemyss, was born and grew up in Neepawa, Manitoba, the Manawaka of her novels. She graduated from the University of Manitoba and spent some years with her Canadian husband in Africa where he was employed as an engineer. She had started writing as a child, but it was her African experience which inspired her first published work. Tree for Poverty *(1954) was a collection of Somali literature translated into English. Returning to Canada in 1957 she published three books about Africa, including her first novel* This Side Jordan *(1960), which won the Canadian Beta Sigma Phi Award. She then began her Manawaka books, receiving the Governor-General's Award of 1966 for* A Jest of God, *subsequently made into the movie,* Rachel, Rachel. *Her short stories have appeared in* The Saturday Evening Post, Tamarack Review, Queen's Quarterly *and* Prism. *She received an Order of Canada Award in 1971. She has a grown son and daughter and makes her home in England and Canada.*

SILVERTHREADS

After supper they baggage me into the car and off we go. I ride in the back seat alone. Bundled around with a packing of puffy pillows, I am held securely like an egg in a crate. I am pleased nonetheless to be going for a drive. Marvin is usually too tired after work. It is a fine evening, cool and bright. The mountains are so clear, the near ones sharp and blue as eyes or jay feathers, the further ones fading to cloudy purple, the ghosts of mountains.

All would be lovely, all would be calm, except for Doris's voice

From: Margaret Laurence, *The Stone Angel* (Toronto: McClelland and Stewart, New Canadian Library, 1968). Reprinted by permission of McClelland and Stewart, the Canadian Publishers.

squeaking like a breathless mouse. She has to explain the sights. Perhaps she believes me blind.

"My, doesn't everything look green?" she says, as though it were a marvel that the fields were not scarlet and the alders aquamarine. Marvin says nothing. Nor do I. Who could make a sensible reply?

"The crops look good, don't they?" she goes on. She has lived all her life in the city, and would not know oats from sow-thistle. "Oh, look at the blackberries all along the ditch. There'll be tons of them this year. We should come out when they're ripe, Marv, and get some for jam."

"The seeds will get under your plate." I can't resist saying it. She has false teeth, whereas I, through some miracle, still possess my own. "They're better for wine, blackberries."

"For those that use it," Doris sniffs.

She always speaks of "using" wine or tobacco, giving them a faintly obscene sound, as though they were paper handkerchiefs or toilet paper.

But soon she's back to her cheery commentary. "Oh, look—those black calves. Aren't they sweet?"

If she'd ever had to take their wet half-born heads and help draw them out of the mother, she might call them by many words, but *sweet* would almost certainly not be one of them. And yet it's true I always had some feeling for any creature struggling awkward and unknowing into life. What I don't care for is her liking them when she doesn't understand the first thing about it. But why do I think she doesn't? She's borne two children, just as I have.

"Dry up, Doris, can't you?" Marvin says, and she gapes at him like a flounder.

"Now, Marvin, there's no call to be rude." Strangely, I find myself taking her part, not that she'll thank me for it.

We fall silent, and then I see the black iron gate and still I do not understand. Why is Marvin turning and driving through this open gate? The wrought iron letters, fanciful and curlicued, all at once form into meaning before my eyes.

SILVERTHREADS

I push aside my shroud of pillows, and my hands clutch at the back of the seat. My heart is pulsing too fast, beating like a berserk bird. I try to calm it. I must, I must, or it will damage itself against the cage of bones. But still it lurches and flutters, in a frenzy to get out.

"Marvin—where are we going? Where are we?"

"It's all right," he says. "We're only—"

I reach for the car door, fumble with the handle, try to release the catch.

"I'm not coming here. I'm not–do you hear me? I want out. Right now, this minute. Let me out!"

"Mother!" Doris grabs my hand, pulls it away from the bright and beckoning metal. "What on earth are you trying to do? You might fall out and kill yourself."

"A fat lot you'd care. I want to go home–"

I am barely aware of the words that issue from my mouth. I am overcome with fear, the feeling one has when the ether mask goes on, when the mind cries out to the limbs, "*Flail against the thing,*" but the limbs are already touched with lethargy, bound and lost.

Can they force me? If I fuss and fume, will they simply ask a brawny nurse to restrain me? Strap me into harness, will they? Make a madwoman of me? I fear this place exceedingly. I cannot even look. I don't care. Has it walls and windows, doors and closets, like a dwelling? Or only walls? Is it a mausoleum, and I, the Egyptian, mummified with pillows and my own flesh, through some oversight embalmed alive? There must be some mistake.

"It's mean, mean of you," I hear my disgusting cringe. "I've not even any of my things with me–"

"Oh, for God's sake," Marvin says in a stricken and apologetic voice. "You don't think we were bringing you here to stay, did you? We only wanted you to have a look at the place, Mother, that's all. We should have said. I told you, Doris, we'd have been better to explain."

"That's right," she parries. "Blame it all on me. I only thought if we did, she'd never agree to even have a look at it, and what's more, you know that's so."

"The matron said we could come and have a cup of tea," Marvin says over his shoulder, in my direction. "Look around, you know. Have a look at the place, and see how you felt about it. There's lots like you, she said, who're kind of nervous until they see how nice it is–"

There is such hopeful desperation in his voice that I am silenced utterly. And now it comes to my mind to wonder about my house again. Has he come to regard it as his, by right of tenancy? Can it actually be his? He's painted the rooms time and time again, it's true, repaired the furnace, built the back porch and goodness knows what-all. Has he purchased it, without my knowledge, with time and work, his stealthy currency? Impossible. I won't countenance it. Yet the doubt remains.

The matron is a stoutish woman, pressing sixty, I'd say, and in a blue uniform and a professional benevolence. She has that look of overpowering competence that one always dreads, but I perceive that some small black hairs sprout like slivers from her chin, so she's doubtless had her own troubles–jilted, probably, long ago, by some rabbity man who feared she'd devour him. Having thus snubbed the creature in my head, I feel quite kindly disposed toward her, in a distant way, until she grips my arm and steers me along as one would a drunk or a poodle.

Briskly we navigate a brown linoleum corridor, round a corner, linger while she flings wide a door as though she were about to display the treasure of some Persian potentate.

"This is our main lounge," she purrs. "Very comfy, don't you think? Now that the evenings are fine, there aren't so many here, but you should see it in the winter. Our old people just love to gather here, around the fireplace. Sometimes we toast marshmallows."

I'd marshmallow her, the counterfeit coin. I won't look at a thing, not one, on the conducted tour of this pyramid. I'm blind. I'm deaf. There–I've shut my eyes. But the betrayers open a slit despite me, and I see around the big fireplace, here and there, in armchairs larger than themselves, several small ancient women, white-topped and frail as dandelions gone to seed.

On we plod. "This is our dining hall," the matron says. "Spacious, don't you know? Very light and airy. The large windows catch the afternoon light. It's bright in here ever so late, way past nine in summer. The tables are solid oak."

"Really, it's lovely," Doris says. "It really is. Don't you think so, Mother?"

"I never cared for barracks," I reply.

Then I'm ashamed. I used to pride myself on my manners. How have I descended to this snarl?

"The leaded panes are nice," I remark, by way of grudging apology.

"Yes, aren't they?" Matron seizes the remark. "Quite recent, they are. We used to have picture windows. But older people don't care for picture windows, don't you know? They like the more traditional. So we had these put in."

She turns to Doris, a stage aside. "They cost the earth, I may say."

Now I'm sorry I praised them. This puts me with the rest, does it, unanimous old ewes?

"We've double and single rooms," the matron says, as we mount the uncarpeted stairs. "Of course the singles run a little more."

"Of course," Doris agrees reverently.

The little cells look unlived-in and they smell of creosote. An iron cot, a dresser, a bedspread of that cheap homespun sold by the mail-order houses.

We descend, matron and Doris gabbling reassuringly to one another. All this while, Marvin has not spoken. Now he raises his voice.

"I'd like to have a word with you in your office, if that's okay."

"By all means. Would Mrs. Shipley–senior, I mean–care for a cup of tea on the veranda, while we chat in here? I'm sure she'd enjoy meeting some of our old people."

"Oh, thanks, that would be just lovely, wouldn't it, Mother?" Doris palpitates.

They look at me expectantly, assuming I'll be overjoyed to talk with strangers just because they happen to be old. Now I feel tired. What use to argue? I nod and nod. I'll agree to anything. Like two hens with a single chick, they fuss me into a chair. Into my hands is pushed a cup of tea. It tastes like hemlock. Even if it didn't, though, I'd have to feel it did. Doris is right. I'm unreasonable. Who could get along with me? No wonder they want me here. Remorsefully, I force the hot tea down my gullet, draining the cup to the dregs. Nothing is gained. It merely makes me belch.

The veranda is shadowy. Awnings have been drawn around the screens and now in the early evening it has that dank aquarium feel that the prairie houses used to have on midsummer days when all the blinds were drawn against the sun.

A young high-bosomed nurse flips open the main door, nods without seeing me, crosses the porch, goes out and down the steps. Being alone in a strange place, the nurse's unseeing stare, the receding heat of the day–all bring to mind the time I was first in a hospital, when Marvin was born.

The Manawaka hospital was new then and Doctor Tappen was anxious to show it off, the shiny enameled walls and the white iron cots, the deathly aroma of ether and Lysol.

I'd rather have had my child at home, a cat in a corner, licking herself clean afterward, with no one to ask who the tom had been. I didn't think there would be an afterward, anyway. I was convinced it would be the finish of me.

Bram drove me into town. I might have known he wouldn't turn at the Anglican Church and go by a side street. Oh no. He had to drive the buggy all the way down Main, from Simlow's Ladies' Wear to the Bank of Montreal, and wave the reins at Charlie Bean, the half-breed hired man who worked at Doherty's Livery Stable, who was sitting on the steps of the Queen Victoria Hotel, beside the cement pots of dusty geraniums.

"What'll you bet it's a son, Charlie?"

Walking across the street, dainty as a lace handkerchief, Lottie Drieser, who'd married Telford Simmons from the Bank, looked and looked but certainly didn't wave.

When we got to the hospital, I told Bram to go.

"You're not scared, Hagar, are you?" he said, as though it had just occurred to him I might be.

I only shook my head. I couldn't speak, nor reach to him in any way at all. What could I say? That I'd not wanted children? That I believed I was going to die, and wished I would, and prayed I wouldn't? That the child he wanted would be his, and none of mine? That I'd sucked my secret pleasure from his skin, but wouldn't care to walk in broad daylight on the streets of Manawaka with any child of his?

"I sure hope it's a boy," he said.

I couldn't for the life of me see why he should care one way or another, except to have help with the farm, but as he only worked in fits and starts, anyway, even an unpaid hired man would have made precious little difference.

"Why should you care if it's a boy?" I asked.

Bram looked at me as though he wondered how I could have needed to ask.

"It would be somebody to leave the place to," he said.

I saw then with amazement that he wanted his dynasty no less than my father had. In that moment when we might have touched our hands together, Bram and I, and wished each other well, the thought uppermost in my mind was–the nerve of him.

If Marvin hadn't been born alive that day, I wonder where I'd be now? I'd have got to some old folks' home a sight sooner, I expect. There's a thought.

Sidling up to me is a slight little person in a pink cotton wrap-around, printed with mignonettes and splattered with the evidence of past meals. What does she want with me, this old old body? Should I speak to her? We've never met. She'd think me brash.

She wafts across the porch, pats at her hair with a claw yellow as a kite's foot, pushes a stray wisp under the blue rayon net she wears. Then she speaks confidingly.

"Mrs. Thorlakson never came down to supper again tonight. That's twice in a row. I watched the blonde nurse take in her supper tray. She never got custard, like the rest of us. She got a cup cake. Can you beat it?"

"Maybe she wasn't feeling well," I venture.

"Her!" The old pink powderpuff snorts. "She's always feeling poorly, so she says. She fancies a tray in bed, that's the long and short of it. She'll outlive the lot of us, you'll see."

I cannot think of anything I would less like to witness. So this is what one may expect in such a place. I look away, but she is un-deterred.

"Last time she got ice cream, when we got lemon Jello. Not only that–you know those ice-cream wafers, the thin little ones like the stuff they use for cones, and icing in between the layers? Well, she got two of them. Two, mind you. I saw."

Really, what a common woman. Doesn't she think of anything except her stomach? It's revolting. How can I get her to go away?

I'm saved the bother. Someone else approaches, and little greedy-guts scampers off, whispering a warning over one shoulder.

"It's that Mrs. Steiner. Once she gets going with those photographs, you'll never hear the end of it."

The new one comes up beside me and scrutinizes me, but not dis-courteously. She's a heavy-built woman and she must have been quite handsome at one time. I take an instant liking to her, although I don't much want to like anyone here. I've always been definite about people. Right from the start, I either like a person or I don't. The only people I've ever been uncertain about were those closest to me. Maybe one looks at them too much. Strangers are easier to assess.

"I see you been talking to Miss Tyrrwhitt," she says. "Who's stolen a march on her this time, may I inquire?"

"She's always that way, then?"

"Every day and all day. Well, it's her way. Who should judge? She looked after an old mother, and now she's old herself. So–let her talk. Maybe it does her good, who knows? You're new?"

"No, no, I'm not staying here. My son and daughter-in-law brought me to see the place. But I'll not be staying."

Mrs. Steiner heaves a sigh and sits down beside me. "That's what I said, too. The exact same thing."

She sees my look. "Don't mistake me," she adds in haste. "Nobody said in so many words, 'Mamma, you got to go there'. No, no, nothing like that. But Ben and Esther couldn't have me in that apartment of theirs–so small, you'd think you walked into a broom closet by mistake. I was living before with Rita and her husband, and that was fine when they had only Moishe, but when the girl was born, where was the space? Here's Moishe and Lynne here–he looks the spitting image of his grandpa, my late husband, the same dark eyes. And smart. The smartest little trick you ever laid eyes on. Look at Lynne. A little doll, isn't she? A real little doll. Her hair is naturally curly."

She holds the photograph out and I examine it. Two perfectly ordinary children are playing on a teeter-totter.

"So I told Rita, 'All right, that's the way it is–what should a person do, spit in God's eye because He never gave you a million dollars you should build some forty-bedroom mansion?' Rita cried, a regular cloudburst, the day they brought me here. 'Mamma,' she says. 'I can't let you go.' I had to shush her like a baby. Even Esther cried, but I must admit she had to work at it. 'Glycerine is how they do it for the movie scene, Esther'–I'm on the point of saying it to her, but why should I bother? She thinks she owes it to Ben to cry, God knows why. A real glamour girl, that Esther, but hard, not like my daughter Rita. So–two years I been here. Rita takes me to town every other week, to get my hair done. 'Mamma,' she says, 'I know your hair's the last thing you'd want neglected.' "

"You're lucky to have a daughter," I say, half closing my eyes and leaning back in my chair.

"It makes a lotta difference," she agrees. "You got–?"

"Two sons." Then I realize what I've said. "I mean, I had two. One was killed–in the last war."

Lapped in the clumsy darkness, I wonder why I've said that, especially as it doesn't happen to be true.

Mrs. Steiner merely sighs her sympathy–tactful in one so talkative.

"A shame," she says at last. "A terrible shame."

"Yes," I can agree to that.

"Well, it's not so bad here," she says, "when all's said and done."

"Do you–" I hesitate. "Do you ever get used to such a place?"

She laughs then, a short bitter laugh I recognize and comprehend at once.

"Do you get used to life?" she says. "Can you answer me that? It all comes as a surprise. You get your first period, and you're amazed–*I can have babies now*–such a thing! When the children come, you think–*Is it mine? Did it come out of me? Who could believe it?* When you can't have them any more, what a shock–*It's finished–so soon?*"

I peer at her, thinking how peculiar that she knows so much.

"You're right. I never got used to a blessed thing."

"Well, you and I would get on pretty good," Mrs. Steiner says. "I hope we see you here."

Then I perceive how I've been led and lured. She hasn't meant to. I don't blame her. I only know I must get out of this place now, at once, without delay.

"You'll not see me here," I blurt. "Oh–I don't mean to be rude. But you'll not see me coming here to stay."

She gives an oriental shrug. "Where will you go? You got some place to go?"

It is then that the notion first strikes me. I must find some place to go, some hidden place.

I rise, frantic to be off. "Good-by, good-by. I must be going."

"Good-by," Mrs. Steiner says placidly. "I'll be seeing you."

The screen door bangs behind me. Down the steps I go, hoping my legs won't let me down. I grip the railing with both hands, feeling my way ahead, testing each step with a cautious foot like someone wading into a cold sea.

Darkness has come, and now I realize that I do not really know where I am going. It is as though I am being led on, and for the moment I am content to follow my feet, certain they are taking me somewhere.

Emerging out of the shadows just ahead of me is a small summer-house. Now I am gifted with sight like a prowling cat and find the darkness not complete after all. The hut seems to be made of logs, rough-hewn, and roofed jaggedly, perhaps with cedar shakes. Some sort of sanctuary, it appears to be. I can see a bench inside where I may rest. Then, about to enter, I catch a tick of movement from within, a momentary tremor slight as a sigh. I look and see a man sitting there. He has not seen me, for his head is lowered. In his hands he holds a carved stick or a cane, and he is twisting it round and round. His glance is fixed on the little groove his stick is making on the earth floor. Round and round it slowly twirls, always on the same place, making its mark, digging itself in.

There are men here, in this place, then, as well as women. The man's shoulders are very wide, and his hair has a kind of shagginess about it. Although his face is hidden, I can see he's bearded. Oh—

So familiar he is that I cannot move nor speak nor breathe. How has he come here, by what mystery? Or have I come to the place he went before? This is a strange place, surely, shadowed and luminous, the trees enfolding us like arms in the sheltering dark. If I speak to him, slowly, so as not to startle, will he turn to me with such a look of recognition that I hardly dare hope for it, and speak my name?

And then he raises his head. I see his face. It is frail as a china teacup, white, the skin stretched thin across the unfamiliar features. His beard looks frayed and molting.

I'm only in a summer-house in some large garden, I and this man, whoever he is. Stupid. Stupid. Thank God I didn't speak. A bell sounds, not the mellow iron of the church bells I remember, but a piercing buzz, a shrill statement of command.

"The curfew," the old man mutters, in a voice slow with rust and disuse. "Time to go."

As he walks away, I hear Doris calling.

"Mother—where are you?"

She sounds alarmed. Idiot—what does she think I've done, flown away? A verse the children used to chant to the tune of *The Prisoner's Song*—

> *If I had the wings of an angel,*
> *Or even the wings of a crow,*
> *I would fly to the top of T. Eaton's*
> *And spit on the people below.*

"I'm here. I'm here. Don't shout so."

Running, she arrives. "Goodness, what a scare you gave us. We didn't know—why, what's the matter? You're not crying, are you?"

"Of course not. It's nothing. I'd like to go home now, if you don't mind. I'd just like to be taken home."

"Well, sure," she says, as though it were a foregone conclusion. "That's where we're going. Come along."

She leads me to the car, and we drive back, back along the highway, back to Marvin and Doris's house.

FURTHER READING

THE "MANAWAKA" BOOKS

The Stone Angel (Toronto: McClelland and Stewart, New Canadian Library, 1968). First published 1964.

A Jest of God (Toronto: McClelland and Stewart, 1966). Also sold under the title, *Rachel, Rachel* (Popular Library Paperback).

The Fire-Dwellers (Toronto: McClelland and Stewart, 1969).

A Bird in the House (Toronto: McClelland and Stewart, 1970).

BOOKS ABOUT AFRICA

This Side Jordan (Toronto: McClelland and Stewart, 1960).

The Prophet's Camel Bell (Toronto: McClelland and Stewart, 1963).

The Tomorrow Tamer and Other Stories (Toronto: McClelland and Stewart, New Canadian Library, 1970).

CRITICISM

Clara Thomas, *Margaret Laurence* (Toronto: McClelland and Stewart, Canadian Writers Series, 1969).

W. E. Swayze, *Margaret Laurence* (Copp Clark Publishers, Studies in Canadian Literature Series).

AUDIO-VISUAL

Canadian Writers on Tape (reel or cassette, includes Margaret Laurence), obtainable from: Publications Sales, OISE, 102 Bloor St. West, Toronto.

Rachel, Rachel, film based on Margaret Laurence's novel, *A Jest of God*.

Percy Janes

Newfoundlander Percy Janes was born in St. John's and grew up in Corner Brook, which was early in the century transformed by the Bowater Pulp Mill from fishing village to company town. A worker's son (but the grandson of Skipper Bill, the famous smuggler), he managed to escape the small town which promised him only a lifetime of manual labour when he won a government scholarship to study at Memorial College (now Memorial University) in St. John's. During the Second World War he served in the Canadian Navy and afterwards studied at Victoria College, Toronto, graduating in 1948. Since then he has travelled a good deal, settling in later years in England where he is now writing.

This excerpt from Percy Janes' contemporary novel, *House of Hate*, which the author has admitted is basically, but not entirely, auto-biographical, exposes the horror of brutality masquerading as discipline. The terminology is judgemental: "this creature called my father . . . seemed to me like some huge emaciated monkey sprung out of the jungle to prey on an innocent world." Juju, from whose point of view the story is told, attempts later on in the novel to fix the guilt for his father's cruelty on the "grimness and battle" of his early life on the east coast of Newfoundland. He wonders if "by some strange process of diffusion this physical misery and the implacable hardness it gave him somehow passed into his moral and emotional and spiritual nature as well." Much of the novel deals with the "venom that flowed" in the Old Man's veins and which "was passed on as a dark legacy to each one of his sons and came out in various forms of abnormality which stunted our growth as human beings."

The very name of the father, Saul Stone–as well as the capitalization of "Old Man"–indicates the ruthless authority behind a king image cut from flint, not granite. Flint is a hard stone, steely-grey, which has the property of giving off sparks when struck with steel. In the encounter between Stone and Racer a destructive flame is indeed kindled. Frederick Philip Grove uses a similar figure of speech in describing John Amundsen in *Settlers of the Marsh*. Ellen's mother in that novel says of her husband that "he is hard . . . as hard as God."

The title of the novel certainly suggests two meanings. Obviously, the Stone family home is literally a "house of hate," but so is, figuratively, Saul Stone himself. The first sentence in the novel is clear on this point, "Hate is the child of fear, and Saul Stone had been afraid of one thing or another all his life."

The silence which was the aftermath of Racer's licking–"they never spoke to each other"–E. J. Pratt well understands in his poem, "Silences":

> But let silent hate be put away for it feeds
> upon the heart of the hater.
> Today I watched two pairs of eyes. One pair
> was black and the other grey. And while the
> owners thereof, for the space of five seconds,
> walked past each other, the grey snapped at
> the black and the black riddled the grey.
> One looked to say–'The cat,'
> And the other–'The cur.'
> But no words were spoken;
> Not so much as a hiss or a murmur came through
> the perfect enamel of the teeth; not so much
> as a gesture of enmity.
> If the right upper lip curled over the canine,
> it went unnoticed.
> The lashes veiled the eyes not for an instant
> in the passing.
> And as between the two in respect to candour of
> intention or eternity of wish, there was no
> choice, for the stare was mutual and absolute.
> A word would have dulled the exquisite edge of
> the feeling,
> An oath would have flawed the crystallization of
> the hate.
> For only such culture could grow in a climate
> of silence–
> Away back back before the emergence of fur or
> feather, back to the unvocal sea and down deep
> where the darkness spills its wash on the thresh-
> old of light, where the lids never close upon
> the eyes, where the inhabitants slay in silence
> and are as silently slain.

Pratt says in the same poem that "There is no fury upon the earth like the fury under the sea."

Another Canadian writer who has used Newfoundland themes and like Pratt describes the sea as vicious, is Norman Duncan. Published under the title *The Way of the Sea*, his collection of short stories about the life of the men who go down to the sea in ships has a more uncompromising realism than Rudyard Kipling's famous novel *Captains Courageous*, the story of a spoiled child of the rich reformed by the example of courage and self-discipline set by fishermen from Newfoundland. It is interesting to note that the two works were published within five years of one another. In his foreword to the 1904 edition of *The Way of the Sea*, Frank T. Bullen of Melbourn, Cambridgeshire, paid this tribute to the author, "With the exception of Joseph Conrad and Rudyard Kipling no writing about the sea has ever probed so deeply and so faithfully into its mysteries as his. The bitter brine, the unappeasable savagery of snarling sea and black-fanged rock bite into the soul, as acid eats into the engraver's plate."

Newfoundland dialect as reproduced by Duncan comes close to Janes' version of island vernacular. Duncan's story, "The Chase of the Tide," tells of a young boy who cries that the sea will not catch him, "He've not cotched me–I woan't let un cotch me!"

In their book on Newfoundland, *This Rock Within the Sea: A Heritage Lost*, Farley Mowat says that he and John De Visser portray the people "in the context of their world in its grimmest and most formidable aspect, in the hard, bleak days of winter."

House of Hate evokes a different chilling bleakness: "the arctic void which the Old Man created around himself."

WHEN RACER GOT HIS LICKIN'

As usual, we males were all served first, then Flinksy sat down with a heaped plateful, and finally Mom appeared ostentatiously bearing a small plate with one or two bits of turnip and potato and a rind or so of meat and took her place at the foot of the table. All this was merely a blind, for we knew she had been eating most of the time the meal was cooking; moreover, I often saw her, as economic conditions gradually improved in the family, take a whole cubic inch of butter on the end of a knife and swallow it straight down with a gulp and a little shudder of sensual delight. She ate and drank with

From: Percy Janes, *House of Hate* (Toronto: McClelland and Stewart, 1970). Reprinted by permission of McClelland and Stewart, the Canadian Publishers.

no more thought of calories than a hungry child let loose on a barrel of ice cream. Her tentative pose at table came from a knowledge that before the meal was over she would be up from one to twenty times for the purpose of tending on Dad or one of the boys until all were satisfied.

On this particular evening some wicked spirit must have got into her or Racer or both of them; or perhaps the showdown came simply because Racer had been made more reckless than ever by his easy escape from the raping incident and felt in a gloating way that nothing could touch him now. As Mom handed him his second help-ing of vegetables, she also gave him a conspiratorial wink. Racer grinned, and from behind his hand he made another face imitating the Old Man in sour mood–mostly for the benefit of Flinksy, Crawfie, and myself. In spite of ourselves we began to giggle and smirk and snort, soon borne along by Racer's bravado to the point where we could not stop even if we had wanted to. A warning from the Old Man took no effect whatever, and he relieved himself for the moment, and had his revenge for being left out of our joke as usual, by reaching out suddenly and giving Crawfie, the least self-controlled of us all, a cuff on the ear with the back of his hand. It was an injustice that brought tears more of indignation than of pain to Crawfie's eyes. "See if that'll shut ye up," said the Old Man coldly.

"Hush up now, all o'ye, and finish yere tea," Mom urged us anxiously, no doubt recognizing danger signals in Dad's manner more readily than anyone else.

Far from recognizing or heeding any danger signals, Racer kept on tormenting us with surreptitious looks and gestures and, at last, in answer to an innocent question from Flinksy, who with a little of Mom's instinct was trying to head off a fuss, he put a match to the gunpowder he had so blithely scattered around himself and all the rest of us. All he said in answer to Flinksy was: "I *hearrrd* diff'rent," but that was more than enough. With a snarl of animal rage the Old Man sprang up, tipping the table and sending most of the food and dishes sliding down to Mom's end in a tinkling ava-lanche. He seized Racer by the hair with his left hand while with the right he began pounding him over the face and head, each blow a grunt of satisfaction and of vengeance achieved.

"Mock me, willya? Mock yer own fawder! And t'ink you can get away wit it, be the Lard Jesus! Shore signs, we'll see about that." He plucked Racer upright until their eyes were almost on a level.

"I . . . I wasn't mockin'," Racer gasped, cowed by the suddenness of the attack. "I wasn't makin' fun." And in truth we others were not at all sure he *had* meant to imitate the Old Man this time. Racer's academic progress to Grade X had softened and toned down the more grotesque of the errors and crudities of speech habitual with us, but by no means removed them entirely.

The Old Man chose to think he had been deliberately mimicked. "Liar!" he yelled. "Bloody liar along wit' all the rest of it." More blows fell now on Racer's head. "You does a t'ing, and then you're not even man enough to own up to it."

"Now that's enough, Dad, that's enough," Mom begged frantically.

"Enough my arse! I'll give him a damn good lickin' while I'm at it. Somet'ing he wunt forget in a hurry. He been askin' for it for years, and now he's goin' to get it." Seeing more punishment coming, Racer tried to pull out of the Old Man's grasp and even raised a clenched hand as though he might be intending to strike back. The mere gesture was taken as an attempt at retaliation.

"Oh, you would, would you? T'ink I'm still not able for you, hey?" The Old Man viciously jerked up his knee and sank it in Racer's belly, dangerously low down. Racer sucked in breath with a kind of rattling gasp and collapsed on the floor.

By now we were all on our feet crying out in protest and staring in horror. Flinksy screamed when Racer fainted, and I saw the blood draining from her face as though someone had stabbed her directly in the heart. When the Old Man raised his boot and made a motion to stamp on Racer, Mom tried to intervene physically but was sent reeling back over the table by a brutal shove. Somehow Flinksy now found the courage to speak out against such violence.

"You shut yer mout'!" the Old Man barked. "And ye too," he rounded on me and Crawfie. "Not a Jesus word, or ye'll get it worse than him. Yes, ye're all alike. Just 'cause ye got a bit o'education ye t'inks yere shit don't stink. But I knows diff'rent. I been out there in the t'ilet right after ye. So don't go givin' me no lip. I should'a did this years and years ago to the whole goddam lot o' ye. Then maybe I wouldn't find ye makin' fun o' yere own fawder right to his face."

During the brief silence that came while the Old Man was recovering his breath, Racer must have come to and perhaps had a brief respite from pain, for suddenly his voice came up from the floor as clear and deliberate as a judge's sentence, startling us all by the manner no less than by the matter of his words.

"You goddam dirty old bastard."

After the first shock of realization had passed, the Old Man leaped for his razor strap that always hung on the wall beside his shaving mirror. This time Mom tried to wrest the weapon from him, but he pulled away and gave her a cut across the front of her dress with the two-tailed heavy leather strap. I saw her already ashen face contract with the pain as she once more fell back from the centre of the struggle.

"If you so much as *touches* him once more," she managed to cry out, "I wunt stay in this house another day. I'll take the two youngsters that's not workin' and I'll clear out o' this cursed hole for good. I'll go back home to Ma in Haystack."

"I don't give a good goddam where you goes. Go to hell, and take yer saucy brats along wit' you. Put that in yer pipe and smoke it. I'm tired tellin' you about the way you goes on wit' 'em. Hulderin' 'em and takin' up for 'em when you should be givin' 'em some discipleen. They're saucy as blacks, every one; but this one is goin' to find out for once he haven't got you to deal wit' this time."

"Oh, I wish Ank was here!" cried Mom in helpless agony. "He'd do something." She looked across the kitchen at her two youngest sons, but it was clear that Crawfie had not the stomach to tackle the Old Man at this time, and as for myself, apart from being too young and delicate for anything to be expected of me in such a situation, I was utterly absorbed, horrified, and fascinated by the spectacle of this creature called my father in the startling transformation of his fury.

His pale eyes protruded from sockets like bags of blood and I noticed how the slack space that always showed between his trousers and his belly opened and closed spasmodically as he panted for breath. When he began to give Racer a thorough lacing with the strap, dancing up and down in the ecstasy of his rage, he seemed to me like some huge emaciated monkey sprung out of the jungle to prey on an innocent world.

Racer threw his arms over his head, drew up his knees, and jack-knifed his whole body into the embryo position to protect himself from the whistling cuts of the strap.

"Will you ever do it again?" the Old Man thundered vengefully. "Will you ever mock me again? Hey? Will you?"

"No, no."

"You better not. I'll have me rights in this house—yes, by the crucified Jesus, I'll have respect from ye, even if I got to swing for ye." He went on like this for quite a while, more or less in time to the strokes of the strap, until fatigue slowed him down, and at last there came a momentary lull in the horror. Racer must have thought this was the end of his torture. He cautiously drew down his arms for an instant, but in that very same instant down came the strap again cutting right across his exposed face. Racer howled, blood spurted, Flinksy screamed again, and the Old Man, stimulated rather than sobered by the sight, kept on lashing at Racer until blood was spattering over himself and the walls, and the kitchen looked more like a slaughterhouse than the centre of our domestic life.

At long last it really was over. Sucking air like a bellows, the Old

Man passed the back of his hand across his forehead to wipe away the blinding sweat, bloodying his whole face with the motion, and then turned to stare at the rest of us as if to demand whether we would like some of the same medicine. We all turned away in disgust, and with a sneer he flung the strap down on top of Racer, muttering contemptuously: "Now get out o' here, the whole bunch o' ye. I'm sick o' the sight o'ye. Get out and leave me alone."

Flinksy managed to rouse Mom from her dazed and terrified state to lead her out of the kitchen while somehow Crawfie and I dragged and supported Racer into our bedroom to examine his wounds and see what could be done for him. The minute we had passed through the kitchen door the Old Man slammed and locked it and then we heard him fall on his couch half-moaning and half-cursing in a totally inarticulate way. His radio remained silent the whole night.

We had to take a jug and go out the front way to get some water for cleaning up Racer's injuries, which however were not nearly as bad as we had thought during the conflict. It was a split lip that had caused all the bleeding, and when we had closed it with plaster and otherwise restored Racer to something like his normally clean, morning-fresh appearance, we were able to hope with some reason that no serious damage had been done. As soon as Mom had quite recovered herself, we broached the question of getting the police after the Old Man; she hesitated, pondered, but after spending a few minutes alone with Racer she decided against it. Apparently Racer's wounds were in a bodily way only superficial, though in another way they would never entirely heal.

That night we had no family prayers nor did any of us boys individually commune with God to thank Him for His general protection in our lives and the particular blessings of this day, fearfully needed though such a communication was in all our minds. From that day came other changes too. Silence was now more noticeable in the kitchen, even if we knew the Old Man was safely down over the hill, and Racer was for many days and weeks less ebullient than we had ever known him. Nowadays he did not pass by the Old Man when they met, but darted around him with eyes averted and his body hunched in a wary manner against possible further punishment. The Old Man was likely to explode again at any moment and for no adequate or predictable cause.

They never spoke to each other. From time to time the Old Man audibly muttered his disgust at Racer being so pig-headed and case-hardened, but still Racer only hung his head and keeping his mouth tight-clamped merely nodded as if to show that now he knew what he knew and there was nothing more to be said. Privately Racer swore to us he was going to get the old bugger and when we told

Ank about the racket, ways and means were discussed; however, I seemed to notice that since he had become a husband and father Ank was not so keen as formerly on condemning the Old Man out of hand, and this time he did not encourage Racer to any positive action or promise any support in the event that Racer should attack on his own initiative.

Racer seeming to be more talk than deeds, the cold war in our home continued cold, but Racer did keep up his campaign of mute resistance and what amounted to silent contempt against paternal domination. Even when the Old Man gave him a direct order he would not acknowledge it by a single word; he would simply jerk his head again and set about his task in a mulish way. For months the whole atmosphere of the house was oppressive as a dentist's breath.

FURTHER READING

SELECTED FICTION: NEWFOUNDLAND

Percy Janes, *House of Hate* (Toronto: McClelland and Stewart, 1970).

Harold Horwood, *Tomorrow Will Be Sunday* (New York: Doubleday and Company, 1966).

Norman Duncan, *The Way of the Sea* (London: Hodder and Stoughton, 1904), out of print.

SELECTED POETRY: NEWFOUNDLAND

D. G. Pitt, ed., *Here the Tides Flow* (Toronto: The Macmillan Company of Canada, 1962).

Peter Buitenhuis, *Selected Poems of E. J. Pratt* (Toronto: The Macmillan Company of Canada, 1968).

PHOTOGRAPHY

Farley Mowat (text), and John de Visser (photography), *This Rock Within the Sea: A Heritage Lost* (Boston: Little, Brown and Company, 1968).